# The Mother's Yoga
### 1956-1973
### Vol. 1, 1956-1967

Author: Loretta Shartsis
Design and Produced by Loretta Shartsis,
loretta@auroville.org.in

First edition February 2011

ISBN: 978-93-95460-10-1 (print)
ISBN: 978-93-95460-11-8 (ebook)

BISAC Code:
OCC026000 BODY, MIND & SPIRIT / Yoga see
HEALTH & FITNESS / Yoga
REF019000, REFERENCE / Quotations

Thema Subject Category:
AKLB, Illustration
VX, Mind, body, spirit

Cataloging-in-Publication Data for this title is
available from the Library of Congress.

Digital Editions produced by:
DMI Systems Pvt Ltd, Vishnupuri,
Aligarh 202001, Uttar Pradesh, India
www.dmi.systems

Published by:
PRISMA, Aurelec/ Prayogshala,
Auroville 605101, Tamil Nadu, India
www.prisma.haus

# INTRODUCTION

This compilation is the record of the Mother's yoga practice during the latter part of her life. It contains her experiences and realizations from 1956 to 1973. In the early 1950's the Mother told Satprem, a French disciple, that she was able to speak to him about many things which she had never said to anyone. For over two decades she spoke to him about many subjects, including, among other topics, her own yoga practice, her life, her work in the Ashram and her universal work in the world.

Satprem recorded these talks and took notes as the Mother told him things which she often said were inexpressible in words. His descriptions of the Mother's body language and gestures help the reader to understand what the Mother was saying. These talks have been published in thirteen volumes in French, 'L'Agenda de Mère' and in English, 'The Mother's Agenda'.

The central line of 'The Mother's Agenda' is her yoga practice to prepare her physical body for the new Supramental consciousness. She related her experiences and realizations in detail as her consciousness went deeper and deeper into physical matter. Her goal was the transformation of her physical body so that she would be able to receive and retain the new consciousness.

Like the central figure of a complex tapestry, the evolving story of the Mother's yoga weaves through the many subjects which she spoke about over the years. In these two volumes of 'The Mother's Yoga', the other subject lines have been omitted so that the reader can follow the Mother's experiences and realizations without having to read about other things.

The Mother wanted to leave this record of her work. She said; 'The Agenda ... is my gift to those who love me.' 'The Mother's Yoga' is also the Mother's gift to those who love her.

3

## February 29, 1956

FIRST SUPRAMENTAL MANIFESTATION

*(During the common meditation on Wednesday the 29th February 1956)*

This evening the Divine Presence, concrete and material, was there present amongst you. I had a form of living gold, bigger than the universe, and I was facing a huge and massive golden door which separated the world from the Divine.

As I looked at the door, I knew and willed, in a single movement of consciousness, that THE TIME HAS COME', and lifting with both hands a mighty golden hammer I struck one blow, one single blow on the door and the door was shattered to pieces.

Then the supramental Light and Force and Consciousness rushed down upon earth in an uninterrupted flow.

Vol. I, p. 69

## September 12, 1956

... A light, not like the golden light of the Supermind: rather a kind of phosphorescence. I felt that had it been night, it would have been *physically* visible.

... And it was denser than my physical body: the physical body seemed to me almost unreal – as though crumbly – like sand running through your fingers.

... I would have been incapable of speaking, words seemed so petty, narrow, ignorant.

... I saw (how shall I put it?) the successive preparations which took place, in certain *anterior* beings, in order to achieve this.

... It felt as if I had several heads.

... The experience of February 29 was of a general nature; but this one was intended for me.

... An experience I had never had.

... I begin to see what the supramental body will be.

... I had had a somewhat similar experience at the time of the union of *the supreme creative principle* with the physical consciousness. But that was a subtle experience, while this was material – in the body.

... I did not *have* the experience, I did not look at it: I WAS it.

... And it radiated from me: myriads of little sparks that were penetrating everybody – I saw them enter *into each one of those present*.

... One more step.

Vol. I, p. 85

## October 17, 1957

There are all kinds of freedom – mental freedom, vital freedom, spiritual freedom – which are the fruits of successive masteries. But a completely new freedom has become possible with the Supramental Manifestation: it is the freedom of the body.

One of the very first results of the supramental manifestation was to give the body a freedom and an autonomy it has never before known. And when I say freedom, I don't mean some psychological perception or an inner state of consciousness, but something else and far better – it is a new phenomenon in the body, in the cells of the body. For the first time, the cells themselves have felt that they are free, that they have the power to decide. When the new vibrations came and combined with the old ones, I felt it at once and it showed me that a new world was really taking birth.

In its normal state, the body always feels that it is not its own master: illnesses invade it without its really being able to resist them – a thousand factors impose themselves or exert pressure upon it. Its sole power is the power to defend itself, to react. Once the illness has got in, it can fight and overcome it – even modern medicine has acknowledged that the body is cured only when it decides to get cured; it is not the drugs *per se* that heal, for if the ailment is temporarily suppressed by a drug without the body's will, it grows up again elsewhere in some other form until the body itself has decided to be cured. But this implies only a defensive power, the power to react against an invading enemy – it is not true freedom.

But with the supramental manifestation, something new has taken place in the body: it feels it is its own master, autonomous, with its two feet solidly on the ground, as it were. This gives a physical impression of the whole being suddenly drawing itself up, with its head lifted high – I am my own master.

We live perennially with a burden on our shoulders, something that bows our heads down, and we feel pulled, led by all kinds of external forces, we don't know by whom or what, nor where to – this is what men call Fate, Destiny. When you do yoga, one of the first experiences – the experience of the *kundalini,* as it is called here in India – is precisely one in which the consciousness rises, breaks through this hard 'lid,' here, at the crown of the head, and at last you emerge into the Light. Then you see, you know, you decide and you realize – difficulties may still remain, but truly speaking one is above them. Well, as a result of the supramental manifestation, it is THIS experience that came into the body. The body straightened its head up and felt its freedom, its independence.

During the flu epidemic, for example, I spent every day in the midst of people who were germ carriers. And one day, I clearly felt that the body had decided not to catch this flu. It asserted its autonomy. You see, it was not a question of the higher Will deciding, no. It didn't take place in the highest consciousness: the body itself decided. When you are way above in your consciousness, you see things, you know things; but in actual fact, once you descend again into matter, it is like water running through sand. In this respect, things have changed, the body has a DIRECT power, independent of any outer intervention. Even though it is barely visible, I consider this to be a very important result.

And this new vibration in the body has allowed me to understand the mechanism of the transformation. It is not something that comes from a higher Will, not a higher consciousness that imposes itself upon the body: it is the body itself awakening in its cells, a freedom of the cells themselves, an absolutely new vibration that sets disorders right – even disorders that existed prior to the supramental manifestation.

Naturally, all this is a gradual process, but I am hopeful that little by little this new consciousness will grow, gain ground and victoriously resist the old forces of destruction and annihilation, and this Fatality we believed to be so inexorable.

Vol. 1, p. 111

### February 3, 1958

Between the beings of the supramental world and men, there exists approximately the same gap as between men and animals. Sometime ago, I had the experience of identification with animal life, and it is a fact that animals do not understand us; their consciousness is so constituted that we elude them almost entirely. And yet I have known domestic animals – cats and dogs, but especially cats – who made an almost yogic effort of consciousness to understand us. But generally, when they watch us living and acting, they don't understand, they don't SEE US as we are and they suffer because of us. We are a constant enigma to them. Only a very tiny part of their consciousness is linked to us. And it is the same for us when we try to look at the supramental world. Only when the link of consciousness has been built shall we see it – and even then, only that part of our being which has undergone the transformation will be capable of seeing it as it is – otherwise the two worlds would remain as separate as the animal world and the human world.

The experience I had on February 3 proves this. Before, I had had an individual, subjective contact with the supramental world, whereas on February 3, I went strolling there in a concrete way – as concretely as I used to go strolling in Paris in times past – in a world that EXISTS IN ITSELF, beyond all subjectivity.

It is like a bridge being built between the two worlds.

This is the experience as I dictated it immediately thereafter:

*(silence)*

The supramental world exists in a permanent way, and I am there permanently in a supramental body. I had proof of this today when my earthly consciousness went there and consciously remained there between two and three o'clock in the afternoon: I now know that for the two worlds to join in a constant and conscious relationship what is missing is an intermediate zone between the existing physical world and the supramental world as it exists. This zone has yet to be built, both in the individual consciousness and in the objective world, and it is being built. When formerly I used to speak of the new world that is being created, I was speaking of this intermediate zone. And similarly, when I am on 'this' side – that is, in the realm of the physical consciousness – and I see the supramental power, the supramental light and substance constantly permeating matter, I am seeing and participating in the construction of this zone.

I found myself upon an immense ship, which is the symbolic representation of the place where this work is being carried out. This ship, as big as a city, is thoroughly organized, and it had certainly already been functioning for quite some time, for its organization was fully developed. It is the place where people destined for the supramental life are being trained. These people (or at least a part of their being) had

9

already undergone a supramental transformation because the ship itself and all that was aboard was neither material nor subtle-physical, neither vital nor mental: it was a supramental substance. This substance itself was of the most material supramental, the supramental substance nearest the physical world, the first to manifest. The light was a blend of red and gold, forming a uniform substance of luminous orange. Everything was like that – the light was like that, the people were like that – everything had this color, in varying shades, however, which enabled things to be distinguished from one another. The overall impression was of a shadowless world: there were shades, but no shadows. The atmosphere was full of joy, calm, order; everything worked smoothly and silently. At the same time, I could see all the details of the education, the training in all domains by which the people on board were being prepared.

This immense ship had just arrived at the shore of the supramental world, and a first batch of people destined to become the future inhabitants of the supramental world were about to disembark. Everything was arranged for this first landing. A certain number of very tall beings were posted on the wharf. They were not human beings and never before had they been men. Nor were they permanent inhabitants of the supramental world. They had been delegated from above and posted there to control and supervise the landing. I was in charge of all this since the beginning and throughout. I myself had prepared all the groups. I was standing on the bridge of the ship, calling the groups forward one by one and having them disembark on the shore. The tall beings posted there seemed to be reviewing those who were disembarking, allowing those who were ready to go ashore and sending back those who were not and who had to continue their training aboard the ship. While standing there watching everyone, that part of my consciousness coming from here became extremely interested: it wanted to see, to identify all the people, to see how they had changed and to find out who had been taken immediately as well as those who had to remain and continue their training. After awhile, as I was observing, I began to feel pulled backwards and that my body was being awakened by a consciousness or a person from here' – and in my consciousness, I protested: 'No, no, not yet! Not yet! I want to see who's there!' I was watching all this and noting it with intense interest ... It went on like that until, suddenly, the clock here began striking three, which violently jerked me back. There was the sensation of a sudden fall into my body. I came back with a shock, but since I had been called back very suddenly, all my memory was still intact. I remained quiet and still until I could bring back the whole experience and preserve it.

The nature of objects on this ship was not that which we know upon earth; for example, the clothes were not made of cloth, and this thing that resembled cloth was not manufactured – it was a part of the body, made of the same substance that took on different forms. It had a kind of plasticity. When a change had to be made, it was done not by artificial and outer means but by an inner working, by a working of the consciousness that gave the substance its form or appearance. Life created its own forms. There was ONE SINGLE substance in all things; it changed the nature of its vibration according to the needs or uses.

Those who were sent back for more training were not of a uniform color; their bodies seemed to have patches of a grayish opacity, a substance resembling the earth substance. They were dull, as though they had not been wholly permeated by the light or wholly transformed. They were not like this all over, but in places.

The tall beings on the shore were not of the same color, at least they did not have this orange tint; they were paler, more transparent. Except for a part of their bodies, only the outline of their forms could be seen. They were very tall, they did not seem to have a skeletal structure, and they could take on any form according to their needs. Only from their waists to their

11

feet did they have a permanent density, which was not felt in the rest of their body. Their color was much more pallid and contained very little red, it verged rather on gold or even white. The parts of whitish light were translucid; they were not absolutely transparent, but less dense, more subtle than the orange substance.

Just as I was called back, when I was saying, 'Not yet ... ,' I had a quick glimpse of myself, of my form in the supramental world. I was a mixture of what these tall beings were and the beings aboard the ship. The top part of myself, especially my head, was a mere silhouette of a whitish color with an orange fringe. The more it approached the feet, the more the color resembled that of the people on the ship, or in other words, orange; the more it went up towards the top, the more translucid and white it was, and the red faded. The head was only a silhouette with a brilliant sun at its center; from it issued rays of light which were the action of the will.

As for the people I saw aboard ship, I recognized them all. Some were here in the Ashram, some came from elsewhere, but I knew them as well. I saw everyone, but as I realized that I would not remember everyone when I came back, I decided not to give any names. Besides, it is unnecessary. Three or four faces were very clearly visible, and when I saw them, I understood the feeling that I have had here, on earth, while looking into their eyes: there was such an extraordinary joy ... On the whole, the people were young; there were very few children, and their ages were around fourteen or fifteen, but certainly not below ten or twelve (I did not stay long enough to see all the details). There were no very old people, with the exception of a few. Most of the people who had gone ashore were of a middle age – again, except for a few. Several times before this experience, certain individual cases had already been examined at a place where people capable of being supramentalized are examined; I had then had a few surprises which I had noted – I even told some people. But those whom I disembarked today I saw very distinctly. They were of a middle age, neither young children nor elderly people, with only a few rare exceptions, and this quite corresponded to what I expected. I decided not to say anything, not to give any names. As I did not stay until the end, it would be impossible for me to draw an exact picture, for it was neither absolutely clear nor complete. I do not want to say things to some and not say them to others.

What I can say is that the criterion or the judgment was based EXCLUSIVELY on the substance constituting the people – whether they belonged completely to the supramental world or not, whether they were made of this very special substance. The criterion adopted was neither moral nor psychological. It is likely that their bodily substance was the result of an inner law or an inner movement which, at that time, was not in question. At least it is quite clear that the values are different.

When I came back, along with the memory of the experience, I knew that the supramental world was permanent, that my presence there is permanent, and that only a missing link is needed to allow the consciousness and the substance to connect – and it is this link that is being built. At that time, my impression (an impression which remained rather long, almost the whole day) was of an extreme relativity – no, not exactly that, but an impression that the relationship between this world and the other completely changes the criterion by which things are to be evaluated or judged. This criterion had nothing mental about it, and it gave the strange inner feeling that so many things we consider good or bad are not really so. It was very clear that everything depended upon the capacity of things and upon their ability to express the supramental world or be in relationship with it. It was so completely different, at times even so opposite to our ordinary way of looking at things! I recall one little thing that we usually consider bad ... actually how funny it was to see that it is something excellent! And other things that we consider important were really quite unimportant there! Whether it was like this or like that made no difference. What is very obvious is that our appreciation of what is divine or not divine is incorrect. I even laughed at certain things ... Our usual feeling about what is anti-divine seems artificial, based upon something untrue, unliving (besides, what we call life here appeared lifeless in comparison with that world); in any event, this feeling should be based upon our relationship between the two worlds and according to whether things make this relationship easier or more difficult. This would thus completely change our evaluation of what brings us nearer to the Divine or what takes us away from Him. With people, too, I saw that what helps them or prevents them from becoming supramental is very different from what our ordinary moral notions imagine. I felt just how ... ridiculous we are.

Vol. 1, p. 137

## May 1, 1958

These days I am having every possible experience in the body, one after the other. Yesterday and this morning ... oh, this morning!

I saw there *(center of the heart)* the Master of the Yoga; he was no different from me, but nevertheless I saw him, and he even seemed slightly imbued with color. Well, he does everything, he decides everything, he organizes everything with an almost mathematical precision and in the smallest details – everything.

To do the divine Will – I have been doing the sadhana for a long time, and I can say that not a day has passed that I have not done the Divine's Will. But I didn't know what it was! I was living in all the inner realms, from the subtle physical to the highest regions, yet I didn't know what it was ... I always had to listen, to refer things, to pay attention. Now, no more – bliss! There are no more problems, and everything is done in such harmony! Even if I had to leave my body, I would be in bliss! And it would happen in the best possible way.

Only now am I beginning to understand what Sri Aurobindo has written in *The Synthesis of Yoga!* And the human mind, the physical mind, appears so stupid, so stupid!

Vol. 1, p. 154

## June 6, 1958

This morning while I was on the balcony, I had an interesting experience: the experience of man's effort, in all its forms and through all the ages, to approach the Divine. And I seemed to be growing wider and wider so that all the forms and all the ways of approaching the Divine attempted by man would be contained in the present Work.

It was represented by a kind of image in which I was as vast as the Universe, and each way of approaching the Divine was like a tiny image containing the characteristic form of this approach. And my impression was this: Why do people always limit, limit themselves? Narrow, narrow, narrow! They understand only when it is narrow.

Take all! Take all within you. And then you will begin to understand – you will begin.

\*     \*     \*

It was in 1910 that I had this sort of reversal of consciousness about which I spoke the other evening – that is, the first contact with the higher Divine – and it completely changed my life.

From that moment on, I was conscious that all one does is the expression of the indwelling Divine Will. But it is the Divine Will AT THE VERY CENTER of oneself, although for a while there remained an activity in the physical mind. But this was stilled two or three days after I saw Sri Aurobindo for the first time in 1914, and it never started up again. Silence settled. And the consciousness was established above the head.

In the first experience [of 1910], the consciousness was established in the psychic depths of the being, and from that poise issued the feeling of no longer doing anything but

15

what the Divine wanted – it was the consciousness that the divine Will was all-powerful and that there was no longer any personal will, although there was still some mental activity and everything had to be made silent. In 1914, it was silenced, and the consciousness was established above the head. Here *(the heart)* and here *(above the head),* the connection is constant.

*Does one exclude the other?*

They exist simultaneously; it's the same thing. When you start becoming truly conscious, you realize that it depends upon the kinds of activities you have to do. When you do a certain kind of work, it is in the heart that the Force gathers to radiate outwards, and when you do another kind of work, it is above the head that the Force concentrates to radiate outwards, but the two are not separate: the center of activity is here or there depending upon what you have to do.

...

As it was the first experience, it started to fade slightly when I began having contact with people; but I really had the feeling that it was a first experience, new upon earth. For I have experienced an absolute identity of the will with the divine Will ever since 1910, it has never left me. It isn't that, it's SOMETHING ELSE. It is MATTER BECOMING THE DIVINE. And it really came with the feeling that this thing was happening for the first time upon earth.

Vol. I, p. 163

### August 7, 1958

Day and night, I am investigating all that has to be transformed ... I can assure you that there is plenty of work!

Last night, I had many dreams (not really dreams, but ... ); I used to find them very interesting because they gave me certain indications, all kinds of things, but when I saw it all now, I said to myself, 'Good Lord! What a waste of time!

Instead, I could be living in a supramental consciousness and seeing things.' So during the night, I made a resolution to change all this too. My nights have to change. I am already changing my days; now my nights have to change. But then all this subconscious in Matter, all this, it all has to change! There's no choice, it has to be seen to.

Once you set to this work, it is such a formidable task! But what can I do?

## September 16, 1958

*(Mother spoke about mantras that have come to her)*

But what is going to come now? I constantly hear the Sanskrit mantra:

*OM NAMO BHAGAVATEH*

It is there, all around me; it takes hold of all the cells and at once they spring forth in an ascension. And Narada's mantra, too:

*Narayana, Narayana ...*

(it is actually a Command which means: now you shall do as I wish), but it doesn't come from the heart.

What will it be?

It will simply spring forth in a flash, all of a sudden, and it will be very powerful. Only power can do something. Love vanishes like water running through sand: people remain beatific ... and nothing moves! No, power is needed – like Shiva, stirring, churning ...

When I have this mantra, instead of saying hello, good-bye, I shall say that. When I say hello, good-bye, it means 'Hello: the Presence is here, the Light is here.' 'Good-bye: I am not going away, I am staying here.'

But when I have this mantra, I believe something will happen.

17

For the moment, of all the formulas or mantras, the one that acts most directly on this body, that seizes all the cells and immediately does this *(vibrating motion) is* the Sanskrit mantra: OM NAMO BHAGAVATEH.

As soon as I sit for meditation, as soon as I have a quiet minute to concentrate, it always begins with this mantra, and there is a response in the body, in the cells of the body: they all start vibrating.

The first syllable of NAMO is pronounced with a short 'a,' as in *nahmo.* The final word is pronounced BHA-GAH-VA-TEH.

This is how it happened: Y had just returned, and he brought back a trunk full of things which he then proceeded to show me, and his excitement made tight, tight little waves in the atmosphere, making my head ache; it made ... anyway, it was unpleasant. When I left, just after that had happened, I sat down and went like this *(gesture of sweeping out)* to make it stop, and immediately the mantra began.

It rose up from here *(Mother indicates the solar plexus),* like this: Om Namo Bhagavateh OM NAMO BHAGAVATEH OM NAMO BHAGAVATEH. It was formidable. For the entire quarter of an hour that the meditation lasted, everything was filled with Light! In the deeper tones it was of golden bronze (at the throat level it was almost red) and in the higher tones it was a kind of opaline white light: OM NAMO BHAGAVATEH, OM NAMO BHAGAVATEH, OM NAMO BHAGAVATEH.

The other day (I was in my bathroom upstairs), it came; it took hold of the entire body. It rose up in the same way, and all the cells were trembling. And with such a power! So I stopped everything, all movement, and I let the thing grow. The vibration went on expanding, ever widening, as the sound itself was expanding, expanding, and all the cells of the body were seized with an intensity of aspiration ... as if the entire body were swelling – it became overwhelming. I felt that it would all burst.

I understood those who withdraw from everything to live that totally.

And it has such a transformative power! I felt that if it continued, something would happen, something like a change in the equilibrium of the body's cells.

Unfortunately, I was unable to continue, because ... I don't have the time; it was just before the balcony darshan and I was going to be late. Something told me, 'That is for people who have nothing to do.' Then I said, 'I belong to my work,' and I slowly withdrew. I put on the brakes, and the action was cut short. But what remains is that whenever I repeat this mantra ... everything starts vibrating.

So each one must find something that acts on himself, individually. I am only speaking of the action on the physical plane, because mentally, vitally, in all the inner parts of the being, the aspiration is always, always spontaneous. I am referring only to the physical plane.

...

So for these mantras, everything depends upon what you want to do with them. I am in favor of a short mantra, especially if you want to make both numerous and spontaneous repetitions – one or two words, three at most. Because you must be able to use them in all cases, when an accident is about to happen, for example. It has to spring up without thinking, without calling: it should issue forth from the being spontaneously, like a reflex, exactly like a reflex. Then the mantra has its full force.

For me, on the days when I have no special preoccupations or difficulties (days I could call normal, when I am normal), everything I do, all the movements of this body, all, all the words I utter, all the gestures I make, are accompanied and upheld by or lined, as it were, with this mantra:

OM NAMO BHAGAVATEH ... OM NAMO BHAGAVATEH ... all, all the time, all the time, all the time.

That is the normal state. It creates an atmosphere of an intensity almost more material than the subtle physical; it's like ... almost like the phosphorescent radiations from a medium. And it has a great action, a very great action: it can prevent an accident. And it accompanies you all the time, all the time.

But it is up to you to know what you want to do with it.

*To sustain the aspiration – to remember. We so easily lapse into forgetfulness. To create a kind of automatism.*

You have no mantras that have come to you, that give you a more living feeling? ... Are their mantras long?

*Yes, they are long. And he has not given me any mantra of the Mother, so ... They exist, but he has not given me any ... I don't know, they don't have much effect on me. It is something very mental.*

That's why it should spring forth from you.

*(silence)*

This one, this mantra, OM NAMO BHAGAVATEH, came to me after some time, for I felt ... well, I saw that I needed to have a mantra of my own, that is, a mantra consonant with what this body has to do in the world. And it was just then that it came. It was truly an answer to a need that had made itself felt. So if you feel the need – not there, not in your head, but here *(Mother points to the center of her heart),* it will come. One day, either you will hear the words, or they will spring forth from your heart ... And when that happens, you must hold onto it.

Vol. 1, p. 194

**April 21, 1959**

Above, beginning with the center between the eyebrows, the work has been done for a long time. There it is blank. For ages upon ages upon ages, the union with the Supreme has been realized and is constant.

20

Below this center is the body. And this body has indeed the concrete sensation of the Divine in each of its cells; but it needs to become universalized. That's the work to be done, center by center. I understand now what Sri Aurobindo meant when he repeatedly insisted, 'Widen yourself.' All this must be universalized; it is the condition, the basis, for the Supramental to descend into the body.

According to the ancient traditions, this universalization of the physical body was considered the supreme realization, but it is only a foundation, the base upon which the Supramental can come down without breaking everything.

Vol. 1, p. 294

## July 24-25, 1959

First penetration of the supramental force into the body.

Sri Aurobindo alive in a concrete and permanent subtle physical body.

Vol. 1, p. 325

## October 6, 1959

For the West, with all its outward development, a few centuries may be needed before the junction between the two worlds can be made. And yet these two worlds – the physical world and the world of Truth – are not distant from one another. They are as if superimposed. The world of Truth is there, close by, like a lining of the other.

Shortly before the 15th of August I had a unique experience that exemplifies all this. For the first time the supramental light entered directly into my body, without passing through the inner beings. It entered through the feet (a red and gold color – marvelous, warm, intense), and it climbed up and up. And as it climbed, the fever also climbed because the body was not accustomed to this intensity. As all this light neared the head,

21

I thought I would burst and that the experience would have to be stopped. But then, I very clearly received the indication to make the Calm and Peace descend, to widen all this body-consciousness and all these cells, so that they could contain the supramental light. So I widened, and as the light was ascending, I brought down the vastness and an unshakable peace. And suddenly, there was a second of fainting.

I found myself in another world, but not far away (I was not in a total trance). This world was almost as substantial as the physical world. There were rooms – Sri Aurobindo's room with the bed he rests on – and he was living there, he was there all the time: it was his abode. Even my room was there, with a large mirror like the one I have here, combs, all kinds of things. And the substance of these objects was almost as dense as in the physical world, but they shone with their own light. It was not translucent, not transparent, not radiant, but self-luminous. The various objects and the material of the rooms did not have this same opacity as the physical objects here, they were not dry and hard as in the physical world we know.

And Sri Aurobindo was there, with a majesty, a magnificent beauty. He had all his beautiful hair as before. It was all so concrete, so substantial – he was even being served some kind of food. I remained there for one hour (I had looked at my watch before and I looked at it afterwards). I spoke to Sri Aurobindo, for I had some important questions to ask him about the way certain things are to be realized. He said nothing. He listened to me quietly and looked at me as if all my words were useless: he understood everything at once. And he answered me with a gesture and two expressions on his face, an unexpected gesture that did not at all correspond to any thought of mine; for example, he picked up three combs that were lying near the mirror (combs similar to those I use here, but larger) and he put them in his hair. He planted one comb in the middle of his head and the two others on each side, as if to gather all his hair over his temples. He was literally COIFFED with these three combs, which gave him a kind of crown. And I immediately understood that by this he meant that he was adopting my conception: 'You see, I embrace your conception of things, and I coif myself with it; it is my will.' Anyway, I remained there for one hour.

And when I awoke, I didn't have this feeling of returning from afar and of having to re-enter my body, as I usually do. No, it was simply as though I were in this other world, then I took a step backwards and found myself here again. It took me a good half an hour to understand that this world here existed as much as the other and that I was no longer on the other side but here, in the world of falsehood. I had forgotten everything – people, things, what I had to do; everything had gone, as if it had no reality at all.

You see, it's not as if this world of Truth had to be created from nothing: it is fully ready, it is there, like a lining of our own present world. Everything is there, EVERYTHING is there.

I remained in that state for two full days, two days of absolute felicity. And Sri Aurobindo was with me the whole time, the whole time – when I walked, he walked with me, when I sat down, he sat next to me. On the day of August 15th, too, he remained there constantly during the darshan. But who was aware of it? A few – one or two – felt something. But who saw? – No one.

And I showed all these people to Sri Aurobindo, this whole field of work, and asked him WHEN this other world, the real one that is there, so near, would come to take the place of our world of falsehood. *Not ready.* That was all he replied. *Not ready.*

Sri Aurobindo gave me two days of this – total bliss. But all the same, by the end of the second day I realized that I could not continue to remain there, for the work was not advancing. The work must be done in the body; the realization must be attained here in this physical world, for otherwise it is not complete. So I withdrew from that world and set to work here again.

23

And yet, it would take little, very little, to pass from this world to the other, or for the other to become the real world. A little click would be enough, or rather a little reversal in the inner attitude. How should I put it? It is imperceptible to the ordinary consciousness; a very little inner shift would be enough, a change in quality.

It is similar with this japa: an imperceptible little change, and one can pass from a more or less mechanical, more or less efficient and real japa, to the true japa full of power and light. I even wondered if this difference is what the tantrics call the 'power' of the japa. For example, the other day I was down with a cold. Each time I opened my mouth, there was a spasm in the throat and I coughed and coughed. Then a fever came. So I looked, I saw where it was coming from, and I decided that it had to stop. I got up to do my japa as usual, and I started walking back and forth in my room. I had to apply a certain will. Of course, I could do my japa in trance, I could walk in trance while repeating the japa, because then you feel nothing, none of all the body's drawbacks. But the work has to be done in the body! So I got up and started doing my japa. Then, with each word pronounced – the Light, the full Power. A power that heals everything. I began the japa tired, ill, and I came out of it refreshed, rested, cured. So those who tell me they come out of it exhausted, contracted, emptied, it means that they are not doing it in the true way.

I understand why certain tantrics advise saying the japa in the heart center. When one applies a certain enthusiasm, when each word is said with a warmth of aspiration, then everything changes. I could feel this difference in myself, in my own japa.

In fact, when I walk back and forth in my room, I don't cut myself off from the rest of the world – although it would be so much more convenient! ... All kinds of things come to me – suggestions, wills, aspirations. But automatically I make a movement of offering: things come to me and just as they are about to touch my head, I turn them upwards and offer them to the Light. They don't enter into me. For example, if someone speaks to me while I am saying my japa, I hear quite well what is being said, I may even answer, but the words remain a little outside, at a certain distance from the head. And yet sometimes, there are things that insist, more defined wills that present themselves to me, so then I have to do a little work, but all that without a pause in the japa. If that happens, there is sometimes a change in the quality of my japa, and instead of being fully the power, fully the light, it is certainly something that produces results, but results more or less sure, more or less long to fructify; it becomes uncertain, as with all things of this physical world. Yet the difference between the two japas is imperceptible; it's not a difference between saying the japa in a more or less mechanical way and saying it consciously, because even while I work I remain fully conscious of the japa – I continue to repeat it putting the full meaning into each syllable. But nevertheless, there is a difference. One is the all-powerful japa; the other, an almost ordinary japa ... There is a difference in the inner attitude. Perhaps for the japa to become true, a kind of joy, an elation, a warmth of enthusiasm has to be added – but especially joy. Then everything changes.

Well, it is the same thing, the same imperceptible difference, when it comes to entering the world of Truth. On one side there is the falsehood, and on the other, close by, like the lining of this one, the true life. Only a little difference in the inner quality, a little reversal, is enough to pass to the other side, into the Truth and Light.

Perhaps simply to add joy would suffice.

I will have to look at this in my body since that is where it is happening, where things are being prepared.

*This other world you speak of, this world of Truth, is it the supramental world?*

My feeling is that this life which Sri Aurobindo is living right now is not the full satisfaction of the supramental life for him.

25

In this other world, there was infinity, majesty, perfect calm, eternity – all was there.

Perhaps it was joy that was missing.

Of course, Sri Aurobindo himself had joy. But I had the impression that it was not total and that this is why I had to continue the work. I felt that it could only be total when things here have changed.

Vol. 1, p. 327

## May 24, 1960

It happened last night. For approximately three hours, the physical ego disintegrated for the first time in such a total way.

Nothing remained but the Force, nothing remained but *Sat-Chit-Ananda,* and not only in the consciousness but in the physical sensation – the divine Satchidananda spreading in a constant flood throughout the universe.

These experiences are always absolute, as long as they last; then, through certain signs that I know (I am accustomed to it), I notice that the body consciousness begins closing up again. Or rather, 'something' – evidently a Supreme Wisdom – decides it's sufficient for this time and that the body has had enough. It ought not to break, which is why certain precautions are taken. So this comes in several little stages that I know quite well. The final one is always a bit unpleasant because my body gets into rather peculiar positions as a result of the work. As it's only a sort of machine, towards the end I have some difficulty straightening my knees, for example, or opening my fingers – I think they even make a noise, like something forced into one position whose life has become purely spontaneous and mechanical. There are plenty of people like that, plenty, who enter into trance and then can no longer get out by themselves; they get themselves into a certain position and someone has to free them. This has never happened to me; I have always managed to extricate myself. But yesterday evening, the experience lasted a very long time. There was even a little cracking at the end, as when people have rheumatism.

And during all this time, approximately three hours, the consciousness was completely, completely different. It was here, however; it was not outside the earth, it was on earth, but it was completely different – even the body consciousness was different. And what remained was very mechanical; it was a body, but it could just as well have been anything. All this power of consciousness that for more than seventy years I've gradually pushed into each of the body's cells so that each cell could become conscious (and it goes on constantly, constantly), all this seemed to have withdrawn – there only remained one almost lifeless thing.

However, I could raise myself up from my bed and even drink a glass of water, but it was all so ... bizarre. And when I went back to bed, it took nearly forty-five minutes for the body to regain its normal state. Only after I had entered into another type of *samadhi* and again come out of it did my consciousness fully return. It is the first time I have had an experience of this kind.

During those three hours, there was nothing but the Supreme manifesting through the eternal Mother.

But there was no consciousness of being Mother, neither eternal nor whatever: it was a continuous and all-powerful flood, and so extraordinarily varied, of the Lord manifesting Himself.

It was as vast as the universe, a continuous movement – the movement of manifestation of something which was EVERYTHING at once, a single whole. There was no division. And such a variety of colors, vibrations, powers – extraordinary! It was one single thing, and everything was within it.

The three Supreme Principles were very clearly there: Existence, Consciousness (an active, realizing consciousness)

27

and Ananda. A universal vastness that kept going on and on and on...

It moves and it doesn't move. How can you explain that? It was in motion, a constant, unceasing motion, and yet there was no shifting of place. I had the perception, or rather there was the perception, of something which WAS forever, which never repeated itself, neither began nor ended, which didn't shift places yet was always in motion.

Words cannot express it. No translation, none, not even the most subtle mental translation can express this. It was ... Even now the memory I have of it is inexpressible. You have to be in it to feel it, otherwise ...

However, to the consciousness it was very, very clear. It was neither mysterious nor incomprehensible, it was absolutely obvious – though untranslatable to our mental consciousness. For they were contradictory, yet they existed simultaneously, indistinguishable: they were not stacked one upon another – it was all simultaneous. How can you explain that?! It's too difficult. It must be experienced.

You see, when something goes beyond thought, a sort of conception of it, or superconception rather, remains behind. But in this case, in my experience, there was no question of thought – it was a question of physical sensation. It was not beyond thought, it was beyond sensation. I was LIVING this thing. And there was no more 'I'. There was nothing but this thing, and yet there was a sensation. I can't explain it!

When I went back to bed, the transitional period lasted 45 minutes. During this time, I tried to locate the role of the individual consciousness on earth. In a flash, I understood its purpose. For you see, as long as the experience lasted, I did not feel any necessity at all of an individuality for this supreme flood to manifest. Then I understood, precisely, that the individuality served to put into contact, in this flood, all that reached out towards what is called 'I' – this individualized representation of the Divine – in order to receive help and

28

support from it, and to be put into contact. I did not say 'put into contact WITH this flood' but 'put into contact IN this flood,' for it was not happening outside – nothing was outside this flood, nothing exists outside it.

And what was really very lovely was the ACCURACY and the power which directed the forces. I watched this for three quarters of an hour: for each thing that presented itself (it could have been someone thinking, something taking place, anything at all), a special little concentration of this flood went exactly onto that point, like a special insistence.

And all this was absolutely egoless, without any personal reaction, nothing; there was nothing but the consciousness of the Supreme Action. It was the only thing existing.

And of course, the whole ordinary and higher mind (as well as the physical mind, it goes without saying, for that must be abolished before going into trance), everything here in the head, above the head, around the head – absolutely immobile.

After all that, towards the end of the night, at two in the morning, only a kind of faint suggestion was left: How can this state – which I knew in trance, in samadhi, and which necessitates lying down – become constant in a physical body which moves about? There is something to discover there. And what form will it take? For in my consciousness, you see, it is constantly like that, this universal flood, but the problem is IN THE BODY: it's the problem of the Force in its most material form.

And during the time my experience lasted, I had no feeling of anything exceptional, but rather simply the fact that after all its preparation, the body consciousness was ready for a total identification with That – in my consciousness it's always the same, a perpetual, constant and eternal state in that it never leaves me. It's like that, and it never varies. What diminishes the immensity of the Vibration are the limitations of the material consciousness which can color it and even sometimes change it by giving it a personal appearance. Thus, when I see someone and speak to him, for example, when my eyes concentrate on the person, I have almost the sensation of this flood flowing from me towards the person or of it passing through me to go onto the person. There is an awareness of the eyes, the body. And it is this which limits or even changes a little the immensity of the thing ... But already this feeling has almost disappeared; this immensity seems to be acting almost constantly. There are moments when I am less interiorized, when I am more on the surface, and it feels like it's passing through a body – moments when the body consciousness comes back a little. And this is what diminishes the thing.

This experience last night also enabled me to understand what X had felt during one of our meditations. He had explained his experience by way of saying that I was this mystic tree whose roots plunge into the Supreme and whose branches spread forth over the world, and he said that one of these branches had entered into him – and it had been a unique experience. He had said, 'this is the Mother.'

And now I understand that what he had seen and translated by this Vedic image was that kind of perpetual flood.

And you see, this experience he had, this contact between him and me, is just a point, a drop, it's nothing; it's merely something the consciousness puts into words, but the THING itself is universal. Last night it was universal; there was no room, no bed, no door – and it was concrete, concrete, so concrete, with such a splendor! There was all the Joy – this perpetual downpour in a limitless splendor.

I was reluctant to speak (because of this problem that remains hanging: to make it permanent, even in the active consciousness), and I said to myself that if I speak, it will create difficulties for me in finding the solution ... But it's all right. I shall simply have to make a still greater effort, because something always evaporates when you speak.

## October 11, 1960

*Doing japa seems to exert a pressure on my physical consciousness, which goes on turning! How can I silence it? As soon as my concentration is not absolute, the physical mind starts up – it grabs at anything, anything at all, any word, fact or event that comes along, and it starts turning, turning. If you stop it, if you put some pressure on it, then it springs back up two minutes later ... And there is no inner consent at all. It chews on words, it chews on ideas or feelings – interminably. What should I do?*

Yes, it's the physical mind. The japa is made precisely to control the physical mind.

I myself use it for a very special reason, because ... You see, I invoke (the words are a bit strange) ... the Lord of Tomorrow. Not the unmanifest Lord, but the Lord as he will manifest 'tomorrow,' or in Sri Aurobindo's words, the divine manifestation in its supramental form.

So the first sound of my mantra is the call to that, the evocation. With the second sound, the body's cells make their 'surrender,' they give themselves. And with the third sound comes the identification of this [the body] with That, which produces the divine life. These are my three sounds.

And in the beginning, during the first months that I was doing the japa, I felt them ... I had an almost detailed awareness of these myriads of cells opening to this vibration; the vibration of the first sound is an absolutely special vibration (you see, above, there is the light and all that, but beyond this light there is the original vibration), and this vibration was entering into all the cells and was reproduced in them. It went on for months in this way.

Even now, when something or other is not all right, I have only to reproduce the thing with the same type of concentration as at the beginning ... for, when I say the japa, the sound and the words together – the way the words are understood, the feel of the words – create a certain totality. I have to reproduce that. And the way it's repeated is evolving all the time. The words are the same, however, the original sound is the same, but it's all constantly evolving towards a more comprehensive realization and a more and more complete STATE. So when I want to obtain a certain result, I reproduce a certain type of this state. For example, if something in the body is not functioning right (it can't really be called an illness, but when something's out of order), or if I wish to do some specific work on a specific person for a specific reason, then I go back to a certain state of repetition of my mantra, which acts directly on the body's cells. And then the same phenomenon is reproduced – exactly the same extraordinary vibration which I recognized when the supramental world descended. It comes in and vibrates like a pulsation in the cells.

But as I told you, now my japa is different. It is as if I were taking the whole world to lift it up; no longer is it a concentration on the body, but rather a taking of the whole world – the entire world – sometimes in its details, sometimes as a whole, but constantly, constantly – to establish the Contact *(with the supramental world)*.

But what you are speaking of, this sort of sound-mill, this milling of words interminably repeating the same thing, I've suddenly caught it two or three times (not very often and with long intervals). It has always seemed fantastic to me! How is it stopped? ... Always in the same way. It's something that takes place outside, actually; it's not inside – it's outside, on the surface, generally somewhere here *(Mother indicates the temples)*, and the method is to draw your consciousness up above, to go there and remain there – white. Always this whiteness, white like a sheet of paper, flat like a plate of glass. An absolutely flat and white and motionless surface – white! White like luminous milk, turned upwards. Not transparent: white.

When this mill starts turning – usually it comes from this side *(Mother indicates the right side of the head)* – it takes hold of any sound or any word at all, and then it starts turning, harping on the same thing. This has happened to me a dozen times perhaps, but it doesn't come from me; it comes from outside, from someone or something or some particular work. So then you take it – as if you were picking it up with pincers, and then ... *(She lifts it upwards),* then I hold it there, in this motionless white – no need to keep it there for long!

Aren't you aware of this thing up above, this white plate at the crown of the head? It's what receives intuitions. It's just like a photographic plate, and it's not even active – things pass right through it without our even realizing it. And then if you concentrate just a little, everything stops, everything stops.

A few days ago, I recall, I wanted to know something that was going to happen. I thought that with the consciousness of supramental time, I could find out ... 'I MUST find out what's going to happen. What's going to happen?' – No answer. So I concentrated on it, which is what I usually do, I stopped everything and looked from above – total silence. Nothing. No answer. And I felt a slight impatience: 'But why can't I know?!' And what came was the equivalent of (I'm translating it in words), 'It's none of your business!!

So I understand more and more. Everything – this whole organization, this whole aggregate, all these cells and nerves and sensors – are all meant uniquely for the work, they have no other purpose than the work; every foolish act that is done is for the work; every stupidity that is thought is for the work; you are made the way you are because only in that way can you do the work – and it's none of your business to seek to be somewhere else. That's my conclusion. 'Very well, as You wish, may Your will be done!' – No, not 'be done'; it IS done. As You wish, exactly as You wish!

And in the end, it's quite fun.

Vol. 1, p. 433

## November 8, 1960

How strange it is! ... You have the feeling of ascending, of a progress in consciousness, and everything, all the events and circumstances of life follow one another with an unquestioning logic. You see the Divine Will unfolding with a wonderful logic. Then, from time to time, there appears a little 'set' of circumstances (either isolated or repeated), which are like snags on the way; you can't explain them, so you put them aside 'for later on.' Some such 'accidents' have been quite significant, but they don't seem to follow this ascending line of the present individuality. They're scattered along the way, sometimes repeated, sometimes only once, and then they vanish. And when you go through such an experience, you sense that they are things put aside for later on. And then, all of a sudden (especially during these last two years when I have again descended to take all that up), all of a sudden, one after another, all these snags return. And they don't follow the same curve; rather, it's as if suddenly you reach a certain state and a certain impersonal breadth that far surpasses the individual, and this new state enters into contact with one of those old 'accidents' that had remained in the deepest part of the subconscient – and that makes it rise up again, the two meet ... in an explosion of light. Everything is explained, everything is understood, everything is clear! No explanation is needed: it has become OBVIOUS.

This is entirely another way of understanding – it's not an ascent, not even a descent nor an inspiration ... it must be what Sri Aurobindo calls a 'revelation.' It's the meeting of this subconscious notation – this something which has remained buried within, held down so as not to manifest, but which suddenly surges forth to meet the light streaming down from above, this very vast state of consciousness that excludes nothing ... and from it springs forth a light – oh, a resplendence of light! – like a new explanation of the world, or of that part of the world not yet explained.

And this is the true way of knowing.

These things are like landmarks along the ascending path: you go forward step by step, and sometimes it's painful, sometimes joyful, or with a certain amount of toil that bears witness still to the presence of the personality or the individuality and its limitations (the *Questions and Answers* are full of this) – but the other thing is different, completely different: the other thing is an overflowing joy, and not only the joy of knowing but the joy of BEING. An overflowing joy.'

Vol. 1, p. 469

## January 10, 1961

Love, in its essence and in its origin, is like a white flame obliterating ALL resistances. You can have the experience yourself: whatever the difficulty in your being, whatever the weight of accumulated mistakes, the ignorance, incapacity, bad will, a single SECOND of this Love – pure, essential, supreme – melts everything in its almighty flame. One single moment and an entire past can vanish. One single TOUCH of That in its essence and the whole burden is consumed.

It's easy to understand how someone who has this experience can spread it and act upon others, since to have it you must touch the unique, supreme Essence of the whole manifestation – the Origin and the Essence, the Source and the Reality of all that is; then you immediately enter the realm of Unity where there is no more separation among individuals: it's a single vibration that can repeat itself endlessly in outer forms.

If you go high enough, you come to the Heart of everything. Whatever manifests in this Heart can manifest in all things. This is the great secret, the secret of divine incarnation in an individual form. For in the normal course of things, what manifests at the center is only realized in the outer form with the awakening and RESPONSE of the will within the individual form. But if the central Will is constantly, permanently represented in one individual, he can then serve as an intermediary between that Will and all beings, and will FOR THEM.

Whatever this being perceives and consciously offers to the supreme Will is replied to as if it came from each individual being. And if individuals happen to be in a more or less conscious and voluntary relationship with this representative being, their relationship increases his efficacy and the supreme Action can work in Matter in a much more concrete and permanent way. This is the reason for these descents of what could be called 'polarized' consciousnesses that always come to earth for a particular realization, with a definite purpose and mission – a mission decided upon before the actual embodiment. These mark the great stages of the supreme incarnations upon earth.

And when the day comes for the manifestation of supreme Love – a crystalized, concentrated descent of supreme Love – that will truly be the hour of Transformation, for nothing will be able to resist That.

But as it's all-powerful, a certain receptivity must be prepared on earth so its effects are not devastating. Sri Aurobindo has explained it in one of his letters. Someone asked him, 'Why doesn't this Love come now?', and he replied something like this: If divine Love in its essence were to manifest on earth, it would be like an explosion; for the earth is not supple enough or receptive enough to widen to the measure of this Love. The earth must not only open itself but become wide and supple. Matter – not just physical Matter, but the substance of the physical consciousness as well – is still much too rigid.

Vol. 2, p. 20

**January 24, 1961**

I have something to tell you now.... We'll work later.

In the middle of the night before last, I woke up (or rather I returned to an external consciousness) with the feeling of having a much larger (by larger I mean more voluminous) and much more powerful being in my body than I usually have. It was as if it could scarcely be held inside me but was spilling over; and SO COMPACTLY POWERFUL that it was almost uncomfortable. The feeling of: what to do with all this?

It lasted the remainder of the night and all day long I had considerable trouble containing an overwhelming power that spontaneously created reactions utterly disproportionate to a human body and made me speak in a way that.... When something was not going well: wham! Such an instantaneous and strong reply that it looked like anger. And I found it difficult to control the movement – it had happened already in the morning and it very nearly happened again in the afternoon. 'That last attack has weakened me terribly!' I told myself, I don't have the strength to contain this Power; it's difficult to remain calm and controlled.' That was my first thought, so I insisted upon calm.

Then yesterday afternoon, when I went upstairs to walk, a couple of things occurred – not personal, but of a general nature – concerning, for instance, certain old-fashioned conventions having to do with women and their particular nature (not psychological, physical) – old ideas like that which had always seemed utterly stupid to me suddenly provoked a kind of reprobation completely out of proportion to the fact itself. Then one or two other things happened in regard to certain people, certain circumstances (nothing to do with me personally: it came from here and there). Then suddenly, I saw a Force coming ('coming,' well, 'manifesting') which was the same as that 'thing' I had felt within me but even bigger; it began whirling upon the earth and within circumstances ... oh, like a cyclone of compact power moving forward with the intention of changing all this! It had to change. At all costs, it must change!

I was above, as usual *(Mother points above her head, indicating the higher consciousness)*, and I looked at that *(Mother bends over, as if looking down at the earth)*, and said to myself, 'Hmm, this is getting dangerous. If it continues like this, it will result in ... in a war or a revolution or some catastrophe – a tidal wave or an earthquake.' So I tried to counteract it by applying the highest consciousness to it, that of a perfect serenity. And I saw especially that this consciousness has been missioned to transform the earth through the Supermind and by the supramental Force, avoiding all catastrophes as far as possible: the Work is to be done as luminously and harmoniously as the earth would allow, even by going at a slower pace if need be. That was the idea. And I tried to counteract that whirlwind power with this consciousness.

*(long silence)*

...

The remainder of the evening passed as usual. I went to bed, and at exactly a quarter to twelve I got up with the feeling that this 'presence' in me had increased even further and really become rather formidable.... I had to instill a great deal of peace and confidence into my body, which felt as though ... it wasn't so easy to bear. So I concentrated, I told my body to be calm and to let itself go completely.

At midnight I was lying in bed. (And I remained there from midnight until I o'clock fully awake. I don't know if my eyes were open or closed, but I was wide awake, NOT IN TRANCE – I could hear all the noises, the clocks, and so forth.) Then, lying flat, my entire body (but a slightly enlarged body, exceeding the purely physical form) became ONE vibration, extremely rapid and intense but immobile. I don't know how to explain this, because it did not move in space but was a vibration (that is, it wasn't motionless); yet it was motionless in space. And the exact form of my body was absolutely the most brilliant white Light of the supreme Consciousness, the consciousness OF the Supreme. It was IN the body and it was as though in EACH cell there was a vibration, and it was all part of a single BLOCK of vibration. It extended this much beyond the body *(gesture indicating about six centimeters).* I was absolutely immobile in my bed. Then, WITHOUT MOVING, without shifting, it began consciously to rise up – without moving, you understand: I remained like this *(Mother holds her two joined and motionless hands at the level of her forehead, as if her entire body were*

38

*mounting in prayer)* – consciously ... like an ascension of this consciousness towards the supreme Consciousness.

The body was stretched out flat.

And for a quarter of an hour, the consciousness rose, rose, without moving. It kept rising up, up, up – until ... the junction was made.

A conscious junction, absolutely awake, NO TRANCE.

Thus the consciousness became the ONE Consciousness: perfect, eternal, outside time, outside space, outside movement ... beyond everything, in ... I don't know, in an ecstasy, a beatitude, something ineffable.

*(silence)*

It was the consciousness OF THE BODY.

I have had this experience before in exteriorization and trance, but this time it was THE BODY, the consciousness of the body.

It remained like that for a certain time (I knew it was a quarter of an hour because the clock chimed), but it was completely outside time. It was an eternity.

Then, with the same precision, the same calm, the same deliberate, clear and concentrated consciousness (absolutely NOTHING MENTAL), I began to come back down. And as I was descending, I realized that all the difficulty I had been fighting the other day and which had created this illness was absolutely ended, ANNULLED – mastered. Actually, it was not even mastery but the non-existence of anything to be mastered: simply THE vibration from top to bottom; yet there was neither high nor low nor any direction.

And it went on like that. After this, slowly, still WITHOUT MOVING, everything went back into each of the different centers of the being. (Ah, let me say parenthetically that it wasn't AT ALL the ascent of a force like the ascent of the Kundalini! It had absolutely nothing to do with the Kundalini movement and the centers, it wasn't that at all.) But while redescending,

39

it was as though WITHOUT LEAVING THIS STATE, without leaving this state which remained conscious ALL the time, this supreme Consciousness began to reactivate the different centers: first here *(Mother points to the center above the head and then touches the crown of the head, the forehead, throat, chest, etc.)* then there, there, there. At each there was a pause while this new realization organized everything. It organized and made the necessary decisions, sometimes down to the most minute details: what had to be done in this case or said in that case; and all of that TOGETHER, at once, not one by one but seen entirely as a whole. It kept on descending – I noted many things, it was extremely interesting – down and down, farther and farther, right to the depths. Everything went on at the same time, simultaneously, and at the same time this supreme Consciousness was organizing everything separately.

This descending reorganization ended exactly when the clock struck one. At that moment I knew that I had to go into trance for the work to be perfected, but until then I was wide awake.

So I slipped into trance.

I came out of this trance two hours later, at 3 a.m. And during these two hours I saw ... with a new consciousness, a new vision, and above all a NEW POWER – I had a vision of the entire Work: all the people, all the things, all the systems, all of it. And it was ... it was different in appearance (this is only because appearances depend upon the needs of the moment), but mainly it differed IN POWER – a considerable difference. Considerable. The power itself was no longer the same.

A truly ESSENTIAL change in the body has occurred.

I see that the body will have to – how can I express it? ... It will have to accustom itself to this new Power. But essentially the change has been accomplished.

It's not ... it is far, very far from being the final change, there's a lot more to be done. But we may say that it's the conscious and total presence of the supramental Force in the body.

*(silence)*

When I got up today, I was going over all this to myself, and my first instinct was not to speak of it, to observe and see what would happen; but then I received a distinct and precise Command to tell it to you this morning. The experience had to be noted down just as it occurred, recorded in its exact form.

In the body now, there is a very clear ... not only a certitude, but a *feeling* that a certain omnipotence is not far away, and that very soon when it sees ('it' sees ... 'it'! There is only one 'It' in this whole affair, which is neither 'he' nor 'she' nor ... ), when it sees that something must be, it automatically will be.

There is still a long, long way to go. But the first step on the way has been taken.

**January 27, 1961**

This time, something has really been achieved.

Since the last experience [January 24] I see it daily. The following day, probably for reasons connected with the body's development and adaptation, I was rather seriously ill – what is usually called 'painfully ill': the body was suffering a lot, or WOULD HAVE suffered a lot had it been in its former normal consciousness. That's where I saw the difference – a fantastic difference!

I was perfectly conscious (now when I say 'I', it refers to my body, I am not speaking of the whole higher consciousness), the body was perfectly conscious of its suffering, the reason for its suffering, the cause of its suffering, everything – and it did not suffer. You understand, the two perceptions were there together: the body saw the disorder, saw the suffering just as it would have felt it a few weeks earlier, it saw all that ('saw,' 'knew'... I don't know how to express it – it was conscious, *it was aware*) and it did not suffer. *The two awarenesses* were absolutely simultaneous.

There is now a kind of VERY PRECISE knowledge of the whole inner mechanism for all things – and what has to be done materially. This is developing, as a flower blossoms: you see one petal open and then another and then another; it is proceeding like that, slowly, taking its time. It's the same process for the Power.

To illustrate this, an interesting thing came up – yesterday, I think. (All these experiences come to show me the difference, as if to give proof of the change.) Someone had had a dream about me whispered to him by the adverse forces for specific reasons (I won't go into the details). He was much affected by it, so he wrote down the dream and gave it to me. I was carrying his letter along with all the others, as I usually do, but suddenly I knew I had to read it right away: I read it. Then I saw the whole thing with such clarity, precision, accuracy: how it had come about, how the dream had been produced, its effect – the whole functioning of all the forces. As I read along and it went on unfolding, I did what was necessary for him (he was present at the time) in order to undo what the adverse forces had done. Then at the end, when I had finished, said everything, explained what it was all about and what had to be done, something SO CATEGORICAL came into me (I cannot verbalize this kind of experience, it is what I call the 'difference' in power: something categorical). I took the letter, uttered a few words (which I won't repeat) and said, 'You see, it's like this: so much for that,' and I ripped the letter a first time. 'Then, that's for that,' I tore it a second time ... and so on. I ripped it up five times and the fifth time I saw that their power was destroyed.

I have done these things before – it's a knowledge I already had – and it always had its effect when I did them; it's not that I am passing from powerlessness to power, not at all. But it's this kind of ... yes, something definite, absolute – a kind of absolute in vision, in knowledge, in action and ABOVE ALL in power – a kind of absolute that doesn't need to conquer obstacles and resistances, but ANNULS the resistance automatically. Then I saw that something had truly changed.

*(After a digression, Mother gives*
*another example of the change:)*

I told you something concerning the power of the will, didn't I?

Well, yesterday I saw R. He was asking me questions about his work and particularly about the knowledge of languages (he's a scholar, you know, and very familiar with the old traditions). This put me in contact with that whole world and I began speaking to him a little about what I had already said to you concerning my experience with the Vedas. And all at once, in the same [absolute] way as I told you, when I entered into contact with that world a whole domain seemed to open up, a whole field of knowledge from the standpoint of languages, of the Word, of the essential Vibration, that vibration which would be able to reproduce the supramental consciousness. It all came, so clear, so clear, luminous, indisputable – but unfortunately there was no tape recorder!

It was about the Word, the primal sound. Sri Aurobindo speaks of it in *Savitri:* the essence of the Word and how it will express itself, how it will bring in the possibility of a supramental expression that will take the place of languages.... I began by speaking to him about the different languages, their limitations and possibilities; and I warned him against the deformations imposed on languages with the idea of making them a more flexible means of expressing something else. I told him how completely ridiculous it all was, and that it didn't correspond at all to the truth. Then little by little I began ascending to the Origin. So yesterday again, I had this same experience: a whole world of knowledge, of consciousness and of CERTAINTY – precluding the least possibility of contradiction, discussion, or opposition; the possibility DOES NOT EXIST, it doesn't exist.

And the mind was absolutely silent and immobile, listening with obvious pleasure because these things had never before come into my consciousness; I had never been concerned with them in that way. It was completely new – not new in principle but completely new in action. The experiences are multiplying.

*A sound that can bring in the supramental Force?*

Yes. While speaking, you see, I went back to the origin of sound (Sri Aurobindo describes it very clearly in *Savitri:* the origin of sound, the moment when what we called 'the Word' becomes a sound). So I had a kind of perception of the essential sound before it becomes a material sound. And I said, 'When this essential sound becomes a material sound, it will give birth to the new expression which will express the supramental world.' I had the experience itself at that moment, it came directly. I spoke in English and Sri Aurobindo was concretely, almost palpably, present.

Now it has gone away.

Vol. 2, p. 47

## January 31, 1961

*(Concerning the experience related on January 24, of the supramental Force reorganizing the activity of each center of consciousness. The experience ended in a deep trance: 'I slipped into trance...')*

I neglected to mention something very important.

At the moment of my coming out of the trance, I had a very concrete, positive perception (not a mental understanding, it didn't come from the being's intellectual part, the part that understands and explains everything and is symbolized, I think, by Indra; it wasn't in any way conveyed through that higher intelligence, it wasn't mental). A kind of perception (not really a sensation, it was more than a sensation) of the

44

almost total unimportance of the external, material expression of the body's condition: the consciousness OF THE BODY was absolutely indifferent to external, physical signs, whether they were like this or like that (the BODY'S consciousness was what had experienced the identity). And this body-consciousness had the perception of the EXTREME RELATIVITY of the most material expression.

I am translating it to make myself understood – it wasn't like that at the time of the experience. Suppose, for example, that there was a disorder here or there in the body, not actually an illness (because illness implies some important inner factor such as an attack or the necessity for some transformation, many different things), but the outer expression of a disorder, such as swollen legs or a malfunctioning liver – not an illness, a disorder, a functional disorder. Well, it was all utterly unimportant: IT IN NO WAY CHANGES THE BODY'S TRUE CONSCIOUSNESS. Although we are in the habit of thinking that the body is very disturbed when it's ill, when something is going wrong, it's not so. It isn't disturbed in the way we understand it.

*Then what is disturbed if not the body?*

Oh, it's the physical mind, this stupid mind! It makes all the trouble, always.

*It isn't the body at all?*

No! The body is VERY enduring.

*Then what suffers?*

Suffering also comes through the physical mind, because if this entity is calmed down, we no longer suffer – exactly what happened to me!

The physical mind, you see, makes use of the nervous substance; if we withdraw it from the nervous substance, we no longer feel anything, for that's what gives us the perception of sensation.... We know something is wrong, but we no longer suffer from it.

This was a very important experience. Afterwards (especially yesterday afternoon and this morning), I gradually began to realize that this kind of indifferent detachment is the ESSENTIAL condition for the establishment of true Harmony in the most material Matter – the most external, physical Matter *(Mother pinches the skin of her hand).*

This experience has been like a stage – an indispensable stage for establishing this complete detachment; an indispensable stage so that the harmony of the body-consciousness (which came with the body's experience of the Divine) might have its effect upon the most external, superficial part of the body.

*(silence)*

This is the logical consequence of the research I have been doing for a long time now on the cause of illnesses and how to overcome them.

This ought to be noted down, because it's important. It has seemed all the more important to me these last two days. Beginning yesterday evening, there was a whole series of experiences, and this morning I came to a certain conclusion, whose starting point, I realized, was that experience I had upon coming out of trance....

The rest will come later.

It was the very moment I was coming out of the trance, at 3 a.m. – I came out of it with that; it was the first contact. I had forgotten to mention this to you because it took on importance only very recently.

Vol. 2, p. 52

**March 27, 1961**

... You remember that type of detachment I spoke of when I had that experience – when the BODY had that experience [January 24, 1961] – well, it has increased to such an extent that it now applies to anything and everything linked with action on earth. This detachment was probably necessary. It

46

began with something like ... things dissolving *(Mother makes a gesture of crumbling something between her fingers);* certain kinds of links between my consciousness and the Work were dissolving (not links with me, because I don't have any, but with the body; the whole physical consciousness, all that attaches it to the things in its environment, to the Work and to the entourage – I spoke to you about that in regard to physical immortality; well, that's what is happening now). It's like things dissolving – dissolving, dissolving, dissolving. And it's more and more pronounced. During these last days, things have been becoming increasingly difficult – difficulties have been coming one after another, one after another. Formerly, I had the power to get a grip on them and hold them *(Mother tightens her grip as though mastering circumstances);* but now that this type of detachment has begun, things drift away everywhere – everywhere, everywhere....

.... What has been affected is a certain confidence in the REALITY of the Power, the REALITY of spiritual action; there seems to be no communication between here *(above)* and there *(below).*

*Does that mean you're breaking all contacts with the earth?*

No, that's not it. Things go on. I don't know, I have no idea. I can't say exactly what it is, but.... It's a.... Don't know. In any case, it seems obvious that the NATURE of the contact must become very different. Because in proportion to this detachment, the reality of the Vibration – and especially the vibration of divine Love – keeps growing and growing (out of all proportion to the body, even) in a FORMIDABLE manner, formidable! The body is beginning to feel nothing but that.

Is this detachment necessary, then, for divine Love to be established? I don't know.

Yes, it's as if I were living, as if the BODY were living (despite all the illnesses and attacks, all the ill will besetting it), living in a bath of the divine vibration – bathing in something ...

47

immense – immense, immense ... limitless, and so stable! The body lives in it like this *(gesture as if Mother were floating)*. So even when there is what we call physical pain, even when there are blows to morale (like having a cashier ask you for money and you have none to give him), well, despite it all, despite all the possible complications (coming all at the same time), EVERYTHING, everything that happens now, even things which seem extremely unpleasant to our mental conceptions or our mental reactions, everything is a bath, a bath of the vibration of divine Love. So much so that if I didn't control my body, I would be smiling at everything all the time like an idiot. A beatific smile for everything (I don't show it because I control myself).

*(silence, the clock strikes the hour)*

...

But you know, it's no *joke,* this transformation!

*(silence)*

Yesterday I had such a strong feeling that ALL constructions, all habits, all ways of seeing, all ordinary reactions, were all crumbling away – completely. I felt I was suspended in something ... entirely different, something ... I don't know.

*(silence)*

And truly, with the feeling that ALL one has lived, all one has known, all one has done, all of it is a perfect illusion – that's what I was living yesterday evening.

And then....

It's one thing to have the spiritual experience of the illusion of material life (some find this painful, but I found it so wonderfully beautiful and happy that it was one of the loveliest experiences of my life); but now the whole spiritual construction as one has lived it is becoming ... a total illusion! Not the same illusion, a far more serious illusion.

If That was not there.... Obviously, That [divine Love] is here, like a mattress placed so you won't break your neck

48

when you fall. That's precisely the feeling: this experience of the vibration of divine Love is the mattress ... so you don't break your neck!

So, petit, don't brood; whatever your difficulties may be *(laughing),* you can tell yourself they are only beginning!

And I'm not exactly a baby; I have been here forty-seven years, and for something like ... yes, certainly for sixty years I have been doing a conscious yoga, with all that memories of an immortal life can bring – and see where I am! When Sri Aurobindo says you must have endurance, I think he is right!

This path is not for the weak, that's for sure.

I believe this body has suffered as much as a body can bear without going to pieces, and it keeps going, it has never asked for mercy – not once has it said, 'No, it's too much,' not once. It says, 'As You will, Lord: here I am.'

And so it continues.

*(Mother gets up to leave)*

Well, I'm never going to tell people that it's just a promenade! No, it's nothing like a promenade. Some say, 'Oh, you're too severe!' But too bad for them; it's better to tell the truth, isn't it?

We mustn't get discouraged.

The absolute certainty of the Victory is unquestionable; but I am not speaking at the scale of our bounded mind. It's up to us to CHANGE TACK – this is what's expected of us, to change tack and not keep going round in circles.

There you are, petit.

It's a process of tempering, you know – we get tempered.

And there's no point in giving up, because it would just have to be started all over again next time. What I always say is: 'Here's the opportunity – go right to the end.' It's no use saying, 'Ah, I can't,' because next time it will be even more difficult.

## July 15, 1961

Some months ago, when this body had once again become a battlefield and was confronting all the obstacles, when it was suspended, asking itself whether ... it wasn't wondering intellectually, but asking for a kind of perception, wanting to touch something: it wondered which direction it was taking, which way things were going to tilt. And suddenly, in all the cells, there was this feeling (and I know where it came from): 'If we are dissolved out of this amalgam, if this assemblage is dissolved and can no longer go on, then we shall all go straight, straight as an arrow' – and it was like a marvelous flame – 'straight to rejoin Sri Aurobindo in his supramental world, which is right here at our door.' And there was such joy! Such enthusiasm, such joy flooded all the cells! They didn't care at all whether or not they would be dissociated.... 'Oh,' they felt, 'so what!'

This was truly a decisive stage in the work of illuminating the body.

All the cells felt far more powerful than that stupid force trying to dissolve them; what is called 'death' left them entirely indifferent: 'What do we care? We shall go THERE and consciously participate in Sri Aurobindo's work, in the transformation of the world, one way or the other – here, there, like this, like that – what does it matter!'

This came more than a year ago, I think. It has never left. Never. All anxiety and all conscious tension have gone.

Only – there is an 'only' in all this – if there were a more liberal proportion between the 'refreshing' (if I may say so) freedom of solitude and the necessity for collective work, there would probably be fewer difficulties.... Towards the end of the first year after I retired upstairs (perhaps even before, but anyway, some time after I began doing japa while walking), I recall having such sessions up there! ... Had there indescribable, absolutely beyond all imaginable or expressible splendor.

And that was when I received the Command from the Supreme, who was right here, this close *(Mother presses her face)*. He told me, 'This is what is promised. Now the Work must be done.'

And not individual but collective work was meant. So naturally, because of the way it came, it was joyously accepted and immediately implemented.

But when I remember that experience and consider what I have now....

*(silence)*

Well, what Sri Aurobindo did by leaving his body is somewhat equivalent, although far more total and complete and absolute – because he had that experience, he had that, he had it; I saw him, I saw him supramental on his bed, sitting on his bed.

*(silence)*

He has written: I am not doing it individually, for myself, but for the whole earth. And it was exactly the same thing for me – but oh, that experience! Nothing counted for me anymore: people, the earth – even the earth itself had absolutely no importance.

*(The clock strikes.)*

*Later, just before leaving:*

But you know, this present state gives me the feeling that actually we know nothing at all, at all, at all – nothing at all. Everything else, everything leading to the spiritual life, to liberation and so forth – well, yes, it's all very well, all very well. But compared to what one must know to do this work....

Perhaps it's better not to know.

Because evidently I can't say that my experiences are the result of a mental aspiration or will or knowledge – I don't what it should be, nor anything at all. I don't know what should be done, I don't know what should not be done – nothing. It's truly a blind march *(gesture of groping along),* in a desert riddled with all possible traps and difficulties and obstacles – all this heaped together. Eyes blindfolded, knowing nothing *(same gesture of groping blindly),* one plods on.

The only thing to do is to be like this *(Mother turns her hands towards the Heights in a gesture of abandonment).* Provided you don't fall asleep! You mustn't enter into a beatific state where you.... No, we must keep moving on.

I don't know what to do. It's not easy.

Vol. 2, p. 263

### August 11, 1961

What's marvelous is that I haven't a single idea in my head – nothing. Not 'idea'; I never have many of them! *(laughing)* No words, mon petit, nothing. I have two of T.'s notebooks here – I read them, said 'Ah!', and put them away. They've already stayed there for two weeks or ... I don't know how long. NOTHING, completely *blank.* But on the lowest plane, some interesting things: suddenly (not from time to time, but all the time, or almost all the time), all the body's cells suddenly seem to participate in a movement of force, a sort of circular movement containing all the vibrations – physical vibrations – right from the most material sensation *(Mother touches the skin of her hands)* to all the feelings of strength, power and comprehension (especially from an active standpoint, the standpoint of actions, movements, influences). It's not at all limited to the body; it's like that, like that, like that ... *(Mother makes a gesture stretching to infinity).* It has neither beginning nor end. The body itself is starting to feel how Energy behaves.

At any moment, if I just pay a little attention, it's like that. And then the body has no more limits – more and more, they seem to disappear.

And for the least little things, the least little things; and ... all taking place within the Supreme, with the ecstasy of His Presence. For the tiniest, tiniest little things: how the Force behaves when you're arranging objects, when you're moving something ... for everything, for food, for....

And it is strangely indifferent to any scale of values or circumstances. Sometimes when I am meeting and speaking with someone, when I am seeing someone, this great universal Light of a perfect whiteness comes streaming in. Well, I must admit, this also occurs for the merest trifles, when I'm tasting some cheese somebody has sent me, for example, or arranging objects in a cupboard, or deciding what things I'm going to use or have to organize. It doesn't come in the same massive way as when it comes directly. When it comes directly it's a mass, passing through and going out like that *(Mother shows the Light descending directly from above like a mass and passing through her head in order to spread out everywhere).* In these small things it's pulverized, as though it came through an atomizer, but it's that same sparkling white light, utterly white. Then, whatever I'm doing, there's a sensation in the body that's like lying on a sea of something very soft, very intimate, very deep and eternal, immutable: the Lord. And all the body's cells are joyously saying, 'You, You, You, You....'

That's my present condition.

The moments of forgetting are brief – plunk! A knock from someone or something – the shock of the ordinary vibration. It's unimportant, you turn your head and push it away. But I don't want that either, it [the movement of rejection] must go away entirely.

From a practical, concrete, effective standpoint, there are

to receive my response very clearly, very precisely. People I don't know at all have written, and they receive my reply even before I write back (they tell this to intermediaries). I had another example only today. It's having results.

The earth is tiny.

## January 12, 1962

*(Note from Mother to Satprem concerning his question of January 9, on the capacities required to gain access to the supramental world. [After Mother spoke about Her experience on the Supramental Ship on February 3, 1958.)*

"Capacity for indefinite expansion of consciousness on all planes including the material."

Limitless plasticity, to be able to follow the movement of becoming.

Perfect equality abolishing all possibility of ego reaction.

(Concerning Satprem's question on the experience of the "supramental ship":)

Did you get my note, petit?

I've said something on the subject somewhere.... Do you remember that gentleman from Madras who had asked a question? There was an indication there....

Because I followed the thread, I put myself back in contact with the experience of the supramental ship, and I noticed that it had a DECISIVE effect on my position: the required conditions were established quite clearly, precisely, and definitively by that experience. In that respect, it was interesting.

Once and for all it has swept away all these notions – not merely ordinary moral notions, but everything people here in India consider necessary for the spiritual life. In that respect, it was very instructive. And first and foremost, this so-called vital movements. Instead of taking these movements and turning them towards the Divine, instead of seeing, that is, the supreme Presence in them (and so letting the Supreme deal with them freely), He is told *(laughing):* "No – it's none of Your business! You have no say in it."

As for the physical, it's an old and well-known story – ascetics have always rejected it; but they also reject the vital. And they're all like that here, even ... X may have changed somewhat by now, but at the beginning he was no different either. Only things classically recognized as holy or admitted by religious tradition were accepted – the sanctity of marriage, for example, and things like that.... But a free life? Not a chance! It was wholly incompatible with religious life.

Well, all that has been completely swept away, once and for all.

This doesn't mean that what's being asked of us is easier! It's probably far more difficult.

I mentioned the principal psychological requirement in my answer to that American: a state of perfect equality. This is an ABSOLUTE condition. Over the years since that experience I have observed that no supramental vibration whatsoever can be transmitted without this perfect equality. The slightest contradiction of that equality – in other words, the least movement of ego, of egoistic preference – and everything is blocked, transmission stops. This is already quite a large stumbling block.

And, over and above this, for the realization to be total, there are two other conditions, which aren't easy either. Intellectually, they're not too difficult; in fact, for someone who has practiced yoga, followed a discipline (I am not speaking here of just anyone), they're relatively easy. Psychologically too, given this equality, there's no great difficulty. But as soon as you come to the material plane – the physical plane – and then to the body, it isn't easy. These two conditions are first, the power to expand, to widen almost indefinitely, enabling you to widen to

55

the dimensions of the supramental consciousness – which is total. The supramental consciousness is the consciousness of the Supreme in his totality. By "totality," I mean the Supreme in his aspect of Manifestation. Naturally, from a higher point of view, from the viewpoint of the essence – the essence of that which in Manifestation becomes the Supermind – what's necessary is a capacity for total identification with the Supreme, not only in his aspect of Manifestation, but in his static or nirvanic aspect, outside of the Manifestation: Nonbeing. But in addition, one must be capable of identifying with the Supreme in the Becoming. And that implies both these things: an expansion that is nothing less than indefinite, and that should simultaneously be a total plasticity enabling one to follow the Supreme in his Becoming. You don't merely have to be as vast as the universe at one point in time, but indefinitely in the Becoming. These are the two conditions. They must be potentially present.

Down to the vital, we are still in the realm of things that are more than feasible – they are done. But on the material level it results in my misadventures of the other day. *(On January 9, 1962, Mother fainted.)*

But even accepting all these misadventures a priori, things remain difficult because there's a double movement: both a cellular transformation and a capacity for '"something" that could replace expansion with readjustment, a constant intercellular reorganization.

The way they are now, of course, our bodies are rigid and heavy – it's unspeakable, actually; if it weren't for that we would never grow old. For instance, my vital being is more full of energy, and thus full of youth and power to grow, than when I was twenty. There's really no comparison. The power is INFINITELY greater ... yet the body is going to pieces – it's really something unspeakable. So a way has to be found to bridge this gap between the vital and the material being.

56

Not that the problem hasn't been partially solved: hatha yogis have solved it, partially – provided you do nothing else (that's the trouble). Yet having the knowledge, we should have the power to do what's necessary without making it our exclusive preoccupation. At any rate, this possibility is certainly not altogether unknown; for the first few months after I retired to my room, when I had cut all contact with the outside, it was working very well ... even extraordinarily so! Lots of disorders in my body were surmounted, and I had many fairly precise indications that if I continued like that long enough I would regain everything that had been lost, and with an even better equilibrium. I mean that the functional equilibrium was far superior. Only when I came back into contact with the world did it all come to a halt and begin to deteriorate – all the more so as it was aggravated by this discipline of expansion making me constantly – CONSTANTLY – absorb mountains of difficulties to be resolved. And so....

With the mind, it's rather easy – you can put things back in order in five minutes, it's not difficult. With the vital it's already a bit more troublesome, it takes a little longer. But when you come to the material level, well.... There's a CONTAGION of wrong cellular functioning and a kind of internal disorganization – things not staying in their proper places. Each vibration absorbed from the outside instantly creates a disorder, dislocates everything, creates wrong contacts and disrupts the organization; it sometimes takes HOURS to put it all back in order. Consequently, if I really want to make use of this body's possibility without having to face the necessity of changing it because it can't follow along, then, materially, I would really need, as much as possible, to stop having to gulp down all sorts of things that drag me years backwards.

It's difficult ... difficult.

So long as there's no question of physical transformation, the psychological and in large part, the subjective point of view is sufficient – and that's relatively easy. But when it comes to incorporating matter into the work, matter as it is in this world where the very starting point is false (we start off in unconsciousness and ignorance), well, it's very difficult. Because, to recover the consciousness it has lost, Matter has had to individualize itself, and for that – for the form to last and retain this possibility of individuality – it has been created with a certain indispensable measure of rigidity. And that rigidity is the main obstacle to the expansion, to the plasticity and suppleness necessary for receiving the Supermind. I constantly find myself facing this problem, which is utterly concrete, absolutely material when you're dealing with cells that have to remain cells and not vaporize into some nonphysical reality, and at the same time have to have a suppleness, a lack of rigidity, enabling them to widen indefinitely.

There have been times, while working in the most material mind (the mind ingrained in the material substance), when I felt my brain swelling and swelling and swelling, and my head becoming so large it seemed about to burst! On two occasions I was forced to stop, because it was ... (was it only an impression, or was it a fact?) in any event it seemed dangerous, as if the head would burst, because what was inside was becoming too tremendous (it was that power in Matter, that very powerful deep blue light which has such powerful vibrations; it is able to heal, for example, and change the functioning of the organs – really a very powerful thing materially). Well then, that's what was filling my head, more and more, more and more, and I had the feeling that my skull was (it was painful, you know) ... that there was a pressure inside my skull pushing out, pushing everything out.... I wondered what was going to happen. Then, instead of following the movement, helping it along and going with it, I became immobile, passive, to see what would happen. And both times it stopped. I was no longer helping the movement along, you see, I simply remained passive – and it came to a halt, there was a sort of stabilization.

*(silence)*

But Sri Aurobindo must have had the experience [of cellular expansion], because he said positively that it COULD be done.

The question, of course, is the supramentalization of MATTER – the consciousness, that's nothing at all. Most people who have had that experience had it on the mental level, which is relatively easy. It's very easy: abolition of limits set by the ego, indefinite expansion with a movement following the rhythm of the Becoming. Mentally, it's all very easy. Vitally.... A few months after I withdrew to my room, I had the experience in the vital – wonderful, magnificent! Of course to have the experience there, the mind must have undergone a change, one must be in complete communion; without exception, any individual vital being that hasn't been prepared by what might be called a sufficient mental foundation would be panic-stricken. All those poor people who get scared at the least little experience had better not dabble with this – they'd panic! But as it happens – through divine grace, you might say – my vital, the vital being of this present incarnation, was born free and victorious. It has never been afraid of anything in the vital world; the most fantastic experiences were practically child's play. But when I had that experience, it was so interesting that for a few weeks I was tempted to stay in it; it was.... I once told you a little about that experience (it was quite a while ago, at least two years). I told you that even during the day I seemed to be sitting on top of the Earth – that was this realization in the vital world. And what fantastic nights it gave me! Nights I have never been able to describe to anyone and never mentioned – but I would look forward to the night as a marvelous adventure.

I voluntarily renounced all that in order to go further. And when I did it, I understood what people here in India mean when they say: *he surrendered his experience.* I had never really understood what that meant. When I did it, I understood. "No," I said, "I don't want to stop there; I am giving it all to

You, that I may go on to the end." Then I understood what it meant.

Had I kept it, oh – I would have become one of those world-renowned phenomena, turning the course of the earth's history upside down! A stupendous power! Stupendous, unheard-of.... But it meant stopping there, accepting that experience as final – I went on.

Well. So now, what can I tell you that's interesting – everything I've just said is a sort of miscellany, and three-fourths unusable.

*But, Mother....*

I didn't say it with the idea of writing an article!

When I read that note you sent me, I immediately reconnected with the experience, and things became clear. I have told them to you as well as they can be told....

*(silence)*

The people on that ship had these two capacities: one, the capacity for indefinite expansion of consciousness on all planes, including the material; and two, limitless plasticity in order to follow the movement of the Becoming.

It was taking place in the subtle physical. The people who had patches on their bodies and had to be sent back were always the ones who lacked the plasticity those two movements required. But the main thing was the movement of expansion; the progressive movement, the movement of following the Becoming, seemed to be a subsequent preoccupation – for those who had landed. The preparation on the boat concerned that capacity for expansion.

Another thing I didn't mention to you when I related the experience was that the ship had no engine. Everything was set in motion through will power – people, things (even the clothes people wore were a result of their will). And this gave all things and every person's shape a great suppleness, because there was an awareness of this will – which is not a mental will

60

but a will of the Self, what could be called a spiritual will or a soul-will (to give the word soul that particular meaning). I have that experience right here when there's an absolute spontaneity in action, I mean when the action – for instance, an utterance or a movement – is not determined by the mind, and not even (not to mention thought or intellect), not even by the mind that usually sets us in motion. Generally, when we do something, we can perceive in ourselves a will to do it; when you watch yourself, you see this: there is always (it can happen in a flash) the will to do. When you are conscious and watch yourself doing something, you see in yourself the will to do it – this is where the mind intervenes, its normal intervention, the established order in which things happen. But the supramental action is decided by a leap over the mind. The action is direct, with no need to go through the mind. Something enters directly into contact with the vital centers and activates them without going through the mind – yet in full consciousness. The consciousness doesn't function in the usual sequence, it functions from the center of spiritual will straight to matter.

And so long as you can keep that absolute immobility in the mind, the inspiration is absolutely pure – it comes pure. When you can catch and hold onto this while you're speaking, then what comes to you is unmixed too, it stays pure. This is an extremely delicate functioning, probably because we're not used to it – the slightest movement, the slightest mental vibration disrupts everything. But as long as it lasts, it's perfectly pure. And in a supramentalized life this has to be the CONSTANT state. Mentalized will should no longer intervene; because you may well have a spiritual will, your life may be the constant expression of spiritual will (it's what happens to all who feel themselves guided by the Divine within), but it still comes through a mental transcription. Well, as long as it's that way, it's not the supramental life. The supramental life NO LONGER goes through the mind – the mind is an immobile

61

zone of transmission. The least little twitch is enough to upset everything.

*(silence)*

So we can say that the Supermind can express itself through a terrestrial consciousness only when there is a constant state of perfect equality – equality arising out of spiritual identification with the Supreme: all becomes the Supreme in perfect equality. And it must be automatic, not an equality obtained through conscious will or intellectual effort or an understanding preceding the state itself – none of that. It has to be spontaneous and automatic; one must no longer react to what comes from outside as though it were coming from outside. That pattern of reception and reaction must be replaced by a state of constant perception and (I don't mean identical in all cases, because each thing necessarily calls forth its own particular reaction) ... but practically free from all rebound, you might say. It's the difference between something coming from outside and striking you, making you react, and something freely circulating and quite naturally generating the vibrations needed for the overall action. I don't know if I am making myself clear.... It's the difference between a vibratory movement circulating within an IDENTICAL field of action, and a movement from an outside source, touching you and getting a reaction (this is the usual state of human consciousness). But once the consciousness is identified with the Supreme, all movements are, so to speak, inner – inner in the sense that nothing comes from outside; there are only things circulating, which, through similarity or necessity, naturally generate or change the vibrations within the circulatory milieu.

I am very familiar with this, because I am now constantly in that state. I never have the feeling of something coming from outside and bumping into me; there's rather the sense of multiple and sometimes contradictory inner movements, and of a constant circulation generating the inner changes necessary to the movement.

This is the indispensable foundation.

I've had that experience for a very long time and now it's completely established. It used to be transitory, but now it's constant.

It is the indispensable foundation.

And in that state, expansion follows almost automatically, necessitating certain adjustments in the body which are difficult to work out. I am still completely immersed in this problem.

Then that suppleness.... It means a capacity for decrystallizing oneself; the whole span of life given over to self-individualization is a period of conscious, willed crystallization, which then has to be undone. To become a conscious, individualized being there has to be a constant, constant, willed crystallization, in everything; and afterwards, again constantly, the opposite movement has to be made – with an even greater will. But at the same time, the consciousness must not lose the benefit of what has been acquired through individualization.

It is difficult, I must say.

For thought, it's elementary, very simple. It's not difficult for the feelings either; for the heart, the emotional being, to expand to the dimensions of the Supreme is relatively easy. But this body! It's very difficult, very difficult to do without the body losing its center (how can I put it?) ... its center of coagulation – without it dissolving into the surrounding mass. Although, if one were in a natural environment, with mountains and forests and rivers, with lots of space and lots of natural beauty, it could be rather pleasant! But it's physically impossible to take a single step outside one's body without meeting unpleasant, painful things. At times you come in contact with a pleasant substance, something harmonious, warm, vibrating with a higher light; it happens. But it's rare. Flowers, yes, sometimes flowers – sometimes, not always. But this material world, oh! It batters you from all sides; it claws you, mauls you – you get clawed and scraped and battered by all sorts of things which ... which just don't blossom. How hard it all is! Oh, how closed human life is! How shriveled, hardened, without light, without warmth ... let alone joy.

While sometimes, when you see water flowing along, or a ray of sunlight in the trees – oh, how it sings! The cells sing, they are happy.

Well, mon petit, that's all I can tell you. If you can make something out of it.... But it's a new experience. Isn't it interesting? I have to put it into the form of an experience – there's no other way for it to be.

But keep it as impersonal as possible!

...

If we continue along this path, we will surely be able to do some worthwhile work, because it's all new. It's quite new – I never spoke of this with Sri Aurobindo because at the time I didn't have those experiences. I had all the psychological experiences, experiences in the mind, even the most material mind, or in the vital or the physical consciousness – the physical CONSCIOUSNESS – but not in the body. That's something new, it started only three or four years ago.

All the rest is easy. Everything up to that point is settled – settled very nicely.

...

Vol. 3, p. 33


## February 13, 1962

Actually, I have noticed one thing: nowadays if I spontaneously say something the way I see it, without trying to adapt myself to people, they don't understand – it's difficult to understand. And I am not speaking of people who know nothing, but of those who have lived and thought with me.

My vision of things – the SAME things – has become very, very different. Very different. When you read these Talks to me it's exactly as though I were listening to someone else saying things – I am transported back into a different person's consciousness. But at least it's accessible, while now....

At that time, I had the sense of a "higher way of living": I used to make a distinction between different ways of life. Now this so-called higher way of living seems so miserable to me – so petty, mean, narrow – that I very often find myself in the same position as those who ask, "But is there really something to it?" And I understand them (even though I have a different will and vision of something to come that is not yet here), I understand the feeling of those who came into contact with spiritual life and asked, "What good is it – what good is it? Is there anything worth living in it?" We are NECESSARILY hemmed in, bound to live in narrowness and pettiness simply to keep alive, for the sake of all the body's needs.

It takes such an effort to bring Light into this poverty, to bring a Force, a Reality, a Power, something, good Lord, something TRUE! Through constant effort and will, constant tension, suddenly, ah! I get two or three seconds ... and then it all ebbs away again.

In that former illusion, there were noble actions, generous actions, great, heroic actions, all adding color to life and capable of giving you some interesting hours. Now that too is gone: I see it all as childishness.

I understand very well that this present state is necessary for getting out of it. For as long as something seems normal, natural, acceptable, there's no escaping it. You have one life on the side and then "this" [the life in the body], that's the way people with a spiritual life always lived: they had their spiritual life and let "this" continue on automatically, without attaching any importance to it – it's very easy.

But what a relief to live the Truth at each instant! ...

I haven't yet found the way.

It will come.

Voilà, petit.

*But will this present period between the old world and the other last a long time? There's nothing in between....*

Not for the moment.

*There's nothing, it's like a no-man's-land. You're no longer on this side and....*

... And you aren't yet on the other. Yes, that's it.

So the tendency is always to step back and go within. But that's not the way! It's a natural movement, but I clearly see that it's false.

Both were there this morning.

Obviously a great, great deal of stability and inner calm is required.... There was a keen sense of the absolute pettiness, stupidity and dullness of all outer circumstances, of this whole bodily life in its external form, and AT THE SAME TIME a great symphony of divine joy. And both states were together like pulsations.

But it makes your head spin. You have to be very careful, it *... it makes you giddy!*

I can't express it – the minute you try to express it, most of it evaporates. And even if I did tell what little I could, surely a good nine and a half people out of ten would say, "She's batty!" If I spoke to the people here that way, they would probably say, "She's soft in the head!"

Strange. This morning it was strange, for both were there: the feeling of physical weakness – almost a physical decomposition – and AT THE SAME TIME, SIMULTANEOUSLY (not even one behind the other, but both together), a glory of divine splendor.

Both together.

Both together.

I always have the most acute experiences when I am getting ready to go down for the balcony [darshan]. That's when they come, during the most prosaic part of daily life. When I am meditating or walking or even seeing someone, it's different: physical things fade away, they lose their significance. But in this case, it's when I am in the very midst of physical life.

It was odd this morning because on one side I felt ("one side" – it's not even a side; I don't know how to explain, they are both together) the body was unwell, most unharmonious (someone in an ordinary consciousness would have said the body was ill, or at any rate very weak, very ... not at all in good condition), and simultaneously, in the SAME PHYSICAL SENSATION: a glory! A marvelous glory of blissfulness, joy, splendor! ... But how could the two be together?

Really, you must stay perfectly, perfectly calm inside; externally, you do things, brush your teeth and so forth, but within you must keep very calm if you don't want to fall over.

*But what prevents the two from joining?*

It's not a joining. It's not a joining: one is to replace the other.

But the other....

You see, it's like trying to alter the functioning of the organs. What is the process? Already the two are beginning to exist simultaneously.... What does it take for one to disappear and the other to remain on its own, changed? ... Changed, because as it is now it wouldn't be enough to make the body function; the body wouldn't perform all the things it must perform, it would stay in a blissful state, delighting in its condition, but not for long – it still has a lot of needs! That's the trouble. It will be very easy for those who come in one or two hundred years; they will only have to choose: not to belong to the old system any more or else to belong to the new. But now.... A stomach has got to digest, after all! Well,

67

that will mean a new way of adapting to the forces of Nature, a new functioning.

*But for that to happen, some beings would have to prepare this new functioning.*

Sometimes I wonder if it's not sheer folly to attempt it.... Shouldn't this body simply be left to dissolve and let others, better fit for the new functioning, be prepared? I don't know.

I don't know. No one has ever done this before, so there's no one to tell me.

So my solution is always the same: I am like this *(gesture of surrender)*, the body saying, "I am quite willing to try, I am trying my best."

Is it folly, or is it really possible? ... I don't know.

## March 6, 1962

*Satprem complains that he feels that he is not making any progress.*

This in itself has to be conquered; I mean, the state in itself represents something to be conquered. Because ... you remember, I told you the other day about having such a tremendous experience in the body-consciousness – this ... this *dull* consciousness in the material world, which really gives the feeling of something inert, unchanging, incapable of responding; you could wait millions and millions of years and nothing would budge. And that experience came at the end of a rather critical passage – it takes catastrophes to get it moving, that's what's so strange! And not only that, but the wisp of imagination it does have (if you can call it imagination) is invariably catastrophic. Whatever it anticipates is always for the worst – the pettiest, meanest, nastiest kind of worst – always the worst. It's ... really, it's the most sickening condition human consciousness and matter can be in. Well, I have been swimming in it for months, and my way of being in it is to go through every possible illness and to have every possible physical aggravation, one after another.

Just recently, as I told you, things truly became a little ... disgusting, dangerous, and for an hour or an hour and a half I did a sadhana like this *(Mother clenches her fists)*, keeping hold of this body and body-consciousness. And the whole time the Force was at work there (it was like kneading a very resistant dough), something was saying to me, "Look, you can't deny miracles any longer." It was being said to this consciousness (not to me, of course), this body-consciousness: " Now you can't deny it – miracles do happen." It was forced to see; there it was, gaping like an idiot being shown the sky – "Ah!" And it's so stupid that it didn't even have any joy of discovery! But it was forced to see, the thing was right under its nose – there was no escaping it, it had to be admitted. But you know what, mon petit, as soon as I let up on the pressure – forgotten!

I remember the whole experience, of course, but the body-consciousness forgot. The slightest difficulty, even the shadow or the recollection of a difficulty, was enough for it to start up all over again: "Oh ... oh! Now what's going to happen?" The same old anxieties and stupidities.

So I realize that we have to keep on trying.

What's annoying, though, is that in order to shake it all up, I have to go through some pretty bad moments physically. So don't worry, I understand how it is for others! I myself never lose either consciousness or contact with ... not with Knowledge, but with the total EXPERIENCE of identification. Only here in Matter does the work have this particular nature. So l understand how it is for people who live heedlessly from day to day, from minute to minute, for whom it's not a constant, permanent work of each second, totally conscious and deliberate.... And besides, this body is so willing – the poor thing, sometimes I have found it crying like a child, imploring, "How do you get out of this mess?" That's exactly why all the people who have achieved the inner realization have called this work "impossible." It's their own impossibility! I know it's not impossible, I know it will come, but ... how long will it take? That I don't know.

My feeling is that if you try to hurry, to rush, to speed things up a little, it jams, it becomes like stone – it turns to stone again. It took the stone a long time to become a man.... So I don't want that. You can't get too impatient – it's not even impatience, but pressure. Beyond a certain pressure, it turns to stone. So I understand people who attain realization and, blissfully enjoying it, kick the whole thing out: "Fine, I'll do without it!"

That's what has always happened.

But I can't do that.

What I always do is say, "Well, all right ..." (I say this to the Lord with a smile), "if You have now decided I should leave, I'll go willingly."

If He ever gave me a slap, that's when I'd get one! I can feel it even while I am saying this.

It's simply to ensure that the consciousness is in a state of perfect equanimity; I mean, whether things turn out like this or like that leaves me completely indifferent: what You will – spontaneously and integrally and exclusively – My Will. I say "My" Will on purpose, to show total adhesion. It's not submission, it has nothing to do with submission; it's like this *(gesture of total abandonment)*. Well, in spite of that, there's not much progress.

Although sometimes, yes, all of a sudden.... Take this example (it may seem a mere trifle, but when you have reached this point ...): the first sudden glimmer of conscious control over a bodily functioning, giving you a glimpse of the time when everything will function through the action of a conscious will. That has begun – but it's a tiny, tiny, tiny beginning. And the slightest mental intrusion from the old movement spoils it all – I mean the old way of behaving with your body: you want this and you want that and you want to make it do this and you want to make it.... The minute that pops up, everything stops. Progress comes to a standstill. One must be in a state of beatific union ... then one can feel the new functioning begin.

But it has become such a delicate play! A MINUTE thing, minute, can throw everything out of gear – one simple ordinary movement. If through habit you slip back into the ordinary functioning (these are infinitesimal things, not easily seen, subtle, tenuous; one must be very, very, VERY alert), if this happens, the whole new thing stops. Then you have to wait. Wait until the ordinary functioning consents to stop, and that means meditating, entering into contemplation – going over the whole path again. Then, when you have caught hold of That again and can stay there for a few seconds, sometimes a few minutes (it's marvelous when it lasts a few minutes).... And then it gets jammed again and everything has to be done over.

I am not saying this to discourage you, but to tell you that one must really and truly be patient. The only possible way to do it is in a sort of passivity: not to WANT the result – WANTING the result brings in an ego movement which spoils it all.

I have been telling you for a long time that we are VERY close – for a long time.

So when people ask me, I say (to tell them something), "We shall see." It's certainly not that I don't know; I know perfectly well how it will be. But *(laughing)* I don't know when! That, I don't know. Even at this point, I don't know when.

In fact, if something wants to know when, then it's still in a hurry.

No, you have to be a saint, mon petit! *(Mother laughs and laughs.)*

*(Satprem grimaces)*

Yes, I know – neither am I!

I used to say the same thing. When Sri Aurobindo was here I used to tell everybody, "I am not a saint and don't want to be a saint!" And look what has happened to me!

You have to be an unsaintly saint.

Without an ounce of saintliness.

You know, all those little rules we're enjoined to follow: "Above all, don't do that; and be sure to do this, don't forget that...." Like ablutions, for instance, or attitudes, or what to eat – there's no dearth of them. A mountain of do's and don'ts – all completely swept away! And swept away to the point where sometimes a rule, something highly recommended ("Be sure to do this, be careful to do that" – an attitude or an action) becomes an obstacle. I hardly dare say it, but one example is having a regular schedule – always making ablutions at the same hour, always doing japa in the same manner and so on. And I am perfectly aware that Sri Aurobindo himself puts all sorts of trivial obstacles in my way – obstacles I could hurdle with a single second of reflection; he sets them up as if in play. Do you remember the aphorism where he says he was quarreling with the Lord and the Lord made him fall in the mud? That's just what I feel. He puts a stick in my spokes and laughs. So I say, "All right, that's enough, I don't give a hoot! I'll do whatever You want, it's not my problem; I can do it or not do it, do it this way or that...." It has all gone up in smoke now.

What has become constant, though.... I shouldn't say it, because it's going to get me into trouble again! But anyway, what's trying to be constant is DISCRIMINATION: taking all circumstances, vibrations, relationships, what comes from the people around me, what responds, and putting each in its proper place. A second-to-second discrimination. I know where things are coming from, why they come, their effect, where they're going to lead me, and so on. It's growing more and more frequent, constant, automatic – like a state of being.

72

That's about the only place where progress is really visible. I hope the fact of having spoken won't get me into trouble again!

But impatience and irritation.... Well, if it makes you feel better.... Some people need it as a safety valve – but it makes you lose a lot of time.

One day I was all tensed up; things had become so "intolerable," as people say, that something in the most material vital went into what's usually considered a fit of rage (it was totally under control – I mean it was working as a safety valve and being observed as such in all its vibrations). I was alone in the bathroom, nobody to see me; I grabbed hold of I don't remember what and smashed it on the floor!

Aah, what a relief!

So there you are.

*But what are we supposed to do in the meantime? What?*

I'll tell you what I do: I say to the Lord, "All right, if that's how it is, well, I am not doing anything any more; I am resting in Your arms and waiting." I actually, concretely (I was about to say "materially") do it – and then I don't stir. "You will do it all, I am not doing anything." And I really stay like that. Immediately, of course, there's a great joy and I don't stir.

For instance, I am completely snowed under with material work, letters, people, matters to arrange and decide, big things to organize, all of it falling on me from every side and trying to take up all my time and energy. At times it really gets too much. So when it's too much, I say, "All right, Lord, now I will nestle in Your arms." And there I am, no longer thinking, no longer bothering about anything, and ... I go into Bliss. Usually after ten minutes everything is fine!

*The trouble is, the mental mechanism isn't there any more. Before, with the mind working, I would take up this thing or do that thing, but now I don't let it function, so there's nothing to make me move!*

Absolutely. But it's a big progress.

*Not necessarily! Maybe there are things I should be doing.*

No. No, it's a big progress, an immense progress.

*All right then; but I feel as if I'm doing nothing ...*

Yes.

*... except the bare minimum, which I do because it has to be done; otherwise.... I have no desire to stir up the mind, I want something else.*

Naturally! Thank god, I tell you, it's an immense progress. You should be delighted.

*Yes, but on a material level I'm doing nothing.*

What does it matter!

You can lie down on a mat, look at a flower or a patch of sky if there's any to see; if need be *(teasingly),* smoke a cigarette to keep yourself busy, and just stay like that, *relaxed.* And if you do your pranayama along with this "relaxation" you will notice yourself growing extremely strong – storing, storing, storing up energies. And then if you have to make an effort, there's nothing to it – it's as easy as pie.

It's that old habit, the old fear of being lazy. It took me.... But Sri Aurobindo cured me of that rather quickly. That's how it was before I met him. And that's the first thing he did: he gave me a tap on the head, and all activity ceased – total silence, all mental constructions and habits swept away ... in the blink of an eye.

I was very careful not to let it come back.

Then, afterwards, well....

He mentions it when he explains mental equality – that a state is reached where one is unable to *initiate* any activity; only the stimulus of an impulsion from above can move you. So you do nothing, you just stay like that, perfectly immobile in your mind (not only physically – especially in your mind): you don't initiate anything.

Before, the mind was always creating, setting actions, wills and movements into motion, producing consequences; and it's very frightening when that stops – you feel you're becoming an idiot. But it's quite the opposite! No more ideas, no more will, no more impulsions, nothing. You act only when something makes you act, without knowing why or how.

This "something" doesn't come from below, of course, it mustn't come from below. But that condition can truly be achieved only when all the work below has been completed.

Vol. 3, p. 107

### April 13, 1962

*(After a perilous month, Mother has suddenly had the formidable, decisive experience, and she gives her first message. She is lying on her bed in the room upstairs, and has become quite thin. It is around ten in the morning. Her voice has greatly changed. Schoolchildren can be heard playing in the distance.)*

Night of April 12-13.

Suddenly in the night I woke up with the full awareness of what we could call the Yoga of the world. The Supreme Love was manifesting through big pulsations, and each pulsation was bringing the world further in its manifestation. It was the formidable pulsations of the eternal, stupendous Love, only Love: each pulsation of the Love was carrying the universe further in its manifestation.

And the certitude that what is to be done is done and the Supramental Manifestation is realized.

Everything was Personal, nothing was individual.

This was going on and on and on and on....

The certitude that what is to be done is DONE.

All the results of the Falsehood had disappeared: Death was an illusion, Sickness was an illusion, Ignorance was an illusion – something that had no reality, no existence.... Only Love, and Love, and Love, and Love – immense, formidable, stupendous, carrying everything.

And how, how to express in the world? It was like an impossibility, because of the contradiction.... But then it came: "You have accepted that this world should know the Supramental Truth ... and it will be expressed totally, integrally." Yes, yes....

And the thing is DONE.

*(long silence)*

The individual consciousness came back, just the sense of a limitation, limitation of pain; without that, no individual.

And we set off again on the way, certain of the Victory.

The heavens are ringing with chants of Victory!

Truth alone exists; Truth alone shall manifest. Onward! ... Onward!

*Gloire à Toi, Seigneur, Triomphateur suprême!*

*(silence)*

And now, to work.

Patience ... endurance ... perfect equanimity. And absolute faith.

*(silence)*

Compared to the experience, whatever I say is nothing, nothing, nothing but words.

And our consciousness is the same, absolutely the same as the Lord's. There was no difference, no difference at all....

We are That, we are That, we are That.

*(silence)*

Later on, I will explain it more clearly. The instrument is not yet ready.

It is only the beginning.

*    *    *

*Mother later added:*

The experience lasted at least four hours. There are many things I will speak of later.

## May 13, 1962

*(This is the first conversation with Mother in two months. She is still reclining on her chaise longue. She looks quite pale and fragile, almost translucent. She enlarges upon the experience she had a month earlier, on April 13. The following text was not taped but noted down from memory and then read out to Mother.)*

I was at the Origin – I WAS the Origin. For more than two hours, consciously, here on this bed, I was the Origin. And it was like gusts – like great gusts ending in explosions. And each one of these gusts was a span of the universe. It was Love in its supreme essence – which has nothing to do with what people normally understand by that word.

And each gust of this essence of Love was dividing and spreading out ... but they weren't forces, it was far beyond the realm of forces. The universe as we know it no longer existed; it was a sort of bizarre illusion, bearing no relation to THAT. There was only the truth of the universe, with those great gusts of color – they were colored – great gusts colored with something that is the essence of color.

It was stupendous. I lived more than two hours like that, consciously.

And then a Voice was explaining everything to me (not exactly a Voice, but something that was Sri Aurobindo's origin, like the most recent gust from the Origin). As the experience unfolded, this Voice explained each gust to me, each span

77

of the universe; and then it explained how it all became like this *(Mother makes a gesture of reversal):* the distortion of the universe. And I was wondering how it was possible, with that Consciousness, that supreme Consciousness, to relate to the present, distorted universe. How to make the connection without losing that Consciousness? A relationship between the two seemed impossible. And that's when that sort of Voice reminded me of my promise, that I had promised to do the Work on earth and it would be done. "I promised to do the Work and it will be done."

Then began the process of descent, and the Voice was explaining it to me – I lived through it all in detail, and it wasn't pleasant. It took an hour and a half to change from that true Consciousness to the individual consciousness. Because throughout the experience this present individuality no longer existed, this body no longer existed, there were no more limits, I was no longer here – what was here was THE PERSON. An hour and a half was needed to return to the body-consciousness (not the physical consciousness but the body-consciousness), to the individual body-consciousness.

The first sign of the return to individuality was a prick of pain, a tiny point *(Mother holds between her fingers a minuscule point in the space of her being).* Yes, because I have a sore, a sore in a rather awkward place, and it hurts *(Mother laughs).* So I felt the pain: it was the sign of individuality coming back. Other than that, there was nothing any more – no body, no individual, no limits. But it's strange, I have made a strange discovery: I used to think it was the individual *(Mother touches her body)* who experienced pain and disabilities and all the misfortunes of human life; well, I perceived that what experiences misfortunes is not the individual, not my body, but that each misfortune, each pain, each disability has its own individuality as it were, and each one represents a battle.

And my body is a world of battles.

78

It is the battlefield.

\* \* \*

(When this text was read to Mother, she gave the following modification.)

I would prefer a word other than "descent," because there was no sensation or notion of descent – none at all.... It could be called the process of materialization or individualization – "transformation of consciousness" would be more exact. It is the process of changing from the true Consciousness to the distorted consciousness – that's it exactly.

*You say it yourself: the transition from the true Consciousness to ordinary consciousness.*

That's it exactly. "Descent" doesn't convey the actual sensation – there was no sensation of descent. None. Neither of ascent nor descent. None at all. Those creative gusts had no POSITION in relation to the creation; it was.... There was ONLY THAT. THAT ALONE existed. Nothing else.

And everything happened within That.

Really, it was.... There was neither high nor low nor within nor without – none of those existed any more. There was only THAT.

It was ... "something" expressing itself, manifesting itself through these gusts. Something that was EVERYTHING. There was nothing else, there was really nothing but THAT. So to speak of high, low, descent won't do at all.

*If you like, we could put "the process of return"....*

Of return to the body-consciousness. Or of materialization.

\* \* \*

*(A bit later, regarding the Talk of August 22, 1956, to be published in the next Bulletin, in which Mother says: "When you are in a condition to receive it, you receive from the Divine the TOTALITY of the relationship you are CAPABLE of having; it is neither a share nor a part nor a repetition, but exclusively and*

*uniquely the relationship each one is capable of having with the Divine. Thus, from the psychological point of view, YOU ALONE have this direct relationship with the Divine." Mother then adds, in a voice that seems to come from far, far away:)*

One is all alone with the Supreme.

Vol. 3, p. 137

## May 15, 1962

*(Satprem ... reads to Mother his notes from the May 13 conversation and asks for further details on the April 13 experience:)*

*About that promise you received....*

I didn't receive a promise – this Voice made me remember a promise I had made. I was saying to myself, "How to connect this true Consciousness to the other one – it's impossible!" And just then I seemed to hear ... not Sri Aurobindo exactly, because then you immediately think of a particular body, but that sort of Voice saying to me, "Your promise. You said you would do the Work." So that's when I said, "Yes, I shall do the Work." And from that moment on the process of materialization began, the entire transition from the true Consciousness to the ordinary consciousness.

I didn't receive a promise, but a reminder of the promise I had made.

*And was that what allowed you to say, "The thing is done"?*

No – it was the experience.

*The experience. When.... I haven't told you this part.*

*(long silence)*

When I was those gusts, those gusts of Love.... When I was conscious of the last one, the one organized outwardly, as it were, by Sri Aurobindo – materializing as the avatar Sri

Aurobindo – then came the absolute certainty that the thing was done, that it was decreed.

And the moment I became aware that it was decreed, I thought, "But how can THAT be translated into that? How can the two be joined?" That was when the words came: "You promised to do it, therefore you will do it"; and slowly the transition began, as if I were again being sent back to do it. Yes, as if ... "You promised to do it and you will do it"; well, that's what I meant by a promise. And I came back towards this body to do it.

I said [on April 3] the body was the battlefield, that the battle was being waged IN this body. And then in that experience [of April 13] I was sent back into the body, because the thing – that last creative gust – had to be realized through this body.

*(silence)*

The experiences are going on....

For instance, I am walking a little now, with someone's assistance, to get the body used to it again. And when I started walking, I became aware of a rather peculiar state ... I might describe it as: what gives me the illusion of a body *(Mother laughs)*.... I entrust it to the person I walk with. In other words, it's not my responsibility: the other person has to make sure it doesn't fall, doesn't bump into anything – you see what I mean. And the consciousness is a limitless consciousness, like a material equivalent or expression of these gusts – it's like waves, but waves with no .... Not separate waves, but a MOVEMENT of waves; a movement of what might be called material, corporeal waves, as vast as the earth, but not ... not round, not flat.... Something giving a great sense of infinity but moving in waves. And this wave movement is the movement of life. And the consciousness (the body-consciousness, I suppose) floats along in this, with a sensation of eternal peace.... But it's not an expanse – that's not the word for it. It is a limitless movement, with a very harmonious and very tranquil rhythm, very vast, very calm. And this movement is life itself.

I walk around the room, and that is what is walking.

And it is very silent – there is no thought; there is barely, barely the ability to observe.... And all kinds of movements, an infinity of movements and vibrations of something that could be the essence of thoughts, move there, rhythmically, in a movement of waves without beginning or end, with a condensation like this *(gesture from above down),* with a condensation like that *(horizontal gesture),* and a movement of expansion *(gesture like a pulsating ocean).* That is, a sort of contraction, concentration, and then expansion, diffusion.

Yesterday I had the total experience – I let myself go completely. It lasted something like forty minutes as I walked around the room.

And actually, apart from the fact of suffering (you know, an ache here, an ache there, a pain here, a pain there, giving the sense of bodily individuality), apart from that, that great undulating movement of life is my normal consciousness. Meaning that I ... what I call Me *(gesture high above),* my consciousness, is completely outside the body. That's what the consciousness of the body is (what I've just been describing), with only points of pain as reminders of what a body usually is: an ache here, an ache there, another ache here.... That's what it's like. And this pain has a small and extremely limited life; it's not general, it's not a body that suffers: it is suffering that suffers. It's a point, a point of pain – a scratch here, a sore there, things like that. That's what is individual and suffers – it's not the body that has a sore, you understand.

It is difficult to express.

But that's my experience. Yesterday I observed it with special care, to be able to tell you about it.

*But are you making a distinction between the body-consciousness and the physical consciousness?...*

Oh yes! The physical consciousness is something very complex; it includes the whole physical, conscious world.

My physical consciousness has been universalized for a long, long time, it encompasses all terrestrial movements; but the body is limited solely to this small concentration of substance *(Mother touches her body)* – that's what I call the body-consciousness.

And when I said, "I have left the body," it certainly didn't mean I have left the physical consciousness – my overall contact with the terrestrial world has remained the same. It concerns only the purely bodily aspect, the specific concretization or concentration of substance giving each of us a different body – a different APPEARANCE.

And a rather illusory appearance, besides. As soon as you rise to a certain height (I saw it quite clearly during that progressive reconcretization), this appearance quickly loses its reality. Our external appearance is very, very illusory. Our particular form (this one's form, that one's form), the form we see with our physical eyes is very superficial, you know. From the vital world onwards, it's completely different.

Well.... I think that's all I can say for today.

Vol. 3, p. 144

**May 18, 1962**

*The other day you said, "What I call Me high above, my consciousness, is completely outside the body." And on April 3, you also said something that gave me a kind of jolt: "I am no more in this body." Why?... Have you really left this body?*

*(very long silence)*

How can I explain it?..

*(long silence)*

I don't know how to explain it....

83

I could almost tell it as a joke: for years and years I felt my consciousness to be outside my body – I always used to say it was there *(gesture above the head),* and not in my body. But from the time of that first experience [April 3], when the doctor said the heart had been physically affected and would stop working if I wasn't careful, from that moment on I felt ... I felt that my body was outside me! It sounds like a joke, but that's how it is.

So to be understood I said, "I am no more in my body." But it isn't that. I hadn't been in my body, my consciousness had been outside my body, for quite a long time! But there was a kind of connection, you know, something that made me feel it as "my body." (If I spoke carelessly, I could now say "what used to be my body," although I know well enough it's still alive!). Well, from April 3 on, when everyone claimed I was so sick and I was forbidden to get out of bed, I had the impression that what was called my body was now outside me.

There was a relation, I kept a link with it, but it took some days to get established (I don't know how many, because for a long time I couldn't keep track of anything). After some days (say ten days, twenty days, I don't know), the will began to function, the body was again under the control of the will. But that didn't happen right away – for some days, the will that deals with the body was annulled (I was entirely conscious and alive, but not in my body). The body was merely something moved around by the people looking after me. Not that it was separate, but I couldn't even say, "it's a body" – it wasn't anything any more! Something.... Having undergone so much preparation, the universalization of the body-consciousness and all that, the experience didn't even seem strange to me (in fact, it was certainly the result of all that preparation). The body was ... "something" like a mass of substance being driven by the will of the three people looking after it. Not that I was unaware of it but.... I wasn't much concerned with it, to tell the truth; but as far as my attention was turned to it, it was a corporeal

84

mass being moved around by a few wills. The supreme Will was in full agreement; the body had been entrusted, in a way (I don't know how to express this) ... yes, it was like something entrusted, and I was simply looking on – I watched it all for I don't know how many days, with hardly any interest.

The one really concrete link was ... pain. That's how the contact was kept.

*When you said, "I am no more in this body," I thought that because of the necessities of the Work some part of you had withdrawn.*

Oh, no! Nothing withdrew – it had already withdrawn a long time ago. The consciousness wasn't at all centered in the body. When I said "I," for instance, it NEVER occurred to me that "I" was this *(Mother points to her body).* I, the I who spoke, was always a will ENTIRELY independent of the body, entirely independent.

But there has been a strange phenomenon [since April 3].... Before, I used to say, "I am outside my body." It was always "I am outside my body." But this time, the body seemed to have been consigned or entrusted – more like entrusted....

It has gradually come back, in the sense that actively.... No, I can't even say that – it's not true. What has come back is the increasingly precise memory of how I had organized the life of this body, the whole formation I had made, down to the smallest details – for the things I was using, how I was making use of them, how I had organized all the objects around the body, all that. What has come back is the memory – is it memory? The awareness of all that has returned, as if I were putting the two back into contact. And so, instead of the body being left totally in the hands of those around me, the formation I had made is coming back, with certain changes, certain improvements and simplifications (but mind you, I had neither the intention nor the will to change anything – those things are simply coming back into

85

the consciousness like that, with certain changes made). In short, it's a kind of conscious formation recrystallizing around this body.

And I have the perception ... a sensation, really, the sensation of ... something not at all me, but entrusted to me. More and more now, there is the feeling of something being entrusted to me in the universal organization for a definite purpose. That's really the sensation I have now (the mind is very calm, so it's difficult to express – I don't "think" all these things, they are more like perceptions). And it's not the usual kind of sensation: the ONLY (I insist on this), the ONLY sensation that remains in the old way is physical pain. And really, those points of pain ... they seem like the SYMBOLIC POINTS of what remains of the old consciousness.

Pain is the one thing I sense the way I used to. Food, for instance, taste, smell, vision, hearing – all that's completely changed. They belong to another rhythm. And this condition has come progressively, like a crystallization of something behind the senses that doesn't come from here – in taste, smell, vision, hearing, touch.... Except this one point.... Even the sense of touch is different now – but PAIN....

Pain is the old world.

It's quite odd, you know; pain is like the symbolic (and rather too concrete!) sign of life in the Ignorance.

And even there I have had an instant (but it was like a flash – the flash of a new experience), an instant when pain disappeared into something else. It has happened three or four times. The pain suddenly became ... something completely different (not a pleasant sensation, not that at all): another state of consciousness.

If that state remained, I would truly be free of the world as it is.

Nonetheless, people can still hear me, can't they? And I can still see, but in a peculiar way – a very peculiar way. At times I see with greater precision than ever before (generally, as I told you the other day, I seem to see from behind a veil; that's constant). I hear things that way too. Certain sounds.... On one occasion I noticed a sound, a seemingly imperceptible sound, coming from about a hundred yards away, and it seemed to be right here. All this has changed – I mean the whole way the organs function. Have the organs themselves changed, or is it their functioning? I don't know. But they all obey another law – absolutely.

And I have the definite impression that that so-called illness was the external and ILLUSORY form of an indispensable process of transformation; without that so-called illness there could be no transformation – it is not an illness, I KNOW it: when people speak of "illness," something in me laughs and says, "What a bunch of geese!"

It is not an illness.

*A disengagement?*

Perhaps.

Perhaps.

It was a bit violent! *(Mother laughs)* ... And yet not so violent, because.... There's something I have never told anyone, but when the doctor was called.... I was constantly fainting, you know: I would take a step and – plop! So the doctor was called and they began watching over me (everything was supposedly going wrong, all the organs, everything breaking down), and he declared I was sick and wasn't to stir from my bed (for a while I wasn't even supposed to talk!).... Well, at that point, something (not exactly what you would call my consciousness; it was far, far more eternal than my consciousness – my consciousness is the consciousness of one form of the Manifestation – well, it was far more than that, beyond that) ... something said YES. And if "That" had not agreed, I could have gone on living almost as usual. "That" decreed, "That" decided – I have never said anything about it.

Otherwise, you know, I would not have consented. If "That" had not agreed, I would have said to my body, "Go on, keep going, move" – and it would have gone on. It stopped because "That" said yes. And then I understood that that whole so-called illness was necessary for the Work. So I let myself go. And then what I told you about happened: this body was consigned to the care of three people, who looked after it marvelously, by the way – really, it filled me with constant admiration – a selflessness, a care ... oh, it was wonderful! I was saying to the Lord the whole time, "Truly, Lord, You have arranged all the material conditions in an absolutely marvelous, incredible way, bringing together whatever is necessary, and placing around me people beyond all praise." For at least two weeks they had a hard time of it – quite hard. The body was a wreck, you know! *(Mother laughs)* They had to think of everything, decide everything, take care of everything. And they looked after it very, very well – really very well.

It's a wonderful story, seen as I see it. And I have observed it very carefully: it isn't an ordinary story seen with an exceptional knowledge, but a true Knowledge and a true Consciousness witnessing an exceptional story. Those three people may not be aware of how utterly exceptional it is, but that's simply because their consciousness is not sufficiently awake. But they too have been, and continue to be, exceptional.

The whole story is a fairy tale.

And the only concrete thing left in this world – this world of illusion – is pain. It seems to me the very essence of Falsehood.

But what feels it feels it very concretely! ... I clearly see it's false, but that doesn't stop my body from feeling it – and there is a reason: it is the battlefield.

I have even been forbidden to utilize my knowledge, power and force to annul the pain in the way I used to (and I used to do it very well). That has been totally forbidden. But I have seen that something else is in sight. Something else is in the making.... It can't be called a miracle because it's not a miracle, but it's something wonderful – the unknown.... When will it come? How will it come? I don't know.

But it's interesting.

*(silence)*

Something really radical has happened, in the sense that.... I tried once just to see if I could do it (I had wisely been told not to try) and I didn't succeed: I can't go back to the old way of relating to my body. It's impossible.

What is coming back is the way "objects" – the whole mass of material substance making up this body's environment – had been organized; that's what is coming back, with some small changes (none of this comes through the head; the head has nothing to do with it). It is a sort of formation reconcretizing itself for life's outer organization.

The old way of relating no longer exists at all.

*(silence)*

It can truly be said that for a short while the body went out of my consciousness completely. I didn't leave my body; the body left the consciousness.

There you have it.

I hope you can cope with this – it's the first time I have tried to explain it. In fact, it's the first time I am looking at it. And it's interesting. An interesting phenomenon.

Vol. 3, p. 149

## May 31, 1962

There's a strange thing that happens to me all the time, at least fifty times a day (and it's particularly clear at night). In its most external form it's like moving from one room to another, or from one house to another, and you go through the door or the wall almost without noticing it, automatically.... Being in one room is reflected outwardly by quite a comfortable condition, a state where there's no pain at all, no pain anywhere, and a great peace – a joyous peace, a state of perfect calm ... an ideal condition, at any rate, which sometimes lasts a long, long time. It's mainly at night, actually; during the day people interrupt me with all sorts of things, but for a certain number of hours at night this state is practically constant. And then suddenly, with no perceptible or apparent reason (I haven't yet discovered the why or the wherefore of it), you seem to ... FALL into the other room, or into the other house, as though you had made a false step – and then you have a pain here, an ache there, you're uncomfortable.

Obviously it's the continuation of the same experience I told you about, [on May 18] but now it has come to this. I mean the two states are now distinct – noticeably distinct; but so far I haven't found either the why or the wherefore.... Is it something coming from outside or just an old rut: yes, it really feels like an old rut, like a wrinkle in a piece of cloth; you know, you iron it out again and again, and the wrinkle comes back. That's more the feeling it gives me – not at all a conscious habit, just an old rut. But might something from outside also be provoking it...?

And the dreams it gives me! Oh, there's a whole series of them, with particular styles and categories.... You start down a flight of stairs – no more stairs; you want to take a certain road – the road closes; you want to catch someone – you can't. All kinds of things. And although these dreams (I have a whole collection of them, in fact) recur with certain minor outward differences, they are all of the same type. It's a well-known type which I now classify as *self-imposed troubles.* When I get out of it and look, I see very clearly that it's only this nasty habit we have of fretting over nothing! *(Laughingly)* Oh, whatever we want to do, immediately there's a complication, a difficulty....

Yes, these dreams arise from the subconscient; they are primarily subconscious habits.... But the pain, the thorns in the garment – it's so clear! *(Mother laughs)* And no way to get comfortable!

In the past, a dream like that would nag me for hours, I would worry, wondering what calamities were going to befall me (this was long, long ago – ages ago). But that was idiotic, as I later understood; it's a certain something in the subconscient, a symbolic form of ... well, of certain bad psychological habits we have, that's all. And I used to torment myself: "How can I get rid of this?" (We're all loaded with a multitude of such weaknesses built into the body.) And then through experience I understood – I saw it was merely certain bad habits.

The only thing to do is not torment yourself and to say to the Lord (in all sincerity, of course), "It's up to You. Rid me of this." And it is very effective. Very effective. At times I have had old things like that dissolved in a flash; certain inveterate little habits – so stupid, but so ingrained you can't get rid of them. Then, while doing japa or walking or meditating or whatever, suddenly the flame flares up and ... (you have really had enough of it; it disgusts you, you want it to change, you really want the change) and you say to the Lord, "I can't do it on my own." (You very sincerely know you can't do it; you have tried and tried and tried and have achieved exactly nothing – you can't do it.) "Well then, I offer it to You – You do it." Just like that. And all at once you see the thing fading away. It is simply wonderful. You know how Sri Aurobindo used to take away someone's pain? It's exactly the same. Certain habits bound up with the body's formation.

One day I will certainly use the same method on those "room changes," but for that it will have to become very clear and distinct, well defined in the consciousness. Because that change of room (intellectually you would call it a "change of consciousness," but that means nothing at all; we're dealing here with something very, very material) ... I have sometimes gone through it without experiencing ANY CHANGE OF EFFECT, which probably means I was centered not in the material consciousness but in a higher consciousness dwelling and looking on from *elsewhere* – a witness consciousness – and I was in a state where everything flows ... flows like a river of

91

tranquil peace.... Truly, it's marvelous – all creation, all life, all movements, all things, and everything like a single mass, with the body in the midst of it all, blending homogeneously with the whole... and it all flows on like a river of peace, peaceful and smiling, on to infinity. And then oops! You trip *(gesture of inversion)* and once again find yourself SITUATED – you ARE somewhere, at some specific moment of time; and then there's a pain here, a pain there, a pain.... And sometimes I have seen, I have witnessed the change from the one to the other WITHOUT feeling the pains or experiencing the thing concretely, which means that I wasn't at all in the body, I wasn't BOUND to the body – I was seeing, only seeing, just like a witness. And it's always accompanied by the kind of observation an indulgent (but not blind) friend might make: "But why? Why that again?" That's how it comes. "What's the use of that?" And I can't catch hold of what makes it happen....

It will come.

It is very interesting because it's very new.

What's happening? What's happening, what's going on?!

*(silence)*

...

The body has been cradled by three Words....

Words that repeat themselves automatically, with no effort of will (but the body itself is quite aware that although these three particular Words happen to have been given to it, it might also have been something else – it was originally the choice of a higher Intelligence). This has become an automatic accompaniment. It is not so much the words in themselves as what they will represent and bring with them in their vibration.... I mean it would be quite inaccurate to say, "Only these Words are helpful," no, not that. But they provide an accompaniment, an accompaniment of subtle, physical vibrations, which has built up a certain state or experience, a sort of association between the presence of those words and this movement of eternal Life, that undulating vibration.

Obviously, another center of consciousness, another (how shall I put it?) ... another concretization, another amalgam, might – would of course – have another vibration.

In ordinary language, the vibration of the mantra is what helps the body to enter a certain state – but it is not particularly THIS mantra: it is the particular relationship established between a mantra (it has to be a true one, a mantra endowed with power) and the body. It surges up spontaneously: as soon as the body starts walking, it walks to the rhythm of those Words. And the rhythm of the Words quite naturally brings about a certain vibration, which in turn brings about the state.

But to say it's these particular Words exclusively would be ridiculous. What counts is the sincerity of the aspiration, the exactness of the expression and the power; that is, the power that comes from the mantra being accepted. This is something very interesting: the mantra has been ACCEPTED by the supreme Power as an effective tool, and so it automatically contains a certain force and power. But it is a purely personal phenomenon (the expression is the same, but the vibrations are personal). A mantra leading one person straight to divine realization will leave another person cold and flat.

What is your experience when you say your mantra? You once told me you felt good saying it....

*I generally find it restful.*

Yes, that's it; that's very good.

*But I don't know what it represents.*

It represents what you put into it – your aspiration, mon petit. No, to me it can represent only ONE thing.... I call it "the Supreme," because you have to call it something, but that Something is the farthest limit of our aspiration, our aspiration in every sense, in all directions, on all occasions. Something that is the supreme summit of our aspiration, WHATEVER

93

that aspiration may be, in whatever direction, in whatever realm – beyond, really beyond, Something beyond any form of activity.

For me, the most concrete approach to this is through the vibration of pure Love; not love for something, a love you give or receive, but Love in itself: Love. It is something self-existent. And it is certainly the most concrete approach for me. (But it isn't exclusive – it contains everything else within itself; it doesn't exclude all the other approaches, all the other contacts.)

Vol. 3, p. 176

## June 6, 1962

But one thing has happened practically without my noticing it. In the past, before that experience [April 13], the body used to feel the struggle against the forces of wear and tear (different organs wearing out, losing their endurance, their power of reaction, and certain movements, for instance, becoming less easy to make). That's what the body felt, although the body-consciousness never sensed any aging, never, none – that simply didn't exist. But in actual material fact, there was some difficulty.... And now, looking at it in the ordinary way, externally, superficially, you might say there has been a great deterioration; well, the body doesn't feel that way at all! What it feels is that a particular movement, effort, gesture or action belongs to the world – this world of ignorance – and isn't being performed in the true way: it's not the true movement, done in the true way. And its sensation or perception is that the state I was speaking of, *soft*, with no angles, has to develop along a certain line and produce effects on the body that will make true action possible, action expressing the true will. With no difference on the surface, perhaps (I don't know about that yet) ... but done in another way. And I am not talking about grandiose things, mind you, but of everyday activities:

94

getting up, walking, taking a bath. I no longer have a feeling of incapacity, but a feeling of (what's the word for it?) ... an *unwillingness* – a bodily *unwillingness* – to do things in the old way.

There is another way to be found.

But not "found" with the head, it's not like that.... A way that is somewhere IN THE MAKING.

I am speaking of the smallest things – take brushing the teeth; there's a difference between the way I brush my teeth now and the way I used to. (In appearance, I suppose it's the same thing.)

And I have difficulty (it's almost an unwillingness too) seeing things the way others see them. It's difficult for me, not spontaneous: it would take an effort I don't care to make.

As for the head, it has learned to keep still.... I walk in the mornings and afternoons, saying the mantra as I did before; but while before I had to drive thoughts away, concentrate and make an effort, now this state comes and takes over everything – the head, the body, everything – and then I walk in that woolly dream (woolly isn't the right word, but it's all I can find!). It's smooth, soft, without angles and supple! No resistance, no resistance.... Oh, that peace!

Very well, petit.

...

*I don't know, but I had the impression it ought to be a POWER rather than a state of consciousness – a power able to CHANGE things. Rather than changing one's attitude, there should be a power that could change Matter, make it more....*

Everything is a power, mon petit! Life is a power – no power, no life.

*Yes, but I mean rather than being something subjective, some thing you "experience," it should be a power that, for instance, could change this material hardness into a softness.*

I haven't changed.

I haven't changed, that's the thing – I haven't changed. Because were it changed, it wouldn't come back; but they coexist. They coexist.

If matter were changeable, it would have changed LONG ago.

*(silence)*

...

*Yes, but that different world you conceive of, will it be different subjectively, or in its material properties?... Will that world be different to us only subjectively, in the way we think of it, or....*

Power ... logically, one has power over things.

I am (how shall I put it?) under way, on the border. But we would need some proof, wouldn't we? Some evidence. For ONESELF, things are unquestionably changing; I have had two or three or four FLASHES of objective change – a change not only for my consciousness, but perceptible to other consciousnesses too. But it's like a flash: "Ah!" And it vanishes in the time it takes to say "Ah! " So it's nothing you can talk about.

Events can be changed: wherever the state of consciousness comes into play, you can change events. I have had hundreds and hundreds and hundreds of examples of that, as I have had the experience of changing a person's state of consciousness and the resulting circumstances of that state of consciousness. All that belongs to the realm of psychological life; but what I am speaking of is this *(Mother vigorously strikes the table).*

...

Two or three times, like a flash, I have seen something ... manifest, change place. But it was over in less time than it takes to tell, so it might be entirely subjective. To make sure, I would have to check it with someone else, wouldn't I?

We will see. Patience.

There you are.

Vol. 3, p. 196

## June 9, 1962

*(In the course of the preceding conversation, Satprem had thought that rather than a subjective change, a change in one's attitude towards things, there should be an objective change, a power capable of changing the very substance of things: their property of hardness, for instance. Here Mother elucidates her previous statement that "if matter were changeable, it would have changed long ago,"*

There is nothing to change! Only the relations between things change....

As an analogy, look at what science has discovered about the so-called composition of matter at the atomic level – there's nothing to change. Nothing to change! The constituent element doesn't change, the relations between things are what change.

Everything has one and the same constituent element, you see; and everything lies IN the interrelations. Well, it's exactly the same for the transformation.

So you speak of "power," but in fact....

*(long silence)*

The notion of "subjective" and "objective" STILL belongs to the old world and to the three, or at most four, dimensions.... It is one and the same Power that changes the interrelations within one and the same element; to put things simply, the Power that gives the subjective experience AND the objective realization is the same; it is only a matter of a greater or lesser totality of experience, as it were. And if the experience were total it would be the experience of the Supreme, and it would be universal.

Does what I am saying make any sense?...

It all practically comes down to a capacity to spread the experience, or to INCLUDE things in the experience (it's the same thing). You really have to forget this business of one person and then another, one thing and then another.... Even if you can't realize it concretely, at least imagine that there is but ONE thing, excessively complex, and (depending on the case) one experience taking place in one spot, or spreading out like oil on water, or embracing everything. This is all very approximate, but it's the only way the thing can be understood. And the sole explanation for "contagion" is in that Oneness.

And power is what makes the difference. The greater the power, you might say (these words are all very clumsy), the farther the experience spreads. How great the power is depends on its starting point. If its starting point is the Origin, the power is ... let's say universal (we won't consider more than one universe for the moment); it is universal. As this Power manifests from plane to plane, it becomes more concrete and limited; on each plane, the field of action becomes more limited. If your power is vital (or "pranic," as it's called here in India), the field of action is terrestrial, and sometimes limited to just a few individuals, sometimes it's a power capable of acting on just one small being. But originally it's the SAME power, acting on the SAME substance ... I can't express it, words are impossible; but I sense very clearly what I mean.

I can affirm that this notion of "subjective" and "objective" still belongs to the world of illusion. The CONTENT of the experience is what may be either microscopic or universal, depending on the specific quality of the power being expressed, or its field of action. The limitation of power can be voluntary and deliberate; it can be a willed, and not an imposed limitation, which means that the Will-Force may come from the Origin but deliberately limit itself, limit its field of action. But it is the same power and the same substance.

Ultimately there is but one power and one substance. There are varying modalities – countless modalities – of power and substance, but there is but ONE power and ONE substance, as there is but ONE consciousness and ONE truth.

*Yes, but when you say that what changes is only "the relations between things," it's still a matter of subjectivity (I use the word for lack of a better one). But when we come down to the brass tacks of transformation – physical immortality in the body, for instance – doesn't it involve more than a simple inner change of relations? Doesn't MATTER itself have to be transformed? So there has to be a power over matter. Not merely a change of relations ... no?*

No; you can't grasp what I mean by the word "relation" unless you take it scientifically. Your body, and my body, this table, this carpet, are all made up of atoms; and these atoms are constituted of the SAME thing. The differences we see – different bodies, different forms – are due to the movements or the interrelations within this same thing.

*Yes, so then it's the interrelations that have to change.*

But this has to be very concretely grasped. Well, I say that the power must change this intra-atomic movement. Then, instead of disintegrating, your bodily substance will obey the movement of Transformation, you follow? But it's all the SAME thing! What must change are the relations among things.

And so it becomes EVIDENT that immortality can be achieved! Things get destroyed simply because of their own rigidity – and even then, it's only a semblance of destruction; the essential element stays the same, everywhere, in everything, in decay just as much as in life.

*It is extremely interesting!*

Ultimately, it's all the constructing Will. This constructing Will is eternal, immortal and infinite – it's obvious – so if it is left to this Will, there's no reason why Its creation shouldn't partake of immortality and infinity – things don't necessarily have to go through the semblance of disintegration to change form, it's not indispensable. It has come to be that way for some reason or other (which is probably none of our business), but it's not indispensable, it could be different.

*(silence)*

The problem is getting out of it: we see, we touch, and we are enslaved. But if you look up THERE *(gesture above the head)* it all seems quite simple!

And looking up THERE, I tell you, I am sure there is no difference between "subjective" and "objective" – except when you give your individuality and your individual consciousness an independent reality; that is, when you cut everything into little bits with your imagination.... Then, of course....

Vol. 3, p. 201

## June 12, 1962

I feel like an egg that has yet to hatch – I mean a certain period of incubation is needed, isn't it?

And I am more and more aware that people really panicked this time; they imagined I was going to die – I could have died, had the Lord willed it. But ... it has been a sort of death, that's for sure – sure, sure, sure – although I don't say so, because.... After all, one must have some regard for people's common sense!

But really, if I let myself go one step further I would say that I was dead and ... have come back to life. But I don't say it.

A lot of people have been praying for me and even taking vows that if I didn't die they would go here or there on a pilgrimage – it's quite touching.

This greatly objectifies my situation, which has nothing to do with an illness to be cured! I can't be cured! It is a work of transformation. At any moment, if the Lord decides it's *hopeless,* it will be *hopeless,* finished; and no matter what happens, if the Lord has decided that I'll go right to the end of the experience, then I'll go right to the end.

That whole way of seeing, feeling and reacting belongs really to another world. Really to another world ... to such a degree that if I had no regard for people's peace of mind I would say, "I don't know whether I am dead or alive." Because there is a life, a type of life vibration that is completely independent of.... No, I'll put it another way: the way people ordinarily feel life, feel that they are alive, is intimately linked with a certain sensation they have of their bodies and of themselves. If you totally eliminate that sensation, the type of relation that allows people to say "I am alive" ... well, eliminate that, but then how can you say, "I am alive," or "I am not alive"? The distinction NO LONGER EXISTS. Well, for me, it has been completely eliminated. That night [April 12-13], it was definitively swept out of me. It has never come back. It's something that seems impossible now. So what they mean by "I am alive" is ... I can't say "I am alive" the way they do – it's something else entirely.

Better not keep this – in the end they'll be worrying about my sanity! *(Mother laughs.)*

But that doesn't matter either!

*(silence)*

You get such a feeling of power, so tremendous, so FREE, so independent of all circumstances, all reactions, all events – and it doesn't depend on whether the body is this way or that. Something else.... Something else....

Only one thing depends on the body: speech, expression ... who knows? ... *(Mother gazes at Satprem for a long time, as though she were considering an unknown possibility.)*

Ah, that's enough for today!

Vol. 3, p. 211


## June 27, 1962

... Personally, I have nothing to say.

This is a period of study and observation. There is absolutely nothing to say. It's a whole world of minute observations which,

I hope, will lead me towards something more ... positive. More exactly, it's a demonstration of the inadequacy of the usual methods when it comes to acting according to Truth – and it goes on night and day.

Two nights ago, I had an experience I hadn't had for perhaps more than a year. A sort of concentration and accumulation of divine Energy in the cells of the body. During a certain period (I don't remember when), every night I had a kind of recharging of batteries through contact with universal forces; I had it again two nights ago, spontaneously. Then last night, when I wanted to look, to study, to understand how it worked, I was given a lavish demonstration of the inadequacy and utter uselessness of all processes of consciousness working through the mind. They are useless, they simply spoil the experience.

Previously, when I had an experience, I took great care to keep everything quiet and still so that it wouldn't be interrupted; but afterwards it was always made use of by the mind in its typical way (not exactly "typical," but typical to the mind), and this appeared to be inevitable. But now it doesn't work in the same way: it's limited to a few inevitable interventions; I mean people speak to me or I to them (I keep as silent as I can, but they still chatter away about every possible subject and I am obliged to answer), and it's limited to that. But as it is, even that ... as soon as I am a bit concentrated, even that seems so ... not wrong or distorted, not that, but INADEQUATE. It expresses absolutely nothing, that's all I can say.

The TRUE thing escapes completely.

So I am in a transitional position – it's all very well to see what's wrong, but there should at least be something that's right!

I have been given certain promises – great promises. Not "promises," but what comes is: "This is how it will be." Great things – concrete manifestations of the divine Power, the divine

Consciousness, the divine Action. And spontaneous, natural, inevitable....

This is obviously being prepared *(Mother touches her body)* so that it won't put the usual obstacles in the way of expression.

But I would much prefer the thing to BE rather than just talk about it. That would be more interesting. So for the moment I prefer to say nothing.

*(silence)*

Many things could happen.... But how much time will it take? I don't know.

*(silence)*

Last night I said to myself, "Now look, that's not so brilliant – if we are still no farther than that...." You see, I was having an experience of (it wasn't an experience, really, but quite a normal state that was continuing and, as far as I could see, was practically continuous) ... a recharging of batteries. But there was also a kind of receiving and observing device – detestable! And I used to think it was excellent! For years before last April, everything was very calm, the mind was always turned this way *(gesture above)*, silent, and there was a sort of functioning – I thought it was very good! Well, I have realized that it's worthless. Mind you, I wish everyone could have what I had! It was extremely handy, far beyond ordinary mental methods – but in fact, it's not true. It is still a ... a gimmick. Not the TRUE thing. It's still one of the things that keep life from being divine, so it's worthless!

But what in our present existence doesn't keep life from being divine? ... Nothing I know of! *(Mother laughs)* happily, Sri Aurobindo and I were the same on this point [a sense of humor]. Effortlessly, from a very young age, something in me has always laughed. It sees all the catastrophes, sees all the suffering, sees it all and can't help laughing – the way one laughs at something that pretends to be but isn't.

In the end, that's how you manage to hold on. It's a great thing.

...

Everything that happened prior to the experience of April 13 has disappeared, as it were, and the usual functioning of the consciousness has been totally annulled; it is trying little by little to create a new mode of operation – not merely trying: it is in the PROCESS of doing so on a truer foundation; a truer foundation, or truer relations, or vibrations, or functionings ... (I don't know the right word for it: all these things at once). That presence the other day [the tall white Being] was nothing essentially new – it had already intervened a good many times; and yet it was new, because the whole functioning was new. It's like my experience two nights ago [the recharging of batteries], I had it for months on end; well, it was new because it was based on a new functioning. And each time (is it out of habit, or to make me understand, to make me see the difference?), each time the old functioning starts up, first of all I really feel I am losing the true contact, that the TRUE thing is escaping, and then I wonder how anybody can function like that without going insane! That's what strikes me now – this feeling of going insane! I mean it grates, it scrapes, it makes no sense – *it misses the point.* It is not the TRUE thing, it's beside the point. It tries to imitate something inimitable. And so I ask myself, "What is this? Am I going crazy? Am I losing my faculties?" And then I realize it's not that at all! Above there's a state of immutable and UNSHAKABLE concentration, constant and almighty, and with but a drop of That, a spark of That, all problems are solved. Then I see clearly that it's only a demonstration to make me see the *inadequacy* of the old, habitual functioning – to really and truly convince me that it's inadequate. It's rather hard to bear, actually. Last night I had it, I have seen it again in recent days: it lasts a few seconds – just enough for a satisfactory lesson! It may also happen to make me understand, but afterwards I wonder, "Well, if everybody is in this state ... they don't know it, but it's just terrible!" And

I realize that the LEAST thing, the slightest circumstance, is COMPLETELY distorted, instantly distorted by the way people ... *work it out,* the way they cause events to develop.

That's an ever-present experience.

But this is still a period of preparation; the best thing to do now is to look and look and look again, observe and observe and observe again; and to have experiences, lots of experiences, because all that is nothing – the thing ITSELF must be grasped. We've got to catch the tail of the true functioning, so it can be substituted for the other at will. That's it exactly.

And that requires minute-to-minute observation.

Someone reads me a letter, for instance, and I have to answer; and there, superimposed, are both functionings: the ordinary reaction coming from above (nothing from here: it comes from above but it's the ordinary reaction) ... and if I follow that and start writing, after a moment comes a kind of sensation that it's inadequate; and then there's the other functioning which is not yet (what's the word? I should be speaking in English!) ... *handy,* not yet at my disposal. I have to keep myself quiet, then it starts operating [the new functioning]. But when there's something to be done, the two are superimposed and I have to keep the old one quiet for the other to come. And the other one ... ohh, it has some unexpected ways! I answer a letter, for example, or I want to say something to someone: my old way is an expression of what comes from above (it is luminous enough, but ADAPTED) ... but then there's that sensation of inadequacy – it won't do. All right. I step back and something else comes; and what comes, I must admit ... it's enough to drive people crazy! It's so MUCH SOMETHING ELSE!

Vol. 3, p. 220

## July 4, 1962

The other day, Pavitra said to me in passing, "Modern science would neither follow nor believe us." According to him, scientists acknowledge only "essential hypotheses," and not having the experience, would take our science for a set of "non-essential" hypotheses. I didn't argue, or else I would have told him, "We don't make any hypotheses, far from it, we simply *state our experiences.*" They are free to disbelieve us or to think we're half crazy or hallucinating – that's up to them, it's their business. But we don't make hypotheses, we speak of things we know and have experienced.

For several hours afterwards I had a vision of this state of mind and found absolutely no need to make hypotheses (you see, Pavitra was speaking of "hypothesizing" the existence of different states of being). It's just as I told you: I have passed that stage; I don't need inner dimensions any more. And observing this materialistic state of mind, it occurred to me that, on the basis of their own experiments, they are bound to admit oneness – at least the oneness of matter; and to admit oneness is enough to obtain the key to the whole problem!

Once again it made me realize that this last experience [of April 13] may in reality have come to free me from ALL past knowledge, and that ... to live the Truth none of it is needed. I need neither all this terminology nor Sri Aurobindo's terminology nor, of course, anyone else's; I don't need all these classifications, I don't need all sorts of experiences – I need ONE experience, the one I have. And I have it in all things and in all circumstances: the experience of eternal, infinite, absolute Oneness manifesting in the finite, the relative and the temporal. And the process of change I am pursuing seems less and less of a problem; after looking like the ultimate problem, it doesn't seem to be one any more, because ... but that ... that can't be uttered – it pleases Him to be that way, so He is that way.

And the secret is simply to be in this "It pleases Him."

To be not merely in what is objectified, but also in That which objectifies.

That's all. With that, I need no other theory.

*(silence)*

Taken to the extreme, if the identification is perfect, it is NECESSARILY omnipotence.

Ultimately, nothing but omnipotence could convert the world, convince the world. The world isn't ready to experience supreme Love. Supreme Love eliminates all problems, even the problem of creation: there are no more problems, I know it since that experience [of April 13]. But the world isn't ready yet, it may take a few thousand years. Although it is beginning to be ready for the manifestation of supreme Power (which seems to indicate that this will manifest first). And this supreme Power would result from a CONSTANT identification.

But this "constancy" isn't yet established: one is identified and then one isn't, is and then isn't, so things get delayed indefinitely. You wind up doing exactly what you tell others not to do – one foot here and one foot there! It just won't do.

*(silence)*

There must be certain laws – laws expressing a Wisdom far beyond us – for the experience seems to follow a sort of curve which, because I am in it, I don't understand. And it won't be understood till the end is reached; but I am right in the middle of it, or maybe at the very beginning....

*(long silence)*

We could say some elegant things, but they don't explain anything; like this feeling, for example, that one must die unto death to be born to immortality.

It doesn't mean anything but it corresponds to something.

To die unto death, to become incapable of dying because death has no more reality.

This is beginning to ... I can't say "crystallize," that's much too hard.... It's like a soft breeze condensing.

Vol. 3, p. 239

## July 11, 1962

Recently, for a short part of my nights, I suddenly find a certain task set before me dealing with this one's or that one's mental constructions. And then I feel I am facing a tremendous, destructive falsehood – a TOTAL contradiction, in fact, of this endlessly unfolding creative vibration.

Some of the people concerned are here, others elsewhere – that is, it's the mental state (even the higher mind in some cases, not necessarily very down-to-earth) of this one or that one or.... It comes individually (and the person's name along with it). And a kind of uneasiness takes hold of my body, as if I were in the presence of ... I don't know, in ordinary life I would say, "Go away! " *(Mother brusquely shoos something away)* But here it is presented for me to do a particular work (I know the people, some are here, others elsewhere; they're people I am in touch with for the yoga). So I am faced with these mental formations and each one is HELD like this *(Mother grips the thing with both hands)* so that I don't simply brush it aside. Then (it's certainly a good opportunity to go completely crazy!) I slowly bring in the divine Vibration, and I hold it like this, without moving *(Mother holds this vibration tight and drives it in like a sword of light),* without moving ... until everything fades away into silence.

I haven't had the chance *(laughing)* to ask them what happened to them!

Probably they were not immediately aware of it, but it's sure to have an effect.

This has never happened before, it's brand-new. Before, there was always that Power transmitted through the higher mind (what Sri Aurobindo calls the Overmind); it was up there, dissolving, dispersing, changing, doing a whole lot of work, without any difficulty, effortlessly *(gesture above the head showing the tranquil, irresistible flowing of a stream),* nothing to it. That was my constant, second-to-second action, everywhere, all the time, for everything that came to me. But

THIS is completely, completely new. It's a sort of imposition, almost like an imposition on the PHYSICAL brain (I presume it must be for changing the brain cells). And I am allowed to do only one thing *(Mother grips the mental construction presented to her);* it's right in front of me like this and won't leave me, it clings like a leech, stock-still. So I have to bring in the supreme, divine Vibration, the Vibration I experienced the other day [April 13], and hold it steadily (sometimes it takes quite a while) ... until all is hushed in a divine silence.

Vol. 3, p. 252

### July 18, 1962

*(Concerning the vibration of supreme Love Mother experienced on April 13:)*

Matter needs quite a preparation to make it strong enough to hold those vibrations, and ... and the body seems to be given a trickle to see how much it can bear. But there's such an immediate intensity of joy in all the cells, in the heart and organs, that it all seems on the verge of exploding.

It comes just to tell you, "See, this is how it is."

I can bring it on at will simply by putting myself in a certain state. But then I notice that someone ("someone" ... well, that's a way of speaking) is dosing it out, allowing the contact for a certain length of time or in a certain amount; and there's nothing to be done about it, it's an Order from above. A mere hint of impatience would spoil everything – the power to establish the contact would probably be lost. I have never done this and I don't intend to.

*(silence)*

It's like an image.... You see, the body is stretched out here on the chaise longue.... You know how it is when experiments are done on animals? It's something like that – the body is there as the "subject" of an experiment. Then there's my consciousness, the part focused on the earthly experience and

the present transformation (it's what I mean when I say "I").
And then the Lord.... I say "the Lord" – I've adopted that
because it's the best way of putting it and the easiest for me, but
I never, NEVER think of a being. For me, it's a simultaneous
contact with the Eternal, the Infinite, the Vast, the Totality of
everything – the totality of everything: all that is, all that has
been, all that will be, everything. Words spoil it, but it's like
that – automatically – with consciousness, sweetness and ...
SOLICITUDE. With all the qualities a perfect Personality can
offer (I don't know if you follow me, but that's the way it
is). And "That" (I use all these words to say it, and three-
fourths is left out) ... is a spontaneous, constant, immediate
experience. So the "I" I spoke of asks that the body may have
the experience, or at least an initial taste, even a shadow of
the experience of this Love. And each time it's asked for, it
comes INSTANTLY. Then I see the three together – in my
consciousness and perception the three are together – and I see
that this Love is dosed out and maintained in exact proportion
to what the body can bear.

The body is aware of this and is a little sad about it. But
immediately comes something soothing, calming, making it
vast. The body instantly senses the immensity and regains its
calm.

This experience I am describing is exactly what happened
yesterday (it happens every day, but yesterday it was especially
clear). And it's still here – I am seeing it as I saw it, it's still
here. Actually, it is always here – always here – though it's
more striking when the body is stretched out, motionless in
the Yoga. The experience is slightly different when walking
because that involves action. When the body walks, it acts on
behalf of everything that's related to it, hence the action is
vaster and more powerful.

But when it is stretched out and asks the Lord to take
possession of it, it really asks with all its aspiration. And the
very intensity of the aspiration brings in the possibility of a
slight emotional vibration. But it is immediately drowned in

... the immobile immensity of matter, which senses the Divine Descent like a leaven that makes dough rise – that's it exactly, the terrestrial immensity of matter and the leavening action of the Divine Descent.... The intensity of these vibrations is above and beyond anything we are used to feeling – the vital seems dull and flat in comparison. And what a Wisdom! ... It knows how to make use of time – that is, it actually changes itself into time – so as to ... minimize the possibilities of damage.

It's plain to see that, left to itself in its full power of transformation and progress, this flame of aspiration, this flame of *Agni* would have scant consideration for the result of the process – the result of the process is that fire burns. And there could be mishaps in the functioning of the organs. All the organs must undergo a transformation, but were it too rapid and too sudden, well, everything would go out of whack. The machine would simply explode. But this Wisdom doesn't come from the universal consciousness (which I don't really think is so wise!), it's infinitely higher: the Supreme Wisdom. Something so wonderful! It foresees things the universal forces in their universal play would overlook – a wonder!

*(silence)*

We mustn't be in a hurry.

*It's hard to imagine how a physical body can, for instance, extend or enlarge itself. It all seems unimaginable.*

It is unimaginable because the body can't do it yet.

No ... and besides, you don't see. If my body resembled its consciousness (because it Is conscious), if what you see with your eyes corresponded to what the body feels, it would probably look monstrous, hideous ... or terrifying!

What the eyes see is so false, so false!

But now the body – the body itself, its very own self – feels it is WITHIN things or WITHIN people or WITHIN an action. There are no more limits, none of this (Mother touches the skin of her hands as if all separation had disappeared). Take this example: someone accidentally bumps me (it does

111

happen) with an object or a part of his body. Well, it is NEVER something external: it happens INSIDE – the body's consciousness is much larger than my body. Yesterday, the table leg bumped my foot; so there was the ordinary outward reaction (it operates automatically and in a curious way – the body jumped), and then the body-consciousness – now I am speaking of the body-consciousness – saw that an unexpected and involuntary collision of two objects had taken place INSIDE ITSELF. And it also saw that if it made a certain movement of concentration at that particular spot, inside itself, some pain or damage would result; but if it made the other movement of ... (how shall I put it?) of union, of abolishing all separation (which it can do very well), well, then the results of the blow would be annulled. And that's what happened, I did it. I was simply sitting down, and I let my body cope with the whole thing (while I watched with keen interest); and I noticed it really did feel the blow inside and not outside – it wasn't that something from outside had struck it, but that there had been an unexpected, or rather an unforeseen and involuntary collision of two things inside itself. And I clearly followed how the body made a more complete movement of identification (you see, someone with the sense of separation had moved the table, so the sense of separation accompanied the blow, and then of course there was all the regret, and so on and so forth); well, the body simply went into its usual state where there's no sense of separation, and the effect vanished instantaneously. Had I been asked, "Where were you hit, what spot?", I couldn't have told, I don't know. All I know, because of words I heard spoken, is that the table leg bumped into my foot. But where? ... I can't say; I couldn't have said even five minutes after the incident – it had utterly disappeared, and disappeared through a VOLUNTARY movement.

This body-consciousness has a will; it is constantly, constantly calling upon the Lord's will: "Lord, take possession of this, take possession of that, take...." There's no question of taking possession of the will, that was done ages ago, but:

"Take possession of these cells, those cells, this, that...." It is the BODY'S aspiration. Well, the blow wasn't caused by this will acting in the body; the blow didn't come directly from the body, but from something that had slipped in through an unconscious element; and the body simply erased, or absorbed, digested this unconsciousness – and the thing vanished without a trace!

And do you know how this body is?... It immediately began wondering (I was quietly watching it all from above), "What if" ("ifs" are always idiotic but it's an old bodily habit), "what if the object had been sharp, would the results have been so easy to annul?" *(Mother laughs)* Then I distinctly heard someone reply (I am putting it into words), "You idiot! That wouldn't have happened in the first place! " That is, the necessary protection would have been there. The protection intervenes only when necessary, not just for the fun of it. "You numbskull," it said (I am translating freely), "how silly can you be! It wouldn't have happened."

But what a world it is – a world of experiences! And the consciousness is somewhere way up high but seeing very clearly, watching with interest.

You just can't imagine – you CANNOT.... When I try to see life as most people see it (it's getting increasingly difficult! but anyhow), the way people ordinarily see it, it becomes a big mishmash! I understand nothing, it makes no more sense – nothing makes sense. Simply, for the sake of the action, I have been warned that nobody can understand – NOBODY can comprehend to what extent the Lord is intermingled, is present and active in all things.

In all things.

*(silence)*

For instance, sometimes He "tells" me (of course it's not external; it's an extremely delicate working, and sort of automatic; no time elapses between the order and its execution: they're not two movements but one single thing) ... when He

113

says "Speak," or when He says "Keep silent" – like the other day when, as you pointed out, I stopped in the middle of a sentence – it's that all of a sudden ... *(Mother makes a gesture as if she were unable to speak, or as if suddenly held by silence).* At other times it pours out like it's doing now. And I don't "hear" an order, I don't "feel" an order: I LIVE the Order; and it's so patently the Lord's that it seems stupid to even mention it.

Vol. 3, p. 262

### September 8, 1962

It's a strange sensation, a bizarre perception of both the true functioning and the functioning distorted by the sense of being an individual body. They're not even ... you can't even say they're superimposed, they're almost simultaneous, and that's why it is so hard to explain.... A number of things are malfunctioning in the body; I don't know if they can be called illnesses (maybe the doctors would call them illnesses ...), but in any case, they're malfunctionings in the body's organs: the heart, the stomach, the intestines, the lungs and so on. And at the same time there's (it can't be called a "functioning") the true state. And thus certain disorders appear only when the consciousness ... as if the consciousness were pulled or pushed or poised in a certain way, and then, those malfunctionings INSTANTLY appear – not as a consequence: I mean the consciousness becomes aware of their existence. And if the consciousness stays in that position long enough, there are what we conventionally call consequences: the malfunctioning has its consequences (tiny things, such as physical discomforts, for instance). And if through (is it yogic discipline, is it the Lord's intervention? ... Call it what you will) ... but if the consciousness regains its true position, the consequences cease IMMEDIATELY. Sometimes, though, it's like this *(Mother makes a gesture of an overlapping or interpenetration by interlacing the*

114

*fingers of her two hands),* in other words, this way, then that, this way, then that *(Mother slips the fingers of her right hand back and forth through the fingers of her left to show the consciousness alternating between two states),* this position, then that position, this one, then that one. This movement takes only a few seconds, so I can almost perceive the two functionings simultaneously. That's what gave me the knowledge of the process, otherwise I wouldn't understand; I would simply think I am falling from one state into another. That's not it, it's just.... The substance, the vibrations, everything is probably following its normal course, you see, and all that is really changing is the way consciousness perceives things.

So pushing this knowledge to its limit – that is, applying it generally – life (what we usually call "life," the physical life of the body) and death are THE SAME THING, simultaneous ... it's just that the consciousness moves back and forth, back and forth *(same gesture).* I don't know if I am making myself clear. But it's fantastic.

And this experience comes with examples just as concrete and as utterly banal as can be. There's no room for imagination or enthusiasm – they are details of the utmost banality. For example (it's only ONE example), this sudden shift of consciousness takes place (something imperceptible, you can't perceive it, for if you had time to perceive it, I suppose it wouldn't happen; it isn't objectified), and ... you feel you're going to faint, all the blood rushes from the head to the feet and: whoops! But if the consciousness is caught IN TIME, it doesn't happen; and if it's not caught in time, it does.

This would tend to show.... I don't know if we can generalize or if this is just one special case being worked out (I can't say), but there's a very distinct impression that what ordinary human consciousness perceives as death might simply be that the consciousness hasn't been brought back to its true position fast enough.

I am quite aware that all this must seem confusing; I can feel how inadequate the words and expression are for describing the experience. When you want to be literary, you say it's a "reversal of consciousness" – but it isn't! That's just literature.

Although perhaps it means we are drawing closer to the knowledge of the thing – by knowledge I mean the power to change it, of course. If you have power over something, it's because you know it; "knowing" a thing means being able to create it, or change it, to make it last or cease to be – in other words it is Power. That's what "knowing" means. All the rest is explanations the mind gives to itself. And I can feel that something ("something"! Well, what Sri Aurobindo calls "the Lord of Yoga": the part of the Supreme concerned with terrestrial evolution) is leading me towards the discovery of that Power – that Knowledge – naturally by the only possible means: experience. And with great care, for I can feel that....

It's going as fast as it possibly can.

Vol. 3, p. 339

## January 9, 1963

But it's very hard for the body to change. Because it lives only from its habit of living. And every time something of the true way of living filters in, then without thinking, without reasoning or anything like an idea, practically without sensation, almost automatically, the cells panic at the newness of it. So, you understand, EVERYTHING has to be changed. It's no longer the heart that has to pump blood and receive the Force, no longer the stomach that has to digest, it's not any of that any more – it all functions in another way. The base must be shifted, the functioning completely changed – but then all those cells are so anxious to see that everything goes ACCORDING TO HABIT....

*(silence)*

116

Terrible. A strange difficulty.

If the inner being – the true being – is the ruler, the power of the true being makes the body act automatically; but then it doesn't grow conscious of its own change, it doesn't collaborate in its change, so for the change to happen it would take ... maybe millennia. The true being has to be like this *(gesture to the background, standing back)* and the body has to do everything BY ITSELF, in other words, contain the Lord, receive the Lord, give itself to the Lord, BE the Lord. It does aspire – oh, it's intense, aflame – that's very good. But the Lord *(smiling)* doesn't conform to the ordinary habit! So all the habits, the minute He just tries to take possession of one function or another, even partially (not totally), all the interrelationships, all the movements are changed instantly – panic. Panic at the particular spot. And the result: you faint, or you are just about to faint, or you have an excruciating pain, or anyway something APPARENTLY breaks down completely. So what's to be done?... Wait patiently until that small number or large number of cells, that little spot of consciousness, has learned its lesson. It takes one day, two days, three days, then the chaotic, upsetting "big" event calms down, is explained, and those particular cells say to themselves (or begin saying to themselves), "God, how dumb we are!..." It takes a little while, then they understand.

But there are thousands and thousands and thousands of them!

You can't overdo it, because disruption is no good, of course! I've been observing that lately. When you came last time, I was – I was going through an upheaval.

The consciousness is there *(gesture, standing back)*, but ... it intervenes only if it is absolutely indispensable. It's just that it tries locally to make the cells ... (not understand, it isn't "understand" because there's no mind) have the right sensation, the right experience – the right experience – until they start saying, "Oh! ... Oh! ..."

Some panic. Some have already had a few experiences, they know better and see clearer, they work to adapt to the new vibration. But others have yet to understand, and they feel so stupid, so stupid! And from above, something watches it all and finds it both (both at once) very funny, because really it's exceedingly ridiculous, and at the same time so sad! It's so sad to see that EVERYTHING is like this: the WHOLE earth, the WHOLE earth! That this body is the object of a special concentration, a special effort, a special CHARGE, a special concern, a special care – this minuscule fragment, minuscule – and there's the whole earth, the whole earth.... And they all think themselves so wonderful, so smart! ...

I could keep talking for hours.

Vol. 4, p. 20

## February 21, 1963

*(Message given by Mother for February 21:)*

"The boon that we have asked from the Supreme is the greatest that the Earth can ask from the Highest, the change that is most difficult to realise, the most exacting in its conditions. It is nothing less than the descent of the supreme Truth and Power into Matter, the supramental established in the material plane and consciousness and the material world and an integral transformation down to the very principle of Matter. Only a supreme Grace can effect this miracle.

The supreme Power has descended into the most material consciousness but it has stood there behind the density of the physical veil, demanding before manifestation, before its great open workings can begin, that the conditions of the supreme Grace shall be there, real and effective.

A total surrender, an exclusive self-opening to the divine influence, a constant and integral choice of the Truth and rejection of the falsehood, these are the only conditions made. But these must be fulfilled entirely, without reserve, without any evasion or presence, simply and sincerely down to the most physical consciousness and its workings."

Sri Aurobindo

Vol. 4, p. 53

**March 23, 1963**

These last few days, while walking in meditation, I said to the Lord, "What do I have? I have no certainty, no foreknowledge, no absolute power, I have nothing." (I don't mean "I," I mean the body – this body.) The body was saying: "Do you see my condition? I am still full of ..." (it was complaining bitterly), "oh, full of the silliest movements." Petty movements of apprehension, petty movements of uncertainty, petty movements of anxiety, petty movements of all kinds of very, very petty things – those who live a normal life don't take any notice, they don't know, but when you observe what's going on deep down with that discernment ... oh, mon petit! It's so petty, so petty, so petty....

Only one thing (which is not even absolute): a sort of equality that has come into the body – not an equality of soul *(laughing):* an equality in the cells! It has come into the body. There is no longer that clash of joy and pain – always and for everything, every minute, every reaction, "You, Lord, to You, Lord." As though the cells were chanting, "To You Lord, to You Lord, to You Lord...." And ... well, that's how it is.

There are enough physical miseries to experience what people call "physical pain" – quite enough (!) Yet, materially, everything is organized to give every possible joy! For example (ever since the age of five it has been like that), whenever the body felt, "Oh, if I had this.... Oh, it would be nice to have that," the thing would come in no time. Fantastic! It has always been that way, only it has become more conscious. Before, it would happen without my noticing it, quite naturally. Now, of course, the body has changed, it's no longer a baby, it no longer has a child's fancies. But when that kind of Rhythm comes, when something says, "Oh, this is fine!" ... mon petit, it comes in TORRENTS from all sides without my saying a word. Just like that. There was a time when the body enjoyed it, it was delighted by it, made very happy by it (even two years ago, a little more perhaps), very happy, it found that amusing – it was lovely, you see. But now: "To You Lord." Only this, a sort of quiet, constant joy: "To You Lord, to You Lord, to You Lord...." And on both accounts: for physical pain as well. In that regard, the body is making progress. Although to tell the truth, its life is made so easy! So easy that it would have to be quite hard to please not be satisfied – the Lord is full of infinite grace.

No, in spite of everything, the body doesn't have that sort of eternal stability, the sense of its immortality (immortality isn't the right word), of its permanence. Not that it has a sense of impermanence, far from it, the cells feel eternal – that much is there. But a certain "something" that would be sheltered from all attacks. It still feels the attacks. It feels an instability, it doesn't have a sense of absolute security, it hasn't yet reached a state of absolute security – that's it: the sense of security. There are still vibrations of insecurity. Yet that seems so mean, so silly! It still lives in insecurity.... Security, the sense of security only comes through union with the Supreme – nothing in life as it is, nothing in the world as it is, can offer the sense of security, it's impossible. But to feel the Supreme's presence so constantly, to be able to pass everything on to Him, "To You, to You, to You," and yet not to have a sense of security! A shock or a blow comes (not necessarily personally, but in life), and there's still a particular vibration: the vibration of insecurity – it still exists. The body finds that disquieting, painful: "Why?" Not that it complains, but it complains about itself, it finds itself not up to the mark.

To know that all is You, that You alone exist, to feel You everywhere, to feel You always, and still to be open to the first thing that comes from outside to give you a blow, a sense of insecurity – how absurd!

120

Of course, with a concentration of the true being *(gesture above),* it disappears instantly – but that means it isn't the body that feels a sense of security! It's the true consciousness (and quite naturally so, for it would not be true if it didn't have that sense). But what we want is the body to exist in ITSELF, by ITSELF, with all qualities WITHIN ITSELF. In other words, God shouldn't need to manifest for the body to live without anxiety!

No, that's not THE thing!

Vol. 4. p. 97

## March 30, 1963

There is a sort of review going on of all the elements of the body consciousness, with a sample of the circumstances of their various manifestations or expressions. All this is passed before me as if to show me all the points in the body's cells that were contrary to or unprepared for the reception of the divine Forces. All that comes up in the form of lived memories – things I had more than forgotten (I could have sworn they no longer existed), but which come back. Un-be-liev-able. And it's not an ego's or a person's memory, but the memory of a force in motion in the general vibrations. So I see ... fantastic things!

But it's erased immediately; as soon as I wake up, my first movement *(gesture of offering)* is to present it all to the Lord: the cause, the effect, the image, the sensation – everything. When it's all seen, I tell Him, "Now it's Yours." And then I forget – fortunately, thank God!

It goes on every night. It takes the form of all sorts of scenes, of symbols, of memories, from words to images. It comes in groups and categories of tendencies, it represents the various human tendencies in detail – it's infinitesimal. It's only because they are multiplied millions of times that they can have some importance – but they're nothing! Mere nothings. Yet that's just what blocks the way.

It really isn't of interest.

*(silence)*

After YEARS of it, there may be a tangible result, who knows? ... Even then, I am not sure it won't be limited. If it were a terrestrial result, it would be worthwhile, but it may also be very limited.

It gives me the impression of a miniature painting done with a magnifying glass and tiny dots – miniatures are painted with a very fine brush, very pointed, and you make tiny dots with a big magnifying glass. It gives me the impression of that work. And it takes many, many, many tiny dots to paint just a bit of cheek.

*(silence)*

Tiny dots, tiny dots.

But it's so dull! So dull, so lackluster, so unchanging, so – uninteresting, really dull – that the slightest light shines like a bright star! The smallest, slightest, tiniest progress seems like an extraordinary thing. Like, for example, the attitude in certain cells towards a physical disorder which, naturally, like all physical disorders, tends to recur. The attitude in the cells changes – not the disorder (!), the disorder changes only because of the cells' reaction, that's what makes it change; but it recurs with clockwork regularity – that's its job. It is the way it's received by the cells, their reaction to it, that brings about the change. And there is now a difference in the cells' reaction. The result of my observation (an impersonal, general observation) is that there are two types of change (I can't call it "progress"), two types of change in the reaction: a change that goes on improving, in the sense that the reaction grows less sharp, the cells are less affected and become not only more conscious but more IN COMMAND of the reaction (something people are not generally conscious of, but which is what brings about the cure). And, on the other hand, deterioration: under the unrelenting attack, the cells panic, become more and more affected and afraid, and it eventually results in a terrible mess and a catastrophe. Well, the whole thing is observed,

122

studied, experienced; but ... (laughing) in ordinary medicine it's explained away in two words! You see, what I see now is the process – they don't know the process, only the result. And, well, I notice that as the consciousness grows, the cells panic less and less and a sort of mastery develops. Of course, it's a pleasing observation, if I may say so, but it doesn't even make me happy! It seems rather obvious.... Also the proportion is such that to get a really telling result, it would take years and years and years! Oh, how many years! How slow things are....

So I don't feel impelled to talk about it. I'd rather concern myself with something else – I do the work, but that's all.

Vol. 4, p. 104

## April 6, 1963

There is progress in the impersonalization of the physical, bodily consciousness, with consequences that are probably interesting, but impossible to explain to people who don't understand. For instance ...

*(silence)*

I am conscious of the body, but it isn't the consciousness of this body *(Mother touches her body):* it's the consciousness of THE Body – it may be anyone's body. I am conscious, for instance, of vibrations of disorder (most often they come in the form of suggestions of disorder) in order to see whether they are accepted and have an effect. Let's take the example of a suggestion of hemorrhage, or some such suggestion (I mention hemorrhage because it will soon come into the picture). Under the higher Influence, the body consciousness rejects it. Then begins the battle (all this takes place all the way down in the cells, in the material consciousness) between what we could call the "will for hemorrhage," for example, and the reaction of the body's cells. But it's very like a real battle, a real confrontation. And all of a sudden, there's something like

123

a general issuing a command and saying, "What's this!"... You understand, that general is conscious of the higher forces, the higher realities and the divine intervention in Matter; and after trying to use the will, this reaction, that feeling of peace and so on, suddenly he is SEIZED by a very strong determination and issues a command – in no time the effect begins to make itself felt, and little by little everything returns to order.

All this takes place in the material consciousness. Physically, the body has all the sensations – but not the hemorrhage, you understand. But it does have the sensations, that is, the effects: all the sensory effects. It goes on for a while and then follows a whole curve. All right. Once the battle is over, I take a look and wonder (I observe the whole thing, I see my body, which has been fairly shaken, mind you), I say to myself, "What in the world is all this?" But just for a second, then I forget about it.

A few days afterwards, I receive a letter from someone very close, who has an ardent faith and really holds on to me with almost perfect faith, exceptional. In the letter: the whole story, the attack, the hemorrhage, how suddenly the being is SEIZED, the consciousness is SEIZED with an irresistible will, and hears words – the very words that were uttered HERE. The result: saved (he was dying), saved, cured.

Just enough time for the letter to reach me.

I remembered my episode ... and began to understand that my body is everywhere!!

You see, it's not a question of just these cells here: it's a question of cells in, well, quite a lot of people, hundreds, maybe thousands – all that clings anywhere and in any way to the higher Consciousness. And since my mind is silent (I deliberately keep the mind absolutely still, trying not to react to all that constantly comes to it from "outside," or trying to react almost subconsciously), nothing is there to think, "Oh, it's this one's body, it's that one's body" – it's THE Body! That's what is so difficult for people to understand. It is THE body – this

124

*(Mother touches her body)* is not my body any more than other bodies (a bit more, in the sense that it is more directly the object of the concentration of the Force). So everything, all the sensations, the movements of consciousness, the battles, all of it is everywhere. And suddenly, with this little affair, oh, I understood a fantastic number of things – and also the difficulty, mon petit!... The difficulty ... because really, after this experience, the body was not ill but very tired. But then it is seized with such things all the time! All the time, all the time, all the time, you know, they spring up, brrm! pounce on it, brrm! from this side, that side, every which way. So I have to keep still *(gesture of stopping, silent, in the midst of other activities),* and then I start waging the battle.

*(silence)*

Which means the body has got its own difficulties (no aggregate of cells is free from difficulties in the present conditions of life), and I think that its capacity to keep still (to an extent) is its only safeguard ... but that doesn't reduce the difficulties at all, since the contact doesn't even depend on the physical presence! But then what tremendous, prodigious power has to be EMBODIED in the physical cells to withstand all that! ...

But there too, a shift is taking place (what I told you once: those abrupt experiences that do not settle in but are first contacts). After the lesson was drawn from this story, suddenly something arose in the body consciousness – which isn't ONE body's consciousness but a general body consciousness – an aspiration, something so pure, so sweet ... so sweet ... something like an entreaty that Truth and Light may at last be manifested here, in this. Not "here in this" *(Mother touches her own body):* it was everywhere.

Then there was a contact – there was a contact – and a pale blue Light, very sweet, very bright, and an Assurance.

It lasted only a second, but it was like a new chapter suddenly opening up.

Mon petit, you are the only person to whom I can say all this — there is not one, not one! Not one able to simply understand. Which makes things more difficult, because I am constantly weighed down by the stupidity of people's thoughts (stupidity in the sense of incomprehension), the thoughts of all those around me, who think I am ("I," what they call "I," you know, "me"), who think I am ill and ... I can't tell them a thing! If I hadn't spoken to you today, it would be gone. I would never have said anything. Well, that's the way it is.

So looking at it from an ordinary viewpoint, it's so ... fantastic, it means such a ... colossal work. Of course, it's the Lord who does it, but will this hold out? *(Mother touches her body)* I can't say.

If He wants, certainly He will find a way for it to hold out. But the thing is rather new....

*(silence)*

My only method is a kind of shield of mental silence (in the ordinary mind), so that all the people's thoughts do not come and pester me all the time, without letup. But they creep underneath! With some people, the moment they enter the room, I feel exhausted, because of their attitude. It doesn't work through thought at all: it's a special vibration in my body.

With others, on the contrary, it's fine.

And I don't try to observe or study or understand — God knows! There is no need to understand: it's self-evident.

Only one thing is always present: to keep intact and POWERFULLY conscious the sense of the divine Presence — that's all. That's the single concern of the cells.

From time to time (Mother laughs), they hold ... a kind of little conference among themselves, they seem to tell each other, "No one can interfere with That!" It makes them happy: "All their thoughts are powerless in front of That!"

That's all, mon petit. More work for you.

*It's stupendous. Stupendous.*

Yes, yes. I had a strong feeling of something ... well, something rather new.

Vol. 4, p. 109

## May 3, 1963

You know, I live from day to day. With only the feeling of "that" moving on very fast. By "that," I mean a large number of things.

It's very hard to say, really.

It's the perception of a terrestrial movement more than anything else. So the details are unimportant in themselves, but they are symptomatic of the whole. I mean that difficulties, obstacles, battles, victories, advances are in themselves nothing but indications of a general movement: at times, the resistance and opposition are formidable; at other times there are fantastic advances or progress, seemingly miraculous. If you see everything together, you feel, you feel a sort of thrust – an overall thrust – in which a small cellular concentration seems really unimportant in itself; its importance diminishes with its lack of resistance, in the sense that the more it allows the Work to be done without hindering or distorting the movement – without hindering it or making it more complicated – the more the sense of its importance diminishes. In other words, it appears important only insofar as it hinders.

There is evidently a twofold movement: on one hand, something that tries to draw less and less the attention and concentration of others, that is, to lessen the sense of intermediary necessary for forces and thoughts to spread (more and more there is an attempt to undo that), and on the other hand, an increase – at times prodigious, staggering – of power. Now and then (seldom, and I must say I don't at all try to make it happen more often), now and then, for a minute – not even a minute: a few seconds – comes a sense of absolute Power; but immediately it is covered over, veiled. The effect at a distance is becoming greater and greater, but that is not the result of a conscious will – I mean there is no attempt to have more power, none at all. Now and then, there's the observation (a very amusing observation, sometimes) that for a moment (but it's a matter of seconds), the Power is absolute, and then the usual hodgepodge takes over again.

The effect on others is increasing considerably, though it too isn't the result of an attempt in that direction, not at all: those things are automatic. Yet, as I said, at certain seconds, there rises ... something that wills. "Wills," but not in the ordinary way: something that ... it's between knowing, seeing and willing. A little something that has something of all three and is ... as hard as diamond ... (oh, how can I explain it? I don't know, there are no words for it), it has something of the emotive vibration, but that's not it; it has nothing to do with anything intellectual, nothing at all; it's neither intellectual vision nor supramental knowledge, that's not it, it's something else. It is ... a diamondlike, live force – live, living. And that's all-powerful. But extremely fleeting – it immediately gets covered over by a heap of things, like visions, supramental vision, understanding, discernment – all this has become a constant mass, you understand.

From the standpoint of sensitivity or sensation (I don't know what to call it), when the body rests and enters the static state of pure Existence ... Before, it was (or gave) a sense of total immobility – not something motionless: a "non-movement," I don't know; not the opposition between something motionless and something in motion, not that – the absence of any possibility of movement. But now, as it happens, the body has the sense not only of a terrestrial movement, but of a universal movement so fantastically rapid that it is imperceptible, beyond perception. As if beyond Being and Non-Being, there were a "something" that's both ... I mean, that doesn't move WITHIN a space but is both beyond immobility and beyond movement, in the sense that it's so rapid as to be absolutely imperceptible to ALL the senses (I don't mean merely the physical senses), all the senses in all the worlds.

This is something new.

When I lie down, I go from one state to the other with extraordinary speed. And I've noticed (the thing is just at its beginning, so I can't really say), I've noticed that in that state, the Movement exceeds the force or power that concentrates the cells into an individual form. And that state seems to be all-powerful, although devoid of conscious will or vision (for the moment). It's a state ... (how can I explain this?) whose characteristics exceed the power that concentrates the cells into an individual body. The effect is automatic (not willed): as soon as something takes the form of a physical pain, it disappears INSTANTLY. But then, and this is most interesting, the second the body reverts to a certain state – its ordinary state, which isn't the ordinary human state, of course, but its ordinary, habitual state – it recaptures the MEMORY of its pain, and along with the memory comes the possibility of reverting to it if a certain number of conditions are not automatically fulfilled. I don't know if what I am saying makes any sense, but that's how the experience is.... It is probably the passage from the true thing to the thing no longer true – not what is meant by Falsehood here on earth (that's something else altogether), but a first alteration compared to the pure Vibration. It gives the impression of a wrong habit, what remains is merely a question of a wrong habit. It's not the principle of distortion that works here, but the wrong habit due to the effect of ANOTHER principle. And something is to be found to check – check, eliminate, prevent – that effect from recurring automatically.

Because it happens CONSTANTLY. It's a constant phenomenon: passing from this to that, this to that, this to that, to such a point – it's so strong – that a second comes, or a minute, or anyway a certain interval of time (I don't know), when you are neither this nor that; then you have a feeling of nothingness. It lasts just an instant; if it lasted longer, it would probably result in fainting or something, I can't say what. But it happens all the time: this, that *(oscillating gesture)*. And between this and that, there is a passage.

Life on the surface (what people see of it, what they are in contact with) is certainly a sort of *mixture* of the two, with something going on behind the screen, but what you see on the screen is a sort of combination of the two – they don't really combine, but the visual effect is odd [for Mother]. By "visual," I don't mean just for the eyes but for the outer consciousness. It's a bizarre life, neither this nor that, nor a mixture of the two, nor a juxtaposition, but as though both were operating through each other. It must be intercellular: something that goes this way *(Mother intertwines the fingers of one hand with the fingers of the other in a continuous movement of interpenetration)*, so that the mixture must be very microscopic, on the surface.

*(Mother remains engrossed, "looking"*
*at the experience)*

But from a much more external viewpoint, the night that followed your arrival there [at Rameswaram, the night of April 21, 1963] was dreadful, in the sense that the consciousness was put in contact with all the most negative and destructive things: like an entire world, yes, of denial, of refusal too, of opposition, of battle, of ill will – the visual appearance was chalk-white, you know, the soulless white of chalk, everything was like that, even black was chalk-white (!). Something absolutely stripped of all soul life. Horrible. I don't know, I would have to go back years and years and years to find anything like it in my memory. And I was right in it, it was forced on me; it was as if I were made to stay there and watch it all.

I forgot: immediately afterwards I swept everything clean. Except for what I've just said, I don't remember what it was – I don't remember what it was because I did NOT want it to exist. But it was horrible. And in the morning, there was such a painful impression! So I thought something was wrong over there, and when I received your letter, I understood. But it isn't limited to one person or another, one place or another: it seems to evoke a universal way of being, that's what troubles me. As if an entire way of being which I've been resisting for ... for, well, more than seventy years at any rate, which I've been keeping at arm's length so it may no longer exist in a real way, as if it were all forced on me. Like a thing from a past that no longer has the right to exist.

Afterwards, it got better. That night was the worst.

But during the morning meditation, I was at a loss.... Is it the symbol of a *clinging to the past?* Possible. But then there are plenty of people like that in the world, who cling to the past, plenty....

*(silence)*

The next morning, for an hour, I had an experience.... Everything always happens as if it were in the body (but this body has become a kind of representative and symbolic object), it always takes place that way, whether it's a sense of imminent death or a sense of perfect immortality. All that always takes place in the body – it is the battlefield, it is the field of victory, it is the Defeat, it is the Triumph, it is everything. So I noted the experience down.

*(Mother hands a slip of paper to Satprem):*

"The Lord is peaceful resignation, but the Lord is also the struggle and the Victory.

"He is the joyous acceptance of all that is; but also the constant effort towards a more total and perfect harmony.

"Perpetual movement in absolute immobility."

This isn't an intellectual reflection, it's the notation of the experience: the constant, twofold movement of total acceptance of all that is, as an absolute condition to participate in all that will be, and at the same time, the perpetual effort towards a greater perfection. And this was the experience of all the cells.

The experience lasted more than an hour: the two conditions.

That's exactly what made a sharp division in the whole spiritual thought or spiritual will of mankind. The point doesn't seem to have been understood. Some, like Buddha and that whole line, have declared that the world is incorrigible, that the only thing to do is to get out of it, and that it can never be otherwise – it changes, but really remains the same. The result is a certain attitude of perfect acceptance. So, for them, the goal is to get out – that is, you escape: you leave the world as it is and escape. Then there are the others, who sense a perfection towards which men strive indefinitely and which is realized progressively. And I see more and more that the two movements complement each other, and not only complement each other but are almost indispensable to each other.

In other words, the change that arises from a refusal to accept the world as it is has no force, no power: what is needed is an acceptance not only total but comprehensive, joyous – to find supreme joy in things in order to have (it's not a question of right or power) ... in order to make it possible for things to change.

Putting it differently, you must become the Supreme in order to help in His action, in the changing of the world; you must have the supreme Vibration in order to participate in that Movement, which I am now beginning to feel in the body's cells – a Movement which is a sort of eternal Vibration, without beginning or end. It has no beginning (the earth has a beginning, so that makes it easy; with the earth's beginning, we have the beginning of the earth's history, but that's not the case here), it has no beginning, it is ... something existing from all eternity, for all eternity, and without any division of time: it's only when it is projected onto a screen that it begins to assume the division of time. But you can't say a "second," or an "instant".... It's hard to explain.... No sooner do you begin to feel it than it's gone: something boundless, without beginning or end, a Movement so total – total and constant, constant – that it is perceived as total immobility.

Absolutely indescribable. Yet it is the Origin and Support of the whole terrestrial evolution.

When you speak of terrestrial things, it's very easy, very easy.

These words *(Mother shows the notation of her experience)* come long after the experience is over. There is a sort of silence, of immobility, and it's like something that settles slowly, slowly; and once it has settled, here is the residue *(Mother shows her note, laughing)*.

Vol. 4, p. 125

## May 29, 1963

*I would like a clarification on a passage from a previous conversation [of May 3], in which you said: "Something tries to draw less and less the attention and concentration of others...." And you added: "That is, to lessen the SENSE OF INTERMEDIARY necessary for forces and thoughts to spread...." What is this "sense of intermediary"? Do you mean your "role of intermediary" in the diffusion of forces? Do you want to lessen that role – to withdraw?*

It isn't "role"! The role is a fact, a sort of ineluctable fact, absolutely independent of the individual will and consciousness – I am more and more convinced of it, fantastically so. The Work is done through a certain number of elements – whether they are aware of it or not, whether they collaborate or not makes little difference. It has been decided that way, it has been chosen that way and it is done that way. Whether you like it or not, whether you are aware of it or not, whether you collaborate or not – very little difference. It's more a question of personal satisfaction!

And inasmuch as the very cells of the body no longer feel their separateness (that is almost entirely gone, even in the sensation), then something is done (or takes place), but without any self-observation. Somewhere *(gesture above)*, something knows, wills and acts; somewhere else, there is a certain number of things in a state of happy receptivity, and absolutely, extraordinarily passive, not interfering. And the less it observes, the better. It remains in an inner contemplation, or rather turned to the Heights (a Height that is everywhere, of course, not just above), a Height perfectly luminous, perfectly conscious, perfectly effective. And that's all that is needed.

The less the consciousness is turned to the outside, the less it perceives obstacles, resistances – all that appears more and more unreal, transient, extremely relative.

In the necessary and unavoidable everyday contact with people, there is a growing perception that whatever the circumstance (which in itself is so simple, simpler than a child, you know – a perfect simplicity), as soon as it comes into contact with the terrestrial human atmosphere, it becomes ever so complicated! And quite unnecessarily. It seems as if the normal human occupation is to complicate all that could be extremely simple. I see this day after day, for all the small events of every day, of each and every minute. With certain consciousnesses – as soon as it touches certain consciousnesses – it is twisted, sometimes into terrible knots. Then it takes a fantastic labor to undo it – the whole thing PERFECTLY unnecessary!

These last few days, in fact, I have been observing it all and wondering, "Why are things this way? ..." It must have been the means – probably the most effective means, I don't know – to emerge from inertia, from *tamas*. If everything worked in that Simplicity, that perfect Quietness, well, human consciousness would be in such a state that it would have simply fallen asleep. It would have reached the state ... not even of an animal, perhaps of a slumbering plant!

That must be the reason.

But when you see it from the other side, it's so absurd – fantastically absurd! To such a point that the meaning of every single word you utter is immediately twisted – automatically, you can't say why. With something clear and obvious, which should have gone smoothly, without hurdles, you are immediately caught in a swirl of complications.

All, all, all activities, all of life is like that.

And then there are little nuances, little differences, which naturally assume considerable proportions in those distorted consciousnesses: they say, "Oh, now everything is fine," and then, "Oh, now everything is going wrong," but that's not true! It's always the SAME thing, only with little nuances.

But the true everything is fine, THE TRUE THING as it is, is so simple! So simple, so quiet, so immediate, so direct that it's almost unthinkable for human thought, much less for human sensation. Voilà.

Vol. 4, p. 153

## June 8, 1963

It was yesterday, I think, in the night (not last night, the night before, the 6th of June, that is), for more than three hours without stop, there was no consciousness of anything any more – not a thought, not a will, not an action, not an observation, nothing. Everything was at a standstill. For instance, all that happens when you have experiences and you work in the subconscient – all that, everything, everything was at a standstill. It was like the action of a Force. Without any thought or idea, only the sensation and a sort of perception (*awareness* is the right word) of a Force, but a stupendous Force, you know, like the Force of the earth – all the combinations of the forces along with an action that came from above and worked on them. It was going through me (especially around the head down to the chest, but it was going on in the whole body, and it was spherical), it went through me and out, and out, and out in this direction, that direction, another direction, innumerable directions, and nothing but movements of Force (there was something like a perception of colors, but not in the ordinary way: like a knowledge that certain vibrations corresponded to a particular color), but it was an incalculable MASS, almost ... indefinite, at any rate, and simultaneous. At first I said to myself *(laughing)*, "What's going on?" Then I thought, "All right, it doesn't matter, I'll just let it happen." And it went on and on and on – three hours without letup.

I didn't know ... I didn't know anything any more, didn't understand anything any more, had no bearings any more; there was only a Force on the move, and what Force! ... It was a Force that came from beyond and acted upon all the forces of the earth: on big things, on small things, on small, precise points, on enormous things, and it was going on and on and on, on this point, that point, all points together and everywhere.... I suppose that if the mind had been associated with the experience, it would have gone a bit mad! It gave that impression, you see, because it was so overwhelming that ... And all the time, all the time in the physical center (the physical center, that is, in the corporeal base), with something in an ecstatic state; it was very interesting how that ecstasy – an ecstasy that sparkled like a diamond – was there, so sweet, so sweet, so peaceful, as though it were there all the while, telling the body, "Don't be afraid, *(laughing)* don't worry, don't be afraid, all is well." As though the supreme Power were saying all the while, "Don't worry, don't worry, leave it to me, leave it to me...." It lasted more than three hours.

I wondered, "What will my condition be like when I get up? Completely dazed, or what?" – Very quiet, nothing different, with only a sort of ... something that was smiling and saying, "Oh, so things CAN be that way."

The mind was absolutely silent, absolutely: all the connections with all that people keep sending from everywhere were cut – all of it was completely gone. There were only the universal forces in action, with something that came from above and impregnated them all, sent them all out. And with it, a point – it was like a point in that immensity – a sparkling point, absolutely ecstatic, in such a peace! An extraordinary ecstasy, which was deliberately saying, "Don't worry; you can see what's going on, can't you, so don't worry, don't worry," because certainly the thing had gone beyond all possible individual proportions.

It's the first time. I've had currents of force, I've had actions on the earth, I've had forces coming to me, all sorts of things; but this was different: it was all of that together. It was everywhere at the same time, everything at the same time, with that Inrush, and it was ... There was certainly something that wanted me to be very quiet and not to worry. It was necessary that I should keep very quiet.

I had a feeling that I was given the awareness of something that's taking place right now. Because at night, generally, I disconnect myself from everything and universalize myself – no, "universalize" isn't the word: I identify myself with the Lord. That's my way of resting. I do it every night, it is the time when I have my deep rest. But now I've been made aware of this Force at work. Often experiences come (there have been a number of them lately), but it's the first time this one has come, because ... It was certainly something happening FOR the earth; but it didn't come from the center of forces that generally acts on the earth. It wasn't the usual working of forces on the earth. It was "something happening." And it gave the sense that the earth was very small – the movement was towards the earth, it was for the earth, but the earth was very small.

Very small.

*(silence)*

There were no psychological perceptions (what I call "psychological perceptions" are, for instance, vibrations of love, vibrations of peace, vibrations of light, vibrations of knowledge, of power), they weren't there in that form, it wasn't that. Still, all that must have been there, because there were many things, many things that were all one thing, but one thing which assumed different forms; but I didn't see the forms, I didn't see the colors. It was only a question of

137

pure sensation. A pure vibratory sensation: only vibrations, vibrations, vibrations, on a ... colossal scale.

It is a new experience.

*(silence)*

Obviously, there was ... there must have been a cause for alarm, because as soon as I became conscious of the experience (it started before I became conscious of it; when I did, it seemed to me it had already been going on for a long time; so when I say three hours, it means three hours during which I was conscious, but it had started long before; it was around eleven at night and lasted till three in the morning), so the second I was made conscious of the "thing," obviously there was a cause for alarm, because immediately I was told, "You see, this is what is going on," and it was thanks to that ecstasy in the body that there was no alarm: "Oh, things are fine, everything is fine." And when the experience was over, it didn't end like an experience exhausting itself; it ended as if, very slowly, the thing were, not exactly veiled to my consciousness, but as if my consciousness were turned away from it, with the feeling, "Don't worry." At the start and at the end. All the same, when I woke up, I thought (because my head felt strange, there was a bizarre sensation as if I had become quite swollen! Swollen, inordinately swollen), I thought, "Maybe when I get up tomorrow morning (I get up at 4:30), I'll find myself in a complete daze!" That's why I observed – but everything was fine, there only remained that sort of feeling of being swollen. I feel (yet it was two nights ago, not last night), I feel as if my head were swollen! But the clear-headedness is the same as ever!! *(laughing)* Nothing's been disturbed!

On the contrary, there is a sort of ... like an acuteness, something more acute in the perception, a little bit ironic – I don't know why. A magnified impression that all the things in the world are much ado about nothing, a lot of fuss about nothing – I've had that feeling for ... for centuries, I could say, but there is in addition something ever so slightly acute and ironic.

But otherwise, crystal clear!

*(silence)*

If someone could tell me ...

But I am not supposed to know, evidently. Probably I am too much of a chatterbox (!), I always tell you all my stories, which probably isn't necessary, so I am not told. But, you know, people are so fond of putting labels on things: "This is what it is, that is what it is...." We don't want that! It sounds so "smart," you know, like newspapers headlines: "The latest development." *(Mother sketches big, sensational headlines)* We don't want that.

You may have an experience for an hour, two hours sometimes, but here there was an impression that ... all of a sudden I was made aware. And that I participated: this *(the body)* was allowed to participate, because for some reason that I don't know (maybe because of the work going on in the body, I don't know, that must be why), it seemed necessary that I should participate. But the impression is that something stupendous is happening right now.

You see, when I had that experience of the pulsations of Love in April last year, I had the perception of the color, the "psychological" perception of the state I was in (how can I explain?), for instance, the quality of the vibration of Love (something that has absolutely nothing to do with earthly things). At the time, I was That, I was those vibrations, but I was fully aware of the quality of those vibrations, and remained so for months – this is completely different! It was nothing but an action. NOTHING but an action. And an action, you know, in which the human body is less than an ant. Much less than an ant: an imperceptible point. Yet there seemed to be ONLY this body! As if this body alone were there and it were going through that. This body was a body ... it was THE body! And that point – that comforting point of ecstasy – was very small.

139

Very small. But it was there, quite insistent, very conscious, telling me, "Don't interfere; leave it to me entirely, all is well – see, all is well." Very small, very small.... Yet it was my body: I tell you, my head still seems swollen!

Strange.

*(silence)*

*But are they new forces, or is it something going on habitually? Is it a new work on the earth, or is it that you have seen something that goes on habitually but of which you were unaware previously?*

I wondered.... But the question isn't put correctly. It is something eternal which, because of what happened at that time (not at that minute, because, as I said, it must have been going on long before and long afterwards) ... it has become something new, for that reason, BECAUSE of what happened. Coming back to all the things we know, we could say (but that's the usual idle talk) that it is something newly manifested.

But my impression was ... an impression of Eternity. An Eternity BEYOND TIME (not something that lasts forever: something timeless), yes, the word would be: "manifesting," "making itself perceptible," or "becoming active" – that's not it, because ... Yes, acting, becoming perceptible because it acts.

That was my impression.

I could also say: something universal which becomes individual; not individual in the sense of a small person, but conscious of itself.

But the remarkable thing is that it had ABSOLUTELY NOTHING to do with all the intellectual activity, high or low – nothing. Nothing. Nothing to do with knowledge, or observation, discernment, intellectual perception, understanding, judgment and whatever.... Nothing, nothing, nothing to do with all that. It was ... a Force in motion.

"Force" means nothing! Force is something very small. It's ... the impression of "something" stupendous!

It had nothing to do with either Knowledge or Light or understanding (the whole angle of light and intellectual knowledge); nothing to do with Love (which I had felt last time and which has its own particular vibration). The best definition we could give is Power. It was Power in its most formidable aspect – crushing. With REAL All-Powerfulness; Power in its all-powerfulness, with that something unshakable, immutable, untouchable. Yes, really Power, that's right.

But Power, you understand ... For example, a hurricane's power is nothing in comparison. All the powers a human being can withstand, even probably imagine, are nothing – nothing ... it's *(Mother blows in the air)* like soap bubbles.

The feeling of something that can be neither withstood nor felt, because of its formidable state.

And it was quite clear that a solicitude, the supreme Solicitude, took great care to reassure me: "All is well." Without that, obviously, the feeling was that everything, everything was going to be dissolved.

So if we use our little wits, maybe we can say it's the supramental Power which has manifested, I don't know.

*(silence)*

But there was no perception of light, nothing that might give a hint; there was no perception of feelings or love to give a hint. There was nothing of the kind, nothing – only something that makes you puff out your cheeks in disbelief (!), so formidable that it's indescribable. Indescribable.

Evidently it's Power.

We always conceive of power acting ON something, ON an object, with an object, WITH A VIEW to realizing something; we cannot separate the two – but it was none of that, it was ... Power in action. But not an action ON something.

I had the feeling it was a decisive turning point which far exceeded my little understanding.

*(silence)*

141

We will know, one day.

But the explanation comes afterwards: it's brought down to our small scale ... *(laughing)* to make us happy!

Vol. 4, p. 162

## July 20, 1963

All the habitual rhythms of the material world have changed.... The body had based its sort of sense of good health on a certain number of vibrations, and whenever those vibrations were present, it felt in good health; when something came and disturbed them, it felt that it was about to fall ill or that it was ill, depending on the intensity. All that has changed now: those basic vibrations have simply been removed, they no longer exist; the vibrations on which the body based its sense of good or ill health – removed. They are replaced by something else, and something else of such a nature that "good health" and "illness" have lost all meaning! Now, there is the sense of an established harmony among the cells, increasingly established among the cells, which represents the right functioning, whatever that may be: it's no longer a question of a stomach or a heart or this or that. And the slightest thing that comes and disturbs that harmony is VERY painful, but at the same time there is the knowledge of what to do to reestablish the harmony instantly; and if the harmony is reestablished, the functioning isn't affected. But if out of curiosity, for instance (it's a mental illness in humans), you start asking yourself, "What's that? What effect will it have? What's going to happen?" (what the body calls "the desire to learn"), if you are unlucky enough to be that way, you can be sure *(laughing)* that you'll have something very unpleasant which, according to the doctor (according to ignoramuses), becomes an illness or disrupts the body's functioning. While if you don't have that unhealthy curiosity and, on the contrary, will the harmony not to be disrupted, you only have to, we could say poetically,

142

bring one drop of the Lord on the troubled spot for everything to be fine again.

The body is unable to know things in the way it did formerly.

So there is a period when you are in suspense: no longer this, not yet that, just in between. It's a difficult period when you have to be very quiet, very patient, and above all – above all – never become afraid or irritated or impatient, because that's catastrophic. And the difficulty is that from all quarters and without letup come all the idiotic suggestions of ordinary thinking: age, deterioration, the possibility of death, the constant threat of illness, of the slightest thing – illness, dotage ... decay. It comes all the time, all the time, all the time; and all the time this poor harried body has to remain very quiet and not to listen, preoccupied only with maintaining its vibrations in a harmonious state.

Sometimes I catch it (that must be something quite common among human beings) in a sort of haste – a haste, a kind of impatience, and also, I can't say fear or anxiety, but a sense of uncertainty. The two together: impatience to get out of the present moment to the immediately next, and at the same time uncertainty as to what that immediately next moment is going to bring. The whole thing makes a vibration of *restlessness* – *what's* the word in French?

*Febrility, agitation?*

That's too much – "agitation" is too much, it's rather a lack of rest. Not agitation really, but something that lacks the rest of certainty. I constantly catch my cells being like that. Naturally I react, but for them it's a very normal state: always straining after the next moment, never the quietude of the present moment. The result (the words I use give a very concrete character to something rather fluid), the result is the feeling that you have to bear or endure, and the haste to get out of that enduring, along with the hope (a very faint and flimsy hope) that the next moment will be better. That's how it is from moment to moment, from moment to moment, from moment to moment. As soon as the Consciousness comes *(gesture of descent)* and concentrates, as soon as I bring the Consciousness into the present moment, everything becomes quiet, immobile, eternal. But if I am not CONSTANTLY attentive, the other condition [of restlessness] comes almost as a subconsciousness: it's always there. And VERY tiring – it must be one of the most important sources of fatigue in mankind. Especially here *(Mother touches her forehead and temples),* it's very tiring. Only when you can live in the eternity of the present minute does it all stop – everything becomes white, immobile, calm, everything is fine.

But it means constant vigilance – constant. It's infinitely more difficult than when one worked even in the vital; in the vital, it's nothing, it's child's play in comparison. But here, phew! ... Because, you see, in the mind or the vital, it's all movements of organization, of action, of choice, of decision – it's very easy to decide, to rule! But that cellular tension is there EVERY SECOND: it's the activity inherent in material existence. It's only when you go into samadhi that it stops. That is, when outwardly you are in trance. Then it stops.

From time to time – two, three times a day – I am given a few minutes of it. It's a marvelous relaxation. But I always come out of it (I mean the BODY comes out of it) with an anxiety, in the sense that it says, "Oh, I've forgotten to live!" Very odd. Only one second, but a second of anxiety: "Oh, I've forgotten to live!" – and the drama starts all over again.

No, it's no fun. It's interesting only for someone who finds interest in EVERYTHING, to whom EVERYTHING is interesting, that is to say, who has the sort of will for perfection that neglects no detail – otherwise, it isn't ... As soon as you enter the mental realm, of course, the mind says, "Ah, no! No, it's a waste of time." It isn't, but the mind regards all that as twaddle.

*(silence)*

I said just now that when I come out of those moments of trance, the body feels, "Oh, I've forgotten to live...." It isn't "live," it's the feeling: I've forgotten to act or concentrate, or to do the thing needed; the feeling of a servant who for a minute has stopped his work – that's it. It's just a flash, then at once comes the sense of the divine Presence, and it's all over.

It's not the word "live," no, it's "To do what one is supposed to do."

It happens especially during daytime (between 12:30 and 1 o'clock – not for long, a few minutes, I can't say; and between 5:30 and 6). At night it's not the same, because (I think I've told you already) as soon as I stretch out, the whole body is like a prayer. It's more than an aspiration, it's an intense need: "Lord, take hold of me ENTIRELY! So there may be nothing but You," and that always brings about a result [the trance] – which may last more or less long, until (how can I put it?) ... the moment "agreed upon" comes! Then when I wake up, or rather when the body emerges from that state, it knows it's agreed upon, it doesn't have that anxiety. I don't know how to explain.... In terms of consciousness it's almost like a child: very simple, very simple. No complications, no complications whatever, very simple: to do what is to be done in the proper way while expressing the supreme Will.... That is, to bring as little mixture as possible to the supreme Will (it's not a question of Will: the Movement, the Vibration), as little mixture or distortion or deterioration as possible to the Vibration – we always translate into words that are too intellectual.

But the body is docile, full of goodwill. Only I find it's a little bit of a whiner (that must be particular to this one, I am sure other bodies are different), it isn't spontaneously joyful. Not that it complains, not at all, but ... Perhaps it's due to that sort of concentration of Force of progress – it's not a blissful satisfaction, far from it. It's a long time since it stopped enjoying ordinary satisfactions, like the sense of taste, of smell: it doesn't enjoy any of that – it is conscious, very conscious, it can discern things very clearly, but in an entirely objective way, without deriving any pleasure from them.

Yet it has a spontaneous tendency to find itself incapable; and it receives the same answer all the time: "That's still the ego." That happens so often, it says to the Lord, "Look how incapable I am of doing what You want," and pat comes the answer, direct, in a flash: "Don't bother about that, it's not your business!" Naturally, I put it into words to express myself, but it isn't words, it's only sensations – not even "sensations": vibrations.

Voilà.

So all that must be having repercussions on the others, like Pavitra, when he told me the other day he was seeking me "up above" and could no longer find me! This very down-to-earth state (we can really call it down-to-earth), this very down-to-earth state of things may also create ... not an increased heaviness (because God knows it isn't heavy! It's so luminous, vibrant, luminous, so vibrant, vibrant), that's not it, but it's really at ground level. At ground level. It has none of the flights and enthusiasms of mental things, visions and all that. So it appears a little monotonous and very much at ground level.

*Yes, but we don't have the sense of participating in something. You are conscious, while we're not.*

Exactly, there's nothing to satisfy you one way or the other!

*Yes, but if we were conscious, at least we would see that something is happening, but as we are unconscious, we aren't aware of anything.*

But how can you say that something is "happening," mon petit!

*We would see a work is being done.... As it is, we don't see anything.*

But, no, you can't "see"! How can you?

*(silence)*

146

I have a kind of certitude (not quite formulated in words: a certitude in sensation, in feeling) that once this work is completed, the result will be ... almost like a thunderbolt. Because the Power's action through the mind gets diluted, qualified, adapted, altered, and so on, and how much reaches down here? *(gesture as of water disappearing into sand)* While the day it acts through this matter *(Mother touches her body)*, obviously it will be overwhelming. There isn't a shadow of doubt. But when will that be? After how long? I can't say. When you see the thing in detail, you know, it appears interminable.

I console myself with the thought that the ways of the Lord are unknown to us, and that the day it pleases Him to declare, "Here, now it's all changed," *(Mother laughs)* all we'll have to do is contemplate!

But when? I don't know. Voilà.

We must have endurance, patience, and trust too – to last and last and last. Because ultimately, whatever way you look at it, that's the only solution. All the roundabout routes people follow *(zigzag gesture as if to show the spiritual disciplines and all the usual human quests)* are simply to give you the illusion that you are doing something. That's quite clear.

*(silence)*

All the same, I have some hope that in February next year [second Anniversary of the Supramental Manifestation] something will be tangible. But ... *(laughing)* Sri Aurobindo says that man lives on hope from the cradle to the grave! Anyhow, mine isn't the same kind of hope: it's a sort of sensation. Something may happen next February – we'll see.

Vol. 4, p. 230


## July 27, 1963

The greatest difficulty is that the body's texture is made of Ignorance, so that every time the Force, the Light, the

Power try to penetrate somewhere, that Ignorance has to be dislodged. Every time the experience is similar, renewed in detail (but not in essence; I mean, every time it's a particular point, but the essence of the problem is always the same): it's a sort of Negation out of ignorant stupidity – not out of ill will, there is no ill will: it's an inert and ignorant stupidity which, by the very fact of what it is, DENIES the possibility of the divine Power. And that's what has to be dissolved every time. At every step, in every detail, it's always the same thing that has to be dissolved.

It's repeated again and again.... It's not as in the realm of ideas, where once you have seen the problem clearly and have the knowledge, it's over; some doubts or absurdities may come back to you from outside, but the thing is established, the Light is there, and automatically things are either repelled or transformed. But this here isn't the same thing! Every single aggregate of cells.... Not that it comes from outside: it's BUILT that way! Built by an inert and stupid Ignorance. An inert and stupid automatism. And so, automatically, it denies – not "denies," there's no will to deny: it is an opposite, I mean it CANNOT understand, it's an opposite – an ESTABLISHED opposite – of the divine Power. And every time, there is a kind of action which really in every detail is almost miraculous: suddenly that negation is compelled ... compelled to recognize that the divine Force is all-powerful. Seen from another angle, it's a sort of perpetual little miracle.

I'll give you an example: last time you were with me, I got (while you were present) a pain here *(gesture to the right side),* a frightful pain of the kind that makes people howl (they think they're very sick, of course!), it came here like that. You didn't see anything, did you, I didn't show anything.

As long as you were here, I didn't bother about it.... I simply thought of something else. But when you left, I thought, "There's no reason to leave that here." So I concentrated – I called the Lord and put Him here *(gesture to the side),* and I saw it all, what I've just told you, that state of stupid negation, and how if you allow the thing to follow what they call its "normal" course, it becomes a good illness *(Mother laughs)*, a serious illness. I call the Lord. (He is always here! But the fact that I concentrate and keep quiet....) And then it's almost instantaneous: the first thing is a reaction – almost a STATE rather than a reaction – which DENIES the possibility of divine Action. It isn't a will, it's an automatic negation. Then there is always a Smile that answers (that's what is interesting, there's never any anger or any force that imposes itself, only a Smile), and almost instantly the pain disappears – "That" settles in, luminous, tranquil.

It isn't final, mind you, only a first contact: the experience recurs on another occasion and for another reason (they aren't mental reasons, they are occasions), it recurs, but there is already a beginning of collaboration: the cells have LEARNED that with That, the state changed (very interestingly, they remember), so they begin to collaborate, and the Action is even more rapid. Then a third time, a few hours away, it recurs once again; but then THE CELLS THEMSELVES call and ask for the divine Action, because they remember. And then That comes in, gloriously, like something established.

Now I've got it – I've got the knack! It's for training the cells, you understand! It's not just like a sick person who has to be cured once and for all: no, it's a training of the cells, to teach them ... to live.

It's wonderful.

That's why with all the consciousness and force, I tell people, "You make yourselves sick with your idiotic fear!" (A subconscious fear – sometimes mental, but then it's utterly stupid – at any rate a fear in the cells, a subconscious fear.) "You make yourselves sick. Stop being afraid and you won't get sick." And I can say that with absolute assurance.

It's interesting.

But constantly (I make the problem more precise for the sake of clarity), there are constantly in the atmosphere, as I have always said, all the suggestions, all that atmosphere of the physical mind which is full of every possible stupidity. You have to be permanently on your guard and sweep it all away: "Go away, don't interfere." The doctors' opinions, the example of other people, that whole ... really, that whole terrible muddle of Ignorance all around, which you have to drive back: "Don't meddle, mind your own business."

*(silence)*

So, regularly, as soon as there comes a pain somewhere or a discomfort or anything, immediately, instantly, the first reaction: "Ah! Lord, what do You want me to learn?" And I become attentive.

If everybody does the same thing, if all those who can do it (sincerely, of course, without pretense) do it sincerely: "Ah! Lord, what do You want me to learn?" and then observe, wait, then things are easier, you put yourself at least in better conditions.

Vol. 4, p. 243


## July 31, 1963

*Mother seems quite shaken and tired, though smiling as always*

I've made a discovery – not positively a discovery, but a confirmation. A rather interesting observation.

There was a sort of periodicity in the attacks – can I call them "physical "? ... They're not physical, although they're on the body. They didn't recur at exactly regular intervals, because the periods of time in between weren't always the same, but there was a sort of analogy, of similarity in the circumstances. And now I have come to a kind of certainty.

The work consists, I could say, in ... either removing or transforming (I am not sure which of the two) all the body's cells that are or have been under the influence of Falsehood (not "lie" but *falsehood)*, of the state contrary to the Divine.

But since probably a radical purge or transformation would have resulted in nothing but the body's dissolution, the work goes on in stages, progressively (I am going very far back in time, to my first attacks). So the sequence is the following: first, a series of activities or visions (but those visions are always activities at the same time: both activities and visions) in the subconscious domain, showing in a very living and objective way the Falsehood that has to be removed (transformed or removed). At first, I took them as adverse attacks, but now I see they are "states of falsehood" to which certain elements in the physical being are linked (at the time, I thought, "I am brought into contact with that because of the correspondence in me," and I worked on that level – but it's another way of seeing the same thing). And it produces ... certainly there is a dissolution – there is a transformation, but a dissolution too – and that dissolution naturally brings about an extreme fatigue or a sort of exhaustion in the body; so between two of those stages of transformation, the body is given time to recover strength and energy. And I had noticed that those "attacks" always come after the observation (an observation I made these last few days) of a great increase in power, energy and force; when the body grows more and more solid, there always follows the next day or the day after, first, a series of nights I could call unpleasant (they are not, for they're instructive), and then a terrible battle in the body. This time I was conscious – naturally, I am conscious every time, but *(smiling)* more so every time.

I had observed lately that the body was getting much stronger, much more solid, that it was even putting on weight (!), which is almost abnormal. Then, I had a first vision (not vision: an activity, but very clear), then another, and then a third. Last night, I was fed a subtle food, as if to tell me that I would need it because I wouldn't take any physical food (not that I thought about it, I simply noticed I had been fed, given certain foods). And with the visions I had the two preceding nights, I knew that at issue were certain elements forming part

151

of the body's construction (psychological construction), and that they had to be eliminated. So I worked hard for their elimination. And today, the battle was waged.

But then, as I had worked hard for the elimination, the battle was quite formidable – when it exceeds a certain measure, the heart has trouble, and then I need to rest. That's how it happened. But it was so clear, so obvious! And the entire process was SEEN from the beginning, every single step of it, it's ... a marvel! A marvel of consciousness, of measure, of dosage, to allow the purification and transformation to take place without disrupting the balance, so that dissolution does not occur. It's based on the capacity to endure and withstand (naturally, if the body were unable to endure, that work couldn't be done).

And now the body KNOWS (in the beginning it didn't, it thought it was "attacks" from the outside, "adverse" forces; and it can always be explained like that, it was true in a certain way, but it wasn't the true truth, the deepest truth), now the body KNOWS where it all comes from, and it's so marvelous! A marvel of wisdom.... It puts everything in its place, it makes you REALIZE that all that play of the adverse forces is a way of seeing things (a necessary way at a given time, maybe – by "necessary," I mean practical), but it's still an illusion; illnesses are a necessary way of seeing things to enable you to resist properly, to fight properly, but it's still an illusion. And now, the BODY itself knows all this – as long as it was only the mind that knew it, it was a remote notion in the realm of ideas, but now the body itself knows it. And it is full not only of goodwill but also of an infinite gratitude – it always wonders (that's its first movement), "Do I have the capacity?" And it always gets the same answer, "It isn't YOUR capacity." "Will I have the strength?" – "It isn't YOUR strength." Even that sense of infirmity disappears in the joy of infinite gratitude – the thing is done with such goodness, such insight, such thoughtfulness, such care to maintain, as far as possible, a progressive balance.

It came with a certitude, an OBVIOUSNESS: this is the process of transformation.

But this time, there was a voluntary collaboration, so maybe it will go faster.

I was unable to do my work: the jolt was too strong. But I said I would see you because I wanted to tell you about it.

*(silence)*

It's odd, when I am in that state, I feel as if to make myself heard I have to lift a staggering weight. I feel (for a few days now) as if I have to speak very, very loudly to be heard; it's almost like a mass ... yes, as though I were buried underground and had to shout very loudly in order to be heard.

Am I speaking very loudly?

*No.*

Because, with everybody, I feel as if I had to shout in order to be heard – and it's an effort, a considerable effort. There is a sort of mass, the color of brownish earth, weighing down on me, as though I were buried and had to shout. All the while I was speaking to you just now, I felt as if I were making an enormous effort to be heard.

Am I shouting or ...?

*No.*

Not at all?

*No, it must be the thickness of consciousnesses that you're feeling?*

Yes! Yes. Yes, it's the air – it's in the air.

*(long silence)*

And I was told something this morning (I think it was this morning, or in the night, I don't remember); it was said to the body, not to me. The body was told that it would go on till complete purification, and that AT THAT POINT it will have the choice between continuing its work or ... You see, once it has attained complete purification from the cellular point

153

of view (not what people call physical "purity," that's not it), from the point of view of the divine Influence, which means that each cell will be under the exclusive influence of the Supreme (that's the work under way now), the body was told that that work would be done, and once it was completed, the body ITSELF, entirely under the Supreme's influence, would decide whether it wants to continue or be dissolved. It was very interesting, because ... dissolution means a scattering, but to scatter (that's easy to understand) is a way to SPREAD the consciousness over a very large area. So the cells will be given the choice either to act in that way *(gesture of diffusion)* or to act in agglomeration *(Mother makes a fist)*.

*(silence)*

It's the first time the problem has been envisaged from that angle, that is to say, from the standpoint of a general work.

*But I don't see how the scattering ... If it is scattered, if it is dissolved, the whole work is dissolved, isn't it?*

No, each cell is perfectly conscious.

*Then they would go into other bodies?*

(Mother remains thoughtful a moment) What happens from the material point of view?... Do they know if it reverts to inert Matter, or what? Does it become dust – what does it become?

*Dust, yes.*

Dust .... They're not cells any more?

*No, I don't think so.*

Then that's not it, because according to what I was told, they were cells – they remained cells. It must be something new. They remained cells, it was the cell that was given the choice either of staying in its present agglomeration or of spreading.

*I don't know, but it seems to me they could persist only in agglomeration with other living beings.*

Are the cells in the human body different from the cells in other bodies, in animals, for instance? Or are they the same?

154

*Except for certain specialized cells, the other cells aren't different, I believe.*

But the specialized cells must be the ones in question, because those in question are fully conscious cells – they are specialized cells.

*So I don't see that they could go into animals, I don't think they're the same kind.*

They could only go into other human organisms.

*Human, yes.*

Maybe it's the difference between ONE being and many beings? ...

It must be something in preparation. We'll see.

So mon petit, I'll let you go now, because ...

\* \* \*

*A few days afterwards, Mother added this reflection:*

It is clearly (according to external logic) a new way of dying that must be possible – no longer death as we regard it. But that ... for the moment, all we could say would be speculative, not a concrete experience. We'll see.

\* \* \*

A few days later, Mother added: "There is also something I left unsaid: an urgent need to cease all material activity in order to enable the body to receive fully – as fully as possible – the divine Force that will replace what has been removed. There is something absolute about that need: to stay totally still, quiet, letting the Force descend – permeate the body, rather. All physical activity must be suspended in some way, and if the material organization, or the habit, tends to make it continue, a kind of material impossibility, an excessive fatigue or discomfort, comes to oblige the body to keep still. Because simply to remove or change what shouldn't be there won't do; it must also be replaced by what SHOULD be there. Otherwise, there would be a dwindling or gradual reduction of substance resulting in dissolution. What has been sublimated or removed

155

has to be replaced by something which is the true Vibration, the one that comes straight from the Supreme."

## August 3, 1963

Physical Matter, physical substance – the very elementary consciousness that's in physical substance – has been so ill-treated (since man's presence on earth, I suppose, because before man, there probably wasn't enough self-consciousness to be aware of being ill-treated; the substance wasn't conscious enough, I suppose, to make a distinction between a normal peaceful state and unfavorable conditions; but anyway, that goes back quite (a long time), so ill-treated that it finds it very hard to believe things can be different. That consciousness has an aspiration – an aspiration especially for a LUMINOUS peace, something that isn't the dark peace of Unconsciousness, which it doesn't like (I don't know if it ever liked it, but it no longer does). It aspires to a luminous peace; not to a consciousness full of various things, not that: simply to a peaceful consciousness, very peaceful, very quiet, very luminous – that's what it wants. Yet at the same time, it has some difficulty believing that it's possible. I am experiencing it: the concrete and absolutely tangible intervention of the supreme Power, supreme Light and supreme Goodness – it [the consciousness in physical substance] has the experience of that, and every time it has a new sense of wonder, but in that sense of wonder I can see something like: "Is it really possible?"

It gives me the impression, you know, of a dog that has been beaten so much that it expects nothing but blows.

It's sad.

Yet the proofs are accumulating. If faith and trust could settle permanently, the difficulty would probably be over.

*(silence)*

That consciousness feels a sort of anxiety towards mental force; the moment a mental force manifests, it goes like this *(gesture of recoil):* "Oh, no! Enough of that, enough, enough!" As though mental force were the cause of all its torment. It feels mental force as something so hard, dry, rigid, ruthless, above all dry – dry, empty – empty of the true Vibration.

That's becoming quite clear. For example, whenever there is no need to do anything outwardly and all activity stops, then there's rest, and there comes that thirst and aspiration for a luminous Peace. It comes, and not only does it come, it seems to be firmly established. But if in that rest something suddenly flags and the old mental activity starts up (an activity of the mind of the cells, the most material mind), immediately that consciousness comes out of its rest with a *jerk:* "Ah, no! Not that, not that, not that!" Instantly the mental activity is stopped, and there is an aspiration for the Presence – "Not that, not that!"

This morning, I had the experience twice; a very slight mental activity, and almost instantly: "Ah, no, no! Not that." That consciousness prefers to act or move or do anything rather than fall into that condition – which it seems to regard as the Enemy.

*(silence)*

This morning there was a kind of vision or sensation of the curve from the animal to man – a spiral curve – then of the return to the state above the animal, in which life, action, movement aren't the result of Mind but of a Force, which is felt as a Force of SHADOWLESS light, that is, self-luminous, casting no shadows, and absolutely peaceful. And in that peace, so harmonious and soft ... oh, it's supreme rest. That disharmony and hardness are the cause of fatigue in life.

I am speaking of the cells' consciousness.

Oh, to get out of that chaos of ideas, wills, conceptions – it's all so petty, so dry, so hollow, and at the same time so irritating in its instability.

...

\* \* \*

157

*(Shortly afterwards, Mother goes into meditation and Satprem follows her:)*

Do you still have a sensation of "descent"? A descent of force?

Me, I no longer feel that it descends: it's there *(gesture around and everywhere).* That is to say, I don't feel "something descending," it's there all the time – what about you?

*I rarely feel a descent, except at times when the Force rushes downward, from below the shoulders downward.*

Yes, in the body.

*Then I feel a descent.*

It [the meditation] was very good, very still and luminous, without any disturbance. Very good.

*But the consciousness doesn't seem to be progressing – the consciousness, you understand.*

Because it doesn't want to be mentalized! You shouldn't worry.

*Oh, I remember, one day (it impressed me much), the Swami told me, "But you should imagine this, imagine that...."*

Oh!

*I said, 'No, I don't want to! I want THE THING TO COME. Then he replied (he said it with great force), "That was your error throughout all your lives."*

Not wanting to imagine?

*Yes, imagine, make use of the mental element.*

But that's quite ... On the contrary, I've had to struggle against that, not in myself but everywhere, against that mania for imagining. That's what gives me such a ... (how can I put it?) both restful and pleasant impression [with you], everything stays still. If one wants to receive the Truth, all that must come to a stop.

*I do understand.... My complaint is rather that the silence doesn't result in a clearer consciousness, for example.*

It will come.

No, that habit of imagining is very, very ... I consider it very baneful.

I had that tendency very strongly in the past; that's what I called "storytelling" – everything, everything became stories: all the work, all that had to be done. But I stopped it completely, completely, as a dangerous thing – it gives a great material power (that's probably why the Swami asked you to do it), what it gives is a material power, but it's VERY bad, it falsifies all that comes from above.

Vol. 4, p. 255

## August 7, 1963

I've noticed that phenomenon: always, when great difficulties crop up – a violent attack, a disorganization – the change isn't progressive: it's abrupt, like a reversal.

Just this morning, it was the same thing for me. You see, when the difficulty comes, there is a kind of general disorganization in the body, with intense pains, and ... (I observe, I want to follow the thing) it's not at all a progressive abatement followed by recovery, that's not how it works: it's absolutely like the reversal of a prism – everything vanishes at one stroke. There remains only that stupid habit the body has of remembering. And in remembering ... the remembrance makes you feel tired and out of sorts – but the thing is over.

The body's remembrance is yet another thing that will have to be worked upon.

There is a state in which you don't feel anything – a state – and a positive one, because it's a state of peace; a kind of very tranquil and very happy peace; a peace which makes you feel like staying that way forever: "Oh, if I could be that way forever! ..." Or else there's a chaos in which everything clashes and denies and quarrels – as though everything were in an uproar. It reminds me of the very first experience I had when

I was – I really lived – that Pulsation of Love and when it was decided I was to take my body again, to reenter my body; well, I had contact with my body, I knew I was in contact with my body, only through a pain. Contact with the body meant suffering.

I said that, in fact.

It seems to me (I've been feeling that for a long time now, more than a year, almost a year and a half), it seems to me that all the work was done only to teach every single element of the body to have a physical, material consciousness, but at the same time to maintain that state of peace – a positive, full, thoroughly comfortable peace: something that can last indefinitely. That is to say, I progressively teach the body what I could call all the divine states; I teach it to feel and live in the divine states. Well, the closest things (two things are close enough, but one is more comfortable, if I may say so – it's the word *ease* in English – than the other; the other is more tense *[Mother makes a fist]*, there is a will in it) the closest things are the sense of eternity and the sense of silence. Because behind the whole creation (I mean the material creation), there is a perfect Silence, not the opposite of noise but a positive silence, which is at the same time a complete immobility – that's very good as an antidote to disorder. But the sense of eternity is still better, and it has a sweetness the other hasn't; the sense of eternity includes the sense of sweetness (but not "sweetness" as we understand it). It's extremely comfortable. That is, there is no reason why it should change – or cease or start anew. It is selfexistent, perfect in itself. And these are the best antidotes to the other state [of disorder]: peace, simple peace, isn't always sufficient.

After all, the body is an utterly wretched thing.... Yesterday, I think, it was complaining, really complaining (I said it was a "whiner," but yesterday it was complaining), really asking, "Why, why was such a wretched thing ever made?" – Incapacity, incomprehension, oh! ... Nothing but limitations and impossibilities. A sterile goodwill, a complete lack of power, and as soon as some little vital power comes, it's turned into violence – disgusting.

*(silence)*

Whenever I complain like that, I can be sure I'll have a night of tension, and the next morning a "jolt."

It would be better to remain quiet, take things as they are and let the Lord do His work without ... without pushing Him all the time like that. I always feel that all our misfortunes are attracted by our impatience or discontent. If we were blissfully content and let things follow their course, "When You will it, it will be, that's all. I am an idiot, I remain an idiot, and when You will it to change ..."

*But can we afford to let things follow their course? If we do, everything goes haywire.*

No.

*We can tell ourselves, "Oh, everything will be fine," and let things sort themselves out, but then they just happen haphazardly.*

They happen haphazardly, but probably there comes a point when they get better.... (Laughing) We don't dare carry out the experiment to the very end!

That belief in us is obviously what makes us struggle. But I am not so sure it is true Wisdom.

I don't know.

Vol. 4, p. 260

**August 10, 1963**

The last experience (which I've had these last few days), in which apparently there was a hitch (it wasn't really one) was a sort of demonstration. I told you what it was, you remember: it's like a purge of all the vibrations that are false vibrations, that aren't the pure and simple response to the supreme Influence (all that in the cells still responds to the

161

vibrations of falsehood, either from habit or from the people around or the food taken – fifty thousand things). Then, with an aspiration or a decision, almost a prayer for purification coming from the body, something happens which, naturally, upsets the balance; the imbalance in turn brings about a general discomfort. The form discomfort takes is habitually the same: first, pains and all kinds of sensations I need not describe; if that state goes on developing, if it is allowed to assume its full proportions, it results ... in the past it resulted in a faint. But this time, I followed the process for about two hours from the moment I got up: the struggle between the new balance, the new Influence that was getting established, and the resistance of all the existing elements forced to go away. That created a sort of conflict. The consciousness remained very clear – the consciousness of the BODY remained very clear, very quiet, perfectly trusting. So for two hours I was able to follow the process (while going on with all my usual activities, without changing anything), until I felt, or rather was told sufficiently clearly that the Lord wanted my body to be completely immobile for a while so that He might complete His work. But I am not all alone: there are other people here to help me and watch over everything (but I don't say or explain anything to them, those are things I don't talk about – I don't say what goes on, I don't say anything), so I sat there wondering, "Is it really and truly indispensable?" *(Mother laughs)* Then I felt the Lord exert a little more pressure, which heightened the intensity of the conflict, so that I had all the signs of fainting – I understood (!) ... I stood up, let my body moan a little to make it plain it didn't feel too well (!) and I stretched out. Then I was immobile, and in that immobility, I saw the work that was being done – a work that cannot be done if you go on moving about. I saw the work. It took nearly half an hour; in half an hour it was over. Which means there is really ... there is a fact I cannot doubt, even if all the surrounding thoughts and forces contradict it: I cannot doubt that the consciousness is increasing more and more – the consciousness in the body. It is growing more and more precise, luminous, exact – QUIET – very peaceful. Yet very conscious of a TREMENDOUS battle against millennial habits. Do you follow?

When it was over, I saw that even physically, bodily, there is a strength: the result is an increased strength. A very clearly increased strength.

But it's still going on. Now, there's a great battle against all the ideas, the habits, the sensations, the possibilities, everything, concerning death – "death" *(laughing)*, not "death" in the sense of the consciousness departing (that, of course, people talk about, but ... those things no longer exist), no: WHAT THE CELLS MUST FEEL. And all the possibilities are presented to me ... With that consciousness (the consciousness accumulated, compressed in all those cells), when the heart stops beating and it's understood that, according to human ignorance, you are "dead," how does the force that groups all those cells together abdicate its will to hold them all together? ... Naturally, I was told right away (because the problem – all the problems – come from everywhere, and it's purposely that I am shown the problem and made to struggle with it; it's not just as an "idea"), I was told right away that that force, that consciousness which holds everything together in really superconscious cells (they don't have at all the ordinary type of consciousness; ordinarily, it's the inner, vital being *[Mother touches the heart center]* that's conscious of oneness, that is, conscious of being a being), that this aggregate of cells is now an aggregate OF ITS OWN WILL, with an organized consciousness which is a sort of collective gathering of that cellular consciousness; well ... Obviously this is an exceptional condition, but even in the past, in those beings who were very developed, outwardly, there was a beginning of willed, conscious cellular gathering, and that's certainly why in ancient Egypt, where occultism was very developed, exceptional beings such as the pharaohs, the high priests, etc., were mummified, so as to preserve the form as long as possible. Even here in

India, generally they were petrified (in the Himalayas there were petrifactive springs). There was a reason.

And I saw for Sri Aurobindo (although he hadn't yet started this systematic transformation; but still, he was constantly pulling the supramental force down into his body), even in his case, it took five days to show the first slight sign of decomposition. I would have kept his body longer, but the government always meddles in other people's business, naturally, and they pestered me awfully, saying it was forbidden to keep a body so long and that we should ... So when the body began to (what's the word?) *shrink* – it was shrinking and contracting, that is, dehydrating – then we had to do it. He had had enough time to come out, since almost everything came into my body – almost everything that was material came into my body.

But the question arose for this body [Mother's], "just to see," you know. And I saw all kinds of things, and finally the answer was always the same (you see, the problem was presented to me to enable me to understand the situation in all its aspects and see the necessities), that naturally everything would be for the best! (*Laughing*) Without a doubt. But I mean it was presented very concretely and, I could say, very "personally" to make me understand the problem. And there was that old thing I was told the other day (old, that is, a few days old! I was told that THE CELLS THEMSELVES would be given a free choice. So the conclusion of all that meditation was that there must be a new element in the consciousness of the cellular aggregates – a new element ... a new experience that must be in progress. The result: last night, I had a series of fantastic cellular experiences, which I cannot even explain and which must be the beginning of a new revelation.

When the experience began, there was something looking on (you know, there is always in me something looking on somewhat ironically, always amused) which said, "Very well! If that happened to someone else, he would think he was quite sick! (*laughing*) Or half mad." So I stayed very quiet and

164

thought, "All right, let it be, I'll watch, I'll see – I'll see soon enough! It has started, so it will have to end! ..." Indescribable! Indescribable (the experience will have to recur several times before I can understand), fantastic! It started at 8:30 and went on till 2:30 in the morning; that is to say, not for a second did I lose consciousness, I was there watching the most extraordinary things – for six hours.

I don't know where this is going....

Indescribable; you know, you become a forest, a river, a mountain, a house – and it's the sensation (an absolutely concrete sensation) OF THE BODY, of this *(gesture to the body)*. Many other things too. Indescribable. It lasted a long time, with a whole variety of things.

So at 2:30 in the morning, I said to the Lord, "That will do, won't it?!" *(Mother laughs)* And He gave me a blissful rest till 4:30.

Good.

...

*I asked myself if for everybody the supramental process will always automatically involve a lot of physical suffering.*

No.

No, because I have a growing proof that those things I have mastered now, in the body, I have the power (I keep receiving letters and notes from here or there, from people here or there who have an illness) ... it is beginning; so far it's only a beginning, a very small beginning: the power to eliminate pain.

You know, on a smaller scale, what happened with your illness.

*Yes, but I didn't mean sick people. I mean people who today or in the future will seek to effect the transformation in themselves.*

No, they ...

*Will they have to go through all that suffering?*

165

No! That Sri Aurobindo wrote very clearly: for all those who have faith and open themselves in *surrender* and faith, the work will be done automatically. As long as he was here, mon petit, all the thirty years I spent with him working, NOT ONCE did I have to make an effort for a transformation. Simply, whenever there was a difficulty, I repeated, *My Lord, my Lord, my Lord* ... I just thought of him – hop! it went away. Physical pain: he annulled it. You know, some things that were hampering the body, some old habits that had come back, I only had to tell him: off they would go. And through me, he did the same for others. He always said that he and I did the Work (in fact, when he was here, it was he who did it; I only did the external work), that he and I did the Work, and that all that was asked from the others was faith and *surrender,* nothing more.

If they had trust and gave themselves in perfect trust, the Work was done automatically.

*In your body's cells, it is therefore a universal progress that is being made, it's the earth that progresses.*

Yes.

*(silence)*

This body was built for that purpose, because I remember very well that when the war – the First World War – started and I offered my body up in sacrifice to the Lord so that the war would not be in vain, every part of my body, one after another (Mother touches her legs, her arms etc.), or sometimes the same part several times over, represented a battlefield: I could see it, I could feel it, I LIVED it. Every time it was ... it was very strange, I had only to sit quietly and watch: I would see here, there, there, the whole thing in my body, all that was going on. And while it went on, I would put the concentration of the divine Force there, so that all – all that pain, all that suffering, everything – would hasten the preparation of the earth and the Descent of the Force. And that went on consciously throughout the war.

The body was built for that purpose.

At the time, there was still a lot of mental activity, and those experiences took all the forms the mind gives to things – very nice, very literary! Now, all that is over – happily, thank God! A complete silence – I don't make speeches on the thing. But the experience of last night! ... And to think that when an experience lasts half an hour, three quarters of an hour, one hour, it's considered extraordinary – it lasted from 8:30 till 2:15, nonstop.

*A sort of ubiquity in the cells?*

Yes, yes.

A oneness – the sense of Oneness.

*(silence)*

It is clear that if this experience becomes natural, spontaneous and constant, death can no longer exist: even for this, I mean *(Mother touches her body)*.

There's something I SENSE there, without being able to express or understand it mentally. There must be some difference, even in the behavior of the cells, when you leave your body.

It must be another phenomenon that takes place.

During all that period of concentration and meditation on what happens in a body after death (I am speaking of the body's experience after what is now called "death"), well, several times the same kind of vision came to me.... I had been told (shown and told) of certain saints whose bodies did not decompose (there's one here, there was one in Goa – fantastic stories). Naturally, people always romanticize those things, but there remains the material fact of a saint who died in Goa, left his body in Goa, but whose body didn't decompose. I don't know the story in all its details, but the body was removed from India, taken away to China and remained buried there, in Hong-Kong, I believe (or somewhere in that region) for a time; then it was taken out, brought back here, buried again. For ten or twelve years it stayed buried in those two places: it didn't decompose. It dried out, became mummified (dried out,

167

that is, dehydrated), but it remained preserved. Well, this fact was presented to me several times as ONE of the possibilities.

Which means, to tell the truth, that everything is possible.

Vol. 4, p. 267

## August 21, 1963

*(Regarding an old "Playground Talk," of January 4, 1951, in which Mother said that one of the essential conditions for transformation is an awareness of the inner dimensions: "It's a total reversal of consciousness, which can be compared to what happens to light when it goes through a prism. Or else it's as if you turned a ball inside out, which can be done only in the fourth dimension. You emerge from the ordinary consciousness of the third dimension to enter the higher consciousness of the fourth dimension, and then an infinite number of dimensions. This is the indispensable starting point.")*

That's what I had told you already: the whole basis of the yogic effort is changed now. Formerly, the work was based precisely on that knowledge of inner dimensions – I can't recapture that any more, I see it as completely outside me.

So I can't add anything to those "Talks": their source is different. Even now for the aphorisms, it's a little bit difficult. I feel I have to come down, to revert to an old frame of mind in order to say something.

*You need not bother about people. Just speak according to your present mode, without bothering whether they understand or not.*

They understand nothing.

*It doesn't matter.*

Then it's no use publishing what I say!

*Some do understand.*

Anyway, what I say nowadays is good for the [Agenda] box.

* * *

*(Then Mother returns to the aphorism on "renunciation."*
*She remains silent. She still appears to be shaken.)*

It's difficult because ...

These days, I don't know whether it has come to the last battle, but it has descended very deep into the cells' worst-lit realm: what still belongs most to the world of Unconsciousness and Inertia and is most foreign to the divine Presence. It is, so to say, the primal substance that was first used by Life, and it has a sort of inability to feel, to experience a reason for that life.

In fact, it's something I had never experienced [that absence of meaning]; even in my earliest childhood, when there was no development, I always had a perception (not a mentalized but a vibrant perception) of a Power behind all things which is the raison d'être of all things – a Power, a Force, a kind of warmth.

It isn't the experience of THIS body's cells: it's an identification with the world in general, with the Earth as a whole. It's an absolutely frightful and hopeless condition: something meaningless, aimless, without raison d'être, without any joy in itself or ... and worse than *disagreeable – meaningless,* insensate. Something that has no raison d'être and yet is. It was ... it is a frightful situation.

I have an impression of being quite close to the bottom of the pit.

Yesterday, it was like that almost the whole day long. But all at once something came (I don't know from where or how ... neither from above nor from within nor from ... I don't know): there is only ONE raison d'être, only ONE Reality, only ONE Life, and there is nothing other than ... THAT. It was THAT (not in the least mentally, there was no intellectual formulation, nothing), it was Something that was Light (far more than Light), Power (far more than power), Omnipotence (far more than Omnipotence), and also an intensity of sweetness, of warmth, of plenitude – all that together – along with that

Something, which naturally words cannot describe. And That came all at once, like that, when there was such a frightful state of anguish, because it was nothing – a nothing you couldn't get out of. There was no way of getting out of that nothing, because it was nothing.

You know, all those who seek Nirvana, all their disgust of life, all that is almost enjoyable in comparison! That's not it. That's not it, it was a thousand times, a million times worse. It was nothing, and because it was nothing it was impossible to get out of it – there was no ... no solution.

At one point, the tension was so great that ... you wonder, "Am I going to burst?"

Then everything relaxed and opened up *(gesture as if the cells opened out)* ... OM.

*(silence)*

I don't know if there's a yet deeper pit but ...

And that relief, that blossoming, that peace ... Everything disappears, except That.

*(silence)*

It's really the first time I had that experience – never, never did I experience that before. And it wasn't in the least, in the least personal to my body, it isn't my body's cells – it's something else....

And that is the basis and foundation of all materialism.

It lasted the whole day long! ...

*(silence)*

The experience came at the time when the condition was most acute in its nothingness.... I don't know how to explain it, it's inexpressible, but it was COMPLETE: there was nothing but that, that sort of meaningless and aimless "nothing," without raison d'être or origin – and, therefore, without remedy. Then it reached the point when ... you know, when everything is about to burst and there is such a tension. (Is it tension? I

170

don't know how to explain.) And all at once, a change as total as you can imagine.

So you understand, those old "Talks," all that's ... a lot of talk!

*(long silence)*

Every time an experience of that kind occurs, the entire vision of things and of the relationship between things is changed *(gesture of reversal)*. Even from a quite practical viewpoint. You see, Life is a sort of chessboard on which all the pawns are arranged according to certain inner laws, and every time it all changes: everything changes, the chessboard changes, the pawns change, the types of organization change. Also the inner quality of the pawns – very much so.

For instance, these last few days I had a whole vision of X, of what he represents, the people around him, his relationship with the Ashram – all that entirely changed. Every element took a new place in relation to all the others. And I have nothing to do with it, I don't "try" to understand, I don't "try" to see, nothing: the thing is simply shown to me. Like pictures that are shown to me. Each thing has its own special flavor, its own special color, its own special quality and its own special relationship with the rest – all the relationships are different.

It's growing very PRECISE, very minute, very sharp, not floating: very accurate to the last detail. And with a great simplicity.

As though the entanglement of forces, of consciousnesses and movements grew clearer and clearer, more and more complete, very, very precise. And very simple too.

Very simple.

All problems, all problems are beginning to be seen in that way.

And always an impression of emerging (what I previously called "clarity" or comprehension is to me now incomprehension and confusion), of emerging from that towards a greater clarity, a more total comprehension. With all sorts of complications that disappear, even though everything is far more complete than before.

Before, there were always hazy spots, some hazy, imprecise, uncertain things; and as that disappears, it all becomes much clearer, much simpler, and MUCH MORE EXACT. And the haziness disappears. There is, you know, a whole world of impressions, of *guessing* (things you imagine, they are imaginations rather than impressions) that fills the gaps; and there were some reference points, things that are known and linked together by a whole hazy mass of impressions and imaginations (it works automatically); and every time, oh, you emerge from it all towards something so light *(gesture above),* and all those clouds evaporate. And it looks so simple! You say to yourself, "But it's so obvious, so clear! There weren't any complications."

Every time, it's like that *(gesture of ascent from stage to stage):* you see farther, you see more things at a glance.

It would seem that a time will come when all the movements of the earth will be like that, very clear and very simple.

And it corresponds to that descent into the pit.

Vol. 4, p. 277


**August 24, 1963**

At times ... For the body it's a constant work – a constant labor – very tiny, of every instant, an unceasing effort, with, so to say, an imperceptible result (externally at any rate, quite nonexistent), so for someone who doesn't have my consciousness, it's perfectly obvious that the body appears to wear out and age, to be slowly heading for decomposition: that's in everyone's atmosphere and consciousness *(Mother laughs),* it's the kind of appreciation and vibration that's being thrown all the time on this poor body, which besides is quite conscious of its infirmity – it doesn't entertain any illusions! But that quiet, peaceful, but UNCEASING endurance in the effort of transformation makes it sometimes yearn for a little ecstasy – not as an abolition or annihilation, not at all, but it seems to be saying, "Oh, Lord, I beg you, let me be You in all tranquillity." In fact, that's its prayer every evening when people are supposed to leave it in peace (unfortunately they leave it in peace physically, but mentally they don't). But that ... I could cut off, I learned to cut off long, long ago, I could cut off, but ... something, I mean somewhere, "someone" doesn't approve! *(Mother laughs)* Obviously what the Someone – the great Someone – wants to see realized is perfect peace, perfect rest, and joy, a passive joy (not too active; a passive joy is enough), a passive, constant joy, WITHOUT forsaking the work. In other words, the individual experience isn't regarded as all-important – very far from it: the help given to the whole, the leaven which makes the whole rise, is AT LEAST equally important. Ultimately, that's probably the major reason for persisting in this body.

Nothing inside asks any questions, there are no problems there; all the problems I am talking about are posed by the body, for the body; otherwise, inside, everything is perfect, everything is exactly as it should be. And totally so: what people call "good," what they call "evil," the "beautiful," the "ugly," the ... all that is a small immensity (not a big immensity), a small immensity that is moving more and more towards a progressive realization – that's the correct phrase – within an integral Consciousness which integrally (how should I put it?) *enjoys*, or I could say, feels the plenitude of what He does – does, is and so forth (it's all the same thing). But this poor body ...

And probably ... It's certain too that one can't go too fast: if the body had that Joy in it, if it had that ecstasy in it, that rapture continually, surely that would bring too rapid a transformation – there are still a lot of things to be changed, a lot, a whole lot of things....

What people see [when they look at Mother's body] is only the appearance, but this appearance is a reflection of something else.... *(silence)* There's a sort of knowledge (is it a knowledge?) or foreknowledge given to the body of how this appearance will be changed. And it sounds so simple, so easy, it can be done in a flash, because it's not AT ALL – it won't AT ALL be done in the way people think or expect.... It's rather like the vision of the TRUE internal movement that would IMPOSE itself in such a way that it would veil the false vision which sees things like that [on the surface]. It's very hard to explain, but it's ... I've felt it several times for a few seconds (I have a sort of sensation of the thing): there is something true, the true Physical, which, although it's not perceptible to our eyes as they see, could make itself perceptible through an INTENSIFICATION. And that intensification would be what would effect the transformation outwardly – that would replace the false appearance with the real form.

But I have no idea whether the false appearance wouldn't still exist for those not ready to see the true thing.... At any rate, it would be an intermediary period: those whose eyes were open would be able to see (what is called "open eyes" in the Scriptures), they would be able to see; and they would be able to see not through effort or seeking, but the thing would impose itself on them. While those whose eyes were not open ... for a time, at least, it would be that way, they wouldn't see – they would still see the old appearance. The two may be simultaneous.

I SAW myself the way I am, and quite obviously ... *(Mother laughs)* my body seems to have been shrunk to enable me to dominate it and exceed it on all sides without difficulty! That's my impression, something that's shrunk! The English word is very expressive *(Mother laughs)*.

Now, of course, when I say that, people imagine it's a psychic or mental vision – that's not it, I don't mean that! I mean a PHYSICAL vision, with these very eyes (Mother touches her eyes). But a TRUE physical vision, instead of the distorted vision we have now.

This means, basically, that the true reality is far more marvelous than we can imagine, because all that we can imagine is always a transformation or glorification of what we see – but that's not it. That's not it!

I am not quite sure that I do not already exist physically with a true body – I say "not quite sure" because the outer senses have no proof of it! But in fact ... I don't try, I have never attempted to see or know, but from time to time, it somehow imposes itself: for a minute, I see myself, feel myself, objectify myself as I am. But it just lasts a few seconds, and pfft! gone – it's replaced by the old habit.

You know, we can only conceive of things changing from one to another: you grow young again, all the signs of aging disappear and so on – that's old hat, that's not how it works. That's not it!

Once, I remember, my body was feeling sorry for itself like a child, it was bemoaning its condition, when it heard a voice – an awesome voice – that said to it, "Why don't you feel yourself AS YOU ARE?" And that experience followed – but it lasted a second. A second, a flash.

And then comes that wonderful reason we reek of (I don't say we're "steeped in," I say we "reek of"), which starts asking: How can that be? And how can I remain efficient? And how can I keep a contact with the rest of the world? And how ... how, how? So I stopped, stopped it all. And what's going to happen to this body? And what will be its mode of existence? ...

We can very well conceive (it's something easy to conceive) that beings may be born in another manner, through a power of concentration, and that those beings may materialize without any of the miseries that beset us – that's all very well, but it's for later. We are in between, that's where the difficulty is.

Vol. 4, p. 284

## August 31, 1963

[O]nce more, I had that experience when the body was again moaning – I say "moaning," but it's not that, it's a kind of aspiration so strong that it becomes like an anguish; and also that sense of incapacity. And the same Response: all at once the body is seized by a formidable power, so great that the body itself feels it could break anything! It comes like a mass. And I recalled a sentence of Sri Aurobindo in which he said, "Before you can be the Lord's lion, you should first be the Lord's lamb," and it was as though I were told, "Enough of being the lamb! *(laughing)* Now become the lion." But it doesn't last.

And I can easily see why it doesn't last! Oh, it's ... You feel as if you're going to tear everything down!

*(silence)*

But the body does profit from the experience, in the sense that it feels stronger afterwards – not much stronger physically, we don't care about that strength! It's a very odd phenomenon: the sense of the "concrete" fades away – it fades farther and farther away. "Concrete" vision, "concrete" sense of smell, "concrete" taste, "concrete" hearing, it all seems far away – far behind in a ... an unreal past. And that kind of dry and lifeless "concrete" is replaced by something that's very supple *(round, global gesture),* very complete in that all the senses function together, and VERY INTIMATE WITH EVERYTHING.

For a while I was shown the two functionings to enable me to perceive the difference: how the senses function now, and how they did formerly: and it gives a fuzzy impression, but it's an impression of something both very intimate and very complete *(same round gesture),* whereas, before, each thing was separate, divided *(choppy, hard gesture),* unconnected with the other, it was very superficial – very precise but very superficial, like a pinpoint. It's not at all that way any more.

And I see very well that if we let ourselves be carried along instead of having that absurd resistance of habit, if we let ourselves be carried along, there would come a sort of very ... *(same round, global gesture)* very soft thing, in the sense of *smooth*, very soft, very complete, very living, and with a very intimate perception of things. Along with a knowledge that becomes ... if there weren't that mixture of the old habit, it would be really extraordinary: the perception of things not as if they were outside, but an INTIMATE perception. When someone enters the room, for instance, or when the clock is about to strike, you know it just (I can't say a second, it's a thousandth of a second), just before it takes place materially; which gives you the feeling of a foreknowledge, but it's not that! It's not a foreknowledge, it's ... It belongs to the realm of sensation, but it's other senses. The FOREMOST feeling you get is one of intimacy, that is to say, there is no more distance, no more difference, no more seer and thing seen; yet, there is in it what corresponds to vision, hearing, sensation, all the perceptions, taste, smell and all of that.

There is here a very concrete change from before, very perceptible.

I understand very well: what prevents the functioning from being perfect is all the old habits. If we could let ourselves be carried along without resisting – without any will to "see well," to "hear well" and so on – we would have the other perception, which is much TRUER. And that intimacy with things ... things are no longer foreign. But there is no thought in it; they speak of "knowledge through identity," you know, but that's all intellectual notions, it's not that! It's ...

And always that feeling of something smooth *(same round gesture)*, smooth, without any clashes, any complications, as though you could no longer bump into things, no longer ... It's quite interesting.

It takes time simply because of the resistance of the old habits. If we could always let ourselves be carried along, things would go much faster – much faster. All the time, a hundred times a day (more than that!), I tell myself, "Why are you thinking of this? Why are you thinking of that?" For example, if I have to answer someone (not always in writing, it can be an [occult] work, to organize something), the Force acts quite naturally, smoothly, without any resistance; then suddenly thought comes into the picture and tries to interfere (I catch it every time and I stop it every time; but it's too often!), and all the old habit returns. That need to translate things into thoughts, to give them "clear" expression.

And then you hinder the entire process.

Oh, to let oneself live simply, simply, without complications....

Vol. 4, p. 294

## September 18, 1963

Above all, there is a kind of coexistence, of juxtaposition of two things that are really opposite states yet always seem to be together: a Peace in which everything is harmonious (I am speaking of the body's cells), everything is harmonious to the point that no disorder can occur, no illness, no suffering, no disorganization or decomposition can occur – impossible; it's a Peace that's eternal, absolutely beyond time (though it is felt in the body's cells); and at the same time, a tremor – an ignorant and bustling and dark tremor, dark in the sense that it's unaware of its ignorance, not knowing what to do and doing useless things all the time. And in that state you find disorder, decomposition, disorganization, suffering and ... at times it becomes acute, acute, all the nerves are tense and it aches all over – and both states are together.

"Are together," I mean to the point that you don't even feel you make a movement of reversal, you don't even know how you go from one state to the other, you ... the reversal is imperceptible.

And they are exactly opposite.

You can, in much less time than a flash, eliminate any pain, any disorder, any illness from your body; and in a flash, it can all come back. And then you can switch from one to the other, from one to the other ... *(back-and-forth gesture)*.

The point not yet grasped or understood is how to stabilize that Peace.

When It's there, you feel as if nothing can alter It: all the attacks in the world fall away, powerless; nothing can alter It. And It disappears the same way It came, there's no knowing how.

If I observe very carefully, I have the impression that the mind of Matter Sri Aurobindo refers to, you know, the thought of Matter, isn't yet pure, it's still mixed; so it only takes one wrong movement for everything to come undone. And in people, that material mind lives in its wrong movement constantly – except a flash once in a while: a reversal. But here [in Mother], there still remains a habit; a habit (almost like a mere memory) of the wrong movement. And it only has to recur even as tiny as a pinpoint for ... brrt! everything to fall back into the old rut.

But when I see the care I've taken for so many years to purify that fellow, I am a little (what should I say?) ... I can't say frightened or anxious, but ... (I can't even say pessimistic), but the condition of people who haven't done all the yoga I've done for years, how difficult it must be! Because the body's cells obey that material mind, which, in its natural state, is a mass of stupid ignorance that thinks it's so smart, oh! ... An almost foul mass of stupidity, and it thinks it's so smart! It thinks it knows everything.

*(silence)*

Because NOTHING in the consciousness budged during those changeovers [back and forth from the true to the false movement]; the consciousness is like that, turned ... not upward, not inward, turned ... simply turned to the Lord, living in His Light, which, in the physical world, becomes a golden splendor. The consciousness is turned to That. There

179

is nothing but That, it's the sole reality, the sole truth. And It vibrates like this *(Mother touches her hands, her arms),* It vibrates in all the cells, everywhere. I go like this *(Mother makes a gesture of collecting "it" in the air around),* as if I picked it up. It isn't ethereal, it's very material; it feels like an air that is thick – but vibrant, very vibrant.... The consciousness is like that. And all this goes on in the body. But with the presence of that old idiot ... which is immediately pessimistic, catastrophic, defeatist – how defeatist, oh ... it sees everything as a calamity. And then that wonderful character, after imagining the worse (in the space of a second, of course), it submits it all to the Lord and tells Him, "Here, Lord, here is Your work, it's all Yours, do what You will with it"! The silly idiot, why did it have to prepare its catastrophes! A catastrophe, invariably a catastrophe, everything is catastrophic – but it offers its catastrophe to the Lord!

And the answer is invariably a smile full of such patience, oh! ... That patience gives me a sense of wonder every second.

Now and then, a great power comes (the body is deliberately given the experience to make it feel and grow aware that "that" exists), a great power comes, and along with it the impression that you would only have to do this *(Mother brings down her two arms in a sovereign gesture)* for everything to change. But ...

It's still much, much too limited and ignorant for that Power to be allowed to act. It [Mother's individuality] sees many sides of the question, but not all. It isn't ... in spite of everything, it has its own angle – as long as there remains an angle, the Power isn't allowed to act.

Though, yes, there was that experience the other day, when all was the Lord, all, with all things as they are, as we see them; when all was That in SUCH a perfect whole, perfect because it was so complete, and so harmonious because it was so conscious, and in a perpetual Movement of progression towards a greater perfection. (That's something odd, things can't stay still for a quarter of a second: they are constantly, constantly, constantly progressing towards a more perfect Totality.) Then, at that moment, if the Power acts (probably it does act), if the Power acts, it acts as it should. But it isn't always there – it isn't always there, there is still a sense of the things that are to fade away and of those that are to come – of the passage; a progression which ... which isn't all-containing.

But in that state, it seems that what you see MUST be – and inevitably (I should say necessarily), it is. And probably instantly so. But you have to see the whole at once for your vision to be all-powerful. If you see only one point (as, for example, when you feel that the action on earth is limited to a certain field that depends on you), as long as you see that way, you can't be all-powerful, it's not possible – not possible. It's inevitably conditioned.

*(long silence)*

There is a growing feeling that all that is, all that happens, outwardly and inwardly (inwardly too) is absolutely necessary for the totality of the whole.

I am thinking, for instance, of that sort of reaction I had the other day.... Naturally there is a part of the being that looks on, that smiles and says, "Oh, aren't you beyond that yet!" And at the same time, I saw, "No, it's necessary – everything is necessary." A special vibration was necessary ... necessary to trigger something else. And everything works like that.

Everything works like that.

*(silence)*

It's a transitional period – but isn't the transitional period constant?! It must be constant. Only, a point comes nevertheless when it becomes absolutely conscious and willed, and then it no longer has the same character.

Basically, once we have emerged from Stupidity, there is ... there should be a rather considerable change.

181

Oh, there would be a world of things to say!

*(silence)*

It is impossible for any change, any change towards perfection (I don't mean a regression, because that's another phenomenon), it's impossible for any change, even in one element or one point of the earth consciousness, not to make the whole earth participate in that change. Necessarily.

Everything is closely knit together. And a vibration somewhere has TERRESTRIAL consequences – I don't say universal, I say terrestrial – necessarily.

Which means there isn't one aspiration, not one effort that isn't useful seen from the terrestrial standpoint (from the individual standpoint, this has been obvious for a very long time), but seen from the terrestrial standpoint, there isn't one effort – not one effort towards the Better, not one aspiration to the True – that does not have terrestrial repercussions, terrestrial consequences.

Vol. 4, p. 314


## November 20, 1963

Everyone is born with ... (what can I call it?) *some special twist (laughing)* – I know my own twist, I know it quite well! (I don't talk about it because it isn't enjoyable.) But that's what remains last of all. With our idiotic human logic, we think, "That's what should go first," but it's not true: it's what goes last! Even when it all becomes clear, clear *(gesture above)*, even when you have all the experiences, the habit stays on and it keeps coming back. So you push it back: it rises again from the subconscient; you chase it away: it comes back from outside. So if for one minute you aren't on your guard, it shows up again – oh, what a nuisance! But Sri Aurobindo wrote about this somewhere, I don't remember the words; I read it very recently, and when I read it, I thought, "Ah, there it is! He knew it was that way." So it comforted me, and I thought, "All right, then." He said that he who has purified his mind and so on and so forth, who is ready to work towards Perfection (it's in the *Synthesis*, "The Yoga of Self-Perfection"), "He is ready and patient for lapses and the recurrence of old errors, and he works quietly, waiting patiently till the time comes for them to leave." I thought, "Very well, that's how it is now." I am patiently waiting for the time when ... (though I don't miss any opportunity to catch them by the tip of their nose, or the tip of their ear, and to say, "Ha, you're still here! ...").

The first thing is to detach your consciousness, that's most important. And to say: I-AM-NOT-THIS, it's something that has been ADDED, placed to enable me to touch Matter – but it isn't me. And then if you say, "That is me" *(gesture upward),* you'll see that you will be happy, because it is lovely – lovely, luminous, sparkling. It's really fine, it has an exceptional quality. And that's you. But you have to say, "That is me," and be convinced that it's you. Naturally, the old habits come to deny it, but you must know that they're old habits, nothing else, they don't matter – that is you.

This movement is indispensable. A moment comes when one must absolutely separate oneself from all this, because only when one has separated oneself and become quite conscious that one is there *(gesture above the head),* that one is THAT, only then can one come down again to change it all. Not to forsake it, but to be its master.

*I've spent nights in sewers, cleaning out sewers.*

Ah, that's good! *(Mother laughs)* Oh, but that's very funny because I've done identical things. Listen! ... Oh, well, it's very funny.

It's all right, it's all right.

We must endure. The victory belongs to the most enduring.

There are times when one is disgusted, and that's just when one should remember this. Now, your disgust may have reasons of its own (!) But you have only to endure. You know, there is one thing, I don't know if you have savored it yet: as soon as you have a difficulty, dissatisfaction, revolt, disgust – anything – fatigue, tension, discomfort, all, all that negative side (there are lots and lots and lots of such things, they take on all kinds of different colors), the immediate movement – immediate – of calling the Lord and saying, "It's up to You." As long as you try (instinctively you try to arrange things with your best light, your best consciousness, your best knowledge ...), it's stupid, because that prolongs the struggle, and ultimately it's not very effective. There is only one effective thing, that's to step back from what's still called "me" and ... with or without words, it doesn't matter, but above all with the flame of aspiration, this *(gesture to the heart),* and something perfectly, perfectly sincere: "Lord, it's You; and only You can do it, You alone can do it, I can't...." It's excellent, you can't imagine how excellent! For instance, someone comes and deluges you with impossible problems, wants you to make instant decisions; you have to write, you have to answer, you have to say – all of it – and it's like truckloads of darkness and stupidity and wrong movements and all that being dumped on you; and it's dumped and dumped and dumped – you are almost stoned to death with all that. You begin to stiffen, you get tense; then, immediately *(gesture of stepping back):* "O Lord...." You stay quiet, take a little step back *(gesture of offering):* "It's up to you."

But you can't imagine, it's wonderful! Immediately there comes – clear, simple, effortlessly, without seeking for it – exactly what has to be done or said or written: the whole tension stops, it's over. And then, if you need paper, the paper is there; if you need a fountain pen, you find just the one you need; if you need ... (there's no seeking: above all don't seek, don't try to seek, you'll just make another mess) – it's there. And that's a fact of EVERY MINUTE. You have the field of experience every second. For instance, you're dealing with a servant who doesn't do things properly or as you think they should be done, or you're dealing with a stomach that doesn't work the way you'd like it to and it hurts: it's the same method, there is no other. You know, at times ... situations get so tense that you feel as if you're about to faint, the body can't stand it any more, it's so tense; or else there's a pain, something wrong, things aren't sorting themselves out, and there's a tension; so immediately you stop everything: "Lord, You, it's up to You...." At first there comes a peace, as if you were entirely outside existence, and then it's gone – the pain goes, the dizziness disappears. And what is to happen happens automatically. And, you see, it's not in meditation, not in actions of terrestrial importance: it's the field of experience you have ALL the time, without interruption – when you know how to put it to use. And for everything: when something hurts, for instance, when things resist or grate or howl inside there, instead of your saying, "Oh, how it hurts! ..." you call the Lord in there: "Come in here," and then you stay calm, not thinking of anything – you simply stay still in your sensation. And more than a thousand times, you know, I was almost bewildered: "Look! The pain is gone!" You didn't even notice how it went. So people who want to lead a special life or have a special organization to have experiences, that's quite silly – the greatest possible diversity of experiences is at your disposal every minute, every minute. Only you must learn not to have a mental ambition for "great" things. Just the other day, I was shown in such a clear way a very small thing I had done ("I," it's the body speaking), a very small thing that had been done by the Lord in this body (that's a long sentence!), and I was shown the terrestrial consequence of that very small thing – it was visible, I mean, as my hand is visible to my eyes – and the terrestrial correspondence. Then I understood.

We are given everything – EVERYTHING. All the difficulties that have to be overcome, all of them (and the more capable we are, that is, the more complex the instrument is, the more numerous the difficulties are), all the difficulties, all the opportunities to overcome them, all the possible experiences, and limited in time and space so they can be innumerable. And it has repercussions and consequences all over the earth (I am not concerned with what goes on in the universe because, for the time being, that isn't my work). But it is certain (because it has been said so and I know it) that what goes on on the earth has repercussions throughout the universe. Sitting there, you live the everyday life with its usual insignificance, its unimportance, its lack of interest ... and it's a WONDERFUL field of experiences, of innumerable experiences, not only innumerable but as varied as can be, from the most subtle to the most material, without leaving your body. Only, you should have RETURNED to it. You cannot have authority over your body without having left it.

Once the body is no longer you at all, once it is something that has been added and TACKED onto you, once it is that way and you look at it from above (a psychological "above"), then you can come down into it again as its all-powerful master.

You must come out of it first, then come down again.

There you are.

And one should also look at all those difficulties, all those bad habits (like, for you, that habit of revolt: it's something that seems to have been kneaded into the cells of your body), one should look at all that with the smile of someone who says, "I am not that. Oh, this was put on me! ... Oh, that was added...." And you know, it was added ... because it's one of the victories you must win.

I've witnessed the most complete panorama of all the idiotic things in this life, they were shown to me as in a complete panorama: passing from one to another, seeing each of them separately and how they combined with each other. And then: Why? Why should one choose this? (A child's question, which one asks immediately.) And immediately, the answer: "But the more" (let's say "central" to be clearer) "the more central the origin and the more pure in its essence, the greater the 'ignoble complexity below,' as we could call it. Because the lower down you go, the more it takes an essential light to change things."

Once you've been told this very nicely, you're satisfied, you stop worrying – it's all right, you take things as they are: "That's how things are, it's my work and I do it; I ask only one thing, it is to do my work, all the rest doesn't matter."

There, mon petit.

Vol. 4, p. 385

## December 7, 1963

I think ("I think," like the scientists' "it appears") I can announce that something is getting organized in the Subconscient – it's beginning to get organized – in the subconscient of individuals as well as in the general Subconscient. It's less unconscious (!) It's a bit more ... yes, a bit more conscious, reflective and organized – a very faint beginning of organization, very little, but a growth in consciousness; it isn't quite so unconscious any more.

It's always the last part of the night that I spend there.... You remember that story of the supramental ship and how things were organized by the will, not by external means? Well, that's the action which is beginning to exist in the Subconscient.

Last night, for instance, early in the morning, there were several layers of cells, as it were, and each cell was I can't say the property, but the possession of someone: what was under his direct control and reflected his "mood," as it is customarily called, his way of being. And there were many levels: you could go upstairs and downstairs.... And the impression I had of myself was that I was much, much taller and that I towered above it all; and I had a different texture, as if I were made

187

of a different substance, not quite the same as the others'. It was as if all that were inside me without being inside me (I can't explain): I was looming over everything and at the same time acting inside. And then, according to the action, people were going upstairs or downstairs, going and coming; but everyone had his own little box – they were BEGINNING to have it, it was beginning to get organized. Each cell was more or less precise: some were very precise, others more blurred, as if on the way to becoming precise. And the whole experience, last night, had a kind of precision about it. I was like something very big, outside, and I was laughing, talking to everyone, but they weren't aware of the action [of Mother]. You see, they seemed to me this tall *(gesture: four inches),* tiny. But quite alive: they were going and coming, moving about.... And I was talking to them, but they didn't know where the voice was coming from. So I laughed, I found it funny, I said to some, "There! You see, that's your idea of things." And it was ... oh, if I compare it to last year, there is a tremendous difference of CONSCIOUSNESS, from the point of view of consciousness. Before, all the movements were reflexes, instincts, as if people were impelled by a force which they were totally unconscious of and considered to be their "character," most of the time, or else Destiny (either their character or Fate, Destiny). They were all like puppets on strings. Now, they are conscious beings – they're BEGINNING, they're beginning to be conscious.

The proportion has changed.

And I was able to show them precisely the proportion between the conscious, willed movement, which can be observed, and that sort of almost unconscious instinct which obeys a COMPELLING Force, that is to say, you know neither where it comes from nor what it means or anything – you just tag along.

188

Some still had quite blurred and cloudy spaces; with others, it was precise, there were even some very precise details. And clear, clear: there was a light – the dawning of a light.

If this goes on, it will be fine. It will change a lot of things.

*It was in the subconscient of individuals?*

Of individuals, yes.

*It wasn't their waking consciousness?*

No, no! It's not individuals as they know themselves – it is their subconscient. It is in the subconscient. The subconscient is a realm just as the material world is a realm – it's in the subconscient.

There have been many efforts, concentrations, meditations, prayers to bring about the clarification and control of all those semiconscious reflexes that govern individuals – a great concentration on that point. And this experience seems to be the outcome.

There are lots of things which people don't even take notice of in life (when they live an ordinary life, they don't take any notice), there's a whole field of things that are absolutely ... not quite unconscious, but certainly not conscious; they are reflexes – reflexes, reactions to stimuli, and so on – and also the response (a semiconscious, barely conscious response) to the pressure exerted from above by the Force, which people are totally unconscious of. It is the study of this question which is now in the works; I am very much occupied with it. A study of every second.... You see, there are different ways for the Lord to be present, it's very interesting (the difference isn't for Him, it's for us!), and it depends precisely on the amount of habitual reflex movements that take place almost outside our observation (generally completely outside it). And this question preoccupied me very, very much: the ways of feeling the Lord's Presence – the different ways. There is a way in which you feel it as something vague, but of which you are sure – you are always sure but the sensation is vague and a bit blurred – and at other times it is an acute Presence *(Mother touches her face)*, very precise, in all that you do, all that you feel, all that you are. There is an entire range. And then if we follow the movement *(gesture in stages, moving away)*, there are those who are so far away, so far, that they don't feel anything at all.

This experience made me write something yesterday (but it has lasted several days), it came as the outcome of the work done, and yesterday I wrote it both in English and in French:

"There is no other sin, no other vice

than to be far from Thee."

Then, the entire world, the universe, appeared to me in that light, and at every point (which takes up no space), at every point of the universe and throughout the universe, it's that way. Not that there are far and near places in the universe, that's not what I mean (it's beyond space), but there is a whole hierarchy of nearness, up to something that doesn't feel and doesn't know – it's not that it is outside, because nothing can be outside the Lord, but it is as if the extreme limit: so far away, so far, so far – absolutely black – that He seems not to reach there.

It was a very total vision. And such an acute experience that it seemed to be the only true thing. It didn't take up any space, yet there was that sensation of nearness and farness. And there was a kind of Focus, or a Center, I can't say (but it was everywhere), which was the climax of Thee – purely Thee. And it had a quality of its own. Then it began to move farther and farther away, which produced a kind of mixture with something ... that was nothing – that didn't exist – but that altered the vibration, the intensity, which made it move farther and farther away to ... Darkness – unconscious Darkness.

And something kept coming again and again to me: there is no other sin ... (because this followed a few lines I read in *Savitri* on the glorification of sin in the vital world, the words came to me because of that) ... there is no other sin, no other vice than to be far from Thee.

190

It seemed to explain everything.

It wasn't I who wrote it! There's no "I" in it: it comes just like that.

The *far from Thee* is so, so intense in its vibration, it has a concrete meaning.

And that's the only thing: all the rest, all moral notions, everything, everything, even the notion of Ignorance ... it all becomes mental chatter. But this, this experience, is marvelous. *Far from Thee....*

Vol. 4, p. 406

## December 11, 1963

There was in the Subconscient a frightful battle in the night from the 8th to the 9th – oh! ... It was like a return of the attack on me when you went to Rameswaram (long ago) [In 1958]; X said it was a Tantric who had made that formation (it happened on December 9 too and I was very sick, I didn't go out). Well, it was an attack of that kind. I don't know if it comes from the same ... I can't say "person," but from the same origin of forces. And very violent, during the night. It went on during the meditation on the 9th: for the first time during those meditations, there was a tremendous battle, in the Subconscient. And the body was in a state ... a not too happy state. It stops the heart, you see, so ... it was unpleasant.

But afterwards, I saw that it did dislodge something, it wasn't useless. It dislodged something. But it's forces with a radical ill will: they are not merely ignorant – a radical ill will.

*But it didn't have a human origin, did it? It wasn't from a human individual?*

No, it's not an individual: it's a universal way of being. It's always that way: things aren't positively impersonal, but they do not belong to one person; they are universal ways of being.

*I mean, there was no human instrument, was there?*

I wasn't conscious of an instrument, but I was conscious of plenty of spots to which the thing clings. It clings not even to beings, but to ways of being of beings: to certain tendencies, certain attitudes, certain reactions – it clings to all that. It's not at all "one" person or "one" will, that's not it, but it's a way of being. It's all universal ways of being that are destined to disappear from the field of activity and are being eliminated.

But the reaction on the body was painful, as it was the first time. The first time (according to X and the Swami), it was supposed to kill me – it didn't even make me seriously ill, but it had a very unpleasant effect. I told you at the time that it was a mantra intended to drain you of all your blood; I've seen several examples of people who died in that way: it was found afterwards to be the result of a mantric formation. In my case, all it succeeded in doing was to make me sick, as if everything came out – I vomited terribly. Then there was something pulling me and I absolutely had to go ... my consciousness told me I had to go and see someone (I was all alone in my bathroom when it happened), a particular person whom I had to go and see; and when I opened the door, Z was there, waiting to prepare my bath, but I didn't see him at all and I absolutely wanted to go somewhere, into the other room, so I pushed against him, thinking, "What's this obstacle in my way?" And he thought I was fainting on him! It caused quite a to-do.

I was completely in trance, you see. I was walking, but completely in trance.

Anyway, things went back to normal fairly quickly at the time. But the other day, the 9th, there was a return of that attack, as though that ill will hadn't been completely eliminated, completely defeated – there was a return. It didn't have the same effect, but it was painful. A curious feeling, as if ... (I was sitting at the table, as I always do on mornings when there is meditation), then at the beginning, in some parts of the body, the cells seemed to be grating. I concentrated, I called, and I saw there was a battle – a formidable battle being waged down below. It was grating, it's curious. A kind of grating of things that aren't smooth. And I wondered, "When will it be able to relax?" Then spasms here, at the solar plexus. And on those days, the doctor and P. always stay here for the meditation; but I was in trance, in my battle, when suddenly I felt a pressure on my pulse *(laughing):* it was the doctor, who had got up from his meditation (I must have been making some strange noises!) and was feeling my pulse – it seems my pulse was fading! But I didn't come out of my trance (I was conscious, but I didn't come out of it), I stayed like that till the end of the meditation, even a little afterwards. Then when the grating diminished, I came out of the trance and saw them both standing in front of me. I gave them a nice smile and told them, "It's all right." And I lay down. Then I went into a deep trance, completely out of the body, and everything returned to normal.

Afterwards I took a look. I wasn't too happy: "To do that during the meditation! ..." And I was "told" that it could be done only during the meditation and not at any other time, in activity or even in concentration, because it's not the same thing: it could be done only in deep meditation. So I said, "Very well." And I was also shown that there was a concrete result, a kind of partial victory over that type of ill will – a very, very aggressive ill will, extremely aggressive, which belongs to another age: it's something that no longer has the right to exist on the earth. It must go.

It's the same thing, moreover, which brought about Kennedy's assassination. And I suppose that's why I had to intervene. Because Kennedy's assassination has upset many things from the point of view of the general work. And it was the same thing, because as soon as I had news of the assassination, I saw the same kind of vibration, the same black force – very, very black – and spontaneously, I said (it isn't "I" who said it), "Oh, that may mean war." In other words, a victory of that force over the one that tries to follow more harmonious paths. But I have been protesting and working since then, and what happened on the 9th is the outcome of it.

But when you're right in it ... it isn't comfortable.

\* \* \*

*(Then Mother reads a handwritten note which is the continuation of the experience she related on December 7, when she spoke of the varying nearness and farness of the Presence.)*

I address it to the Lord:

"It is as if You flowed with the blood, You vibrated with the nerves, You lived with the cells...."

It isn't "in" or "by": it's "with," it's identified. As if You flowed with the blood. And the sensation was absolutely concrete: this Presence of the Lord FLOWS with the blood, VIBRATES with the nerves, and LIVES ("lives," meaning Life, the essence of Life) with the cells.

That's the best time! *(Mother laughs)*

Well, just recently, since that attack of the 9th, the Presence has increased [in the body]. And that's how I know that something has been won. I mean it has increased in duration, in frequency, and in the promptness of its response, of the time needed to get it.

*(silence)*

The difference between before and after the 9th is that before the 9th there was a constant pressure of adverse suggestions.... "It's all an illusion, it's all imagination...." A constant harassment. And sometimes it even takes very precise forms: "You think you're integrally conscious of the Lord – not in the least! It's just a little bit in your head, vaguely, and so you imagine it's true." When I heard that, it annoyed me very much, and I said, "All right, I'll see." And it is after that kind of battle in the Subconscient that the voice stopped and I had this experience: "It flows in the blood, it vibrates in the nerves, it lives in the cells...."

And everywhere, you see, not just my cells, not just the cells of this body: when the experience comes, it is quite widespread; I have an impression of many bloods, many cells, many nerves.... Which means that the CENTRAL consciousness isn't always aware of it, the individual isn't always aware of it (it has an extraordinary feeling, but it doesn't know what it is), while the cells are aware of it, but they cannot express it.

I felt that several times: when the experience comes, it isn't limited to one body. Only, the consciousness – the observing consciousness – isn't the same everywhere: there are DEGREES of consciousness, and here [in Mother's body] it appears to be a MORE CONSCIOUS center of consciousness, that's all; but otherwise ... For the consciousness itself it's that way too: at times it is very much awake, at other times not so awake.... Ultimately, all this is an experience of Oneness, of multiplicity in Oneness, and this experience depends on the degree of nearness and intensity. But it is the all – the all which is one – and seen from the standpoint of the Lord's consciousness.... You know, what we call "the Lord" is that which is fully conscious of itself; and the more the consciousness diminishes, the more you feel it's no longer the Lord – but it is the Lord all the same!

That's how it is.

*(silence)*

When we speak of "perception or knowledge through identity," it is still something that projects itself, identifies itself and OBSERVES itself while doing so; and it is conscious of the result. But my experience now isn't like that; it isn't something projecting itself: it's an overall perception. So instead of being able to say, "You think this way, THIS ONE thinks that way, THAT ONE feels this way," one thinks it or feels it with more or less clarity in the perception, more or less precision in the perception, but it's always "one" – you don't feel like saying "I"; there's no "I," it's "one," it's something. Listen, I'll give you an example: this morning I received that Italian, he started speaking, making gestures, telling me things – NOT ONE sound reached my ears ... yet I knew perfectly well what he was saying. And I answered him in the same way, without speaking. I didn't feel it was someone else talking to me and that I was answering him: it was a totality of movements more or less conscious of themselves, a totality and an exchange, an interchange of movements more or less conscious of themselves, with some vibrations more conscious, some less conscious, but the whole thing very living, very active. But then, in order to speak, I would have had to put myself in the ordinary consciousness in which the Italian was over there and I was here – but it didn't mean anything any more, it wasn't true. So there was something answering within, very actively, very distinctly, and all of it went on together *(gesture showing movements of consciousness or waves of vibrations),* and at the same time, there was a consciousness – a very, very vast consciousness – which was watching it all [those exchanges of vibrations] and exerting a sort of control, a very, very slight but very precise control, so as to put each vibration in its place.

That's how it is now when I see people. And it seems to be becoming more and more constant.

The other state, the state in which there is "me" and "other people," is becoming unpleasant; it brings things the consciousness disapproves of, reactions the consciousness disapproves of: "Still this? Still this smallness, still this limitation, still this incomprehension, still this darkness?..." All the time like that. So, immediately, something within goes like this *(gesture of inner reversal),* and it becomes the other way. And the other way is so soft, oh! ... So soft, so smooth, without clashes, without friction, without unpleasant reactions – that's what happened when there was that very painful "grating" during the meditation on the 9th, it was because the individual reactions of the cells were not in accord with the general harmony.

It's becoming a little interesting. It's a little new.

And there is a kind of joy, an unobtrusive joy, always like a kind of smile ... a smile not ironic, but a little ...

Putting it into words takes a sort of contraction, which is a pity – a pity. I don't know when there will be a means of expressing ourselves without that contraction. ... it wasn't at all one person saying to another, "It's time to go," it's as if I said to myself, "Now it's time to go." It's very odd. Rather new. Because it has become much more conscious; it had been like that in a sort of natural and spontaneous way of being for a long time, but now it's becoming conscious.

And when there is ... For example, when there is a relaxation in someone, or when there is a tensing up, I feel it: something in me relaxes, or tenses up; but not "in me" here, like this *(Mother in her armchair):* in me THERE *(Mother in the "other" person).*

And I know the very minute it takes place, you see. But those [tensing up, relaxation] are big movements, so it becomes obvious, but I realize that it goes on all the time – it's like that all the time.

To the point that what happens in the body isn't (oh, it's been that way for a long time, but it's becoming more and more that way), isn't familiar like something that happens in a particular body: it's just one way of being among all the others. It's becoming more and more like that. The reaction here [in Mother's body] isn't any more intimate than the reaction in others. And it's barely more perceptible: it all depends on the state of attentiveness and concentration of the consciousness (it's all movements of consciousness). But the consciousness isn't – is NO LONGER individual AT ALL. I am positive about that. A consciousness ... which is becoming more and more total. And now and then – now and then – when everything is "favorable," it becomes the Lord's Consciousness, the Consciousness of everything, and then it's ... a drop of Light. Nothing but Light.

Vol. 4, p. 410

## December 21, 1963

I have a feeling that something is pressing to eliminate in my active consciousness that discernment which is so sharp, so imperative – sharp, you know, with a vision ... (like the vision I had the other day of the nearness and farness), a vision almost microscopically exact. Obviously, this is helpful to get rid of all the things that shouldn't be, but now there is a will for this attitude to move into the *background,* and for the active consciousness to see constantly and almost exclusively only WHAT SHOULD BE.

Which means there are movements of elimination, of rejection, movements (for a second) of transformation, and also movements of construction – it seems the time has come to step into the movement of construction.

The body consciousness is still very timid, very timid in the sense that it doesn't have confidence in itself. It feels that if it isn't constantly vigilant, watching, watching, observing, discerning, some things *(gesture below)* may get through that shouldn't get through. That's what hinders. And that is why this certainty comes more and more: no criticism, no criticism at all, none at all, don't see what shouldn't be – see only WHAT SHOULD BE.

It's a great victory to be won – a great victory.

Vol. 4, p. 425

## January 15, 1964

There is a curious transitional state in the most material consciousness, the body consciousness. A transition from the state of subjugation, of helplessness, in which one is constantly at the mercy of forces, vibrations, unexpected movements, all sorts of impulses – to the Power. The Power that asserts and realizes itself. It's the transition between the two; and there is almost a swarm of experiences of all types, from the most mental part of that consciousness down to the darkest, most material part.

And when I want to say something, there immediately comes from all corners a swarm of things that want to be said and rush in all at the same time – which, naturally, prevents me from speaking.

It's a curious state.

The passage from an almost total helplessness – a sort of Fatality, like the imposition of a whole set of determinisms against which you are powerless, which weigh down on you – to a clear, definite Will, which, the MOMENT It expresses itself, is all-powerful.

*(silence)*

But, as a whole, it gives a sense of treading a very sharp ridge between two precipices.

**January 29, 1964**

For a long time people have been like bubbling champagne, you know, always wanting to know, "What's going to happen? What can we expect?" A big to-do. I answered, "I don't know." I don't know – I am not trying to know, I am not looking at it, I am not concerned with it: when it comes, it will come. Then, several times (while I was writing birthday cards or letters), several times, it was as if clearly dictated to me, "Prepare yourself for the Truth-Light that is descending." And it's clearly this: the Truth-Light that is going to manifest ... the Truth-Light that is descending ... the Truth-Light that is preparing its manifestation – all sorts of sentences kept coming to me like that, but always "the Truth-Light." Then I understood that this was what was going to happen.

And now ... it's something as solid as cement (which means it's material) and ab-so-lute-ly EVEN, you know, even, not one ripple of form, absolutely flat as a slab of marble, and without beginning or end – limitless, you can't see its end:

it's everywhere. Everywhere, and everywhere the same. Everywhere the same. A color ... like a sort of gray (a gray, the gray of Matter) that would contain a golden light, yet doesn't shine: it doesn't shine, it doesn't have a luminosity of its own, but it contains light. It doesn't radiate, it isn't luminous, yet it's a gray with a golden light in it – the gray of the most material Matter, of stone; gray, you know. But it contains that light: it's not inert, not insensitive, not unconscious, yet it is MATTER.

I have never seen that before.

It has been there for two days. What is it going to be? What is it going to bring about? ... I don't know.

Vol. 5, p. 43

## January 31, 1964

*Mother reads the text of a message she has just given:*

I wrote it in English yesterday:

The only hope for the future is in a change of man's consciousness and the change is bound to come. But it is left to men to decide if they will collaborate in this change or if it will have to be enforced upon them by the power of crushing circumstances.

Then, at the end, I put:

So, wake up and collaborate.

There seems to be a "push from behind" – I don't know how I could explain it to you.... I feel something, as if from behind a veil something were pushing and saying, "Come on! Move on, now!" As if everything were almost completely asleep and there, behind, something pushing very forcefully.

Vol. 5, p. 46

## March 4, 1964

....[O]n the morning of the 29th, I woke up ("woke up," I mean "got up") with the consciousness the Vedic Rishis called the "straight consciousness," the one that comes straight from the Lord – the Truth-Consciousness, basically. It was absolutely quiet, calm, but with a sort of supersensation of an absolute well-being. Well-being, security – yes, a security – an indescribable peace, without the contrast of opposites. And it lasted about three hours, continuously, solidly, effortlessly (I didn't make any effort to keep it). I only had a definite perception that it was what they called the consciousness of truth and immortality, along with a perception (an observation, rather), fairly clear and precise, of the way in which it becomes *crookedness* (you know their word).

I hadn't tried to have that experience, I hadn't thought about it or anything – it came as something massive, and it stayed. But I had the feeling it was individual: I didn't feel it was something descending on earth. I felt it was something given to me, given to this body. That's why I didn't attach much importance to it. The feeling of a grace given to this body. And it didn't leave till – it hasn't left, but it has been little by little and very slowly veiled by ... you know, that chaos of work, which has never been so chaotic and feverish at the same time. For about two weeks, it has been appalling. We haven't come out of it yet. It has veiled that state FOR ME. But I clearly felt it was something GIVEN to this body.

During the meditation on the 29th, I noticed (I looked), I noticed that for about two days, the atmosphere had been full of a sparkling of white stars, like dust – a twinkling dust of white stars. I saw it had been there for three days. And at the time of the meditation, it became extremely intense. But it was widespread, it was everywhere.

There seemed to be nothing but sparkling dots – dots that glittered like diamonds. It was like sparkling diamonds everywhere, absolutely everywhere. And it had a tendency to come from above downward. It lasted not just hours, but days; others saw it (yet I didn't say anything to anyone), others saw it and asked me what it was.

But there was nothing stunning or magnificent or astounding about it: nothing of the kind, nothing spectacular, nothing to give the feeling of a "great experience" – very quiet, but very, very self-assured. Very quiet.

Once it was over, after the balcony, when I came back from the balcony, I said spontaneously, "Very well, then, we'll have to wait another four years."

Something in me was expecting ... I don't know what, which didn't happen – maybe something that would have created havoc!

It was very quiet, very peaceful – very quiet, especially very quiet, and nothing marvelous or miraculous, nothing of the sort. So I said, "Very well, we'll wait four years, another four years," but for what, I don't know ... the something I was expecting and which didn't happen.

But the external, material life had become very difficult – there were 3,000 extra people from outside. So it made a sort of confusion in the atmosphere, which isn't over yet.

*(silence)*

I heard from some people that a great number of little miracles had occurred, but I didn't listen, it doesn't interest me (people tell me, but my thoughts are elsewhere). It's possible: the atmosphere was highly charged. In people's consciousness, it may result in little phenomena – a number of little phenomena which they call "miraculous," but which to me are childishly simple and elementary: it's just "the way things are."

Vol. 5, p. 69

## March 7, 1964

I told you last time that when I returned from the balcony on the 29th, it was as if in my concentration I said to the Lord, "Well, we'll wait another four years." That was the impression. And since then (today is the same day as the 29th, it was just a week ago), everything has been like this *(quivering gesture in the atmosphere)*, like hosts of little promises – but promises that haven't come to fruition, in other words, it's always something that IS to come, something that IS to be, something that IS to be realized; something that's drawing near, but nothing tangible. And last night, when I awoke from my usual concentration (it's almost always at the same time: between midnight and half past midnight), I felt something special in the atmosphere, so immediately I let myself flow into it and made contact with it.

I noticed (I've known it for some time, but it was quite concrete this time) that in my rest, as soon as I am at rest, the body is completely identified with the material substance of the earth, that is to say, the experience of the material substance of the earth becomes its own – which may be expressed by all sorts of things (it depends on the day, on the occasion). I had known for a long time that it was no longer the individual consciousness; it isn't the collective consciousness of mankind: it's a terrestrial consciousness, meaning it also contains the material substance of the earth, including the unconscious substance. Because I have prayed a lot, concentrated a lot, aspired a lot for the transformation of the Inconscient (since it is the essential condition for the "thing" to happen) – because of that there has been a kind of identification.

Last night it became a certainty.

And something began to descend – not "descend": to manifest and permeate; permeate and fill this terrestrial consciousness. What a force it had! What a power! ... I had never felt that kind of intensity in the material world. A stability, a power! Everything in the sense of a power, everything in the sense of a thrust forward – a thrust forward: progress, evolution, transformation. Everything like that. As if everything, everything were filled with a power of transformation – not "transformation," not transmutation, I don't know how to explain it.... Not the final transformation that will change the appearance, not that: it was the ananda of progress. The ananda of progress, like the ananda of progress of the animal becoming man, of man becoming superman – it wasn't transformation, it wasn't what will respond to that progress: it was progress. And with a plenitude, a constancy, and No RESISTANCE ANYWHERE: there was no panic anywhere, no resistance anywhere; everything was enthusiastically participating.

It lasted more than an hour.

And with the feeling that it was something unceasing, but that the consciousness [of Mother] was only changing its position because of the necessities of the work. And this change of position took place in a few minutes, quickly enough, without the sense of losing the other experience; it simply remained there, behind, in order for the work to be done outwardly in a normal way, that is, without too abrupt a change. And the consciousness seemed to revert to a sort of superficial bark: it gave exactly the impression of something hard, rather inert, very artificial, extremely thin, dry, with just an artificial transcription of life – and that was the ordinary consciousness, the consciousness that makes you feel you are in a body.

...

It's the same thing with that necessity of returning to the superficial consciousness. In the beginning, in the very beginning, when I identified myself with that pulsation of Love that creates the world, for many days I refused to resume entirely the ordinary, habitual consciousness (to which I was just referring: that sort of surface consciousness which is like bark), I no longer wanted it. That's why I was outwardly so helpless; in other words, I refused to make any decisions *(Mother laughs)*, the others had to decide and do things for me! That's what convinced them that I was extremely ill!

204

Now I understand all this very well.

At any rate, last night's experience was decisive in that it coordinated all those scattered little promises, all those scattered little advances, and gave a TERRESTRIAL meaning to all those little things that came making a promise of progress here, a promise of consciousness there – all those promises have suddenly been coordinated within a sort of totality on the scale of the earth. I didn't feel it as something crushing in its immensity, not at all: it was still something dominated by my consciousness. A little thing *(Mother holds up a ball in her hands)*, which my consciousness dominated but which was (for the moment) the exclusive object of my concentrations. And when I returned to the external consciousness (there was a moment when I had both consciousnesses at once), then I saw that the supposedly individual or personal consciousness, the consciousness of the body – of the body – was no more than a sort of convention necessary for maintaining contact. With the feeling that a step or two more – not many – will give THE Will (the supreme Will, that is) full power to act on this body.

It [this body] wasn't much more interesting or important than many other bodies – it didn't at all have the sense of its importance. Even, in the overall vision of the Work, its present imperfections were quite simply tolerated, even accepted, not because they are unavoidable, but because the amount of concentration and exclusive attention necessary to change them does not appear to be important enough to stop or reduce the general work. That's how it was ... there was a smile for lots of little things. Finally, as for "the Thing" (the great thing from the "artistic" point of view of the material appearance, great too from the point of view of public faith, which only goes by appearances, of course, and which will be convinced only when there is an obvious transformation), it appeared to be, for the moment, at any rate, something secondary and not urgent. But there was a fairly clear perception that soon (how can I put it?) the state of being or way of being (I think they say the "modus vivendi") of the body, of this fragment of terrestrial Matter, could be altered, ruled, entirely driven by the direct Will. Because it was as if ALL the illusions had fallen away one after another, and every time an illusion disappeared it produced one of those little promises that came in succession, announcing something that would come about later. So that prepared the final realization.

When I got up this morning, I had the feeling that a corner had been turned. But not at all – oh, not at all! – a subjective thing, not at all: a corner has been turned FOR THE EARTH. It doesn't matter in the least if people aren't aware of it.

*(silence)*

Amidst all that – that mass of experience – there was, standing out from the rest, the impression of the gorilla, of the fantastic power of progress that would turn him into a man.... It was very odd, it was an extraordinary physical power, with an intense joy of progress, of the thrust forward, and it made a kind of simian form moving forward towards man. And then it was like something repeating itself in the spiral of evolution: the same brute power, the same vital force (there's no comparison, of course, man has lost all that completely), the fantastic force of life that's found in those animals was coming back into the human consciousness and, probably, into the human form, BUT with all that has been brought by the evolution of Mind (a painful enough detour), and transformed into the light of a higher certitude and a higher peace.

And, you know, it wasn't a thing that came, diminished and came back again, it wasn't like that. It was ... an immensity, a full, solid, ESTABLISHED immensity. Not something that comes and presents itself to you to tell you, "This is how it will be," it wasn't that – it was HERE.

And I didn't feel it went away: it's I who left it, or rather, to say things accurately, I was made to leave it in order to concentrate on this bark, for the necessities of the work.

But it hasn't gone – it's here.

This morning I noted the experience through the same process I told you I was using for revelation. I wanted to note exactly how the experience could be defined *(Mother reads out a note):*

"The penetration and permeation into material substance of the Ananda of the power of progress in Life."

It wasn't a permeation into the Mind: it was a permeation into Life – into Life, into the material, earthly substance, which had become alive. Even plants participated in last night's experience: it isn't something that was the privilege of the mental being, it's the whole vital substance (vitalized material substance) of the earth that received this ananda of the power of progress – it was triumphant. Triumphant.

And when I came back (it took me perhaps five or six minutes to come back), it was with a sort of quiet certainty that the return was a necessity, and that something else would occur thanks to which it won't be necessary to leave one state for the other (that's the trouble, we still have to leave one state for the other). It hasn't left, but it's in the background – it should be in the front.

And then I realized ... When I got up, I asked myself, "Am I again going to come up against all the same material drawbacks that come from this sort of ... not even contagion, of identification with the people and things around?" The slightest thing causes a reaction....

*Yes, I'm familiar with it.*

Then one has to hold still, put the Force and ... Now, I am conscious of where it comes from, of what it is, of who it is (when it comes from someone), of all that. And the response can be perfectly conscious and willed. And when I restore order here *(gesture to the abdomen),* it restores order there, too.

This, in the realm of thought, is something that has been there for a very long time – very long, years and years: the shock that comes from outside exactly as if it were ... it's YOUR thought, but it comes from over there, it isn't actually here; and then the response. Since soon after the beginning of the century, this work has been going on. Afterwards, there was all the psychic work, in the same way *(gesture of widening):* the identification and the response. Then the vital work, which I began with Sri Aurobindo when we were staying over there [at the Guest House]; then the physical work, but there it's ... gropingly learning one's job. Now there is a sort of certainty (not absolute and constant, but not far away), a sort of certainty: you see, you come into contact with something, and then you know instantly what should be done and how it should be done; the vibration comes, meets a response, and goes back – and this is going on every minute, all the time.

A sort of assurance and confirmation came last night with that experience.

But we must be patient. And we mustn't think that we've reached the goal – we're still far from it! There is always the joy of the first step, the first step on the path: "Ah, what a lovely path!" *(Mother laughs)* ... We have to go right to the other end!

*(silence)*

It was luminous – luminous the whole time. That diamond-like sparkling turning into something much more compact, but less intense, that is, less bright – far more powerful. There was, above all, that sense of power: a power that can crush everything and rebuild everything. And in such an Ananda! But with nothing, absolutely nothing that had the slightest excitement, nothing of that bubbling which comes from the mind – the mind was like this *(gesture, both hands open towards the Eternal),* peaceful, peaceful, quiet, absolutely quiet. And while the experience went on, I knew (because the consciousness above was watching it all), I knew that only when the flash – the dazzlingly intense flash of the mental transformation through the supramental descent – only when the Light, the burst of Light, joins the ananda of Power will there occur things that will be a bit ... indisputable.

208

Because in an experience of this type, only the one who has it can be sure. The effects are visible in tiny details that can be observed only by those who are already well-disposed, that is (to translate), by those who have faith – those who have faith can see. And I know that because they tell me: they see examples of those tiny miracles of every minute (they aren't "miracles") multiply; they're everywhere, all the time, all the time – little facts, harmonies, realizations, concords ... all of which are quite unusual in this world of Disorder. But while the experience was there, I knew there would be another one, which is yet to come (God knows when!), and which would join with this one to form a third. And it is that junction that will then probably cause something to be changed in the appearances.

When will it come? I don't know. But we shouldn't be in a hurry.

Voilà.

Vol. 5, p. 73

### March 25, 1964

*... The true perception of the physical world – of trees, of people, of a stone – what would it be like to a supramental eye?*

That's exactly what cannot be said! When you have the vision and consciousness of the Truth-Order, of that which is DIRECT, the direct expression of the Truth, you immediately feel something inexpressible, because all words belong to the other sphere; all images, all comparisons, all expressions belong to the other sphere.

I had precisely that great difficulty (it was on February 29): all the time while I was living in that consciousness of the DIRECT manifestation of the Truth, I tried to formulate what I was feeling, what I was seeing – it was impossible. There were no words. And immediately, merely formulating things made me instantly fall back into the other consciousness.

On that occasion, the memory of this aphorism on the sun and the earth came back to me.... Even to say a "change of consciousness" ... a change of consciousness is still a movement.

I don't think we can say anything. I don't feel capable of saying anything, because all that you can say is uninteresting approximations.

*But when you are in that Truth-Consciousness, is it a "subjective" experience, or does Matter itself really change in its appearance?*

Yes, everything – the whole world is different! Everything is different. And the experience has convinced me of one thing, which I am still feeling constantly: that both states [of Truth and Falsehood] are simultaneous, concomitant, and there's only ... yes, a "change of consciousness," as he calls it, which means that you are in this consciousness or in that consciousness, and yet you're not moving.

We are forced to use words of movement because, for us, everything moves, but that change of consciousness isn't a movement – it isn't a movement. So then how can we speak about it and describe it?...

Even if we say "a state that takes the place of another" ... takes the place ... we immediately introduce movement – all our words are like that, what can we say?...

Yesterday again, the experience was quite concrete and powerful: it isn't necessary to move, or to move anything, for this Truth-Consciousness to replace the consciousness of deformation or distortion. In other words, the capacity to live in and be this true Vibration – essential and true – seems to have the power to SUBSTITUTE this Vibration for the vibration of Falsehood and Distortion, to such an extent that ... For instance, the outcome of Distortion or of the vibration of distortion should naturally have been an accident or catastrophe, but if, within those vibrations, there is a consciousness that has the power to become aware of the Vibration of Truth and therefore manifest the Vibration of Truth, it can – it must –

cancel the other vibration. Which would be translated, in the external phenomenon, by an intervention that would stop the catastrophe.

There is a growing feeling that the True is the only way to change the world; that all the other processes of slow transformation are always at a tangent (you draw nearer and nearer but you never arrive), and that the last step must be this – the substitution of the true Vibration.

There are partial proofs. But as they are partial, they aren't conclusive. Because, to the ordinary vision and understanding, you can always find explanations: you can say it was "foreseen" and "predestined" that the accident would miscarry, for example, and that consequently that intervention isn't at all what made it miscarry – it was "Determinism" that had decided it. And how do you prove anything? How do you even prove to yourself that it is otherwise? It's not possible.

You see, as soon as we express things we enter the mind, and as soon as we enter the mind there's that kind of logic, which is frightful because it is all-powerful: if everything has already been existing and coexisting from all eternity, how can you change one thing into another?... How can anything at all "change"?

We are told ... that to the Lord's consciousness there is neither past nor time nor movement nor anything – everything is. In order to translate, we say "from all eternity," which is nonsense, but anyway, everything IS. So everything is *(Mother folds her arms),* and then it's all over, there's nothing more to be done! You understand, this conception, or rather this manner of speaking (because it's only a manner of speaking) nullifies the sense of progress, nullifies evolution, nullifies ... We are told: it's part of the Determinism that you should strive to progress – yes, all this is rhetorical gibberish.

And, mind you, this manner of speaking is one minute of experience, but it's NOT the total experience. For a moment you feel this way, but it's not total, it's partial. It's only ONE way of feeling, it isn't all. There is in the eternal consciousness something far deeper and far more inexpressible than this – far more. This is only the first stupefaction you have when you emerge from the ordinary consciousness, but it isn't all. It isn't all. When the memory of this aphorism came back to me these last few days, I felt it was only a little glimpse you have all of a sudden and a sense of opposition between the two states, but it isn't all – it isn't all. There is something other than this.

There is something else, which is something altogether different from what we understand, BUT WHICH IS TRANSLATED INTO WHAT WE UNDERSTAND.

And That we cannot say. We cannot say what it is because ... it's inexpressible – inexpressible.

It amounts to feeling that all that, in our ordinary consciousness, becomes false, distorted, crooked, is ESSENTIALLY TRUE for the Truth-Consciousness. But how is it true? This is precisely something that cannot be said with words, because words belong to the Falsehood.

*Does this mean that the materiality of the world wouldn't be canceled by this Consciousness, but would be transfigured?... Or would it be another world altogether?*

*(silence)*

We should be clear on one point.... I am afraid that what we call "Matter" is precisely the world's false appearance.

There is something that CORRESPONDS, but ...

You see, this aphorism would eventually lead to an absolute subjectivity, and only that absolute subjectivity would be true – well, it's NOT like that. Because that means "pralaya," it means Nirvana. Well, there isn't only Nirvana, there is an objectivity that's real, not false – but how can you say what it is! ... It's something I have felt several times – several times, not just in a flash: the reality of ... (How can we express ourselves? We are always deceived by our words) ... In the perfect sense of Oneness and in the consciousness of Oneness there is room for the objective, for objectivity – one doesn't destroy the other, not at all. You may have the sense of a differentiation; not that it isn't yourself, but it's a different vision.... I told you, all that we can say is nothing, it's nonsense, because the purpose of words is to express the unreal world, but ... Yes, that may be what Sri Aurobindo calls the sense of "Multiplicity in Unity" (maybe that corresponds a little), just as you feel the internal multiplicity of your being, something of that sort.... I don't at all have the sensation of a separate self anymore, not at all, not at all, not even in the body, yet that doesn't prevent me from having a certain sense of an objective relationship – well, yes, it leads us back to his "change in the relation of sun-consciousness and earth-consciousness." *(Laughing)* Maybe that really is the best way of putting it! It's a relation of consciousness. It isn't at all the relationship between oneself and "others" – not at all, that's entirely canceled – but it might be like the relation of consciousness between the various parts of one's being. And it gives objectivity to those various parts, obviously.

*(long silence)*

To come back to that very easily understood example of the aborted accident, we may very well conceive that the intervention of the Truth-Consciousness had been decided "from all eternity" and that there isn't any "new" element; but that does nothing to alter the fact that this intervention is what stopped the accident (which gives an exact image of the power of this true consciousness over the other one). If we project our way of being onto the Supreme, we may conceive that He enjoys carrying out many experiments to see how it all plays (this is something else, it doesn't follow that there isn't an All-Consciousness that knows all things from all eternity – all this with utterly inadequate words), but that does nothing to alter the fact that, when we look at the process, this intervention is what was able to make the accident miscarry: the substitution of a true consciousness for a false consciousness stopped the process of the false consciousness.

213

And it seems to me it occurs often enough – much more often than people think. For example, every time an illness is cured, every time an accident is avoided, every time a catastrophe, even a global one, is avoided, all that is always the intervention of the Vibration of Harmony into the vibration of Disorder, allowing Disorder to cease.

So the people, the faithful, who always say, "Through the Divine Grace this has happened," aren't so wrong.

I only note the fact that it is this Vibration of Order and Harmony that intervened (we're not concerned with the reasons for its intervention, this is only a scientific observation), and of this I've had a fairly large number of experiences.

*So that would be the process of transformation of the world?*

Yes.

*An increasingly constant embodying of this Vibration of Order.*

Yes, exactly, that's it. Exactly.

Even from that point of view, I have seen ... You know, the ordinary idea that the phenomenon [of transformation] must necessarily occur first in the body in which the Consciousness is expressed the most constantly seems to me quite unnecessary and secondary. On the contrary, it occurs at the same time wherever it can occur the most easily and totally, and this aggregate of cells *(Mother points to her own body)* isn't necessarily the most ready for this operation. It may therefore remain a very long time as it apparently is, even if its understanding and receptivity are special. I mean that this body's *awareness,* its conscious perception is infinitely superior to the one all the bodies it comes into contact with can have, except for a few minutes – a few minutes – when other bodies, as if through a grace, have the Perception. While for it, it's a natural and constant state; it's the effective result of this Truth-Consciousness being more constantly concentrated on this collection of cells than on others – more directly. But the substitution of one vibration for another in facts, in actions, in objects, occurs wherever the result is the most striking and effective.

I don't know if I can make myself understood, but it is something I have felt very, very clearly, and which one cannot feel as long as the physical ego is there, because the physical ego has the sense of its own importance, and that disappears entirely with the physical ego. When it disappears, one has a clear perception that the intervention or manifestation of the true Vibration doesn't depend on egos or individualities (human or national individualities, or even individualities of Nature: animals, plants and so on), it depends on a certain play of the cells and Matter in which there are aggregates particularly favorable for the transformation to occur – not "transformation": the substitution, to be precise, the substitution of the Vibration of Truth for the vibration of Falsehood. And the phenomenon may be very independent of groupings and individualities (it may happen in one part here, another part there, one thing here, another thing there); and it always corresponds to a certain quality of vibration that causes a sort of swelling – a receptive swelling – and then, the thing can occur.

Unfortunately, as I said at the beginning, all words belong to the world of appearances.

*(silence)*

This has repeatedly been my experience lately, with a vision and a conviction, the conviction of an experience: the two vibrations are like this *(concomitant gesture indicating a superimposition and infiltration),* all the time – all the time, all the time.

Maybe the sense of wonder comes when the quantity that has infiltrated is large enough to be perceptible. But I have an impression – a very acute impression – that this phenomenon is going on all the time, all the time, everywhere, in a minuscule, infinitesimal way *(gesture of a twinkling infiltration),* and that in certain circumstances or conditions that are visible (visible to this vision: it's a sort of luminous swelling – I can't explain), then, the mass of infiltration is sufficient to give the impression of a miracle. But otherwise, it's something going on all the time, all the time, all the time, continuously, in the world *(same twinkling gesture)*, like an infinitesimal amount of Falsehood replaced by Light ... Falsehood replaced by Light ... constantly.

And this Vibration (which I feel and see) gives the feeling of a fire. That's probably what the Vedic Rishis translated as the "Flame" – in the human consciousness, in man, in Matter. They always spoke of a "Flame." It is indeed a vibration with the intensity of a higher fire.

The body even felt several times, when the Work was very concentrated or condensed, that it is the equivalent of a fever.

Two or three nights ago, something like that occurred: in the middle of the night, early morning, there was a descent of this Force, a descent of this Truth-Power; and this time it was everywhere (it's always everywhere), but with a special concentration in the brain – not in this brain: in THE brain. And it was so strong, so strong, so strong! The head felt as if it were about to burst – yes, as if everything were going to burst – so that for about two hours I simply had to keep calling for the widening of the Lord's Peace: "Lord, Your widening, Your peace," like that, in the cells. And with the consciousness (which is always conscious, of course *[gesture above]*) that this descent into an unprepared brain would be enough to drive you completely mad or absolutely daze you (at the very best), or else you would burst.

This experience, like the other one, hasn't left.

It's everywhere, you understand.

And I saw (because I wanted to see, and I saw) that the other experience was still there but it was beginning to be almost habitual, almost natural, while this one was new. It was the result of my old prayer: "Lord, take possession of this brain."

Well, that's what is happening – happening everywhere, all the time. So if it happens in a large enough aggregate, it gives the appearance of a miracle – but it is the miracle of the whole EARTH.

But one must hold out, because it has consequences: it brings a sensation of Power, a Power which very few people can feel or experience without their balance being more or less upset, because they don't have an adequate basis of peace – a vast and very, very, VERY quiet peace. Everywhere, even here at the School, children are in a state of effervescence (I was informed that the best-behaved and generally most regular children had become like that). I said, "There is only ONE answer, one single answer: you must be still, still, and even more still, and increasingly still. And do not try to find a solution with your head because it cannot find any. You must only be still – still, still, immutably still. Calm and peace, calm and peace.... It is the ONLY answer."

I am not saying it's the cure, but it's the only answer: to endure in calm and peace, endure in calm and peace....

Then something will happen.

*(silence)*

But this experience (this is between ourselves) is an experience I had never had in my life. I always had the impression of a sort of control over what was going on in the brain, and that I was always able to answer with the "blank," you know, the calm, still blank – the still blank. This time *(laughing)*, it wasn't that! And it became so formidable that even the mantra (the words of the mantra) were shooting past like cannonballs! *(Laughing)* It all seemed like a frightening hail of bullets!

There was only this to be done: I kept perfectly still, calling – calling for the Lord's Peace and Calm, that ever-widening Peace. The Infinite of the Lord's Peace.

217

Then it became possible to bear the Vibration.

Now, what it does, its work — that's not our business, it's His. We cannot understand. But that it is at work goes without saying.

But without a doubt, if at that moment there had been a doctor to take my temperature, he would have found there was a tremendous fever — though nothing even remotely like an "illness"! No, it was miraculously wonderful, it gave the feeling that ... it was something the earth did not know.

That's how it always expresses itself: something the earth did not know, something new. It is new to the earth. That's why it's hard to bear! Because it is new.

Even now *(Mother touches her skull)*, it feels all swollen, and with a vibration inside *(gesture of a trepidation)* as if the head were twice as big as before.

Vol. 5, p. 90

## July 22, 1964

Human love, what people call "love," even at its best, even taking it in its purest essence, is something that goes to one person, but not to another: you love SOME people (sometimes even you love only certain qualities in some people); you love SOME people, and that means it's partial and limited. And even for those who are incapable of hatred there is a number of people and things that they are indifferent to: there is no love (in most cases). That love is limited, partial and defined. It's unstable, moreover: man (I mean the human being) is unable to feel love in a continuous way, always with the same intensity — at certain times, for a moment, it becomes very intense and powerful, and at other times it grows dim; sometimes, it falls completely asleep. And that's under the best conditions — I am not speaking of all the degradations, I am speaking of the feeling people call "love," which is the feeling closest to true love; that's how it is: partial, limited, unstable and fluctuating.

Then, immediately, without transition, it was as if I was plunged in a bath of the Supreme's Love ... with the sensation of something limitless; in other words, when you have the perception of space, that something is everywhere (it's beyond the perception of space, but if you have the perception of space, it's everywhere). And it's a kind of homogenous vibratory mass, IMMOBILE, yet with an unparalleled intensity of vibration, which can be described as a warm, golden light (but it's not that, it's much more marvelous than that!). And then, it's everywhere at once, everywhere always the same, without alternations of high and low, unchanging, in an unvarying intensity of sensation. And that "something" which is characteristic of divine nature (and is hard to express with words) is at the same time absolute immobility and absolute intensity of vibration. And That ... loves. There is no "Lord," there are no "things"; there is no subject, no object. And That loves. But how can you say what That is?... It's impossible. And That loves everywhere and everything, all the time, all at the same time.

All those stories those so-called saints and sages told about God's Love "coming and going," oh, it's unspeakably stupid! – It's THERE, eternally; It has always been there, eternally; It will always be there, eternally, always the same and at the highest of its possibility.

It hasn't left, and now it won't be able to leave.

And once you've lived That ... you become so irrevocably conscious that everything depends on the individual perception, entirely; and naturally, that individual perception [of divine Love] depends on the inadequacy, the inertia, the incomprehension, the incapacity, the cells' inability to hold and keep the Vibration, anyway all that man calls his "character" and which comes from his animal evolution.

*(silence)*

It is said that divine Love doesn't manifest because, in the world's present state of imperfection, the result would be a catastrophe – that's a human vision. Divine Love manifests, has manifested eternally, will manifest eternally, and it's the incapacity of the material world ... not only of the material world, but of the vital world and the mental world, and of many other worlds that aren't ready, that are incapable – but HE is there, He is there, right there! He is there permanently: it's THE Permanence. The Permanence Buddha sought is there. He claims he found it in Nirvana – it is there, in Love.

*(silence)*

Since that experience came, there has no longer even been in the consciousness that sort of care I took for years not to concentrate too much Force or Power, or Light or Love, on beings and things for fear of upsetting their natural growth – that seems so childish! It's there, it's there, it's there – it is there. And it's for things themselves that it's impossible to feel more of it than they can bear.

*(silence)*

As soon as I have one minute to meditate, that is to say, as soon as I am not assailed from every side by people, things, events, as soon as I can simply do this *(gesture of drawing within)* and look, well, I see that the cells themselves are beginning to learn the Vibration.

It is obviously the agent of the creation.

And I said that that sort of "rain of Truth-Light" which came a few months ago announced something – it has obviously prepared, started this kind of permeation of a superior Harmony into the material vibrations. It has prepared not a "new descent," but the possibility of a new perception, a perception that allows an outward and physical action.

...

But it's clear that in my consciousness the [supreme] contact has been made (with some degree of limitation, but still it has been made), and nothing takes place – nothing, absolutely nothing, not even the most totally in-sig-nif-i-cant things – without, I can't even say the "thought" or the "sensation" (in English they say *awareness*, but it's much fuller than that), the feeling (another impossible word), without the feeling of the Lord's Presence, the supreme Presence, being there twenty-four hours a day. Throughout that activity of the night I've just told you about, He was there, the Lord's Presence was there all the time, every second, directing everything, organizing everything – BUT THAT WASN'T THERE. And That, which I call Love, that Manifestation, is so formidably powerful that, as I once said, it is intolerant of anything else – That alone exists.... That exists, That is – and it's finished. Whereas the Lord (the "Lord," what I call the Lord) is something else altogether; the Lord is all that has manifested, all that hasn't manifested, all that is, all that will be, and all, all is the Lord – it's the Lord. But the Lord *(laughing)* is necessarily tolerant of Himself! ... All is the Lord, but all is perceived by the Lord through the limitations of human perception! But everything, everything is there – everything is there; everything, as it is every second; and with the perception of time, every second is different, in a perpetual becoming. This is supreme Tolerance: there is no more struggle, no more battle, no more destruction – there is only He.

Those who have had this experience have generally stopped there. And if they wanted to get out of the world, they chose the Lord's "aspect of annihilation"; they took refuge there and stayed there – all the rest no longer existed. But the other aspect ... the other aspect is the world of tomorrow, or of the day after tomorrow. The other aspect is an inexpressible glory. So all-powerful a glory that it alone exists.

It's ONE way of being of the Lord.

*(silence)*

This experience is a milestone on the road.

Vol. 5, p. 133

## August 11, 1964

There was an experience the night of the 8th, which lasted at least two hours by the clock, maybe more. An experience I had never had before. In fact, it wasn't at all the experience of a "person," because I was very conscious of the return to the personal consciousness, and in a very interesting way: everything was felt as a diminishing. The return lasted nearly half an hour. It's inexpressible with words.

For two hours, it was the experience of Omnipotence – of THE LORD'S Omnipotence – for two hours, with all the decisions that were made then, that is to say, the expression of what was going to be translated in the earth consciousness. There was such a simplicity about it! Such obviousness – what we customarily call "natural." So obvious, so simple, so natural, so spontaneous, without even the memory of what might be an effort – the constant effort you have to make in material life just to live, just to keep all those cells together.

The strange thing is that (I was very conscious, perfectly conscious; the "Witness" consciousness is never canceled, but it isn't in the way) is that I knew, I saw (yet my eyes were closed, I was lying in my bed), I saw my body moving – it had movements of such a Rhythm! ... You see, every movement, every gesture, every finger, every attitude was a thing that was being realized. Then what I studied, what I saw during the half-hour that followed (with my eyes closed, seeing much more clearly than with my ordinary eyes) was the difference in the body – the difference in the body's movements between that moment [during the experience] and after [when Mother returned to the personal consciousness]. At that moment, the movements were ... it was creation! And with an EXACTNESS, a majesty! *(Mother stretches out her arms and moves them slowly in a vast Rhythm.)* I don't know what other people

222

might have seen, I have no idea, but as for me, I saw myself; I saw especially the arms because it was the arms that acted: they were like the realizing intermediaries ... I don't know how to put it. But it was as vast as the world. It was the earth (it's always the earth consciousness), not the universe: the earth, the earth consciousness. But I was conscious then of the universe and of the action on the earth (both things), of the earth as a very small thing in the universe *(Mother holds a small ball in her hands)*. I don't know, it's hard to say, but when it expressed itself, there was also the perception of the difference in vision between that moment [during the experience] and afterwards.... But all this is inexpressible. Yet it is an absolute knowledge − it's another way of knowing. Sri Aurobindo explained this, that all mental knowledge is a seeking: you seek; while this knowledge has another quality, another flavor. And then the power of the Harmony is so wonderful! *(Mother again depicts a great Rhythm, her arms outstretched)* So wonderful, so spontaneous, so SIMPLE. And It stays there, as if It supported the entire world as it is; it is a kind of inner support of the world − the world leans on it.

But outwardly, that sort of film ... it's like a thin film of difficulties, of complications, added on by the human consciousness (it's much stronger with man than with the animal; the animal doesn't have that, very little − it has it more and more because of man, but very little; it's something specific to man and the mental function), it's something very thin − as thin as an onion skin, as dry as an onion skin − yet it spoils everything. It spoils everything ONLY FOR THE HUMAN CONSCIOUSNESS. At the time [of the experience], it was unimportant. Unimportant, in the sense that it takes away all the Beauty, all the Power, all the Magnificence of the thing − for the human consciousness. For man, it is of paramount importance. But for the Action, it's almost negligible. Basically, it's rather that it makes it difficult for man to become conscious and PARTICIPATE; otherwise, my feeling is that truly the time has come for things to get done:

that experience was a NEW descent, that is, something new entering the terrestrial manifestation; it wasn't that I became conscious of how the world is: I WAS the Lord's Will coming into the world to change it. That's what it was. And that action was only very slightly affected (assuming it was affected at all) by that stupid "onion skin" of human mentality.

In fact, that was the interesting point: when you come back to the other side (it's not even "coming back to the other side," it's a curious thing that happens ..), I remember, when I became conscious again of this body, its gestures had become dry, sterile, thin – stupid. And yet it was still in an intense Bliss and a total self-giving: it was at the height of its joy; and yet what it was doing, its appearance, oh, it all seemed so silly!

Those oppositions are really what gives the consciousness an interesting knowledge. Because I have a feeling that that Action wasn't at all limited to the moment when the consciousness that acts here took part in it: it's going on all the time. If for just a second *(gesture of interiorization)* I stop speaking or acting, I feel that golden Glory behind – "behind," it's not behind, not within, it's ... supporting everything – it is there. But in that experience, I was given two hours of TOTAL participation: there was nothing left but That, nothing existed anymore but That. And all the cells were given an unforgettable joy: they had become That.

What I don't know is, if someone had been looking, what would he have seen? I don't know.

Anyhow, the work is being done very fast. This is truly what Sri Aurobindo called "the Hour of God": it's being done very fast.

Vol. 5, p. 153

## August 22, 1964

Something peculiar happened to me.... It was the other day, the last time you came. I looked peculiar that day, didn't I?

*You were tired.*

It's not that! It's never "tired," never "ill" – it's never that, it's something else. But it takes me a few days to find out what it is.

It's that the center of the body consciousness moved (usually it's in the head, in the brain). The body consciousness, the cellular consciousness, the one that responds to the workings of Nature and governs the whole functioning – suddenly it moved, it went out of the body.

I had the experience (I knew what it was, but I didn't know the consequences or how to express it), I had the experience of my body consciousness going completely out of the body (that must be what happens when one dies, mustn't it?), and for ... apparently for ten or fifteen minutes, I don't know, it was over, the physical world no longer existed, the body no longer existed. But I was very conscious of a movement of forces and of an action; that corporeal consciousness was even repeating its mantra, that was very interesting: it was repeating its mantra and watching the effect of the mantra on the vibrations of forces. But the consciousness left the body over there *(gesture to the bathroom)* and came back into it here *(on the bed)*. I was carried .. and what happened between the two, I don't know. But when you reenter your body (that is, when the most material part of the consciousness has left the body, when you faint or go into a state of cataleptic trance, and then reenter your body), it's very painful, very painful – all the nerves hurt. So then, suddenly, I felt a lot of pain like that (it lasts two seconds, that's nothing), and then I felt that I was lying on cushions! *(Laughing)* My last impression was of standing over there!

It's the first time in my life that has happened. Always, whenever I fainted, I would remain conscious of what was happening to my body; often, I would even see it – I would see it lying on the floor, for instance; but I would remain conscious. This is the first time.

But the effect afterwards was queer, as if all the functionings had lost their (what can I call it?), their captain – they no longer knew what to do. And in the head, at first it felt as if it had grown very, very big, and then there were vibrations ... You know, I often mention those Vibrations of Harmony that try to enter the vibrations of Disorder (it's something I often see now, even with my eyes open: they come through, enter, there are formations, all sorts of things), but that was going on in my head. My head was big (!), and inside, there were all those dots of the white light of Harmony, moving about with a great intensity and power, within a dark gray medium. It was interesting. But I was conscious only of that – the entire relationship with the body had vanished. And the whole day long I had the feeling of a lack of government in the body, as if everything followed its own impulsion; it was very hard to keep it all together.

That's how it was – very strong. The second day, it was a little less strong; the third day ... But there is something that has changed and isn't coming back. And that something gives the sense of a distance (it's the word *aloofness)* from the natural body consciousness that makes the body automatically do all it has to do. It is as if that consciousness were now at a distance, had almost lost interest in what's happening – not "lost interest," because it's laughing! I don't know why, I feel it's laughing, as if it were making fun of me, of this body – the poor old thing! *(laughing)* It has a lot of difficulties, it is made to do some strange things.

*And that center hasn't returned to its normal place?*

No, no! Nothing has returned of what was before.

It's very different from what it was before for so many years – very different. I feel a sort of ... Oh, it's an impression equivalent to the one I had when Sri Aurobindo gave my mind silence. It became perfectly blank and empty *(gesture to the forehead),* blank and empty, and there was nothing anymore: I couldn't think anymore, not one idea, not one system anymore, nothing – in a word, total imbecility! It never came back. You see, it went up above, and here there was nothing. Well, this time, it was the same thing for the body consciousness: before, it was everywhere like something holding everything together (to such a point that when there was a difficulty, I only had to stop bothering about it all and let that act, and the difficulty would automatically be sorted out by that body consciousness, which knows far better than our active thought what the body should do), and that day it left DELIBERATELY. The decision had been made the night before, but I was resisting it, as I knew the normal consequence was fainting. But "that" willed it so and "that" chose its own time (when there was no danger, when no accident could happen and someone was there to help me), "that" chose its own time and "that" did it deliberately – gone. And it has never returned.

So the first day, I was almost dazed; I was constantly groping for the way to do things. Yesterday, it was still strong. And this morning, suddenly I began to understand (what I call "to understand" is to have control), I understood: "Ah, that's it!" Because I was wondering, "But what on earth does all this mean? How can I do my work?" ... I remember, yesterday I had to see a host of people, people who aren't close and whose atmosphere isn't good: it was very difficult, I had to keep a hold on myself, and I must have looked strange, very absent – I was very far away, in a very deep consciousness, so that my body wouldn't be ... you know, that gave it discomfort of sorts – discomfort, yes – it was hard to bear. Yesterday the body was still that way the whole morning; towards evening it got better. But the night wasn't good, oh! ... In the night, I am always given a state of human consciousness to put right, one after another – there are millions of them. And there are always all the images and events that illustrate that particular state of consciousness. At times, it's very hard going: I wake up tired, as after a long period of work. And last night, that's how it was; it's always the various, multiple ways which men have of complicating the original Simplicity: of turning a simple vibration into extremely complicated events – where the thing should be simple and flow naturally, there are endless complications, and such difficulties! Unbearable and insuperable difficulties. I don't know if you have experienced that: you want to go somewhere, but there are hindrances everywhere; you want to go out of a room, but there is no way out, or there is one, but you have to crawl on the ground under kinds of rocks ... and then something in the being refuses, "No, I won't do it." And with a sense of insecurity, as if at any moment the thing could topple over and crush you.... There are people who want to help you, but they can't do anything at all, they only make the complication still more complicated; you start on a road with the certainty of reaching a particular place, then all of a sudden, in the middle of it the road changes, everything changes, and you have your back to the place you wanted to go.... All kinds of things like that. The symbolism of it is extremely clear. But then, it makes for a lot of work.

Anyway, I got up in that state and began to wonder, "Won't there be an end to it?"... It's always, always, always like that. And more and more I have an inner conviction that it isn't a thing you can obtain through effort and progressive transformation – it would take millions of years! It's only ... the Grace. When the Lord decides, "It's finished, now it's going to be like that," it will be like that. Then you find rest and tranquillity.

I offered Him my whole night and all the difficulties and all the complications, as I always do. Then a sort of Peace came into me, and in that Peace, I saw what it was and said, "That's odd! The center of the body consciousness isn't there anymore."

From that moment on, it got much better. The sort of vague uncertainty this poor body was in went away. Because, naturally, that center was immediately replaced by the clear Consciousness from above, and I hope that little by little it will have complete control over the body.

In fact, it must be – theoretically it must be to replace the natural, automatic consciousness by a conscious consciousness.

It isn't a consciousness that sees the details: it's a consciousness that establishes and maintains a Harmony.

There. I thought it was amusing to tell.

Otherwise, it's endless! ...

Everybody is falling ill. And for me, it's the same thing: it isn't an illness – it isn't an illness, it's a very strong action on the consciousnesses.

Vol. 5, p. 169

## September 23, 1964

*I don't know what is the fruit of the japa and what is simply the fruit of a sedimentation: I can't tell. I know that when I am doing my japa, there is a rather concentrated force, but I don't know if that comes from the japa or, quite simply, from the fact that I concentrate. I can't tell.*

Oh, you mean the words of the japa – those words have only the power given by the generations that have repeated them.

*(silence)*

There is ONE sound which, to me, has an extraordinary power – extraordinary and UNIVERSAL (that's the important point): it doesn't depend on the language you speak, it doesn't depend on the education you were given, it doesn't depend on the atmosphere you breathe. And that sound, without knowing anything, I used to say it when I was a child (you know how in French we say, "Oh!"; well, I used to say "OM," without knowing anything!). And indeed, I made all kinds of experiments with that sound – it's fantastic, even, fantastic! It's unbelievable.

So then, if around this you build something that corresponds to your own aspiration – certain sounds or words that FOR YOU evoke a soul state – then it's very good.

All that is traditional benefits from the power of tradition, that goes without saying, but it's necessarily very limited – personally, it gives me the feeling of something shriveled and withered, as if all the juice it could contain had been squeezed out (!) Except if, spontaneously, the sounds correspond to a soul state in you.

*I have noticed that this japa automatically triggered the physical mind into a great activity.*

The physical mind!

*Yes, that is to say, when I begin the japa, I am assailed by a number of material questions, tiny little material things that happened during the day and come back. Uninteresting things. The japa seems to act on that mind, on that bit of physical mind.*

Yes, it WANTS to act there. That's why its action is stupefying – it is meant to stupefy that mind. But there are people who can't be stupefied, mon petit! ... It's very good for average humanity, it can help average humanity, but on those who have an intellectuality, it cannot act.

...

... There is a whole part of the most material consciousness, the utterly physical consciousness (precisely the one that participates in incalculable, minuscule activity of every day) which, of course, is very hard to bear. In ordinary life, it's tolerable, it's bearable because you take interest in it and sometimes pleasure – all that life on the surface that makes you ... you see a pretty thing, it gives you pleasure; you have something tasty in your mouth, it gives you pleasure; anyway, all these little pleasures that are so futile, but help people bear existence. Those who don't have the inner consciousness and the contact with what's behind all that wouldn't be able to live if they didn't have little pleasures. So a host of tiny little problems crop up, problems of material existence, which explain perfectly well that those who no longer had any desire, and therefore no longer took any pleasure in anything, had one single idea: "What's the use of it all!" And indeed, if we didn't have the feeling that all that must be borne because it leads to something else of an altogether different nature and expression, it would be so insipid and puerile, so petty that it would become quite unbearable. That's certainly what explains the aspiration for Nirvana and the flight from this world.

So there is this problem, a problem of every second, which I must solve every second by the corresponding attitude that leads to the True Thing; and at the same time, there is the other attitude of acceptance of all that is – for instance, of what leads to disintegration: the acceptance of disintegration, defeat, decomposition, weakening, decay – all things that, naturally, to the ordinary man, are detestable and against which he reacts violently. But since you are told that everything is the expression of the divine Will and must be accepted as the divine Will, there comes this problem, which crops up almost constantly and every minute: if you accept those things as the expression of the divine Will, quite naturally things will follow their habitual course towards disintegration, but what is the TRUE ATTITUDE that can give you that perfect equanimity in all circumstances, and at the same time give a maximum of force and power and will to the Perfection that must be realized?

As soon as we deal with even the vital plane, even the lower vital, the problem doesn't arise, it's very easy; but here, in the cells of the body, in this life? In this life of every minute, which is so constricted, so shriveled, so microscopic.... What should you do when you know that you mustn't bring into play a will to reject all that is a decay, and when, at the same time, you can't accept decay because you don't see it as a perfect expression of the Divine?

It's very subtle ... there is something to be found; and it's something that, obviously, I haven't found because it keeps coming back again and again.... At times, I even say, "Oh, for Peace, Peace, Peace ..." but then I feel it is a weakness. I say, "To let myself go, not thinking of anything, not trying to know anything," but then something instantly rises there, somewhere, and says, *Tamas*.

*(silence)*

You see, on the mental level, it isn't a problem, all that has been solved and it's very fine. But it's HERE, inside here – I can't even say in the sensation because I don't live in the sensations. It's a problem of consciousness, of the consciousness of this body.

And I clearly feel that the problem could disappear only if the supreme Consciousness truly took possession of the cells and made them live, act, move, like that, so they had the sense of the Omnipotence taking hold of them; then it would be over, they would no longer be responsible for anything. This seems to be the only solution. Then comes the prayer, "When will it come?"

"Aspire intensely, but without impatience...."

It's not even that I have the feeling of the years going by – there is nothing like that, it's not that! It's the problem of living from second to second, from minute to minute. I don't at all think, "Oh, the years are going by ... ," it's a long time since all that has been over. It's not that, it's ... the easy path of passive acceptance, which evidently leads ("evidently," I mean not through reasoning, but THROUGH EXPERIENCE), which leads to increased decay; or else, that intensity of aspiration for the Perfection that must manifest, for all that must be, an aspiration which keeps everything at a standstill in that expectation. It's the opposition between these two attitudes.

The problem is made worse by the fact that the goodwill of the cells (a necessarily ignorant goodwill) doesn't know if one attitude is better than the other, if it should choose between the two, if both should be accepted – they don't know! And as it isn't mentalized or formulated or with words, it's very difficult. Oh, as soon as the words are there ... all that has been said comes back, and it's over. It's not that, it's not that anymore. Even if strong sensations or a vital force come up, it's not a problem anymore. The problem is only HERE, in this *(Mother strikes her body).*

Nights, for instance, are a long awareness, a great action, a discovery of all kinds of things, a taking stock of the situation as it is – but there aren't any problems! But the minute the body (I can't say "wakes up" because it isn't asleep: it's only in a state of rest sufficiently complete for its personal difficulties not to interfere), but from time to time, what we'll call "waking up" takes place, that is to say, the purely physical consciousness comes back – and the whole problem comes back instantly. Instantly the problem is there. And without your remembering it: the problem doesn't come back because you remember it, it's that the problem is there, in the very cells.

And in the morning, oh! ... All mornings are difficult. It's odd: life as a whole goes by with almost dizzying speed – weeks and months go by like that – and mornings, about three hours every morning, last like a century! Each minute is won at the cost of an effort. It is the time of the work in the body, for the body, and not just one body: for instance, all the vibrations from sick people, all those problems of life come from everywhere. And for those three hours, there is tension, struggle, acute seeking for what should be done or for the attitude to be taken.... It's at that time that I have tested the power of the mantra. For those three hours, I repeat my mantra automatically, without stopping; and every time the difficulty increases, a kind of Power comes into those words and acts on Matter. And that's how I know: without the mantra, that work couldn't be done. But that's why I say it has to be YOUR mantra, not something you received from whomever – the mantra that arose spontaneously from your deeper being *(gesture to the heart),* from your inner guide. That's what holds out. When you don't know, when you don't understand, when you don't want to let the mind intervene and you are ... THAT is there; the mantra is there; and it helps you to get through. It helps to get through. It saves the situation at critical moments, it's a considerable support, considerable.

For those three hours (three or three and a half hours), it's constant, constant, without stop. So then the words well up *(gesture from the heart)*. And when the situation becomes critical, when that disorder, that disintegration seem to be gaining in power, it's as if the mantra were becoming swollen with force, and ... it restores order.

And that wasn't just once, or for a month, or a year: it has been like that for years, and it goes on increasing.

But it's hard work.

And afterwards, after those hours, the contact with outside starts again: I start seeing people again and doing the outer work, listening to letters, answering, making decisions; and every person, every letter, every action brings its own volume of disorder, disharmony and disintegration. It's as if all that were dumped by the truckload on your head. And you have to hold out.

Then, at times, it becomes very difficult. You have to hold out.

When you can remain still and quiet, it's fine, but when you have to make decisions, listen to letters, answer ... So when it's too much at once and when people who bring it all bring their own disorder in addition, at times it's a bit much.

But it's so subtle in its nature that it is incomprehensible for people around you; you seem to be making a lot of fuss about nothing. Those are things which, in their unconsciousness, they don't feel at all, not at all – it takes shouting and quarrels and battles, almost, for them to notice that there's disorder!

Voilà.

Vol. 5, p. 201

## September 30, 1964

It is like the beginning of a new phase.

Previously, the whole action always used to come from here *(radiating gesture above the head),* in the highest, vastest and purest Light; but for a few days now, whenever something or other goes wrong, when, for instance, people don't do what they should or their reactions are wrong, or when there are difficulties in circumstances, anyway when things "grate" and Disorder gets worse, now there comes into me a sort of Power, a VERY MATERIAL Power, which goes like this *(gesture of pummeling),* which goes at things and pushes terribly hard – oh, what a pressure it makes! ... And it comes without my willing it, it goes without my knowing it.

Naturally, the inner Power is put into action (that Power which obviously is always increasing), but it never used to be exerted in that way, in detail, on tiny things of that sort, like someone's wrong attitude or an action that doesn't conform to the Truth, anyway lots of things ... pitiable things, which I used to watch: I would smile, put the Truth-Light on them *(gesture from above),* and would leave them. But now, it's not that way: "that" comes, and it's like something that comes and says to people, things, circumstances and individuals *(in an imperative tone): "You* shall do what the Lord wills – you shall do what He wills. And beware! you shall do what He wills." *(Mother laughs)*

It makes me laugh, but it must be having some effect!

It is very material, it's in the subtle physical. And it always takes that form; it doesn't say, "You should do this" or "You should do that," or "You shouldn't do this" ... – nothing like that: "You SHALL do what the Lord wills," just like that, "You SHALL do ... and, you know, you shall do it, so beware!"

It is a strong Light, with what looks like precise little details (which probably must be translated as details of action, I don't know): they are like lines that make little marks like this *(gesture).* It's a formation.

It's a force that isn't ordinary in the material world.

235

You remember, I had that in the past (a few months or years ago), I told you, it was something that would suddenly make me bang my fist ... it was so terrible that I felt as if everything would be smashed – it's the same thing, but now organized for a definite aim: it comes fully ready, then it acts, and when it's finished, it goes. It comes, and sometimes it stays long enough: it insists and insists, as though it were pummeling the resistance; and then suddenly it stops, it's finished, it's gone. It comes into the consciousness spontaneously, it goes out of it spontaneously, and I am like a witness. Just a witness who is used as a link – an electric plug.

It goes towards the person (I see it with the inner vision, you understand) or towards the circumstances or towards the event, and it pummels it without letting go of it: "You will do what the Lord wills, it will be as the Lord wills."

I put it into words, but ...

And it's completely outside – outside – human feelings, human thoughts, human perceptions, which means it can go to someone very close, very intimate, just as it can go to someone very remote; it can go to someone full of goodwill just as it can go to someone full of ill will – with perfect impartiality. It's very interesting, there are no nuances in its action, no nuances. There may be a dosage, but the dosage seems to be measured according to the resistance. But no nuances, which means that, for its action, everyone and everything is IDENTICAL – absolutely identical; there aren't those "for" and those "against," that doesn't exist anymore; there's only something that isn't as it ought to be: it isn't as it ought to be – bang! *(Mother laughs)*

It came again just yesterday.

Generally, I have to be resting or at any rate quiet for it to come (or maybe for me to perceive it).

Voilà, mon petit.

Vol. 5, p. 216

## October 7, 1964

... Do you have a question to ask?

*No ... a question of sadhana, perhaps.... Isn't the true attitude at present to try and be as transparent as possible?*

Transparent, receptive.

*I ask myself the question because you feel that that transparency is transparent indeed, but it's a bit ... nothing – a nothing that's full, but still is nothing: you don't know. You don't know if it's a kind of higher "tamas" or...*

Above all, one should be trusting.

The big difficulty, in Matter, is that the material consciousness, that is to say, the mind in Matter, was formed under the pressure of difficulties – difficulties, obstacles, suffering, struggle. It was, so to speak, "worked out" by those things, and that gave it an imprint almost of pessimism and defeatism, which is certainly the greatest obstacle.

This is the thing I am conscious of in my own work.

The most material consciousness, the most material mind, is in the habit of having to be whipped into acting, into making effort and moving forward, otherwise it's tamas. So then, if it imagines, it always imagines the difficulty – always the obstacle, always the opposition, always the difficulty ... and that slows down the movement terribly. So it needs very concrete, very tangible and VERY REPEATED experiences to be convinced that behind all its difficulties, there is a Grace; behind all its failures, there is the Victory; behind all its pain and suffering and contradictions, there is Ananda. Of all the efforts, this is the one that has to be repeated most often: you are constantly forced to stop, put an end to, drive away, convert a pessimism, a doubt or a totally defeatist imagination.

I am speaking exclusively of the material consciousness.

Naturally, when something comes from above, it goes vrrm! like that, so everything falls silent and waits and stops. But ...

I well understand why the Truth, the Truth-Consciousness, doesn't express itself more constantly: it's because the difference between its Power and the power of Matter is so great that the power of Matter is as if canceled – but then, that doesn't mean Transformation: it means a crushing. It doesn't mean a transformation. That's what used to be done in the past: they would crush the entire material consciousness under the weight of a Power that nothing can fight, nothing can oppose; and then they would feel, "Here we are! It's happened!" It hadn't happened at all! Because the rest down below remained as it was, unchanged.

Now, there is a will to give it the full possibility of changing; well, for that, it has to be given free play, without bringing in a crushing Power – this I understand very well. But it has the obstinacy of stupidity. How many times at the moment of a suffering, for instance, when a suffering is there, acute, and you feel it's going to become intolerable, there is in the cells a little inner movement of Call: the cells send out their S.O.S. Everything stops, the suffering disappears. And often (now it's becoming more and more like that), the suffering is replaced by a feeling of blissful well-being. But the first reaction of that stupid material consciousness, its first reaction: "Ha! Let's see how long it's going to last." So, naturally, with that movement, it demolishes everything. Everything has to be started again.

I think that for the effect to be lasting (not to be, as I said, a miraculous effect that comes, dazzles, and goes away), for it to be truly the effect of a TRANSFORMATION, one has to be very, very, VERY patient. We are dealing with a very slow, very heavy, very obstinate consciousness, which cannot move on rapidly, which holds on tight to what it has, to what has seemed to it to be a "truth": even if it is a very small truth, that consciousness holds on tight to it and doesn't want to budge anymore. So to cure that takes a great deal of patience – a great, great deal of patience.

The whole thing is to endure – endure and endure.

Sri Aurobindo said it several times, in various forms: *Endure and you will conquer.... Bear – bear and you will vanquish.*

The triumph belongs to the most enduring.

And then *(Mother points to her own body),* this seems to be the lesson for these aggregates (bodies, you know, seem to me to be simply aggregates). And as long as there is, behind, a will to keep this together for some reason or other, it stays together, but ... These last few days (yesterday or the day before), there was this: a sort of completely decentralized consciousness (I am always referring to the physical consciousness, of course, not at all to the higher consciousness), a decentralized consciousness that happened to be here, there, there, in this body, that body (in what people call "this person" and "that person," but that notion doesn't quite exist anymore), and then there was a kind of intervention of a universal consciousness in the cells, as though it were asking these cells what their reason was for wanting to retain this combination (if we may say so) or this aggregate ... while in fact making them understand or feel the difficulties that come, for example, from the number of years, wear and tear, external difficulties – from all the deterioration caused by friction, wear and tear. But they seemed to be perfectly indifferent to that! ... The response of the cells was interesting enough, in the sense that they seemed to attach importance ONLY TO THE CAPACITY TO REMAIN IN CONSCIOUS CONTACT WITH THE HIGHER FORCE. It was like an aspiration (not formulated in words, naturally), and like a ... what in English they call *yearning, a longing* for that Contact with the divine Force, the Force of Harmony, the Force of Truth and ... the Force of Love, and [the cells' response was] that because of that, they valued the present combination.

It was an altogether different point of view.

I am expressing it with the mind's words because there's no other way, but it was in the field of sensation rather than anything else. And it was very clear – very clear and very continuous, without fluctuations. And then, at that moment, the universal Consciousness intervened, saying, "But here are the obstacles...." And those obstacles were clearly seen: that kind of pessimism of the mind (a formless mind that's beginning to be born and organized in these cells). But the cells themselves didn't care a whit! To them it was like a disease, they said, "Oh, that ..." (the word distorts, but it was felt as a sort of "accident" or an "inescapable disease or something that DID NOT FORM A NORMAL PART of their development and had been forced on them), "Oh, that, we don't care about it!" And then, at that moment, a sort of LOWER power to act on that mind was born; it gave the cells a MATERIAL power to separate themselves from that and reject it.

From that point of view, it was interesting. And it was after that that there was the turning point I told you about: a turning point in things as a whole, as if something truly decisive had taken place. There was a sort of trusting joy: "Ah! We're free from that nightmare."

Usually, I don't say anything until it's firmly established, because ... But anyway, that's how it was.

And at the same time, a relief – a physical relief – as if the air were easier to breathe.... Yes, it was a bit like being shut inside a shell – a suffocating shell – and ... at any rate, an opening has been made in it. You can breathe. I don't know if it's more than that, but at any rate, something has been as if torn open, and you can breathe.

It was a totally, totally material and cellular action.

But as soon as you descend into that realm, the realm of the cells and even of the cells' constitution, how much less heavy it seems! That sort of heaviness of Matter disappears: it becomes fluid and vibrant again. Which would tend to show that the heaviness, the thickness, the inertia, the immobility, is something that has been ADDED ON, it's not an essential quality of Matter – it's false Matter, Matter as we think or feel it, but not Matter itself as it is.

That was very perceptible.

The best one can do is not to have any prejudices or preconceived ideas or principles – oh, moral principles, fixed codes of conduct, "what must be done" and "what must not be done," and preconceived ideas with regard to morals, with regard to progress, and then all the social and mental conventions – there's no obstacle worse than that. I know people who wasted dozens of years trying to overcome one of those mental constructions!

If one can be like this, open – truly open in a simplicity ... you know, the simplicity of ignorance that knows it's ignorant ... like this *(gesture, hands open),* ready to receive all that comes ... then, perhaps, something will happen.

Naturally, the thirst for progress, the thirst to know, the thirst to transform yourself, and above all the thirst for Love and Truth – if you can keep that, then you go faster. Really a thirst, a need, you know, a need.... All the rest doesn't matter, what you need is THAT.

*(silence)*

To cling to what you think you know, to cling to what you feel, to cling to what you like, to cling to your habits, to cling to your so-called needs, to cling to the world as it is, that's what binds you hand and foot. You must undo all that, one thing after the other. Undo all the bonds.

This has been said thousands of times, but people go on doing the same thing.... Even those who are, you know, very eloquent, who preach this to others, they CLING – they cling to their own way of seeing, their own way of feeling, their own habit of progress, which to them is the only possible one.

No more bonds – free, free, free, free! Always ready to change everything, except ONE thing: to aspire. That thirst.

I quite understand: some people don't like the idea of a "Divine" because it immediately gets mixed up with all the European or Western conceptions (which are dreadful), and so it makes their lives a little bit more complicated – but we don't need that! The "something" we need, the Perfection we need, the Light we need, the Love we need, the Truth we need, the supreme Perfection we need – and that's all. The formulas ... the fewer the formulas, the better. A need, a need, a need ... that THE Thing alone can satisfy, nothing else, no half measure. That alone. And then, move on! Move on! Your path will be your path, it doesn't matter; any path, any path whatever, even the follies of today's American youth can be a path, it doesn't matter.

As Sri Aurobindo said, if you can't have God's love (I am translating), well then, find a way to fight with God and have a wrestler's relationship with Him.

Vol. 5, p. 222

## October 14, 1964

... These last few nights, an experience has been developing. There is a sort of objectification, like scenes unfolding in which I am one of the characters; but it isn't "me," it is some character or other that I play in order to have the double consciousness, the ordinary consciousness and the true consciousness at the same time. There was a whole series of experiences to show simultaneously the True Thing and the sort of half-death (it's his word that makes me think of this – "I am too dead ..."), the half-death of the mind. In those experiences, the state of ordinary mentality is something dry (not exactly hard because it's crumbly), lifeless, without vibration – dry, cold; and as a color, it's always grayish. And then, there is a maximum tension, an effort to understand and remember and know – know what you should do; when you go somewhere, know how you should go there; know what people are going to do, know ... Everything, you see, is a perpetual question of the mind (it's subconscious in the mind – some are conscious of it, but even in those who are apparently quiet, it's there constantly – that tension to know). And it's a sort of superficial thing, shallow, cold and dry, WITHOUT VIBRATION. At the same time, as

242

if in gusts, the true consciousness comes, as a contrast. And it happens in almost cinematographic circumstances (there is always a story, to make it more living). For instance, last night (it's one story among many, many others), the "I" that was conscious then (which isn't me, you understand), the "I" that was playing had to go somewhere: it was with other people in a certain place and had to go through the town to another place. And she knew nothing, neither the way nor the name of the place she was going to, nor the person she had to see – she knew nothing. She knew nothing, but she knew she had to go. So then, that tension: how, how can you know? How can you know? And questioning people, asking questions, trying to explain, "You know, it's like this and like that ...," innumerable details (it lasts for hours). And now and then, a flood of light – a warm, golden, living, comfortable light – and the feeling that everything is prearranged, that all that will have to be known will be known, that the way has been prepared beforehand – that all you have to do is let yourself live! It comes like that, in gusts. But then, there is an intensity of contrast between that constant effort of the mind, which is an enormous effort of tension and concentrated will, and then ... and then that glory. That comfortable glory, you know, in which you let yourself go in trusting happiness: "But everything is ready, everything is luminous, everything is known! ... All you have to do is let yourself live." All you have to do is let yourself live.

It's as if a play were performed to make it more living, more real – one subject, another subject, this, that.... If you enter a certain state, then another time enter the other state, you can remember the difference and it's useful, but in this form of a play, with the double consciousness, the opposition becomes so real, so concrete that ... you come out of it wondering, "How can you go on living in this aberration when you have once TOUCHED – touched, experienced the True Thing?"

It's as if the body were being dealt with like a child who has to be educated. Because that mind I am talking about is the physical mind, the material mind (not the speculative mind: the vibration isn't the same at all), it's the mind OF THE EARTH, the mind of everyday life, the mind you carry along in your every movement and which tires the body so much! ... Such a tension, an anguish – living is an anguish. Yes, the feeling of a living death.

This morning, when I came out of it, I said to myself, "That's odd...." But the body is learning its lesson; that way, it's learning its lesson. And yet it goes on with that nasty habit of wanting rules, of wanting to know in advance what it should do, of wanting to know in advance how it should do it, of organizing its life within a straitjacket, instead of letting itself live.

...

It is building an iron cage for yourself and getting into it.

It was exactly that.

Trying to explain to someone, "You know, it's a place like this or like that, and the person there is like this – you know, that person who did such and such a thing...."

You try out a number of landmarks ... in order to build yourself a cage. And then, suddenly, a breath – a luminous, golden, warm, relaxed, comfortable breath: "Oh, but it's obvious, that's how it is! But I will be CARRIED quite naturally to the place – what's all this complication!?"

It is the body learning its lesson. It's learning its lesson.

It's also learning the lesson of "illness" – of the illusion of illness. Oh, that's very, very amusing. Very amusing. The difference between the thing itself, as it is, the particular kind of disorder, whatever it is, and the old habit of feeling and receiving the thing, the ordinary habit, what people call an illness: "I am ill." That's very amusing. And ALWAYS, if you stay truly still (it's difficult to be really and truly still – in the vital and mind, it's very easy, but in the body's cells, to be perfectly still WITHOUT BEING TAMASIC is a little difficult, it has to be learned), but when you are able to be truly still, there is ALWAYS a little light – a warm little light, very bright and wonderfully still, behind; as if it were saying, "You only have to will." Then the body's cells panic: "Will, how? How can I? The illness is on me, I am overcome. How can I will? It's AN ILLNESS" – the whole drama (and that wasn't in sleep: I was completely awake, it was this morning), it's "an illness." Then something with a general wisdom says, "Calm down, calm down, *(laughing)* don't remain attached to your illness! Calm down. As if you wished to be ill! Calm down." So they consent – "consent," you know, like a child who has been scolded, "All right, very well, I'll try." They try – immediately, that light comes again: "You only have to will." And once or twice, for one thing or another (because the Disorder is something general: you may suffer at any spot, have a disorder at any spot if you accept a certain vibration), on THIS POINT, you consent – the next minute, it's over. Not the next minute: a few seconds and it's over. Then the cells remember: "But how come? I had a pain here ..." – pop! It all comes back. And the whole drama unfolds like that, constantly.

So if they really learned the lesson ...

Things come from outside, you can't always stop them from coming; it's like what I told you, those little black darts (you don't keep guard, you don't spend all your time protecting yourself!). But if, at that moment, you had the true attitude ... It was curious enough, because it came to the throat, and it rather bothered me, I don't like it when it comes there; so I concentrated so it wouldn't be there, and it didn't come there ... (laughing) it turned into a cold!

Oh, they are learning their lesson all the time, all the time. Everything, all that happens is ALWAYS a lesson – always. Always, always: all the quarrels, all the difficulties, all the troubles, all the so-called illnesses, everything, all the disorders are to make you learn a lesson – as soon as you've learned the lesson, it's over! But then, you are so slow and heavy, you take so much time to realize that it's a lesson that it drags on and on and on.

And for everything, ... it was a lesson to be learned. But it isn't an individual lesson, you understand; the trouble is that it doesn't depend on one individual: it depends on groups, or on a certain type of individual, or on a way of being of human life, or ... It's the WHOLE that has to learn the lesson.

Maybe ... maybe if there is a symbolic being (it's what I am beginning to ask myself), if there is a symbolic being who has the power (it takes a great deal of endurance!), the power to CONTAIN the representation of all those disorders and to work on that symbolic representation, it must help the whole. Because if an entire human way of being has to change for the Victory to be won, it's going to take millions of years! That may be why there are symbolic beings.

That's what I am now asking myself.

In the realm of ideas, there aren't any problems, everything was resolved long ago – the problem is in the fact, in the material fact of the body.... It is beginning to learn its lesson. It's beginning to learn. And then, instead of the selfish answer that consists in saying, "Ah, no! I don't want that, I don't want any of it! *(Laughing)* I am above that weakness and disorder," let it come, accept it and see what the solution is. In other words, instead of the old problem – rejection of life, rejection of the difficulty, rejection of the disorder and the flight into Nirvana – it's the acceptance of everything – and Victory.

This is really (as far as I know) the new thing Sri Aurobindo has brought. Not only the idea that it's possible, but that it's the true solution, and the idea that we can start now. I am not saying we'll reach the end now, I don't know, but the idea is that we can begin right now, the time has come when we can begin, and it's the only true solution, the other solution is no solution – well, it was a necessary experiment in the universal march, but flight is no solution: the solution is Victory. And the time has come when we can try.

All ordinary common sense (which is still triumphant in this world) tells me, "What illusions you nurse, my child! You arrange things to your satisfaction, you're sugarcoating the pill for yourself," and so on, it comes like that, regularly, in waves. Well ... it's also part of the problem. But a time will come when certain truths will be acknowledged as true and no longer disputed; then the Work will be easier. But in order to get there, there has to be at least a beginning of experience, a beginning of realization that enables you to say, "But here is the proof."

This seems to me to be the process under way.

It is a rather obscure labor that's going on at the moment.... I remember the day when Sri Aurobindo told me (we were still in the other house), he told me, "Yes, you are doing an overmental work, a creation of the Overmind, you will work heaps of miracles and the whole world will admire you! ... But that is not the Truth we want." I told you the story. Well, this memory very often comes to my aid. I said, "That's right, we don't care for the fanfare of popular victory!"

It's without glory. But it doesn't need any glory at all! I said to him, "I don't need glory and I don't care a whit for public admiration! *(Laughing)* That has no place in my consciousness."

But I understand.... Oh, how there are deeper ways to understand things!

The body is learning its lesson.

...

Life is on the verge of becoming wonderful – but we don't know how to live it. We still have to learn. When we truly learn, it will be something.

Vol. 5, p. 237


## October 21, 1964

On the 18th, I had an interesting experience. It was the doctor's birthday and I gave him a meditation, and after the meditation, he asked me to write for him what I had seen during the meditation. I had no intention of doing so, but an hour later, that is, at lunch time ...

To be clear, I should tell the whole story from the beginning.

Before the meditation, I told him, "You will let me know when you have finished – I don't want to let you know." So I finished what I had to do, then I took a look and said to myself, "Let's see now, let's try." And I simply made a formation and put it on him, saying, "Now, it's over." Then I didn't move, I stayed very quiet. It took about half a minute, even less; he opened his eyes, and then it was over. But when I saw him again at lunchtime, I asked him, "When you indicated to me it was over, what did you feel?" He told me, "I felt *(Mother laughs)* the Force was going, so I thought it was over..." Well, his answer showed me the exact difference.... He should have felt, "Mother is calling me, Mother is telling me it's over," but he felt the Force was going.

Then, as he saw I was talking to him, he took the opportunity to ask me, "I would really like to have visions." I answered him all that had to be answered, and I told him that, in the last analysis, it's only the Lord who decides when we should have visions, when we shouldn't have them, when we are making progress, when we aren't, and so on. Then, in the most hypocritical tone *(laughing),* like someone who says something to be polite but doesn't believe a word of it, he said, "Oh, then we are indeed fortunate, because we have the Lord among us." I pretended to believe he was sincere, and I answered him, "No, no, no! You can't say that, it's not possible – I AM NOT the Lord!" And I explained a little the consciousness I have of the Lord, I said, "You shouldn't think I am the Lord ..." (in my thought, it was: "I am not the Lord as YOU imagine Him"), "because if I were the Lord *(Mother smiles, amused),* you would have visions and you would be cured."

This took place around 11:30. In the afternoon, usually I take my bath and stretch out a little, a good while, over there.

I said to the Lord, "And after all, why *(laughing)* can't I do something for people like this who are really nice? Why can't I work miracles?" I asked Him this half seriously, half in jest. Then all of a sudden, it became very serious. All of a sudden, the Presence was very intense and it was very serious. Then I felt something that said in an absolutely positive way (it was translated into words), "You MUST NOT have powers." And the total understanding.

You must not have powers.

And it was a world of ... Incidents of this kind bring about a world of parallels, of experiences and so on. So I began writing (it came, as always, through successive "sedimentations"). The first sedimentation gave this:

If you approach me in the hope of obtaining favours, you will be frustrated, because I have no powers at my disposal.

It came in French too:

"Ceux qui s'approchent de moi avec l'intention d'obtenir des faveurs seront déçus, parce que je ne dispose pas de pouvoirs."

But the true version is this one (I replaced *s'approchent* with *viennent* and *dispose* with *détiens,* and I put the present tense), it's from the last sedimentation:

"Ceux qui viennent a moi avec l'intention d'obtenir des faveurs sont déçus, parce que je ne détiens pas de pouvoirs."

And what's almost fantastic is that a whole ARMY OF ADVERSE FORCES WERE REDUCED TO SILENCE – immediately. And the atmosphere was clarified, relieved.

Then, taking a good look, I understood that it is that mixture in people's thoughts, in people's feelings, in their approach to spiritual life, which is catastrophic – they always "want" something, they always "demand" something, they always "expect" something. In fact, it's a perpetual bargaining. It's not the need to give yourself, not the need to melt into the Divine, to disappear into the Divine – no: they try to take, to obtain what they want.

And for several hours (it lasted several hours, from that moment till night) the atmosphere was clear, light, luminous – and my body, my body was in such joy! As if it were floating in the air.

Afterwards, everything came back – not "everything": something didn't come back, which was definitely settled, but one part of the attacks was clarified.

It was so concrete! I have never felt it so concretely, something seemed to have been completely swept away.

*But how is your renouncing or your having no powers sufficient to sweep the adverse forces away?*

No, it's the fact that I ANNOUNCED it.

*That you announced it?*

No powers – I knew very well I had no powers! And I couldn't have cared less because I understood perfectly well that what is being attempted now isn't miraculous events at all, but the LOGICAL and normal and inevitable CONSEQUENCE of the supramental transformation – that is the whole point. That I know and knew, and that's why I didn't even bother about powers; anyway it hadn't even remotely occurred to me that I might work a miracle for the doctor or for this or that other person who approaches me – I didn't think about it, it didn't enter my consciousness. Only, on the 18th, through that occasion it entered my consciousness, and so I asked the question to find out why I never thought about it: "Why?" And I was positively told: "You MUST NOT wield powers, because that's not the way things should be done."

*I do understand, but...*

But there was a whole mass of adverse forces (I saw all sorts of things, I don't want to go into details) that were trying to PREVENT me from declaring it. And I had to make an effort *(Mother makes a gesture of driving back an obstructing mass)* ... not an effort to fight, but an effort to overcome something, as when you are hemmed in, an effort to break a shell so as to be able to proclaim it. And the minute I did that, the minute I took my paper and started writing – pfft! it all went, as if swept away! ... That, yes, that I understand! That's the Lord's Power. No intermediate power can do that – it was a splendor, you know! As if all of a sudden the physical world had become a solar world, splendid and radiant, and so light, so harmonious! It was a marvel. For hours.

And it made me understand that one of the most considerable obstacles is that deviation of aspiration into a thirst for something. But who doesn't deviate? ... You see, I always start by looking at myself and at all that I know of this being's conscious life (that's my first observation), and all the images come; well, the self-offering, the perfectly pure aspiration that doesn't expect any result – absolutely free from the slightest idea of result – the aspiration in its essential purity ... that's not frequent. It's not frequent.

Now the conditions are totally different, but I see the mass of aspirations, of approaches, and I always compare with my attitude towards Sri Aurobindo at that time, when it was he who, to me, represented the Intermediary; well, I understand ... I understand that the absolutely pure thing, that is, free of all mixture with the ego consciousness (it's the ego consciousness), free of all mixture with the ego consciousness, is ... it's still rare.

And it's this mixture with the ego consciousness (I am speaking here not from the personal, but from the general standpoint) that, when the words were written, was swept away by something as powerful as a hurricane, without the violence of a hurricane – scattered, dissolved, swept away! All those things that were pressing, against which I constantly had to strive in order to move on – swept away! And they didn't come back completely.

That state didn't remain (that state was a state of Victory). But things haven't come back as they were, and they will never come back as they were. Something has really been clarified. And it isn't a personal, individual question: it's something general.

You understand, the word "favor" is deliberate. It's quite deliberate, it really means a favor – to be helped in making the necessary progress is all very well, but what they want is the result WITHOUT HAVING TO WALK THE PATH, and that's what is impossible, that's what must not be.

Basically, that's always what men ask of religions; the "God" of religion is a god who must do them favors: "I believe in You, therefore You must do this for me" (it isn't formulated so bluntly, but it is like that), it isn't the aspiration to be guided on the path in order to do exactly what should be done for the Transformation to take place. And that's what I was clearly told: "It MUST NOT be miraculous powers." The power of the Help is there, fully, of course, but the miraculous power that does things without their being the result of a progress achieved, that must not be.

*(Mother goes on copying her note)*

And I replaced the future tense with the present, deliberately too, because it isn't something new: it has always been that way; it isn't that I now announce they will be disappointed – they have always been disappointed. And asserting this fact is what had the power of dispelling a whole mass of formations: not only formations of beings of the vital or hostile beings, but the false mental formations of human beings.

And here, I wrote: *Je ne détiens pas de pouvoirs* ["I possess no powers"], which is better than *Je ne dispose pas de pouvoirs* ["I have no powers at my disposal"]. I had chosen the word *dispose* in French (chosen, I mean, not mentally), but the word *dispose* came along with the meaning that the power wasn't at my disposal – there is a nuance. I mean that if, by some aberration (it would really be an aberration), if by some aberration I had the desire to work a miracle, I wouldn't be able to – it would be contrary to the supreme Will. It isn't

252

that I am deliberately making the choice, "No, I won't work miracles" – I can't, that's not the way, it MUST NOT be like that.

*You'll have a lot of difficulty driving that into people's heads!*

Oh, but there has been a dreadful revolt in the Ashram's atmosphere! Not in their conscious mind, but in the subconscient – a terrible revolt. In order to write down my declaration, in order to formulate it, I had to overcome a whole mass of things, it was extraordinary! There have even been individual reactions: "Then I am going away." I said, "Very well, here is the exact proof."

It was interesting.

The doctor himself received it as a blow – he was trembling inside.

*No, what should be asked, since we're always asking for something, is for the substance to become conscious enough to receive the Force and itself work its own "miracle," get cured, or this or that, anyway do the work.*

Yes, it mustn't be a "favor." "Give me the Force to be what I should be," that, yes.

Vol. 5, p. 249

## October 30, 1964

I feel we are turning a corner.

It's very narrow. Do you know mountain roads?... All of a sudden, you come to a corner, a sharp turn, and you can't see the other side – below is a precipice, behind is the rock – and the path ... it would seem to have grown narrower in order to turn the corner, it's become quite narrow. I've encountered that in the mountains – often. And now, I feel we are turning the corner; but we are beginning to turn it, in the sense that we are beginning to see the other side, and the consciousness (always the body consciousness) is on the verge of a bedazzlement, like the first glimpses of something marvelous – not positively unexpected because that is what we wanted, but truly marvelous. And at the same time, there is that old habit of meeting difficulties at every step, of receiving blows at every step, the habit of a painful labor, which takes away the spontaneousness of an unalloyed joy; it gives a sort of ... not a doubt that things will be that way, but you wonder, "Has it already come? Have we reached the end?" and you don't dare think you have reached the end. That attitude, naturally, isn't favorable, it still belongs to the domain of the old reason; but it receives support from the usual recommendations: "You shouldn't give free rein to wild imaginings and hopes, you should be very level-headed, very patient, very slow to get carried away." So there is an alternation of a sort of crouching, timorously moving forward step by step in order not to slide down into the hole, and a glorious sense of wonder: "Oh, are things really that way?!"

This has been the body's feeling for three or four days.

But it keeps increasing, and that sort of "crouching" is greatly lessened by the knowledge and experience that if you are per-fect-ly calm, all goes well – always, even in the worst difficulties.... Very recently, the day before yesterday, there was (always on the physical level; it can't be called "health," but it's the body's functioning) a rather serious attack, which found expression in a rather unpleasant pain; it came with unusual brutality. Then, immediately, the body remembered and said, "Peace, peace ... Lord, Your Peace, Lord, Your Peace ..." and it relaxed in Peace. And in an objectively perceptible way, the pain went away.

It tried to come back and then went away, tried to come back and went away.... The process lasted the whole night.

But it was extraordinarily obvious! The physical conditions were absolutely the same, and one minute earlier, there was an almost intolerable pain, which went away like that, in the Lord's Peace.

It's already two days since it went away, and it hasn't come back. I don't know if it will come back.

But then, the body is learning one thing, and learning it not as an effort that has to be made, but as a spontaneous condition: it's that ALL that happens is for progress. All that happens is for reaching the true state, the one that is expected of the cells so that the Realization may be accomplished – even the blows, even the pains, even apparent disorganizations, all that is on purpose. And it's only when the body takes it in the wrong way, like a fool, that it gets worse and insists; whereas if the body immediately says, "Very well, Lord, what do I have to learn?" and responds with calm, calm, the relaxation of calm, immediately the difficulty becomes tolerable, and after a moment, it gets better.

*(silence)*

If the work were limited to a single body, a single mass or quantity, a single aggregate of cells, it would be very easy by comparison, but the interchange, the union, the reciprocity is automatic and spontaneous, and constant. You feel that the effect going on here [in Mother's body] naturally, necessarily and spontaneously has its consequences very far and wide; only, it makes difficulties worse, and that's why it takes a lot of time. There is a correspondence, you see: something new occurs in the body, a new pain, a new disorganization, something unexpected, and after some time, I learn that this person or that person has the very same thing!

That, too, the body knows, and it doesn't protest – that goes without saying, it's the way things are. But it prolongs the work considerably.... Probably there will be a corresponding endurance. Because there is neither regret nor revolt nor fatigue; really, the body is ready to be very happy, all it wants is to be very happy – it dare not be yet, that's the only point. It's something it dare not be: "Are things ... are they really as good as that!" It dare not. But it's very happy: "I have no cause for complaint, everything is fine; there are difficulties, but without difficulties there is no progress."

255

Yes, what it still has is the fear of joy – not positively "fear," but ... a timidity in the face of joy. Sometimes waves of an intense Bliss come to it, waves of Ananda, in which all the cells begin to swell with a joyous golden light, and then ... it's as if one dared not – one dare not. That's the difficulty.

The people around me don't help. Those immediately around me have no faith.

So that doesn't help, because the mental atmosphere isn't favorable. Mentally, you look at it and smile; but the body feels it a little bit, it feels a little the pressure of defeatist formations around. But it knows why those around are like that – from the material point of view, those around are just what is needed, just what is needed; the body needs such an atmosphere so that material difficulties aren't made worse. So it's perfectly happy, only it dare not be joyous; it immediately says, "Oh, it's still too beautiful a thing for life as it is!"

I don't know how long it will last.

*(silence)*

Now and then, when I am perfectly at rest and perfectly quiet (when I know, for instance, that I have half an hour of perfect quiet and no one will disturb me), at such time, the Lord becomes very close, very close, and often I feel Him saying (not with words), saying to my body, "Let yourself go, let yourself go; be joyous, be joyous, let yourself go, relax," and the immediate result is that it completely relaxes, and I go into a bliss – but I no longer have any contact with the outside! The body goes into a deep trance, I think, and it loses all contact; for instance, the clock strikes, but I don't hear it.

One should be able to keep that bliss while being quite active and hard at work. I am not referring to the inner joy, not at all, there's no question of that, it's out of the question, it's immutably established: I am referring to that Joy IN THE BODY ITSELF.

That sort of quiet satisfaction which it feels, now it feels it even when there are sharp pains, with the trusting feeling

256

that it's all with a view to transformation and progress and the future Realization. It no longer worries – it no longer worries at all, it no longer frets at all, it no longer even has the sense of the effort to be made in order to endure: there's a smile.

But the glimpses of the True Thing, all of a sudden, are so wonderful that ... Only, the gap between the present state and THAT is still wide, and it seems that for THAT to settle in once and for all, It must become natural.

Voilà.

## November 4, 1964

For the first time yesterday, I had in a flash – it lasted just a flash – for the first time in my life, I had the PHYSICAL experience of the Supreme's presence in a personal form. It wasn't a defined form, but it was a personal form. And it came in the wake of a series of experiences in which I saw the different attitudes of different categories of people or thinkers, according to their conviction. And it came as if that form were saying to my body (it was a PHYSICAL presence), as if it were saying, really with words (it was a translation; the words are always a translation – I don't know what language the Supreme speaks (!), but it is translated, it must be translated in everyone's brain according to his own language), as if He were telling me, "Through you" (that is, through this, the body) "I am charging ..." (it was like a conquest, a battle), "I am charging to conquer the physical world." That's how it was. And the sensation was really of an all-powerful Being whose proportions were like ours, but who was everywhere at once, and really of a physical "charge" to chase away all the dark little demons of Ignorance, and those little demons were like black vibrations. But He had something like a form, a color ... and above all, there was a contact – a contact, a sensation. That's the first time.

I have never tried to see a personal form, and it always seemed to me an impossibility, as if it were childishness and a diminishing; but this came quite unexpectedly, spontaneously, stunningly: a flash. I was so astonished.... The astonishment made it go away.

The first time in my life.

It was a physical presence, with a form, but a form ... It was odd, it was a form ... As soon as you try to describe it, it seems difficult. But I still have the memory of having seen a sort of form with a quite special – but MATERIAL – light and quality, and which ... Yes, maybe it is *(Mother looks silently)* ... maybe that is the form of the supramental being?... It was very young, but with such power! A power, almost a muscular power (but there were no "muscles"), and there was a charge: he literally charged down on people and things, and everything was immediately scattered and upset. And he laughed! He laughed, there was such joy! A joy, a laughter, and, yes, he said, "Through you ..." (it was through my physical presence), "I am charging ... ," I am charging down on Darkness or Falsehood, or whatever – words come afterwards and spoil everything – but the idea was ... (no, it wasn't an idea, it was something that was said). It lasted just long enough for me to notice it – a flash. Then I said, "Ah! ... " I had, you know, that reaction of astonishment.

The first time – completely unexpected.

And now, during the whole meditation, the presence was there, that presence was there, but so concrete! So concrete, so powerful. Maybe it is ... maybe there is a will to make me see the supramental form? It's possible. It was PHYSICAL – it was physical. And there was that CONTACT, the physical contact. But the contact, I have it all the time – as soon as I stop, there is a massive contact, and weightless at the same time.

Didn't you feel anything particular?

*Yes, I feel this massive thing present.*

A presence.

*Yes, very strong.*

That's right. Oh! ...

Yes, it's like what you can see in a flash. It was a form – a form derived from the human form; it wasn't something that contrasted sharply with the human form, but it had something the human form doesn't have: a suppleness and power in the movement. And it was radiant, a little radiant, as though it emanated a little light; but not something that gives you the feeling of the supernatural: not like apparitions in paintings, not that – it was material, it was ...

It's the first time. I was sitting like this, as I was just now, the same thing, nothing particular. And it filled me with something inexpressible, a sense of fullness, of joy – of triumph, you know.

It was so brief that I didn't intend to talk about it, because words ... You're always afraid of adding to the experience. But this presence was so concrete just now, during the meditation, and time passed so extraordinarily quickly, like a flash. And I had the same feeling, oh, such a fullness! ...

He said (it was translated into words: I heard them, in what language I don't know, but I understood very well), I heard the words and he said to me: "Through you, I am charging...." I am charging, as if he were launching into a battle against the world's Falsehood. "Through you, I am charging ..." that's perfectly clear, and it was against ... I saw little aggregates of black dots being scattered.

But at that moment, I felt something like the representation of certain states of mind, certain intellectual conditions, a whole series of things that represented doubts, negations, ignorant attitudes, revolts ... and all at once, this came.

And I still see the form I saw: like that, as if he were launching into battle – but only what you can see in a flash.

Vol. 5, p. 268

## November 7, 1964

*Mother looks very pale.*

For the past three days there has been a constant phenomenon: something ... I don't know what it is ... as if the whole head were being emptied *(Mother shows the blood going downward).* Physically, that's what you feel before fainting, as if all the blood were leaving the head: the head empties, and then you faint.

The first time it came was the day before yesterday; I was resting (after lunch I rest for half an hour), and at the end of my rest, suddenly I see myself – I see myself standing near my bed, very tall, with a magnificent dress, and with someone dressed in white beside me. And I saw this just when I seemed about to faint: I was at once the person standing and the person on the bed who was watching, and at the same time I felt that thing flowing downward, flowing downward from the head – the head empties completely. And the person standing smiled, while the person in the bed wondered, "What! I am fainting – but I am in my bed!" There. And as it was time for me to "wake up" (that is, to return to the outer consciousness), I came back.

And I was left with this problem: who was standing there? ... Very tall, with a splendid dress, and then a person (who was a human person, but much shorter), a white person beside me, all white. And just when I become conscious of this, when I see this, the head empties completely of something, and the face of the person standing (who was me) smiles. And then, the other part of me that was lying down in my bed said, "What! It's odd, I am fainting; how is it that I am fainting? – I am in my bed!"

I got up and didn't feel anything physically, it didn't correspond to anything.

I haven't had any explanation. I don't have any clue. What does it mean? I don't know.

Obviously, it's something!

But since then it has been like that, and particularly last night when it was terribly cold [monsoon + windstorm], I was completely still in my bed, with an almost constant feeling of that "something" flowing downward – of the head emptying.

It continued this morning, a very bizarre impression. Yet, physically, I feel fine, I took my food, I ...

*But you look very pale.*

Very pale?

*Yes, it struck me. You're very pale, as if you didn't have much blood.*

But in the beginning when you arrived and I sat down, it came very strongly – very strongly, as if everything ... vrrt! were going away.

So I'm pale, am I?

*Yes, you were more so ten minutes ago.*

Because I have concentrated.

It's always the same thing, you know: I strongly feel that the explanation, or even the physical phenomenon, is the translation of something going on elsewhere. But I don't know what it is.... It is a new process.

*But once, you had a similar experience with all the symptoms of fainting: when the center of your physical consciousness left you.*

Yes, but that's not ...

*(long silence)*

I feel it as something linked to the circulatory system, but ...

*(Mother goes into a meditation, looking for the real cause)*

I don't understand. And those things keep recurring until you have understood ... So that's troublesome.

\* \* \*

*At the end of the conversation, Mother consults her appointment book:*

261

There's a crush of people.... I ought to have some peace.

When I have some peace, I am perfectly well. But ...

There's obviously something going on, but I don't know what it is.... It seems to be going quickly now, a little more quickly.

But the mind (if we can call that "mind"), the physical stupidity cannot understand the process: what's happening, what's going on, it doesn't understand. The body only has, as soon as it is at peace, the feeling of bathing in the Lord. That's all. But in the body (not in its attributes, I mean when neither force nor energy nor power or any of that is there), in it there is, not something powerful, but a very gentle tranquillity. But not even the feeling of a certainty, nothing. It's negative, rather: the sensation of an absence of limits, something very vast, very vast, very tranquil, very tranquil – very vast, very tranquil. A sort of – yes, like a gentle trust, but not the certainty of transformation, for instance, nothing of that kind.

It's strange, it isn't a passivity; it isn't passive, but it's so tranquil, so tranquil, with a sort of – yes – gentleness.

I don't know. We'll see, maybe by the next time I will have found out?

Vol. 5, p. 270

### November 12, 1964

With those faintings of sorts I told you about the other day, I observed (it went on the whole day), and I saw (saw with the inner vision): it is like the travel – at times as quick as a flash, at other times slow and very measured – of a force that starts from one point to reach another one. That force travels along a precise route, which isn't always the same and seems to include certain cells on its way: the starting point and the arrival point *(Mother draws a curve in the air)*. If you aren't on your guard, if you are taken by surprise, during the passage of the force (whether long or short) you feel the same sensation ("you," meaning the body), the same sensation as before fainting: it's the phenomenon that precedes fainting. But if you are attentive, if you stay still and look, you see that it starts from one point, reaches another point, and then it's over – what that force had to do has been done, and there is no APPARENT consequence in the rest of the body.

I mentioned (not with so many details) the fact to the doctor, not in the hope that he would know, but because (it's amusing) when I speak to him, he tries to understand, of course, and then there is the mirror of his mental knowledge, and in that mirror, sometimes I find the key! *(Laughing)* You understand, the scientific key of what's going on.

As a matter of fact, it was after I spoke to him (I mentioned it to him as a sort of dizzy spell) that I was able to perceive precisely those "routes." I wondered if it wasn't the projection on a magnifying screen of phenomena taking place between different brain cells? Because those sorts of dizzy spells always follow (today there hasn't been anything at all), they always follow a moment or a day of intense aspiration for the transformation of the brain. It may be that.... You know, all those brain cells in there are hitched together, and if those "hitchings" are disturbed, generally people become deranged; and it gave me the impression of a magnifying projection enabling me to follow the connections established between certain brain cells, so that the functioning may not be the automatic, semiconscious functioning of the old state anymore and the brain may truly become the instrument of the higher Force. Because the formula of my aspiration is always, "Lord, take possession of this brain," and it's always after this intense aspiration that those kinds of phenomena occur. So it is to prepare the brain to be the direct expression of the higher Force.

This is what I have learned these last few days.

I also noted something down, an experience I had this morning. It lasted half an hour, and during that half-hour ... *(Mother looks for her notes among a series of little scraps of paper)* ... You know that with people who have a revelation, their state of consciousness changes all at once, and at that moment they have the feeling that everything is changed; then, the next moment, or after a certain time, they realize that all the work ... (how should I put it?) of working out the experience remains to be done; that it was only like a flash lasting a certain length of time and that they have to *work it out* through a process of transformation. This is the usual idea.

And all of a sudden, I saw – that's not it at all! When they have the experience, at the time of the experience, it is the thing ITSELF, the perfection ITSELF that has been reached, and they are in a state of perfection; and it is because they COME OUT of it that they feel they have to slowly prepare themselves for the result.... I don't know if I am expressing myself clearly, but my notation was like this: perfection is there, always, coexisting with imperfection – perfection and imperfection are coexistent, always, and not only simultaneous, but in the SAME PLACE *(Mother presses her two hands together),* I don't know how to put it – coexistent. Which means that at any second and in any conditions, you can attain perfection: it isn't something that has to be gained little by little, through successive progress; perfection is THERE, and YOU change states, from the state of imperfection to the state of perfection; and it is the capacity to remain in that state of perfection that grows for some reason or other and gives you the feeling that you must "prepare" yourself or "transform" yourself.

That was very real and very concrete.

*(Mother gives the text of her note:)*

The perfection is there coexistent with the imperfection and attainable at each and any moment.

Yes, it isn't something that becomes: perfection is an absolute state that can be attained at any moment.

And then, the conclusion is very interesting *(Mother looks for another scrap of paper)....* You remember, I told you that

264

for the body consciousness, the problem that remains hard to solve is that notion (to me, it has become just a notion, it isn't a truth), of the preexistence of all things: of the state in which each thing IS, even in its unfolding.... You understand, it would be as if all the POINTS of the unfolding were preexistent.

I was on the threshold of an understanding (an "understanding": I am not talking about a mental understanding, I am talking about the experience of the fact). The experience of the fact is the experience of the coexistence of the static state and the state of development – of the eternal static state and the state of eternal unfolding (indefinite, rather, not to use the same word). Then, at that point, there was this vision *(Mother holds out a note):*

"When the truth manifests, the false vibration disappears ...

Disappears, it is CANCELED ("CANCELED" is the word).

"... as if it had never existed, before the vibration of truth that replaces it. This is the real basis of the theory of Illusion."

Yes, all of a sudden I understood what they really meant when they said that the physical world as it is is illusory.

You can say it is illusory only if it has no lasting existence, of course. And this experience – which I saw, felt, lived – is that the vibration of truth literally CANCELS the vibration of falsehood, which doesn't exist – it existed only as an illusion for the false consciousness we have.

I don't know if I am making myself understood, but it's very interesting.

*It isn't the world that's illusory, it's the perception ...*

It's the perception of the world that's illusory – the perception of the world, the perception we have of it, is illusory. The world has a concrete, real existence in what we could call the Eternal's Consciousness. But we, the human consciousness has an illusory perception of this world.

And when the Vibration of Truth triumphs, you see and have the sense of the true reality of the world; and as I said, that illusory perception disappears immediately. it is canceled.

Which means that their way of saying or thinking or understanding that "all that is has existed from all eternity" isn't ... it isn't "all that is" as they see it and conceive of it, it isn't even the principle of all that is, it is ... it is the ONE Truth that's eternal, and the unfolding ... It's difficult to say.... The unfolding follows a law and a process that are quite different from what we conceive or from what we perceive.

It's the same thing again: Truth is there, Falsehood is there *(Mother presses her two hands together);* perfection is there, imperfection is there *(same gesture);* they're perfectly coexistent, in the same place – the minute you perceive perfection, imperfection disappears, the Illusion disappears.

Only, I am not speaking here of a mental conception of some vague and general state: I am referring to that state of infinitesimal vibration (which they discovered when they tried to find the makeup of Matter: that's what they are trying to reduce Matter to), it is that state of vibration, it is THERE, it's in that state of vibration that, for the concrete world, imperfection must be replaced by perfection. Do you understand what I am saying? Or does it make no sense?

*I don't see. You mean it's at that stage, at that level that ...*

Yes, it's at that level that the change must take place. At the mental or even vital level, it's a psychological question, it's nothing, it's not really THE THING (it's the thing expressed in a HUMAN consciousness). Because the other day ... the other day, suddenly I went out of humanity. My consciousness went right out of the human consciousness. And then I said to myself, "But ... all that they say, all that they know, all that they have attempted, all that so-called knowledge which has been accumulated on earth, it's nothing! It's something that belongs only to MAN – eliminate man ... and everything exists!

And all the explanations man has given about things are like zero." That's it: everything exists.

I had the experience of the universe outside the human perception of that experience; and then the vanity of that human experience was so obvious, you know, that at that point a door began to open onto something else.

All this is perhaps the Lord taking possession of the brain?

It's hard to explain, but as an experience it was extraordinary. You see, we live INSIDE a formation, which was the human – human – formation, all human knowledge.... Because I was beginning to try to find what we know of human life and life on earth: it's almost nothing at all, a very small thing (Sri Aurobindo wrote somewhere that there were billions of years BEFORE). So what we know is practically nil. All right. So, to get out of that. And it led me quite naturally to go out of humanity – out of the earth, of the universe; of the earth that has been the product of all that we know (at any rate we are explaining what happened, what was there). And then suddenly, yes, the futility, the vanity of that knowledge appeared very clearly, and there was a sort of flash of something else.

*(Mother goes into that flash*
*and remains in contemplation)*

Vol. 5, p. 274

## March 20, 1965

You know, problems of illness, problems of possession (vital and mental possession), problems of egos that refuse to yield (and this results in circumstances which, humanly, are described in the ordinary way: such and such a thing has happened to so-and-so – but that's not how it comes into the consciousness), well, if you look at things in a sufficiently general way, those problems REMAIN problems. There is indeed something, but a "something" that is still elusive (elusive in its essence): it has to do with feeling, with sensation, with perception, also with aspiration – it has to do with all that, and it is ... what we habitually call divine Love (that is, essential Love, that which is expressed by Love and seems to be beyond the Manifestation and Nonmanifestation, which, naturally, becomes Love in the Manifestation). And That would be the ALL-POWERFUL expression. In other words, That is what would have the power to transform into divine consciousness and substance all the chaos we now call "world."

There was the experience of That [the experience of the great pulsations], but it was an experience ... (how can I put it?) of a drop that would be an infinite, or of a second that would be an eternity. While the experience is there, there is absolute certitude; but outwardly, everything starts up again as it was one minute before – That *(gesture of pulsation for a second)*, puff! everything is changed; then everything starts up again, with perhaps a slight change that's perceptible only to a consciousness (perceptible to the consciousness, but not concretely perceptible), and with, generally, violent reactions in the Disorder: something that revolts.

So, to our logic (which is obviously stupid, but anyway), it means that the goal is still very far away, that the world isn't ready.

You see, all of a sudden, through the intensity of the aspiration, of that sort of thirst for "the Thing," contact is made – contact is made; it isn't even a contact between two different things, it is ... That which is all. But it is in Time that the Thing is expressed, and then it doesn't last, so much so that even the resulting effect doesn't seem to be able to last. Although there is something there that contradicts: the effect is lasting, but imperceptible as long as it isn't general; so immediately it's a translation into the world of Time, Space, and so on.

Whereas "That" is beyond Time and Space. When you have gone from the Creation to Noncreation (which do not follow each other, they are concomitant), if you go beyond, you encounter this "something" which, I don't know why, I call Love.... Probably because the vibration of true Love (what I call divine Love, which is at work in the world) bears the closest resemblance to That. It is something absolutely inexpressible, which belongs neither to "receiving" nor to "giving," neither to uniting nor to absorbing, nothing like all that.... It's something very particular.

*(long silence)*

I remember, that night I spoke of, I WAS that Pulsation, and each burst of pulsation created. Well, it was the first expression of That in the Manifestation; and it was already in action, it was already in movement. But the Vibration BEHIND that is ... I might say the potentiality of everything – of everything that becomes perceptible to us through the Manifestation; because it is everything that in our consciousness gets divided into various possibilities, like truth, love, life, power, etc. (but all that is nothing, of course, it's dust in comparison). And it's everything together; not the union of different things: it's EVERYTHING – everything, and it is absolutely ONE, but everything is there. And That is what one finds beyond the Manifestation and the Nonmanifestation – the Manifestation almost looks like child's play in comparison. That Pulsation was the origin of the Manifestation.

And Nonmanifestation is blissful Immobility – it's more than that, but it's essentially that: blissful Immobility. It's the supreme and supremely divine essence of rest. And both [Manifestation and Nonmanifestation] are together, and they come from That.

I have a very strong feeling that it's only That, only with That that things can change, all the rest is inadequate.

And if I remember right, Sri Aurobindo said that this manifestation (which he too calls Love) would take place AFTER the supramental manifestation, didn't he?

*First Truth, then Love.*

Then Love.

Yes, he said there were different "levels" in the Supramental – but that *(smiling)* is the sauce that makes things more easily digestible (!) Everyone says things in the way he finds the easiest to assimilate.

But the experience – the experience – is always beyond words, always.

*(silence)*

And it's rather strange: all these cells have in their aspiration an Ananda of Light, of Truth, but that doesn't satisfy them completely, that is, they still have a sensation of helplessness.... Of course, it's all the Darkness, all the Falsehood, all the Disorder, all the Disharmony of the world that you constantly absorb every time you breathe (not to speak of all that you absorb with food, and all the rest – the worst of all – that you absorb mentally through contact with others, mentally and vitally). And all that has to be changed, transformed, constantly. Well, the cells feel their helplessness to face the work if That, that Vibration, isn't there. They find that Vibration irresistible, they find it's the only irresistible one.

Naturally, there is a progress (a work that can be noted, discerned) in the consciousness of the cells, in their receptivity and their resistance to Disorder; but it's just a progress, meaning that the possibility, and even the recurrence of disorder, decomposition, disharmony, wrong functioning, none of that is conquered at all, not at all.... There is a growing feeling of being the docile instrument of the supreme Will, to such a point that the cells feel that whatever they may be asked to do they can do, but there is at the same time the very clear perception that the field of what is asked of them is still very limited – very limited – and that they would be unable to do better or more. And that's what gives weight to the notion of wear and tear, of aging – not that they feel like that, but in material fact, what is asked of them is very limited.

Vol. 6, p. 54

## March 24, 1965

*... I am quite submerged in matter.*

That's right.

*It's no joke.*

No, but don't you want to get out of it?

*Oh, I am assailed! And then, my body also doesn't help me much.*

Oh, no, the body never helps. Now I am convinced of it. You can, to some extent, help your body (not to a great extent, but up to a point, anyway), you can help your body, but the body doesn't help you. Its vibration is at ground level, always.

*Yes, it's heavy.*

Without exception. Without exception, it brings you down, and above all it's something that makes you dull, so dull – something that doesn't vibrate.

*It's heavy.*

But with this sadhana I am doing, there are some threads that lead you along, and I have some sentences by Sri Aurobindo.... For the other sadhanas, I was used to it: all that he said was clear, it showed the way, you didn't have to look for it. But here, he didn't do it; he only said or made certain remarks now and then, and those remarks are helpful to me. (There is also my meeting him at night, but I don't want to count too much on that, because ... you grow too anxious for the contact, and that spoils everything.) There are in that way several remarks that have remained with me and are, yes, like leading threads. For instance, "Endure ... endure."

Let us assume you have a pain somewhere; the instinct (the instinct of the body, of the cells) is to tense up and try to reject – which is the worst thing to do: it invariably increases the pain. So the first thing that must be taught to the body is to stay still – not to have any reactions. Above all no tensing up, and not even a movement of rejection – a perfect stillness. That's corporeal equanimity.

A perfect stillness.

After perfect stillness, there is the movement of inner aspiration (I am always referring to the aspiration of the cells – I am using words to describe something wordless, but there is no other way to express oneself), the *surrender,* that is to say, the SPONTANEOUS AND TOTAL acceptance of the supreme Will (which is unknown to us). Does the total Will want things to go this way or that way, that is, towards the disintegration of certain elements or towards ...? And then again, there are endless nuances: there is the passage from one height to another (I am speaking of cellular realizations, of course, don't forget that), I mean that you have a certain inner equilibrium, an equilibrium of movement, of life, and it's understood that in order to go from one movement to a higher movement, there is almost always a descent, then a new ascent – there is a transition. So does the shock received impel you to go down in order to climb up again, or does it impel you do go down in order to abandon old movements? Because there are cellular ways of being that have to disappear in order to give way to others; there are others that climb down in order to climb up again with a higher harmony and organization. This is the second point. And you should wait and see WITHOUT POSTULATING IN ADVANCE what has to be. There is especially, of course, the desire: the desire to be comfortable, the desire to be in peace and all that – that must cease absolutely and disappear. You must be absolutely without any reaction, like this (*gesture of immobile offering Upward, palms open*). And then, when you are like that ("you," meaning the cells), after a while the perception comes of the category the movement belongs to, and you just have to follow the perception, whether it is that something must disappear and be replaced by something else (which one doesn't know yet), or whether it is that something must be transformed.

And so forth. And it's like that all the time.

...

272

[T]he thought is absolutely still, everything takes place directly: questions of vibrations. Well, that's the only way to know what has to be done. If it goes through the mind – especially through that physical thought, which is absolutely idiotic, absolutely – you can't know; as long as that works, you are always driven to do what you shouldn't do, particularly to have the wrong reaction: the reaction that helps the forces of disorder and darkness instead of contradicting them. And I am not talking about anxiety because it's a long, a very long time since my body stopped having any anxiety – a long time, years – but anxiety is like swallowing a cup of poison.

This is what is called physical yoga.

To get over all that. And the only way to do it is for all, every one of the cells, every second, to be *(gesture of immobile offering Upward)* in an adoration, an aspiration – an adoration, an aspiration, an adoration, an aspiration.... And nothing else. Then, after a time, there is joy, too, and then it ends with blissful trust. When that trust is established, everything will be fine. But ... it's much easier said than done. Only, for the moment, I am convinced that it is the only way, there is no other. There. Give your hands....

Vol. 6, p. 60

## March 27, 1965

*I find that all those meats they have given me to "build me up" make me heavy, especially with the hot days starting again. Couldn't I go back to vegetarian food?*

It doesn't really have an action on the consciousness, I am absolutely certain of that. Meat can give the body a feeling of great solidity, but in my opinion, solidity is most important, most important – I don't believe in a spirituality that "etherealizes," that's the old falsehood of the past.

273

No, the body's heaviness ... You must not only conceive but understand and accept that the purpose of this heaviness is to repair the body's internal damage, and the body must in fact change this heaviness into a sort of constant tranquillity so that order is restored everywhere.

I don't believe that the impression of being "light" is a good impression. Because both the so-called lightness and the so-called heaviness have ABSOLUTELY nothing to do with the yoga and the Transformation. All those are human sensations. The truth is quite different from and quite independent of those things. The truth, of course, is the cells' conscious aspiration to the Supreme; it is the only thing that can actually transform the body; and it is very, very independent of the domain of sensations.

On the contrary, it's good for the nerves to calm down, and I think that when the nerves strengthen, their first movement is to calm down, and that gives the impression of a heaviness, almost the impression of a tamas, but it's a sort of quiet stability, which is necessary. There. That's how I see it.

Basically, in order to cure the misdeeds of that physical mind, it's not bad to become ... we could say in jest, vegetarian in the sense of becoming a plant – the peaceful life of a plant, like that *(gesture, stretched out in the sun).*

Yes, there is a kind of vegetative immobility which is excellent for overcoming the agitation – the frantic agitation – of that physical mind.... Oh, look, it's the sensation of a waterlily floating on water: those large leaves spreading out like that – a very quiet, still water, and a waterlily.

The waterlily is the white flower opening up to the light, above those large, floating leaves.... Oh, how good it is to be carried.

When the nerves have really calmed down because one has eaten well, one can go into a blissful contemplation – don't be occupied with anything, above all don't try to think: like this *(gesture of floating, offered),* invoking the Lord and his

Harmony – a luminous harmony – and then lying like that at least half an hour, three quarters of an hour after the meal. It's very good, it's excellent. Don't fall asleep: blissful – nothing, being nothing. Nothing but a blissful tranquillity. That's the best remedy.

I think that's easier after eating well!

Try to be a waterlily.... A waterlily, that's pretty!

Even watching animals is very pretty – they know far better than men how to rest.

We could make a slogan: if you want to keep well, be a waterlily! *(Mother laughs)* ... I see the picture of a pond in the sun.

In reality, I deserve some credit for asking people to eat well.... You know that I had difficulties: for two days, it was nearly impossible for me to eat – and I am so glad! But I always scold myself: it's a weakness – a moral weakness. I am in a very good position to say so, because I have the same difficulty as you with those questions of food, and that's very bad. It's not out of personal taste for food that I am preaching (!), but in order to react against the other tendency. Every time something comes and prevents me from eating, immediately, spontaneously, the body says, "Oh, thank you, Lord, I don't have to eat!" I catch myself and give myself a slap.

Vol. 6, p. 64

## April 10, 1965

I have been asked a question *(Mother looks for a note):*

*How can I love the Lord? I have never seen Him and never He speaks to me.*

This is my answer:

*It is not what one sees or hears that one loves, it is love that one loves through the forms and sounds, and of all love the most perfect love, the most loving love is the Lord's love.*

When I wrote it, it was an extraordinarily intense experience: one cannot love anything but love, and it is love that one loves behind all things – it is love that one loves. It is Love that loves itself everywhere.

### April 17, 1965

*You said there had been a step forward. Is there something new?*

I had always said that there were two points on which the future hadn't been revealed to me. First, what the first form of supramental life on earth would be exactly, that is to say, the stage that will follow man as he is – just as there was a stage that followed the animal (and which, in fact, disappeared), what is the stage that will follow man, and will perhaps be destined to disappear, too? Then the other point, which was more personal: could the transformation of this body go far enough to allow an indefinite prolongation, or would the work on the cells be somehow partly wasted?

I can't say I have answers, but in both directions there has been some opening, as it were. The feeling that I was in front of a wall and it's opening up, I am allowed to proceed. Well, the conclusions aren't there yet, but in both directions we have actually taken a step forward because it's open – there isn't a wall any longer, it's open.

Especially that feeling of being stuck has gone away.

The first discoveries aren't worth telling because they aren't precise or concrete or definitive enough. There is just this sense of relief: instead of standing in front of something that blocks your way, phew! you can breathe and walk on.

The consequences will be for later.

*(long silence)*

The transition between the two appears really possible only through the entry – the conscious and willed entry – of a supramentalized consciousness into a body that we could call an "improved physical body," in other words, the human physical body as it is now, but improved: the improvement produced, for instance, by a TRUE physical training, not in its present exaggerated form but in its true sense. It's something I have seen fairly clearly: in an evolution (physical training is developing very fast nowadays, it's not even half a century since it started), in evolution, that physical training will bring an improvement, that is, a suppleness, a balance, an endurance, and a harmony; these are the four qualities – suppleness (plasticity), balance between the various parts of the being, endurance, and harmony of the body – that will make it a more supple instrument for the supramentalized consciousness.

So the transition: a conscious and willed utilization by a supramentalized consciousness of a body prepared in that way. This body must be brought to the peak of its development and of the utilization of the cells in order to be ... yes, consciously impregnated with the supreme forces (which is being done here [in Mother] at the moment), and this to the utmost of its capacities. And if the consciousness that inhabits that body, that animates that body, has the required qualities in sufficient amount, it should normally be able to utilize that body to the utmost of its capacity of transformation, with the result that the waste caused by the death of decomposing cells should be reduced to a minimum – to what extent?... That's precisely what still belongs to the unknown.

That would correspond to what Sri Aurobindo called the prolongation of life at will, for an indefinite length of time.

But as things are at present, it would seem there is a transitional period in which the consciousness has to switch from this body to another, better prepared body – better prepared outwardly, physically (not inwardly); "outwardly," I mean, having acquired certain aptitudes through the present development, which this body doesn't have, of the four qualities – which it doesn't have in sufficient amount and *completeness*. That is to say, those four qualities must be in perfect accord and in sufficient amount to be able to bear the work of transformation.

I don't know if I can make myself understood....

*Yes, but you are talking about "switching" to a new body?*

In that case, one would have to switch to a new body. But a switching (from the occult point of view, that's a known thing), a switching not to a body to be born, but to an already formed body. It would take place through a sort of identification of the psychic personality of the body to be changed with the other, receiving body – but that, the fusions of psychic personalities, it's possible, *(laughing)* I know the procedure! But it requires the abolition of the ego – yes, the abolition of the ego is certainly necessary; but if the abolition of the ego is sufficient in the supramentalized individuality (can I use the word individuality? I don't know ... it's neither "personality" nor "individuality"), in the supramentalized being, if the abolition of the ego is done, completed, that being has the power to completely neutralize the presence of the ego in the other being. And then, through that neutralization, the shrinking that always comes from a reincarnation would be canceled – that's the dreadful thing, you see, that time lost in the shrinking into a new being! While through that conscious passage – willed and conscious – from one body to the other, the being whose ego no longer exists has an almost total power to abolish the other ego.

All that occult mechanism needs to be developed, but for the consciousness it's almost rational.

That would be the procedure.

The conditions for the almost indefinite prolongation of the life of the body are known, or almost known (they are more than sensed – they are known), and they are learned through the work that must be done to counteract the EXTREME

FRAGILITY of the physical balance of the body undergoing the transformation. It's a study every minute, as it were, almost every second. This is the extremely difficult part. It is difficult because of all the reasons I have already explained, because of the intrusion of forces that are in a state of imbalance and have to be, as they come along, brought back to the new state of balance. That's where you find the sign of the unknown.

Voilà. It's there.

But it's not blocked anymore. The path is open, one can see – one can see.

It will come.

But the transition which is really hard to perceive is the transition from the animal creation (which is perpetuated, of course) to the supramental formation; that transition hasn't taken place yet. The passage from that creation to the supramental creation of a body – that's what we don't know. It is the passage from one to the other: how? It still is a somewhat more difficult problem than the passage from animal to man, you understand, because the process of human creation is refined, but it is the same ... Oh!

*(The conversation is cut short by the doctor's entry)*

... While here, it is a new form of creation.

Vol 6, p. 71


**April 21, 1965**

*About the last conversation, a quotation from Sri Aurobindo came to mind.*

Which quotation?

*You were speaking of the first form of supramental life.*

On the earth.

*Yes, in an "improved physical body." I wondered about that ... especially when you speak of "switching to a new body."*

What were you wondering?

*This, in particular: The difference between the present human body and the supramental creation is so considerable, the substance must be so different...*

Of course.

*... that I am wondering to what extent even an improved physical body could be of use? Because the thing is going to be so different. Whether this body is old and bent or young and very supple, does it really make any difference, since ...*

That's not what I meant by "improved." Whether the body is young or old doesn't make any difference, because the advantages are balanced by drawbacks. I have also looked at the problem – it doesn't make any difference.

Switching to a new body may become a necessity, that's all, but it's secondary.

What I meant by an "improved physical body" is that sort of mastery over the body that's being gained nowadays through physical training. I have seen lately magazines showing how it had started: the results in the beginning and today's results; and from the standpoint of the harmony of forms (I am not talking about excesses – there are excesses everywhere – I am talking about what can be done in the best possible conditions), from the standpoint of the harmony of forms, of strength and a certain sense of beauty, of the development of certain capacities of endurance and skill, of precision in the execution combined with strength, it's quite remarkable if you think of how recent physical training is. And it's spreading very quickly nowadays, which means that the proportion of the human population that is interested in it and practices it is snowballing. So when I saw all those photos (for me, it's especially through pictures that I see), it occurred to me that through those qualities, the cells, the cellular aggregates acquire a plasticity, a receptivity, a force that make the substance more supple for the permeation of the supramental forces.

Let's take the sense of form, for example (I am giving one example among many others). Evolution is openly moving towards diminishing the difference between the female and the male forms: the ideal that's being created makes female forms more masculine and gives male forms a certain grace and suppleness, with the result that they increasingly resemble what I had seen all the way up, beyond the worlds of the creation, on the "threshold," if I can call it that, of the world of form. At the beginning of the century, I had seen, before even knowing of Sri Aurobindo's existence and without having ever heard the word "supramental" or the idea of it or anything, I had seen there, all the way up, on the threshold of the Formless, at the extreme limit, an ideal form that resembled the human form, which was an idealized human form: neither man nor woman. A luminous form, a form of golden light. When I read what Sri Aurobindo wrote, I said, "But what I saw was the supramental form!" Without having the faintest idea that it might exist. Well, the ideal of form we are now moving towards resembles what I saw. That's why I said: since there is an evolutionary concentration on this point, on the physical, bodily form, it must mean that Nature is preparing something for that Descent and that embodiment – it seems logical to me. That's what I meant by an improved physical form.

The other point is quite secondary, it's incidental, it isn't in the line of evolution. I am only saying that it's a method that CAN be used, and it has been used in the past.

*Switching to a new body?*

Switching to a new body. The method may be used again, IF IT IS FELT TO BE NECESSARY. It wasn't the central idea, it was perfectly incidental – it may happen. And all I said was that the consciousness of these cells having lost the sense of ego (I think they have lost it, though this body was formed without the sense of ego – at any rate, if it was necessary at a given time, it no longer is), having lost the sense of ego, it finds no difficulty in manifesting in another body. And this is a perfectly practical and material experience, I mean I have had multiple experiences of this consciousness using that body, this body, that other body ... for certain things; of course it was momentary, not in a permanent way, but at will and anyway lasting long enough to make me experience it concretely.

But this is a personal affair, it has nothing to do with the public or collectivity, while the other point is interesting: I have a feeling it is Nature's collaboration, pushing humanity in that direction in order to prepare a matter more receptive to the ideal that wants to manifest.

*When I thought about the last conversation again, it seemed to me that the gap between the two creations, the animal and the supramental, is so huge that it doesn't make much difference whether the body is more supple and so on.*

The gap isn't so huge. The gap is huge in the MODE OF CREATION, that's where there is a huge gap. That's where it is difficult to conceive how we will switch from one to the other and how there can be intermediaries.

*Exactly, I suddenly remembered in this connection a quotation from Sri Aurobindo that seemed to me interesting. It's in "The Human Cycle," at the end of "The Human Cycle." Here's what he says: "It may well be that, once started, it [the supramental endeavour] may not advance rapidly even to its first decisive stage; it may be that it will take long centuries of effort to come into some kind of permanent birth. But that is not altogether inevitable, for the principle of such changes in Nature seems to be a long obscure preparation followed by a swift gathering up and precipitation of the elements into the new birth, a rapid conversion, a transformation that in its luminous moment figures like a miracle."*

This is very interesting.... Yes *(laughing),* he said this to me a few days ago!

It is true.

Basically, once there is a body formed, precisely, by an ideal and an increasing development, a body with sufficient stuff and capacities, sufficient potential, there may very well be a rapid Descent of a supramental form, just as there was one with the human form. Because I know that (I know it from having lived it), I know that when the transition – a very obscure transition – from the animal to man (of which they have found fairly convincing traces) was sufficient, when the result was plastic enough, there was a Descent – there was a mental descent of the human creation. And they were beings (there was a double descent; it was in fact particular in that it was double, male and female: it wasn't the descent of a single being, it was the descent of two beings), they were beings who lived in Nature an animal life, but with a mental consciousness; but there was no conflict with the general harmony. All the memories are absolutely clear of a spontaneous, animal life, perfectly natural, in Nature. A marvelously beautiful Nature that strangely resembles the nature in Ceylon and tropical countries: water, trees, fruits, flowers.... And a life in harmony with animals: there was no sense of fear or difference. It was a very luminous, very harmonious, and very NATURAL life, in Nature.

And strangely, the story of Paradise would seem to be a mental distortion of what really happened. Of course, it all became ridiculous, and also with a tendency ... it gives you the feeling that a hostile will or an Asuric being tried to use that to make it the basis for a religion and to keep man under his thumb. But that's another matter.

But that spontaneous, natural, harmonious life – very harmonious, extremely beautiful and luminous and easy! ... A harmonious rhythm in Nature. A luminous animality, in fact.

That's how we began, and it began that way because there was a descent of the higher human mental consciousness into the form that existed. The phenomenon may recur in the same way, with the difference that it can be more conscious and willed – there may be the intervention of a conscious will. It would, or it could happen through an occult process – well, I don't know, there are all sorts of possibilities, one of which could be the conscious passage of a being who has used the old human body for his development and his yoga, and who would leave that form once it became unnecessary in order to enter a form capable of adapting to the new growth.

Here, the two possibilities meet.

But for the time being, there is no question of that because although the development of physical training is extremely rapid, it's still clear that it may take hundreds of years.

There is a quotation from Sri Aurobindo in which he says that the first point to be acquired is prolongation of life at will – it isn't directly immortality: it is prolongation of life at will. He wrote it in the articles on *The Supramental Manifestation*.

Vol.6, p. 74

## May 5, 1965

*You look pale.*

I am not feeling very well.

*(silence)*

I feel as if I am not here, and this has been going on since ...

My body is far away from me.

Last time, in the afternoon of the day you came, the 30th, I was rather in a poor condition [Mother had "heart" troubles]. And since then I have felt as if ... I am rather far away from my body.... I am in a very, very diluted consciousness *(widespread gesture)*, very diluted.

*(Mother goes into meditation)*

I have a feeling that only one thing exists: making contact – putting the divine Vibration in contact with Matter. And this is the only thing which is REAL. Things seem to have clarified these past few days, since the 30th; and this morning when I got up, it was so strong that it was really the only thing existing. To such a point that there was a spontaneous perception that whatever thought clothes this thing in, or whatever the organization of life, it's totally unimportant – it's only men who attach importance to that, but from the standpoint of the Work, only this matters: being in this state I am in (which is a very particular state), in which the vibration, the vibration of Matter is put in contact, united – united – with the divine Vibration.

All the rest ... unreal.

*(long silence)*

I feel as if the circulation isn't working, I don't know how to explain it.

*Mother goes into concentration)*

It's like this *(vast, expansive gesture)*, im-mo-bile.... But with a great intensity of vibration – the vibration that doesn't move.

...

*(long meditation)*

It can go on like that indefinitely.

So what are we going to do? If it goes on, it'll be a long time before we've finished our work!

*We have time.*

Indeed we have – when one thinks one has time, it takes years! Anyway, I am not doing it deliberately – it's thrust upon me, and then there's nothing that can be done.

But are things better for you?

*Yes, Mother.*

*(silence)*

There is a growing sense of a Power that's beginning to be limitless. But that state is in fact linked with those difficulties [heart or circulatory troubles]. And, you know, I don't make any decisions, I don't do anything [to attain that state]: I am like this *(immobile gesture, palms open to the Heights)*, in "something" that feels as if it could be eternally like that.

But within it, I perceive waves, movements (and sometimes concentrations, when it has to do with world events) that have a stupendous power.

We just have to keep still and, well, we'll see what will happen anyway.

Vol. 6, p. 87

## May 8, 1965

It has been a revolution in the atmosphere, that's why I am telling you about it. Because all the experiences described [in *Savitri*] are precisely the experiences I have. So then, suddenly, in the body .. I was over there in the music room, and H. was reading to me; then when she had finished reading, all of a sudden the body sat up straight in an aspiration and a prayer of such intensity! It was a dreadful anguish, you know: "See, the whole experience is here [in Mother], complete, total, perfect, and because this thing [the body] has lived too long, it no longer has the power of expression." And it said, "But why, Lord? Why, why do You take away from me the power of expression because this has lived too long?" It was a sort of revolution in the body's consciousness.

Things have been much better since, much better. There has been a decisive change.

You see, it was the exact description of the body's present state, yet it constantly feels fragile, in a precarious balance. And then, with all its aspiration, it said, "But WHY? Why? ... See, the experience is all there – why isn't it expressed?"

As always *(laughing)*, I had the feeling that the Lord was laughing and saying to me, "But since such is your will, it will be that way!" Meaning simply: it's you who CHOSE to be like that.

And it's perfectly true. All our incapacities, all our limitations, all our impossibilities, it's this idiotic Matter that chooses them all – not with intelligence, but with a sort of feeling that "that's how things must be," that they are "naturally" like that. An adherence – an idiotic adherence – to the mode of the lower nature.

Then there was laughter, tears, a whole revolution, and afterwards all was fine.

But nobody on earth will be able to convince me it isn't because this material nature chooses to be that way that it is that way.

And the Lord looks on, smiles, waits ... *(laughing)* for the body to be cured of its idiocy.

He does all that is needed, but ... we don't take any notice.

It's the trigger of FAITH that's not there, that famous faith Sri Aurobindo always mentions.

When people write me long letters (what letters I receive! laments all the time: my health is going wrong, my work is going wrong, my relationships are going wrong – laments all the time), and I always see, behind, that Consciousness, luminous, magnificent, marvelous – sun-filled, you know – exactly as if to say, "Whenever will you be cured of that mania!" The mania of the tragic and the lower.

Somewhere in the reason, one understands – it isn't that reason doesn't understand, but the reason has no power to make this matter obey.

And every minute, I have now the feeling of a choice between victory and defeat, sun and shadow, harmony and disorder, the easy solution ... truly, the comfortable or pleasant and the unpleasant; and the feeling that if you don't intervene with authority, there's a sort of ... oh, it's a combination of cowardice and spinelessness: it's something limp – limp, you know, slack.

When I speak like this, it's very simple and it seems very easy, but EVERY MINUTE you are hanging between three possibilities (generally three) for the body: the fainting or the acute suffering, the indifferent, mechanical movement, or the glorious Mastery. And I am talking about washing your eyes, rinsing your mouth, doing any of those absolutely indifferent little things (in big things it always goes well because nature is in the habit of thinking that one should bear oneself "properly" to rise to the occasion – all that is ridiculous), but in little things, that's how it is. So the head whirls, and hup! ... And you can see – you can see with extreme precision – the three possibilities, and if you aren't constantly attentive *(gesture of a closed fist, of authority and control),* the physical nature, with such repulsive spinelessness, you know, absolutely disgusting, lets itself go.

This repeats itself hundreds upon hundreds of times a day.... So if this isn't called "sadhana," I don't know what a sadhana is! You see, eating is a sadhana, sleeping is a sadhana, washing is a sadhana, everything is a sadhana. What's a sadhana least of all is, for instance, receiving someone, because the body immediately keeps quite still – it calls the Lord and says, "Now be here," and then everything is fine (because it keeps still). The visitor comes, the body smiles, everything is fine – the Lord is there, so of course everything goes very smoothly. But when we're dealing with what we call "material" things, the things of daily life, it's hell, because of that idiot.

...

But what to people is unconscious, what they don't understand or call "illness," is to me as clear as daylight; and it's always a CHOICE, there is always a choice every minute (for the material nature), and if the will isn't unshakable, if you aren't holding on to the higher Will with desperate and unrelenting eagerness, you let yourself go; and then the body becomes stupid: it faints, it has pains.... That same day when I couldn't eat (after lunch I always rest for some time to ... well, those are the hours when I put the body in direct reception of the Force – it doesn't last very long, I don't have much time), but as soon as I lay down on the chaise longue, such pains! Howling pains that take hold of you ... *(gesture to the waist)* at those spots that are open to the adverse attacks. I was lying down, but I was fully conscious then and I said to myself, "Oh, very well! You want to make a big scene.... All right, I will bear everything and I won't make a sound – and I won't budge, and you're going to keep still." Then I started repeating my mantra quietly, as though the body weren't in any pain. And after a while, the pain went away. The body saw it was no use, so it went away!

And I KNOW it's the same for everything, for all "illnesses," without exception. I see, I know the "origin" of illnesses, of the various disorders, all that is now crystal clear (it's a story that it could take hours and days to tell), and that's how it is. So when, in a more or less dogmatic or literary way, the sages say, "Disorder occurs because the nature has decided to be in disorder," it's not so silly.

It's ... oh, a spinelessness which is one of the things most contrary to the divine Glory. The spinelessness that accepts illness, you know. And I am saying this to my body, not to anyone else – others, that's not my business, it's their work, not mine; I mean, I am present [in them] only as the divine Consciousness, and then it's very easy, a very easy work; but the work here, the sadhana in here ...

But sick people ... when I tell them, "Be sincere," I know what I mean: if they REALLY want the Divine, all that must stop. That's all.

...

You know what's called *self-pity?* *(Mother caresses her cheek)* "Poor little thing, how you suffer! How you are to be pitied!" Well, the material nature is like that, it says, "I want to be like You, Lord; but then why do You leave me in this condition?" – a good slap and march!

## June 2, 1965

*Mother tries to read a paper with a magnifying glass:*

It's quite peculiar, it doesn't help me anymore.... Is it clean? *(Mother holds out the magnifying glass to Satprem)* There seems to be a haze.

*Yes, it's clean.*

It's rather strange, this eyesight. There always seems to be a veil between me and things, constantly; I am so used to it; I see everything very well, but as if there were a slight veil. Then all of a sudden, without any apparent reason (an outwardly logical reason, I mean), a thing becomes clear, precise, sharp *(gesture: leaping to the eyes)* – the next minute, it's over. Sometimes it's a word in a letter or written somewhere, sometimes it's an object. And it is a different quality of vision, a vision ... (how can I explain it?) as if light were shining from within things instead of shining on them: it isn't a reflected light. It isn't luminous, it isn't like a candle, for instance, or a lamp, not that, but instead of being lit by a projected light, things have their own light, which doesn't radiate.

It's becoming more and more frequent, but with perfect illogic. Which means that I don't understand the logic of it at all; I don't know why this thing ["lights up"] rather than that thing, or that rather than this: suddenly something leaps to the eyes – "Ah!" – and it's gone in a flash. And the vision is so precise! Extraordinary, with the full understanding of the thing seen while you are seeing it. Otherwise, everything is as if behind ... is it a veil? I don't know.

Sometimes (often), the same thing happens to me with speech. I feel as if I am speaking from very far away or from behind a woolly substance that blunts the precision of vibrations. In its extreme form, it's because of this that I sometimes don't hear – nothing: when some people speak to me, I hear absolutely nothing. With others, I hear the drone of a sound devoid of meaning. And with other people, I hear EVERYTHING they say. But it's a different way of hearing:

what I hear is the vibration of their thought and that's what makes it very clear.

I have the same thing with hearing, the same thing with sight. It begins with taste, but that doesn't interest me much, so I don't take notice, I don't pay attention. But a few days ago I had the experience that the quality of tastes had changed: certain things had an artificial taste (the usual taste is an artificial taste) while others carried in themselves a TRUE taste; so this is very clear – very clear and very precise. But it's not so interesting a subject, so I am not occupied with it so much.

What struck me the most is sight. Hearing ... for a very, very long time – years – I've had the feeling that when people don't think very clearly, I can't hear. But that's not quite the point: it's when their consciousness isn't ALIVE in what they're saying – it's not so much a question of "thought," it's their consciousness that isn't ALIVE in what they're saying; it's a mental machine; then I don't understand anything at all – nothing. When their consciousness is alive, it reaches me. And I have noticed, for instance, that people whom I don't hear think it's because I am deaf in the ordinary way, so they start shouting – which is even worse! Then it's as if they were throwing stones in my face.

There must be an action on the organs.

But it's my eyes that I find the most interesting. For instance, I noticed this while washing early in the morning: I go into the bathroom before turning the light on, because I turn it on from inside; but I see just as clearly as when the light is on! It makes no difference. And then everything was as if behind a kind of veil. Then I turned my attention (or rather my attention was drawn) and I said to myself, "But all this is becoming so lackluster, it's completely uninteresting!" And I started thinking (not thinking, but becoming aware of one thing or another), and suddenly, I saw that phenomenon of a bottle in the cupboard becoming so clear, so ... with an inner life (gesture as if the bottle lit up from inside). "Oh!" I said – the next minute, it was over.

But I seemed to be told, "Yes, you can. You no longer see this way, but you can see that way; you no longer see the ordinary way, but you can see ..." *(inward gesture).* I have been left with enough vision to be able to move around freely, but this is clearly the preparation for a vision through the inner light rather than projected light. And it is ... oh, it's warm, living, intense – and of such precision! You see everything at the same time, not only the color and shape, but the character of the vibration: in a liquid, the character of its vibration – it's marvelous. Only, it lasts a moment, it's like promises that come and tell you (like when you make a promise to someone to comfort him and give him heart), "It will be like this." Very well. *(Mother laughs)* In how many centuries, I don't know!

But when I used to use this magnifying glass, I could read very well (I stopped because of those hemorrhages, though my eyes seem to be well again), but now it's absolutely no use! *(Mother looks at a file with the magnifying glass)* It doesn't grow any clearer, there is always the same cloudiness. It's bigger, that's all. *(Mother looks again)* Strange, it's bigger but it's the same thing, there is the same veil ... of unreality.

As for the sense of smell, the nature of my sense of smell changed long, long ago. To begin with, I practiced this (a long time ago, years, many years ago): being able to smell only when I wanted to and only what I wanted to. And it was perfectly mastered. It already prepared the instrument a great deal. I can see it was already a preparation. I can smell things ... I can smell the vibratory quality of things rather than simply their odor. There is a whole classification of odors: there are odors that lighten you, as if they opened up horizons to you – they lighten you, make you lighter, more joyful; there are odors that excite you (those belong to the category of odors I learnt not to smell); as for all the odors that disgust you, I smell them only when I want to – when I want to know, I smell them, but when I don't want to know, I don't. Now it's automatic. But my sense of smell was very much cultivated even when I was just a child, very long ago: at that time I cultivated the eyes and the sense of smell, both. But my eyes have been used for everything, for all the visions, so it's something much more complex, while the sense of smell has remained as it was: I can smell people's psychological state when I come near them; I can smell it, it has an odor – there are very special odors ... a whole gamut. I've had that for a very, very long time, it's something that's quite dominated, mastered. I am able not to smell anything at all: when, for instance, there are bad odors that upset the body's system, I can cut off the connection completely.

But I don't notice a great change in this domain because it had already been cultivated very much, while my eyes are much more ... (how can I put it?) ahead, in the sense that there is already a much greater difference between the old habit of seeing and the present one. I seem to be behind a veil – that's really the feeling: a veil; and then, suddenly, something lives with the true vibration. But that's rare, it's still rare.... Probably *(laughing)* there aren't many things worth seeing!

Oh, listen, it was Y.'s birthday the other day. I told her to come. She came: her face was exactly like her monkey's! She sat down in front of me, we exchanged a few words, then I concentrated and closed my eyes, and then I opened my eyes – she had the face of the ideal madonna! So beautiful! And as I had seen the monkey (the monkey wasn't ugly, but it was a monkey, of course), and then that, "Ah!" it struck me, I thought, "What wonderful plasticity." A face ... oh, a truly beautiful face, perfectly harmonious and pure, with such a lovely aspiration – oh, a beautiful face! Then I looked a few times: it was no longer one or the other, it was ... it was something (what she usually is, I mean), and it was behind the veil. But those two visions were without the veil.

And for me that's how it is, I don't see people, I no longer see (but that has been going on for a long time), I no longer see the way people do, the way they are used to seeing. At times someone tells me, "Have you noticed, so-and-so is like this or like that?" I answer, "No, I haven't seen anything."

And at other times I see things no one else sees! It's a much more complete development than simply switching from one vision to the other.

But my senses of smell and vision were developed a lot between the ages of twenty and twenty-four. It was a conscious, willed, methodical education, which had interesting results. And which did a great deal to prepare the instrument for now.

## July 21, 1965

There is a slight hope that this material mind, the mind of the cells, will be transformed.

*This is good news!*

Isn't it! I am quite astonished. I noticed it yesterday or the day before. I wasn't well, anyway things weren't pleasant, and all of a sudden, here was all this mind saying a prayer. A prayer ... you know how I used to say prayers before, in *Prayers and Meditations:* it was the Mind saying prayers; it would have experiences and say prayers; well, here we are, now it's the experience of all the cells: an intense aspiration, and suddenly all this starts expressing it in words.

I noted it.

And then, interestingly enough ...

It was dinner time; there had been (there always is) a fatigue, a tension, the need for more harmony in the atmosphere ... it's becoming a little heavy going; and there I was, sitting, when all of a sudden, all this straightened up like a flame, oh, in a great intensity, and then it was as if this body-mind, on behalf of the body (it was the body beginning to be mentalized), were saying a prayer ... *(Mother looks for a note)* And it very much has the sense of the oneness of Matter (this has been very strong for a long, long time, but it's becoming very conscious: a sort of identity); so there was the sense of the totality of

294

Matter – terrestrial, human Matter, human Matter – and it said:

"I am tired of our unworthiness. But it is not to rest that this body aspires ...

And this was felt in all the cells.

"... it is not to rest that this body aspires, it is to the glory of Your Consciousness, the glory of Your Light, the glory of Your Power, and above all ...

Here, it became still much more intense:

"... to the glory of Your all-powerful and eternal Love."

And all these words had such concrete meaning!

I wrote this very fast, then I left it there. But here's this mind showing itself to be like the other ... *(Mother looks for a second note),* it has a sort of concern for perfection in the expression; and in the afternoon of the next day (it generally happens after my bath; there is a sort of special activity at that time), after my bath it was in that state and I had to write this (it had become quite like a prayer):

"OM, supreme Lord,

God of kindness and mercy,

OM, supreme Lord,

God of love and beatitude ...

When it came to "beatitude" ... all the cells seemed to be swollen.

"... I am tired of our infirmity. But it is not to rest that this body aspires, it aspires to the plenitude of Your Consciousness, it aspires to the splendor of Your Light, it aspires to the magnificence of Your Power; above all, it aspires to the glory of Your all-powerful and eternal Love."

There is a sort of concrete content in the words, which has nothing to do with the mind. It is something lived – not just felt: lived.

And then, in the afternoon, it was no longer a prayer, but the observation of a fact *(Mother looks for a third note)*.... I found it was becoming interesting. It said:

"The other states of being ...

If you knew with what sort of disdain it spoke, such a superior air!

"The other states of being, the vital, the mind, may enjoy the intermediate contacts ...

In other words, all the intermediate states of being, also the gods, the entities and all those things. And it spoke with a power and a sort of dignity – yes, it was dignity, almost pride, but not an arrogant pride, nothing of the sort. It was the sense of a nobility.

"... The supreme Lord alone can satisfy me."

And then, there was suddenly such a clear vision that the supremely perfect alone can give this body plenitude *(gesture of junction between the High and the Low)*.

I found that interesting.

It's the beginning of something.

*(silence)*

It started with disgust – a disgust ... a sickening disgust – at all this misery, all this weakness, all this fatigue, all this discomfort, all this friction and grating, oof! ... And it was very interesting because there was that disgust, and along with it came a sort of suggestion of Annihilation, of Nothingness: of eternal Peace, you understand. And it swept all that away, as if the whole body straightened up: "Hey, but that's not it! That's not what I want. I want ..." (and then there was a dazzling burst of light – a dazzling golden light) ... "I want the splendor of Your Consciousness."

That was an experience.

*(silence)*

There is still a bit of friction, but anyway it's better. Just before you came ... You know, there are two, three of them hurling at me everyone's demands, the work to be done, the answers to be given, the checks to be signed; it's quite a task ... you are harassed, mauled as though by claws. And there is this fatigue I feel every day, always, and because of which I need to be left absolutely undisturbed (you seem to be clawed); and I saw it was because all the work this body is made to do doesn't come from That to which it aspires – it doesn't come from up above: it comes from here, from all around, and that's why it grates, as if something were being ground. Then, very consciously, this mind called on that aspiration and on equanimity, on cellular equality: "Well, this is the time to be in equality," and instantly a sort of quiet immobility was established, and things were better, I was able to go to the end.

I feel as if the tail of the solution had been caught. Now, naturally, we must *work it out*.

Anyway, there is some hope.

I had always been under the impression of what Sri Aurobindo said: "This instrument [the physical mind] is useless, it can only be got rid of...." It was very difficult to get rid of it because it was so intimately linked to the aggregate of the physical body and its present form ... it was difficult; and when I tried and a deeper consciousness tried to manifest, it used to cause fainting. I mean that the union, the fusion, the identification with the Supreme Presence without that, without this physical mind, by annulling it, caused fainting. I didn't know what to do. Now that it's collaborating, and collaborating consciously (and with a great power in the sensation, it seems), maybe things are going to change.

Everything that was mental ... I remember very clearly the state I was in when I wrote those *Prayers and Meditations*, especially when I wrote them here (all those I wrote here in 1914): it seems to me cold and dry ... yes, dry, lifeless. It's luminous, it's lovely, pleasant, but it's cold, lifeless. Whereas

this aspiration here [in the cellular mind], oh, it has a power –
a power of realization – quite an extraordinary power. If this
becomes organized, it will be possible to do something. There
is an accumulated power there.

Vol. 6, p. 184

## August 7, 1965

This morning, for, oh, at least a good hour, an experience
came: the true attitude and true role of the material mind –
lived, not thought. Lived. It was interesting. A sort of tranquil
beatitude.... It was about the relationship between the constant
state and the action that keeps coming from outside and
interrupts (or has the habit of interrupting when it shouldn't),
interrupts this constant state. There were examples, and the
first that came was you, the relationship with you, and the way
out of the "state of illness," I might say, and also the complete
blossoming of the consciousness, the harmony of the whole
being – what this new realization can do to change all that.

It lasted a good hour. ... it was between 4:30 and 5 this
morning.

But it was truly interesting! I understood; I said to myself,
"If life becomes constantly like this, then, then ... we will no
longer complain about anything."

And all the disorders were not only erased in their unpleasant,
disagreeable effects (that is to say, the pain had disappeared, to
speak their ordinary language), but were consciously TAKING
PART in the progress of the being. Then it becomes splendid!

... [W]hen I talk it stops the experience and I have to wait
for some time before it recurs – it never recurs in the same
way. Which means that the experience I had today, now it's
finished. I have talked about it, it's finished. I have to move
ahead towards something better. If you don't talk, you can
keep the experience for a time, till the effect is extinguished.

When you talk, it's finished; it belongs to the past and you have to move ahead towards something new.

Something is always, always, always pushing me towards the new – one more step. That's good.

*But what was it about? An action of the material mind?*

An attitude.

*An attitude of the material mind?*

An attitude, but ... oh, not willed or concerted, nothing like that: simply it had understood.

It had learned to keep silent and act.

To keep silent and act. Oh, it was lovely!

*(silence)*

Every time I express it, it recedes farther into the past.

... *(Mother looks at Satprem:)* You have a question? Ask.

*No, I didn't have any question, I was immersed in what you were saying.*

It followed a long curve.... It began with a deep disgust for its [the material mind's] habitual activity; I started catching (not now: it's been going on for weeks), catching all its routine and almost automatic activities – I have said it several times: this material mind is defeatist, always pessimistic, meddlesome, grumbling, disgruntled, lacking in faith, lacking in trust.... Even when it tends to be joyful and content, something comes and says, "Ah, stop it, because you'll get another knock." That sort of thing. It went on for weeks, and a continuous, constant work.... It always ended in the offering. There was a beginning of progress when ... No, first I should tell all that happened before. To begin with, the japa, the mantra, for instance, was taken as a discipline; then from the state of discipline it changed into a state of satisfaction (but still with the sense of a duty to be done); then from that it changed into a sort of state of constant satisfaction, with the desire (not "desire," but a will or an aspiration) for it to be more frequent, more constant, more exclusive. Then there was a sort of repugnance to and rejection of all that comes and disturbs, mixed with a sense of duty towards work, people and so on, and all that made a muddle and a great confusion. And it always ended in the transfer to the Supreme along with the aspiration for things to change. A long process of development.

Recently there was a sort of will for equality towards activities that had been tolerated or accepted only as an effect of the consecration and in obedience to the supreme Will. And then, all of a sudden they became something very positive, with a sense of freedom and a spontaneity of state, and a beginning of understanding of the attitude with which the action must be done. All this came very, very progressively. And then this morning, there was the experience.

*(silence)*

I may express it in this way: the capacity to fall silent and to intervene only on the Impulse from above.

To intervene only when set in motion by the supreme Wisdom, for every action to be done.

And it gave the exact meaning of the purpose of this material mind; because there was always, in the background of the consciousness, that sentence of Sri Aurobindo's which said it was an impossible instrument and would probably have to be got rid of. It had remained. And I saw there was something wrong: in spite of all the criticism, all the offering, all the disgust, even all the rejection, this material mind was preserved. Only, it has been transformed slowly, slowly, and now the first step has been made, a step on the road to transformation, with the experience of the cessation of its automatic activity.

That was the experience of this morning.

I am not saying it is final, far from it, but it's much more under control. The cessation lasted perhaps an hour or two, I don't remember, but its activity isn't so mechanical anymore.

You know that sort of mental silence in which everything falls flat *(immobile, horizontal gesture);* well, it can now be done with this material mind – it falls flat, turned upward.

But it is a beginning, just the beginning.

Only, there is a certainty. Even if it had occurred for just a few minutes, one could be sure that it would be – it occurred for much longer than that. Consequently this material mind will be part of what will be transformed.

And it gives a tremendous power! When it stops, the Vibration of Love can manifest in its plenitude.

It came this morning, in a glory.

It's for later.

Vol. 6, p. 207

## August 21, 1965

Since the 15th, there has been a whole work of preparation for the transformation .... What could I call it? ... A transfer of power.

The cells, the whole material consciousness, used to obey the inner individual consciousness – the psychic consciousness most of the time, or the mental (but the mind had been silent for a long time). But now this material mind is organizing itself like the other one, or the other ones, rather, like the mind of all the states of being – do you know, it is educating itself. It is learning things and organizing the ordinary science of the material world. When I write, for instance, I have noticed that it takes great care not to make spelling errors; and it doesn't know, so it inquires, it learns, it looks up in the dictionary or it asks. That's very interesting. It wants to know. You see, all the memory that came from mental knowledge went away a long, long time ago, and I used to receive indications only like this *(gesture from above).* But now it's a sort of memory being built from below, and with the care of a little child who educates himself but who wants to know, who doesn't want to make errors – who is perfectly conscious of his ignorance, and who wants to know. And the truly interesting thing is that it knows this knowledge to be quite ... more than relative, simply conventional, but it is like an instrument that would like to be free of defects, like a machine that would like to be perfect.

It is a rather recent awakening. There has been a sort of reversal of consciousness.

And at night it corresponds to thoroughly strange activities: a completely new way of seeing, feeling and observing people and things. Last night, for example, for over two hours there was a clear vision – an active vision (through action, that is) – of the way in which human consciousnesses make the most simple things complicated and difficult. It was fantastic – fantastic. And then, this consciousness was spontaneously impelled by the divine Presence, but it followed the others' human movements with the clear perception of the simple thing and of the way in which it becomes complicated. It was symbolic, with images; an activity in images in the sense that it wasn't purely material, physical as we know it here, but in a symbolic, imaged physical (in which the material world is seen as clay). It was very interesting.

Only, there was a very great intensity of transformation, and (how can I explain?) ... It's like a shift in the directing will. And then, there was materially, physically, a sort of surprise, and a need to identify with the new direction – it's a little difficult. It's difficult to explain, too.... It's no longer the same thing that makes you act – "act" or anything, of course: move, walk, anything. It isn't the same center any longer. And then if, by habit, you try to reconnect with the old center, oh, that creates a great disorder, and you must be very careful not to let habit, the old habit, express itself and manifest.

It's hard to express it. It is still too much just an action.

## August 28, 1965

*(Regarding the conversation of August 21 and the experience of the "transfer of power" to the cellular consciousness:)*

I said the other day that this aggregate of cells had changed its initiating power. It struck me as a unique experience, as something that had never occurred before. Unfortunately, it didn't last long. But the experience has left a kind of certitude in the body: it is less uncertain about the future. As if the experience came to tell the body, "This is how things will be."

If it stays on, it clearly means immortality.

I remember, when I told that experience, it was no longer something personal at all: if you can catch that....

Vol. 6, p. 228

## August 31, 1965

*(Regarding the conversations of August 21 and 28 on the "transfer of power":)*

*How do you define this physical mind, the one that underwent the transfer of power?*

That isn't the physical mind. The physical mind, it's a long time since ... It is the material mind – not even the material mind: the mind OF MATTER. It is the mental substance that belongs to Matter itself, to the cells. That's what was formerly called "the spirit of the form," when it was said that mummies kept their bodies intact as long as the spirit of the form persisted. That's the mind I mean, that completely material mind. The other one, the physical mind, has been organized for a long time.

*So what is the difference between this material mind and the physical mind? How would you define the physical mind in contrast with this material mind?*

The physical mind is the mind of the physical personality formed by the body. It grows with the body, but it isn't the

303

mind of Matter: it is the mind of the physical being. For instance, it is the mind that makes one's character: the bodily, physical character, which is in large part formed by atavism and education. What is called "physical mind" is all that. Yes, it's the result of atavism, of education and of the formation of the body; that's what makes the physical character. For example, some people are patient, some are strong and so on – physically, I mean, not for vital or mental reasons, but purely physically everyone has a character. That's the physical mind. And it is part of any integral yoga: you discipline this physical mind. I have done it for more than sixty years.

*But then, that mind, for instance, which is spontaneously defeatist, which has all sorts of fears and worries, which sees the worst, repeats the same things forever, is that the physical mind or the material mind?*

It is the most unconscious part of the physical mind, and that's what connects the physical mind with this material substance. But that's already an organized mind, you understand? It is the most material part, the one that borders on the mind ... (what can we call this mind?), we can't even call it "corporeal mind": it is the mind of the cells, a cellular mind.

This cellular mind exists in animals, and there is even a faint beginning (but very faint, like a promise) in plants: they respond to a mental action. They respond. As soon as Life manifests, there is already the beginning, like a promise of mind, of mental movement. And in animals, it's very clear. Whereas that physical mind really began to exist only in man. That's what a very small child already has: it already has a physical mind; so that no two very small children are alike, with identical reactions: there is already a difference. And it is especially what is given you with the special FORM of your body, by atavism, and then fully developed by education.

No, the physical mind, as soon as you do an integral yoga, you are obliged to deal with it, while this material, cellular mind, I can assure you that it's absolutely new! Absolutely new.

It is the mind that was like an uncoordinated substance, with a constant, unorganized activity *(Mother gestures to show a constant tremor)*. This is the mind which is being organized. That's what is important, because Sri Aurobindo said it was unorganizable and the only thing to do was to reject it from existence. And I was under that impression, too. But when the transforming action on the cells is constant, this material mind begins to become organized, that's the wonderful thing! It begins to become organized. And then, as it becomes organized, it learns to FALL SILENT – that's the beautiful thing! It learns to keep calm, silent, and to let the supreme Force act without interfering.

The most difficult part is in the nerves, because they are so habituated to that ordinary conscious will that when it stops and you want the direct Action from the highest height, they seem to become mad. Yesterday morning I had that experience, which lasted for more than an hour, and it was difficult; but it taught me many things – many things. And all this is what we may call the "transfer of power": it is the old power that withdraws. But then, until the body adapts to the new power, there is a period which is, well, critical. As all the cells are in a state of conscious aspiration, it's going relatively fast, but still ... the minutes are long.

But there is increasingly a sort of certitude in the cells that everything that happens is with a view to this transformation and this transfer of the directing power. And at the very moment when things are materially painful (not even physically: materially painful), the cells keep that certitude. And so they withstand, they endure the suffering without being depressed or affected in the least, with that certitude that it is to prepare for the transformation, that it is even the process of transformation and of the transfer of the directing power. As I said, it's in the nerves that the experience is the most painful (naturally, since they are the most sensitive cells, those with the sharpest sensation). But they have a very great receptivity, and very spontaneous, a spontaneously strong receptivity –

and effortless – to the harmonious physical vibration (which is very rare, but still it exists in some individuals), and that physical vibration ... what we could call a physical FORCE, a harmonious physical vibration (spontaneously harmonious, of course, without the need for mental intervention – like the vibrations of a flower, for instance; there are physical vibrations that are like that, that carry in themselves a harmonious force), and the nerves are extremely sensitive and receptive to that vibration, which immediately puts them right again.

It's very interesting, it explains many, many things. A day will come when all this will be explained and put in its proper place. Now isn't the time to reveal it yet, but it's very interesting.

I really have the feeling that it's beginning to be organized, that the work is beginning to be organized.

Naturally, care must be taken to avoid letting a mental organization intervene, which is why I am not trying to explain things too much. The mind comes, and then that's not it anymore.

Vol. 6, p. 229

## September 25, 1965

The whole night (not last night, the night before) was very, very critical, and with such a clear perception of the futility of the present procedure ... and of this slavery that comes from a habit several thousand years old and more.

There was in fact in the body a struggle between the two tendencies: one that was by habit subject to the old movement, and one that was trying to drop that habit, with the perception of the new way. It was ... it was extremely painful, difficult and absolutely grotesque all at once. And then, this body found itself to be a sort of battlefield, and that wasn't pleasant.

And the body consciousness (which is now taking form more and more clearly), even the one that is subject to the old habit, is conscious of the divine existence, I might say (the existence of the Divine and almost the divine existence), but it still has a sense of helplessness, and also, within that helplessness, of a complete surrender to the divine Will: "If we aren't ready, it will be like that" [= the dissolution]. And there is a part that feels ready, that understands and knows how things must be and wants them that way, and the two clash. It's not that one is for the Divine and the other against, nothing of all that old business is there any longer: there is the complete acceptance of the Divine, but the sensation of not being ready – the sensation that the world isn't ready (it wasn't at all an individual affair, not at all, it was a terrestrial consciousness).

And you clearly feel in this struggle (which lasted the whole night and the whole morning – yesterday, I wasn't in too brilliant a state), you clearly see, it's visible that it's not a question of a forceful will or ... it's not that: the SUBSTANCE must be ready. If the substance isn't ready, a forceful, powerful action visibly causes a dissolution. And then all that has been built has to be rebuilt. This idiotic death, you see, reduces it all to nothing, and the whole work is wasted – what goes out is what came in ... with a little more experience, that's all. That's nothing.

*(silence)*

If even one very small aggregate of cells could succeed in having the complete experience of transformation right to the end, that would be more effective than great upheavals – much, much more effective.

But it's more difficult. Much more difficult. And it doesn't cause big dazzling "events" that make a great to-do.

*Yes, it's linked to the general state of the world.*

Absolutely.

*And there really doesn't seem to be any progress. The feeling, on the contrary, is that men, heads of state, human consciousnesses are getting tinier and tinier.*

Yes, perfectly correct.

*Pygmies. It strikes me how in twenty years all that has been growing more and more dwarfish.*

That's perfectly correct. But I mean that according to my vision (which I don't think is mine, it's not a personal vision), nights and days like yesterday (which aren't pleasant) obviously give you a knowledge, and upheaval [Kali] still belongs to the old method – it's accepting that the world hasn't changed. While this sort of apparent shrinking is in fact perhaps the proof that the earth consciousness has changed and is putting pressure on what resists, which gets smaller and smaller, but harder and harder.

*Harder and harder, that's right.*

As if all that's conscious and living were being extracted, and what remains becomes more and more stony.

*(silence)*

The conscious perception of the two elements (the body is becoming a representative object; not just symbolic: representative), the perception of the state of consciousness of those elements that belong to the past, to the past evolutionary movement, and of those that are open to the new method, if I may say so, is clearer and clearer; it's perceptible as clearly as, more clearly than external physical things, than the external form (this distinction is physical, but it belongs to the inner construction). Outwardly, it results in fever. It's a battle. And not a battle of ill wills, it's not that: it's a sort of incapacity. And it's not with violence that we will succeed. You know, the only thing that can triumph is this supreme Vibration of Love, but there is an incapacity to receive, and then (it's a strange phenomenon), this incapacity to receive causes a sort of sifting, and it's only elements that are as if watered down that can pass through – the Thing in itself in its true essence cannot.... If you look at it from below, you feel as if That refuses to give itself, but it's not true, because when you ARE That *(laughing)*, there is no sense of being watered down: That manifests in its plenitude. And see what happens [the sifting]!

And it's clear (you can see it in very small details) that if there were direct contact, something would be as if shattered – it would cause something to be shattered. Yes, too abrupt, too sudden a change, like something that's shattered.

There have been microscopic experiences, sorts of microscopic demonstrations; well, if those microscopic demonstrations, along with their result, occurred in sufficient quantity or sufficient number, yes, that would necessarily cause what, for us, would be a dissolution.

And that was an experience lived every second, for about six hours nonstop. Six hours nonstop and in stillness (not stillness, but the possibility of physical immobility on the bed), then the continuation for more than an hour after getting up, with the activities (limited, but ordinary activities), but then it became terrible! And I say: all, all the elements, whatever they are, whether they belong to the old movement or to the other one, all the elements had the same sense of adoration. Therefore it isn't a moral attitude: the same sense of adoration. Only, some, in their adoration, accepted annulment, while others wanted the Victory, the transformation – it's not that they "wanted": they FELT the victory: and the others accepted the dissolution. And both together ... Very likely, if I had expressed that (I wasn't in a fit state to do so!), if I had expressed it at the time, I would have been accused of acute delirium – I was perfectly conscious. And there, I mean, THERE, above the body, the most wonderful Peace one can imagine, a smiling Peace and ...

And the fever is going on. [Mother had a fever the day before]. Which is to say that I am very, very conscious that this is the maximum of what can be done to advance swiftly towards transformation.

This fever that everybody has [several hundred cases in the Ashram for the past few months] is the same thing, except that

309

it's diluted in an unconsciousness. But it's the same thing: it's a "cellular" affair (I've had the experience of this because I have been able to stop it abruptly in a few through a process of isolation from the general movement).

Vol. 6, p. 255

## October 10, 1965

Oh, there's a whole work going on at night. Oh! ... The whole petty subconscious working of habits, with all the gradations of the importance it assumes in the general consciousness, and, very interestingly, according to the proportion of the importance, it gives the scale. There was the whole scale, from the little manias people have, which of course are very superficial and mere habits, to the known maniacs or half-mad – the whole scale, along with the whole working. And then, the perception that it's just a question of dosage: we all belong to the same substance! It was seen so concretely that it was quite interesting. And in conclusion, one saw how to put that under the direct Influence of the supreme Force and Consciousness so as to break the inescapable chain of habits. It was very interesting.

Those are all the things that are considered "unimportant," and it's all that, the whole mass of all that, which prevents the physical transformation.

And because they are very small things (that is, APPARENTLY very small things, without any importance from the viewpoint of thought, for instance, and considered negligible), they are the worst obstacles.

Naturally, if the consciousness is warped, it must first be set right, but I am talking about enlightened consciousnesses that live in the Truth, that have aspiration and that wonder why this intensity of aspiration produces such poor results – now I know. The poor result is because they don't attach enough importance to those very small things that belong to the subconscious mechanism and because of which in thought you are free, in sentiment you are free, even in impulse you are free, and physically you are a slave.

One must undo all that, undo it, undo it.

And when the cells are goodwilled ... By "goodwilled," I mean that as soon as their attention is turned to the supreme Force (or supreme Presence or supreme Existence or supreme Reality – whatever, words are nothing but words), as soon as their attention is turned to That, a burst of joy: "That's it! That's it!" In the cells that are truly not only goodwilled but thirsting for the Truth: a burst of joy. And then ... the old habits start up again. And the cells say (it recurs periodically, that is, very often, thousands of times a day), "But we only have to will!" or "We only have to aspire" or "We only have to think of That" (it's not "think" as we understand it), "We only have to turn our attention" – "Oh, but it's true!" Like that. "Oh, such joy!" And then, brrf! all the old habits come back again. It's fantastic ... fantastic.

The fear of the unknown is gone (doubt went away a very long time ago), the fear of the unknown, of the new, the unexpected, is gone; there only remains the mechanism of habit. But it holds on, it clings, oh! ...

It will go.

And now and then (now and then: quite rarely), a spark, so to say, of the true Consciousness making an attempt, descending, but it still causes ... (gesture of upheaval and turmoil). It isn't yet received and manifested in the supreme Peace, so it goes away.

If previously (before the work on the cells), if the body was able to remain calm when the Force descended, without being overwhelmed, it was because of the tremendous amount of tamas that was inside it! That's right! A tamas that didn't respond, so it was calm. But now, it responds.

And you realize that if all this Power, this tremendous Force manifested – the force that is conscious, which is there,

311

conscious – if it manifested, oh, *(Mother laughs)* you feel as if everything were about to start dancing and jumping!

We must be patient, that's what I keep saying to myself a hundred and fifty, a thousand times a day: we must be patient.

Vol. 6, p. 269

## October 30, 1965

Something amusing has happened. You know that there is a new comet? ... This morning around four, I saw the comet, and suddenly I found myself in a state above the earth, and I saw a being who seemed to be associated with this comet. He had red hair (but not an aggressive red), a white body, but not pure white: a golden white, as if he were naked, but he didn't give an impression of being naked, or of wearing any clothes either (I have noticed this several times already), sexless – neither man nor woman. And it was a young being, charming, full of a sort of joy, like the joy that came a little in the music just now, and he was spreading in the earth atmosphere a sort of substance that was heavier than Matter – not heavier, but denser – and jelly-like. It was as though he had taken advantage of the comet passing near the earth to spread that substance. And at the same time, I was told it was "to help for the transformation of the earth." And he showed me how to make that substance circulate in the atmosphere.

It was charming: a young being, full of joy, as if dancing, and spreading that substance everywhere.

It lasted a long time. For several hours I remained in it.

Vol. 6, p. 281

## November 6, 1965

At night, the last two or three nights, but especially last night (in the middle of the night, after midnight), and for at least two hours, I am carried away in a movement, but a frightfully swift movement! I am lying on something which is a sort of silvery light – a silvery light. And I am lying on it, enveloped in it, and carried away in such a dizzying movement that ... you feel as if your head is going to break.

And there are people with me – you are one of them.

*Really?*

Yes!

Last night it lasted two hours. And you feel like holding on to something, because it's so dizzying.... I don't know, last night, in the middle of the experience I became a little conscious, and it was ... *(gesture expressing a fantastic movement)*. But the Command came: "Quiet, quiet, don't move, quiet," so I didn't move. And it lasted almost two hours. And the movement is head first (not feet first), head first, it's the head that's pulled.

All I know is that it has to do with the transformation of the body. But how does one know that it's fast? There is nothing but the movement and the body's sense of being carried away dizzyingly.

And I noticed a few people – you were there. Prrtt! at full speed, like that. I said to myself *(laughing)*, "It must be to cure him!" But a movement ... I tell you, the consciousness just woke up, I wanted to start observing, and immediately the Command came, "Quiet, quiet, don't move, quiet, nothing must move."

It must be at the time of the night when you really sleep. It's after midnight and before two in the morning.

But there is nothing to remember: one seems to be whisked along, like that – maybe it's the speed of comets! I told myself it was a *drastic* treatment, as they say in English.

But the other night (it had come two or three times already), it wasn't so strong. Last night, it was so strong and it lasted such a long time....

313

...

You've been in a car at more than sixty miles an hour, haven't you? ... It feels motionless in comparison to that Speed. It wasn't physical since my bed wasn't moving, but it was so swift, so swift that you could feel the friction of speed. And head first: it went head first. It didn't go feet first because I was lying and I didn't go feet first: I went head first, brrf! I as if sucked along by something. And my eyes were open. But naturally, the body wasn't moving – visibly, at least, it wasn't moving! ... Oh, I remember, yes, the night before, it was the house that was moving; I was in a room that was moving with that same swiftness, and I was watching everything hurtling and hurtling past, it was fantastic! And yesterday, it wasn't the house, it was only ... a sort of column ... how can I explain? It wasn't a column – a strip. I was there on that strip, but I was very tall, I took up a lot of room; there were lots of people, and they were small *(Mother draws small figures)*, a lot, brrf!

Yes, yes, I remember, the previous night, it was the room that was moving: a square room; and there weren't any walls, there were just windows, and it was rushing and rushing, what a race it was! ... Then everything stopped abruptly, finished – not finished, not stopped: the consciousness changes, there is a reversal of consciousness, so it's over.

Yes, I remember now. First a room without anything – anything – an absolute empty space; there was nothing except that strip.

Oh, do you remember those moving walkways? Something like that, but instead of a walkway, it was a strip of silvery light, and it was the strip that was moving. A strip of silvery light with little sparkles. I was lying on it (quite a few people were lying on it, too), and it was zooming! ...

## November 15, 1965

You must sleep well. Yes, I have noticed that it's important to sleep a long time. As soon as you feel tired, let yourself drift into sleep, don't resist. That's important. I am saying this from personal experience, because all of a sudden ... When there is a length of time (it lasts an hour, two hours, it depends) during which the atmosphere is all vibrant with this light-force-joy I spoke of the other day, and you are as if ... it's absolutely full, absolutely full; and then all of a sudden *(gesture of inward plunge)*, and after a time you ask yourself, "Well, well, where have I been?..." There are times like that when you go into a sort of sleep. The first few times, I thought I had lapsed into unconsciousness (although that has rarely happened to me!), but anyway, I wondered what it meant. Then I took a good look and I saw it was a necessary period of assimilation. It's very necessary. It's in a sort of stillness of the cells' consciousness that they assimilate the new force. So when it comes, don't resist. Generally, it doesn't last very long: fifteen minutes, twenty minutes. A period of assimilation. You know, the atmosphere is charged, charged, increasingly charged. So if suddenly you feel something pulling, don't resist, let yourself go – it's better not to be standing up!

Vol. 6, p. 298

## November 23, 1965

*Regarding the message Mother will give for the November 24 darshan:*

"It is certainly a mistake to bring down the light by force – to pull it down. The Supramental cannot be taken by storm. When the time is ready it will open of itself – but first there is a great deal to be done and that must be done patiently and without haste."

*Sri Aurobindo*

315

That's good for sensible people. They will say, "There, he doesn't promise any miracles."

*Why? Are there lots of people who tend to "pull"?*

People are in a hurry, they want to see results right away.

So then, they think they are pulling the Supramental down – and they pull some little vital entity that leads them on and afterwards plays nasty tricks on them. That's what happens most often, ninety-nine times out of a hundred.

A little individuality, a vital entity that puts on a big show and creates dramatic effects, lighting effects; so the poor devil who has pulled is bedazzled, he says, "Here's the Supramental!" and he falls into a hole.

It's only when you have touched, seen somehow or other, and had a contact with the true Light that you can discern the Vital, and you realize that it's absolutely like lighting effects on a theater stage: theatrical effects, an artificial light. But otherwise people are bedazzled – it's dazzling, it's "magnificent," and so they are misled. It's only when you have SEEN and had a contact with the Truth ... "Ah!" then it makes you smile.

It's showing off, but you have to know the truth in order to discern the showing off.

Basically, it's the same for everything. The Vital is a sort of super-theater giving performances – very alluring, dazzling, deceptive performances – and it's only when you know the True Thing that immediately, instinctively, without reasoning, you discern and say, "No, I don't want that."

And for everything, you know. The one point in human life where it has assumed cardinal importance is love. Vital passions and attractions have almost in every case taken the place of the true feeling, which is tranquil, while that makes you bubble with excitement, it gives you the feeling of something "living".... It's very deceptive. And you can know this, feel it, perceive it clearly only when you know the True Thing; if you have touched true love through the psychic and through divine union, then it [vital love] appears hollow, thin, empty: an appearance and a drama – more often a tragedy than a comedy.

All that you can say about it, all that you can explain about it is perfectly useless, because the one who has been caught will instantly say, "Oh, it's not like with others" – what happens to you is never like what happens to others (!) What's needed is the "Thing," the true experience ... then the whole Vital is seen as a masquerade – not an alluring one.

And when people pull down, oh, it's much more than ninety-nine times out of a hundred – it's one case in a million in which the True Thing happens to be pulled down; which proves the person was ready. Otherwise, what's pulled down is always the Vital: the appearance, the dramatic representation of the Thing, not the Thing itself.

Pulling down is always an egoistic movement. It's a distortion of aspiration. True aspiration involves a giving – a self-giving – while pulling down is wanting for oneself. Even if you have in your thought a vaster aspiration – the earth, the universe – it makes no difference, those are mental activities.

*(long silence)*

When things are put mentally, all those who have tried to explain things mentally have made an opposition, and so people imagine that one is the very opposite of the other [the True Thing and its distortion]; in that case it would be so easy to discern. But that's not at all how it is! ... I am now studying the way in which Matter, the body, can be in constant harmony with the divine Presence. And it's so interesting: it's not at all an opposition, it's a tiny little microscopic distortion. For instance, there is this frequent experience (and generally people don't know why it is so – now I know): on some days or at certain times all the gestures you make are harmonious, all the things you touch seem to respond harmoniously to the will that touches them, everything works out (I am talking

317

about the very small things of life – of everyday life), each thing seems to be in its place or to find its place naturally: if you fold a paper, it folds itself as though spontaneously, as it should; if you look for something, you seem to spontaneously find the thing you need; you never knock against anything, never upset anything – everything seems harmonious. And then, without any appreciable difference in the overall state of consciousness, at other times, it's the exact opposite: if you want to fold a paper, you fold it the wrong way; if you want to touch some object, you drop it – everything seems disharmonized or off balance or bad-willed. You are yourself more or less in the same state. But now, with the present keen and fine observation, I see that in one case, there is a sort of inner silence in the cells, a PROFOUND quietude, which doesn't prevent movement, even rapid movement, but the movement seems to be founded on an eternal vibration; and in the other case, there is that inner precipitation *(gesture of tremor),* that inner vibration, that inner restlessness, that haste to go from one moment to the next, that constant hurry (why? There's no knowing why), always, always hurrying and scurrying; and everything you do is wrong. And in the other case, with that inner serenity and peace, everything is done harmoniously, and MUCH FASTER in material time: there is no time lost.

And that's why it's so difficult to know how one should be. Because in thought you can be in the same constant state, even in aspiration you can be in the same constant state, in the general goodwill, even in surrender to the Divine, it all can be the same thing, in the same state – it's in here *(Mother touches her body),* and this makes the whole difference. I can very well conceive that there may be people in whom this opposition persists in the mind and the vital, but there it's so obvious.... But I am talking of something absolutely material. Some people say and think, "How come? I have such goodwill, such a desire to do the right thing, and then nothing works, everything jars – why? I am so good (!) and yet things don't respond." Or those who say, "Oh, I have made my surrender, I have such goodwill, I have an aspiration, I want nothing but the Truth and the Good, and yet I am ill all the time – why am I ill?" And naturally, one small step more, and you begin to doubt the Justice that rules the world, and so on. Then you fall into a hole.... But that's not it, that's not what I mean. It's much simpler and much more difficult at the same time, because it isn't blatant, it isn't evident, it's not an opposition from which you can choose, it's ... truly, totally and integrally leaving the entire responsibility to the Lord.

Vol. 6, p. 300

## January 31, 1966

All discoveries are always graces – wonderful graces. When you discover that you can't do anything, when you discover that you are a fool, when you discover that you have no capacity, when you discover that you are so petty and mean and stupid, well ... "Oh, Lord, I thank You so much, how good You are to show me all this!" And then, it's over. Because the minute you discover it, you say, "Now this is up to You. You will do what has to be done for all this to change." And the best part of it is that it does change! It does change. When you do like this *(gesture of offering to the Heights)*, sincerely: "Oh, take it, take it, take it, rid me of it, let me be ... only You" ...

It's wonderful.

There.

Vol. 7, p. 33

## February 26, 1966

What's interesting is that now that this mind of the cells has been organized, it appears to be going with dizzying speed through the process of human mental development all over again, in order to reach ... the key, precisely. There is of course

319

the sense that the state we are in is a false unreality, but there is a sort of need or aspiration to find, not a mental or moral "why," nothing of the sort, but a HOW – how it got twisted this way *(Mother bends her wrist in one direction),* in order to straighten it out *(gesture in the opposite direction).*

The pure sensation has the experience of the two vibrations [the false and the true, the twisted and the straight vibrations], but the transition from one to the other is still a mystery. It's a mystery, because it cannot be explained: neither when it goes this way *(gesture to the false direction)* nor when it goes that way *(gesture to the true direction).*

So there is something that says like Théon, "Learn to BE that way [on the true side] and stay that way." But there is an impression that the "stay that way" must depend on knowing why one is that way or how one is that way?

I don't know if I make myself understood! ...

Vol. 7, p. 45

## March 9, 1966

*There's a question I'd like to ask you. It's in fact the question I wanted to ask you last time.... When one is in that eternal Consciousness, to be with or without a body makes little difference, but when one is "dead," as it is called, I'd like to know if the perception of the material world remains clear and precise, or if it becomes as vague and imprecise as might be the consciousness one has of the other worlds when one is on this side, in this world? Sri Aurobindo speaks of a play of hide and seek, but the play of hide and seek is interesting if one state of being doesn't deprive of the consciousness of the other states?*

Yesterday or the day before, the whole day from morning to evening, something was saying, "I am ... I am or have the consciousness of a dead person on earth." I am putting it into words, but it seemed to say, "This is how the consciousness of a dead person is in relation to the earth and physical things....

320

I am a dead person living on earth." According to the stand of the consciousness (because the consciousness changes its stand constantly), according to the stand of the consciousness, it was, "This is how the dead are in relation to the earth," then, "I am absolutely like a dead person in relation to the earth," then, "I am the way a dead person lives without any consciousness of the earth," then, "I am quite like a dead person living on earth ..." and so on. And I went on speaking, acting, doing as usual.

But it has been like that for a long time.

For a very long time, more than two years, I saw the world like this *(ascending gesture, from one level to a higher level)*, and now I see it like this *(descending gesture)*. I don't know how to explain it because there's nothing mentalized about it, and non-mentalized sensations have a certain haziness that's hard to define. But words and thought were a certain distance away *(gesture around the head)*, like something that watches and appreciates, in other words, that tells what it sees – something around. And today, it has been extremely strong two or three times (I mean that that state dominated the whole consciousness): a sort of impression (or sensation or perception, but it's nothing like all that) of, "I am a dead person living on earth."

How can I explain that?

And then, with vision, for instance, the objective precision is missing *(Mother makes a gesture of not seeing through her eyes)*. I see through and with the consciousness. With hearing, I hear in a totally different way; there is a sort of "discrimination" (it isn't "discernment"), something that chooses in the perception, something that decides (that decides, but not arbitrarily – automatically) what is heard and what isn't heard, what is perceived and what isn't perceived. It's already there in vision, but it's still stronger with hearing: with certain things, all that's heard is a continuous drone; others are heard very clearly, as clear as crystal; still others are blurred, half heard. With sight, it's the same thing: everything is behind a sort of luminous fog (very luminous, but it's a fog, which means there is no precision), then all at once, a particular thing will be absolutely precise and clear, seen with a most precise vision of detail. The vision is generally the expression of the consciousness in things. That is, everything seems to become more and more subjective, less and less objective.... And they aren't visions that impose themselves on the sight, or noises that impose themselves on the hearing: it's a sort of movement of consciousness that makes certain things perceptible and keeps others as if in a very imprecise background.

*The consciousness chooses what it wants to see.*

There's nothing personal – nothing personal. There is obviously the sense of a choice and a decision, but there is no sense of a personal choice and decision – moreover, the "personal" is reduced to the necessity of making this *(Mother pinches the skin of her hand)* intervene. With eating, for example, it's very odd – very odd.... It's like someone who is watching over a body (which isn't even a very precise and defined thing, but a sort of conglomerate holding together), a spectator of ... something happening! No, it's really an odd state. Today, since I got up and till now, it has been very strong, dominating the whole consciousness. And there are even times when you feel that a mere nothing could make you lose contact *(gesture of disconnection, as if the link with the body were severed),* and that only if you remain very still and very indifferent – indifferent – can it continue.

In the consciousness of the people, the whole morning, it was translated by (all this is perceived very clearly), by the thought, "Oh, Mother is VERY tired." But there is that sort of state of indifference, unreceptive to the vibration around, which enables you to go on, otherwise you feel that ... *(same gesture of disconnection)* something would be seriously disrupted. Once or twice I had to draw within and become still. And it's going on. And in fact, while it was like that something came and told me (but all this wordlessly), "When Satprem is here, you will understand." Then there was tranquillity, because the moment was ... (what shall I say?) very uncertain. And there was a sort of relaxing: "You will understand when he is here, you will have the explanation."

Those experiences are always preceded by the Supreme Presence drawing near in a very intimate and inner way, with a sort of suggestion, "Are you ready for anything?" (that was two nights ago). Naturally I answered, "Anything." And the Presence takes on such a wonderful intensity that there is a sort of thirst in the whole being for it to be constantly like that. Nothing but That exists anymore, nothing but That has a raison d'être anymore. And in the middle of it comes this suggestion: "Are you ready for anything?"

I am talking about the body. It's not the inner beings, it's the body.

And the body always says yes, it does like this *(gesture of surrender)*. No choice, no preference, no aspiration, even: a total, complete surrender. So then, things of that sort come to me; yesterday, all day long, it was: "A dead person living on earth." With the perception (not a very pronounced perception yet, but clear enough) of a vast difference between the way of life [of this body] and that of other people, of all the others, the people who talk to me, the people with whom I live. It isn't clear-cut yet, or sharp or very precise, but it's very clear – very clear, very perceptible. It's another way of life.

*One would tend to say that it's not a gain from the standpoint of consciousness, since things become blurred. I don't know, is that way of being a gain?*

It can only be a transition. It's a transitory mode.

From the standpoint of consciousness, it's a tremendous gain! Because all slavery, all bonds with external things, all that is finished, it has completely fallen off – completely fallen off: there's absolute freedom. In other words, That alone remains, the Supreme Master is the master. From that point of view, it can only be a gain. It's such a radical realization.... It seems to be an absolute of freedom, something that's considered impossible to realize while living the ordinary life on earth.

It corresponds to the experience of absolute freedom one has in the higher parts of the being when one has become completely independent of the body. But the remarkable point (I lay great stress on this) is that it's the consciousness OF THE BODY that has those experiences ... and it's a body that's still visibly here (!)

Of course, there is nothing left of what gives human beings "trust of life." There doesn't seem to be any support from the outward world left; there is only ... the supreme Will. To put it into ordinary words, well, the body feels it lives only because the supreme Lord wants it to live, otherwise it wouldn't be able to live.

*Yes, but it seems to me that a state of perfection should embrace everything, so that one can be in the supreme state without its abolishing the material state.*

But it doesn't abolish it.

*No, but still you say it's "far away," "behind a veil," that it no longer has its exactness and precision.*

That's a purely human and superficial perception. I don't at all feel that I have lost anything, on the contrary! I have the sense of a state much superior to the one I had.

*Even from the material standpoint?*

What the Lord wants is done – that's all; it begins there and ends there.

If He told me ... Whatever He wants the body to do, it can do; it no longer depends on physical laws.

*What He wants to see it can see; what He wants to hear it can hear.*

Undeniably.

*And when He wants to see or wants to hear materially, it sees perfectly and hears perfectly.*

Oh, perfectly! At times the sight is more precise than it ever was. But it's fleeting: it comes and goes; probably because it's only as an assurance of what will be. But, for instance, the perception of people's inner reality (not what they think they are or what they pretend to be or what they appear to be – all that disappears), the perception of their inner reality is infinitely more precise than formerly. If I see a photograph, for example, there's no question anymore of seeing "through" something: I almost exclusively see what the person IS. The "through" decreases to such a point that at times it no longer exists at all.

Naturally, if a human will wanted to exert itself on this body, if a human will said, "Mother must do this" or "Mother must do that," or "she must be able to do this, she must be able to do that ... " it would be totally disappointed, it would say, "She has become useless," because this body wouldn't obey it anymore. And human beings constantly exert their will on each other, or they themselves receive suggestions and manifest them as their own will, without realizing that it's all the external Falsehood.

*(silence)*

There is a sort of certitude in the body that if, for the space of just a few seconds, I lost contact ("I," meaning the body), if the body lost contact with the Supreme, it would die that very moment. It's only the Supreme that keeps it alive. That's how it is. So naturally, to the ignorant and stupid consciousness of human beings, that's a pitiable condition – and to me, it's the true condition! Because for them, instinctively, spontaneously and in a so to say absolute way, the sign of perfection is the power of life, of ordinary life.... Well, that no longer exists at all – it's completely gone.

Yes, quite a few times, several times, the body did ask the question, "Why don't I feel Your Power and Your Force in me?" And the answer was always a smiling answer (I am putting it into words, but it's wordless), the answer is always: "Patience, patience, you must be READY for that to be."

Vol. 7, p. 58

## March 26, 1966

... The nerves began only a few months ago their work of "transfer of power." (What I call "transfer of power" is that instead of the nerves being moved by and obeying complex and organized forces of Nature, of the character, of the material consciousness in the body, they attune themselves to and directly obey the divine Will.) It's the transfer from one to the other that's difficult: there is the entire old habit, and then the new habit to be formed. It was a rather difficult moment. But now there remain enough old vibrations to be able to gauge exactly (and this has nothing to do with thought, it isn't expressed in words or thoughts or anything like all that: just vibrations), to know exactly the state people near me are in. From that point of view the lesson is going on, it's very interesting. And what's wonderful is that more often than not the most receptive vibration, conforming the most to what it should be, is in children, but the very small ones, the tiny tots.... I see lots of people, but now I understand why: I learn enormously that way, through that contact (with people whom I don't know, sometimes whom I see for the first time, or whom I haven't seen for years). It's very interesting.

But when nobody is there or I am alone, or when I don't speak or I am not busy with other people, it's the inner lesson: the whole change in the vibration and how the world is organized. This morning, it was really extraordinarily amusing to see the mass of things that lie behind this appearance, an appearance that seems complicated enough as it is, but it's nothing! It's thin, flimsy, without complexity in comparison with the MASS of things behind, which ... *(drilling gesture)* which bore their way through to reach the surface. It's amusing. But certainly ninety-nine people in a hundred would be seized with panic if they knew, if they saw. I had always been told (I read it, Sri Aurobindo often said it to me, Théon too often said it to me, so did Madame Théon) that it's the Grace that keeps people from knowing. Because if they knew, they would be terrified! All, but all the things that are constantly there, moving behind – behind the appearances – all the complexities that are the true causes of or the instruments for all those small events, which to us are absolutely unimportant, but because of which one day you feel everything is harmonious, and another day you feel it takes a labor to do anything at all. And that's how it is. And naturally, when you know, you have the key. But if you know before you have the key, it's ... a little frightening. I think that when people take leave of their senses, it's because they are put in contact with the vibrations before having the knowledge, the sufficient knowledge, the sufficient state of consciousness.

...

*But how is the transition made? The transition that materializes? What is the secret of the passage from that very subtle physical to the physical proper? How is the passage made from one side to the other?*

Mon petit, I don't know what comparison I should use, but I am certain there are some things that are invisible this way *(Mother rotates her wrist in one direction),* and visible that way *(gesture in the other direction).* My impression is that what we see as a considerable difference between the tangible, the material, and the invisible or the fluid, is only a change of position. Perhaps an internal change of position because it isn't a physical, material change of position, but it is a change of position. Because I have experienced this I don't know how many times, hundreds of times: like this *(gesture in one direction),* everything is what we call "natural," as we are used to seeing it, then all of a sudden, like that *(gesture in the other direction),* the nature of things changes. And nothing has happened, except something within, something in the consciousness: a change of position. Do you remember that aphorism in which Sri Aurobindo says that everything depends on a change in the relation of the sun-consciousness and the earth-consciousness? When I read it the first time, I didn't understand, I thought it was something in the very subtle realms; and then, very recently, in one of those experiences, I suddenly understood, I said, "But that's it!" It isn't a shift since nothing moves, yet it is a shift, it is a change of relation. A change of position. It's no more tangible than that, that's what is so wonderful! Oh, the other day, I found another sentence of Sri Aurobindo's: "Now everything is different, yet everything has remained the same." (It was on one of my birthday cards.) I read that and said to myself, "Oh, that's what it means!" It's true, now everything is different, yet everything has remained the same. We understand it psychologically, but it's not psychological: it's HERE *(Mother touches matter)*. But until one has a solid base ... From the standpoint of concrete, physical, material things, I don't think there's anyone more materialistic than I was, with all the practical common sense and positivism; and now I understand why it was like that: it gave my body a marvelous base of equilibrium. It prevented me from having the very sort of madness we were talking about earlier.

[Aphorism 102: "To the senses it is always true that the sun moves round the earth; this is false to the reason. To the reason it is always true that the earth moves round the sun; this is false to the supreme vision. Neither earth moves nor sun; there is only a change in the relation of sun-consciousness and earth-consciousness."]

The explanations I asked for were always material, I always sought the material explanation, and it seemed obvious to me there's no need of any mystery, nothing of the sort – you just explain things materially. Therefore I am certain this isn't a tendency to mystic dreaming in me, not at all, not at all, this body had nothing mystic! Nothing ... Thank God!

I saw that (not in my head, because for me there are no such limits), in this sort of conglomerate, here: the nearest explanation is a "shift" – a shift, the angle of perception becoming different. And it's not really that, words are incorrect, because it's far more subtle and at the same time far more complete than that. I have watched the change several times; well, this change gives you, to the outward consciousness, the sense of a shift. A motionless shift, meaning that you don't change places. And it's not, as we might be tempted to think, a drawing within and a drawing without, it's not that at all, not at all – it's an angle of perception that changes. You are in a certain angle, then you are in another.... I have seen small objects of that sort for the amusement of children: when those objects are in a certain position, they look compact and hard and black, and when you turn them another way, they are clear, luminous, transparent. It's something like that, but it's not that, that's an approximation.

*But if we know the way in which the change is effected, we can ...*

Ah!

*... we can stop the entry of bad vibrations?*

As for me, I have only one method (but I can conceive that this is simply because that's the way my nature is), I have only one method, it's self-abolition, the idea (not an "idea") that the Supreme alone exists.

Vol. 7, p. 72

### March 30, 1966

The same Consciousness as this consciousness I had in what we can call the "material mental" (that is, the collective consciousness of the cells), but this morning it was in the cells themselves, this Consciousness [the eternal Consciousness] ... the same Consciousness. And it was truly miraculous. With the impression that with THAT there [in the cells], there is nothing impossible.

It comes, it stays in spite of everything, whatever I do, even if I speak, and it goes. And when it's gone it's gone, I can make an effort, it doesn't come back. But so long as it is there, it is all-powerful, it dominates everything and ... yes, the whole world seems to change. And yet everything is the same. You remember this sentence of Sri Aurobindo: "All was changed and yet everything was the same"? That is exactly that.

*"And then, it becomes just a choice: you choose things to be like this or like that ..."*

Yes, this same thing, this same experience in the cell-consciousness. What the human beings call "life" and "death," the continuation of this present organization or its cessation, it was absolutely a question of choice (something like a choice – there are some who say "the Divine's Will" or "the Supreme's Will"; it is a way of saying, but it is ... it is something that chooses). And there was at the same time the exact ... it was more than a feeling, it was a lived knowledge of what is the individual and why the individual and in what way the Supreme becomes the individual and how He can continue to be the individual or stop to be the individual.... Now that the experience is gone, naturally what I say has no meaning, but at that time it was the exact perception: the individual is that *(gesture)*, that position taken by the Supreme, and if He chooses to continue it continues.

It becomes quite material, you see, no more mental at all (it is very difficult to express because of that). It becomes a living experience of just what makes the individual and how this individual can remain individual although it is united perfectly, united in perfect consciousness with the Supreme.

It lasted about fifteen to twenty minutes in complete stability and I continued doing my normal activities (it was during the time of my toilet – I wash my mouth and gargle), purposely it comes at that time to show that it is absolutely independent from the activity. And it comes more often at that time than when I sit in meditation. When I sit in meditation generally begins a kind of all-around-the-earth activity or even universal activity, it becomes conscious of that, but this body's experiences are not there – to have the body experience you must live in your body! It is why the ancient sages or saints didn't know what to do with the body, because they went out of it and sat, and then the body is no more concerned. But when you remain active, then it's the body that has the experience.

That is the secret.

Vol. 7, p. 77

## May 14, 1966

But everything, absolutely everything is becoming strange. As if there were two, three, four realities *(superimposed gesture)* or appearances, I don't know (but they are rather realities), one behind another or one within another, like that, and in the space of a few minutes it changes *(gesture as if one reality were surging forward to overtake and replace another)*, as though one world were just there, inside, and emerged all of a sudden. When I have peace and quiet, there is a slight ... not a movement, I don't know what it is: it might rather feel like pulsations, and depending on the case, there are different experiences. For instance, customary things take a usual amount of time when nothing abnormal happens, and then you have an exact sense of the time they take. So then, I am "given" the following experience, of the same thing done in the same way, accomplished a first time in its normal duration, and another time, when I am in another state, that is, when the consciousness seems to be placed elsewhere, the thing seems to be done in a second! – Exactly the same thing: habitual gestures, things you do absolutely every day, quite ordinary things. Then, another time (and it's not that I try to have it, I don't try at all: I am PUT in that state), another time I am put in another state (to me, it doesn't make much difference, they are like very small differences in the concentration), and in that state, the same thing, oh, takes a long, long time, an endless time to get done! Just to fold a towel, for instance

(I am not the one who does it), someone folds a towel or someone puts a bottle away, wholly material and absolutely simple things devoid of any psychological value; someone folds a towel that's on the floor (I am giving that example): there is a normal time, which I perceive internally after a study; it's the normal time, when everything is normal, that is, usual; then, I am in a certain concentration and ... without my even having the time to notice it, it's done! I am in another state of concentration, with absolutely minimal differences as far as the concentration is concerned, and it's endless! You feel it takes half an hour to get done.

If it occurred just once, you'd say, "Never mind," but it takes place with persistence and regularity, as when someone is trying to teach you something. A sort of insistence and regular repetition as if someone wanted to teach me something.

Vol. 7, p. 106

## May 28, 1966

*(Mother takes her face in her hands and looks exhausted.)*
Are you all right?
*Are YOU tired?*
No, it's worse than tired, it's worse....

A whole work of adjustment is going on, which has become very, very difficult, very difficult *(Mother makes a gesture of churning).*

I am practically unable to eat any longer, I force myself, otherwise all I would do is drink. And it's not caused by the stomach, it's not that, it's ... *(same gesture of churning).*

I don't feel tired, but I've had for a long time and increasingly (the last few days it has become very acute) the impression of walking forward, moving on *(gesture in a precarious balance),* and that the slightest false step would hurl me into the chasm. I seem to be on a ridge between two chasms.

And that's something going on in the body's cells. There's nothing moral to it, nothing even to do with sensation.

One is compelled to constant vigilance. The slightest slackening, you know, is ... catastrophic.

*(long contemplation)*

So I'll see you on Thursday? Well, I hope it'll be over and I'll be out of it!

The consolation is that the Supreme's action is growing increasingly clear and evident. You know, I am like a speck of ... *([Mother makes a gesture in the hollow of a Hand]* how can I explain it?...) of dust, but a dust that suffers, that's the trouble. Very sensitive. But the play of forces is growing increasingly clear and powerful, and over an increasingly extensive field. And directly HERE [in matter], with extraordinary precision and force. It's a consolation.

Let's just not bother about it.

## June 2, 1966

Oh, I've had an experience, a new experience. I mean, it's the cells of the body that have had a new experience.

When I lie down on my bed at night, there is an offering of all the cells, which regularly *surrender* as completely as they can, with an aspiration not only for union but for fusion: let there remain nothing but the Divine. It's regular, every day, every single day. And for some time, these cells or this body consciousness (but it isn't organized as a consciousness: it's like a collective consciousness of the cells), it seemed to be complaining a little, to be saying, "But we don't feel much. We do feel" (they can't say they don't feel: they feel protected, supported), "but still ..." They are like children, they were complaining that it wasn't spectacular: "It HAS to be marvelous." *(Mother laughs)* Ah, very well, then! So two nights ago, they were in that state when I went to bed. I didn't

333

move from the bed till about two in the morning. At two in the morning I got up, and I suddenly noticed that all the cells, the whole body (but it really is a cellular consciousness, not a body consciousness; it isn't the consciousness of this or that person: there's no person, it's the consciousness of a cellular aggregate), that consciousness felt bathed in and at the same time shot through by a MATERIAL power of a fan-tas-tic velocity bearing no relation to the velocity of light, none at all: the velocity of light is something slow and unhurried in comparison. Fantastic, fantastic! Something that must be like the movement of the centers out there ... *(Mother gestures towards faraway galactic space).* It was so awesome! I remained quite peaceful, still, I sat quite peaceful; but still, peaceful as I could be, it was so awesome, as when you are carried away by a movement and are going so fast that you can't breathe. A sort of discomfort. Not that I couldn't breathe, that wasn't the point, but the cells felt suffocated, it was so ... awesome. And at the same time with a sensation of power, a power that nothing, nothing whatsoever can resist in any way. So I had been pulled out of my bed (I noticed it) so that the BODY consciousness (mark the difference: it wasn't the cells' consciousness, it was the body's consciousness) would teach the cells how to *surrender* and tell them, "There is only one way: a total *surrender,* then you will no longer have that sensation of suffocation." And there was a slight concentration, like a little lesson. It was very interesting: a little lesson, how it should be done, what should be done, how to abandon oneself entirely. And when I saw it had been understood, I went back to bed. And then, from that time (it was two, two:twenty) till quarter to five, I was in that Movement without a single break! And the peculiar thing was that when I got up, there was in that consciousness (which is both cellular and a bit corporeal) the sense of *Ananda* [divine joy] in everything the body did: getting up, walking, washing its eyes, brushing its teeth.... For the first time in my life I felt the Ananda (a quite impersonal Ananda), an Ananda in those movements. And with the feeling, "Ah, that's how the Lord enjoys Himself."

334

It's no longer in the foreground (it was in the foreground for an hour or two to make me understand), now it's a bit further in the background. But, you understand, previously the body used to feel that its whole existence was based on the Will, the surrender to the supreme Will, and endurance. If it was asked, "Do you find life pleasant?", it didn't dare to say no, because ... but it didn't find it pleasant. Life wasn't for its own pleasure and it didn't understand how it could give pleasure. There was a concentration of will in a surrender striving to be as perfect – painstakingly perfect – as possible, and a sense of endurance: holding on and holding out. That was the basis of its existence. Then, when there were transitional periods ... which are always difficult, like, for instance, switching from one habit to another, not in the sense of changing habits but of switching from one support to another, from one impulsion to another (what I call the "transfer of power"), it's always difficult, it occurs periodically (not regularly but periodically) and always when the body has gathered enough energy for its endurance to be more complete; then the new transition comes, and it's difficult. There was that will and that endurance, and also, "Let Your Will be done," and "Let me serve You as You want me to, as I should serve You, let me belong to You as You want me to," and also, "Let there remain nothing but You, let the sense of the person disappear" (it had indeed disappeared to a considerable extent). And there was this sudden revelation: instead of that base of endurance – holding on at any cost – instead of that, a sort of joy, a very peaceful but very smiling joy, very smiling, very sweet, very smiling, very charming – charming! So innocent, something so pure and so lovely: the joy which is in all things, in everything we do, everything, absolutely everything. I was shown last night: everything, but everything, there isn't one vibration that isn't a vibration of joy.

That's the first time.

So then, the result ... (laughing) is that the body is a little better! It no longer feels that tension so much. But it has been advised to be very peaceful, very peaceful, above all no excitement, no "joy" as one usually has it (the vital joy that is aware of itself and expresses itself), not that, nothing of all that: very peaceful, very peaceful. It's something so pure, oh! ... So translucent, transparent, light....

It's the first time I have felt this physically. Meaning it's the first time these cells have had this experience.

You see, previously, they always felt the Lord's support in the power and the force, they felt they existed because of Him, they existed through Him, they existed in Him; they used to feel all that. But to be capable of feeling it, they had to have endurance – absolute endurance – to endure everything. Now it's not that; it's not that, there is something that smiles, but smiles so sweetly, so sweetly, and is, oh, extraordinarily amused, behind it all, and it's light, light, so light – all the weight of that tension has disappeared.

And it's the result of that awesome "flow": a flow that carried the cells along; it wasn't that the cells were immobile and it was flowing through them: they were IN the movement, they were moving with that same velocity – a fantastic velocity with a dazzling luminosity and unimaginable speed, felt materially, like that. It was beyond all possibility of ordinary sensation. It lasted for hours.

Vol. 7, p.125

## June 8, 1966

*(Regarding an old Talk of 19 April 1951 in which Mother said: "You seem to be on an inner hunt, you go hunting for the dark little corners.... You offer the difficulty, whether it is in yourself or in others, whatever the seat of its manifestation, to the Divine Consciousness, asking It to transform it.")*

That's precisely what I have been doing for two days! For the last two days I have spent all my time seeing all that ... oh, an accumulation of heaps of sordid little things we constantly

336

live in, sordid tiny little things. And then, there is only one way – only one way, always the same: to offer it.

This Supreme Consciousness almost seems to put you in contact with quite forgotten things that belong to the past – that are even, or that were or seemed, completely erased, with which you no longer had any contact: all kinds of little circumstances, but seen now in the new consciousness, in their true place, and because of which all life, all human life is such a pathetic, miserable, mean whole. And then, there's a luminous joy in offering all that for it to be transformed, transfigured.

Now it has become the movement of even the cellular consciousness. All the weaknesses, all the response to adverse suggestions (I mean the tiny little things of every minute, in the cells), it sometimes comes in waves, to such a point that the body feels it's going to buckle under the onslaught, and then ... there's such a warm, deep, sweet light, so powerful, which restores order everywhere, puts everything in its place and opens the road towards transformation.

These phases are very difficult times for the body's life; you feel as if there only remains one thing that decides: the supreme Will. There's no support left – no support; from the support of habit to the support of knowledge and the support of will, all the supports have disappeared: there is only the Supreme.

*(silence)*

The aspiration in the cellular consciousness to the perfect sincerity of the consecration.

And the lived experience – intensely lived – that only that absolute sincerity of the consecration allows existence.

The slightest pretense is an alliance with the forces of dissolution and death.

So it's like a chant in the cells – but they mustn't even have the insincerity to watch themselves – the chant of the cells: "Your Will, Lord, Your Will ..."

And the immense habit of depending on the will of others, the consciousness of others, the reactions of others (of others and of all things), that sort of universal playacting everyone does for everyone and everything does for everything must be replaced by a spontaneous, absolute sincerity of consecration.

It is obvious that that perfection in sincerity is possible only in the most material part of the consciousness.

That's where you can be, exist, act without watching yourself be, without watching yourself exist, without watching yourself act, with perfect sincerity.

*     *     *

*Soon afterwards*

This Talk [of April 19, 1951] interests me immensely. It's exactly the same focus as the present effort.

This constant correlation between the inner and the outer work is very interesting, like the preparation of this *Bulletin*, for instance.

I can clearly see that the initial cause always comes from outside ("outside" with regard to this body), in the sense that the focus of the effort depends on the state of health of the people around me, on a certain set of circumstances, and also on an intellectual work (like this *Bulletin*); those are the causes. Because here *(gesture to the forehead),* there's really a tranquil and silent stillness. So there's only what comes from outside.

And the body is increasingly conscious: it has a very acute perception of the vibrations coming from the old habits, from the old ways of being and from the opposition, and of the presence of the True Vibration. So it's a question of dose and proportion, and when the amount, the sum total of the old vibrations, the old habits, the old responses, is too great, that creates a disorder which takes stillness and concentration in order to be overcome, and which gives such a clear and intense perception of how precarious the equilibrium and existence

338

are. And then, behind: a Glory. The Glory of the divine Light, the divine Will, the divine Consciousness, the eternal Motive.

## July 9, 1966

*There's a question I'd like to ask you in connection with the last aphorism....*

121 – The love of inaction is folly and the scorn of inaction is folly; there is no inaction. The stone lying inert upon the sands which is kicked away in an idle moment, has been producing its effect upon the hemispheres.

*You started saying that regardless of all the unnecessary overactivity of people, there was underneath that great current of irresistible Power DOING things despite everything, despite people....*

So, what's your question?

*But that great current of Power needs instruments in order to express itself, doesn't it?*

A brain.

*But not just a brain, precisely. That Power can express itself, as in the past, in a mental or overmental way; it can express itself vitally through force; it can express itself through muscles; but how can it express itself physically (because you often speak of a "material power"), purely, directly? What's the difference between the Action up above and true Action here?*

Every time I have been conscious of the Power, the experience has been similar. The Will from above is expressed by a vibration, which certainly gets clothed in vital power but acts in a subtle physical. There is a perception of a certain quality of vibration, which is difficult to describe but gives a sense of something coagulated (not broken up), something that feels denser than air, extremely homogeneous, with a golden luminosity, an AWESOME power of propulsion, and which expresses a certain will – it doesn't have the nature of human will but more the nature of vision than that of thought: it's like a vision imposing itself in order to be realized, in a domain very close to material Matter, but invisible except to the inner vision. And That, that Vibration, exerts a pressure on people, on things, on circumstances, in order to fashion them according to its vision. And it's irresistible. Even people who think the opposite, who want the opposite, do what is willed without wanting it; even things that are opposed in their very nature are turned around.

For national events, relations between nations, terrestrial circumstances, that's how it acts, constantly, constantly, like an AWESOME Power. So then, if you are yourself in a state of union with the divine Will, without the thought and all the conceptions and ideas interfering, you follow, see, and know.

The resistance of inertia in consciousnesses and in Matter are the reason why that Action, instead of being direct and perfectly harmonious, becomes confused, full of contradictions, shocks and conflicts. Instead of everything working out "normally," I might say, smoothly (as it should), all that resisting, opposing inertia causes things to start clashing together in a tangled movement, with disorder and destruction, which are made necessary only by the resistance but were NOT indispensable: they might not have been – they should not have been, to tell the truth. Because that Will, that Power, is a Power of perfect harmony in which each thing is in its place, and It organizes everything wonderfully: It comes as an absolutely luminous and perfect organization, which you can see when you have the vision. But when It descends and presses down on Matter, everything starts seething and resisting.

So to want to ascribe to the divine Action and the divine Power the disorder and confusion and destruction is yet more human nonsense. It's inertia (not to speak of ill will), it's inertia that CAUSES the catastrophe. It isn't that the catastrophe is willed, or even that it's foreseen: it is CAUSED by the resistance.

Then, added to this is the vision of the action of the Grace that comes and mitigates the results wherever possible, that is to say, wherever it's accepted. And that's what explains that the aspiration, the faith, the complete trust of the human, terrestrial element, have a power of harmonization, because they allow the Grace to come and mend the consequences of blind resistance.

It's a clear, very clear vision, clear even in the details.

If one wanted to, one could prophesy by telling what one sees. But there is a sort of supercompassion preventing that prophecy, because the Word of Truth has a power of manifestation, and to express the result of resistance would make that state more concrete and would lessen the action of the Grace. That's why even when one sees, one cannot speak, one MUST NOT speak.

But Sri Aurobindo certainly meant that this Power or this Force is what does everything – everything. When you see It or are one with It, at the same time you know, and you know that That is the only thing that really acts and creates; the rest is the result of the field or the world or the matter or the substance in which It acts – it's the result of resistance, but it's not the Action. And to unite with That means that you unite with the Action; to unite with what's below means that you unite with the resistance.

So then, because they fidget, stir, bustle, want to do this and that, think, make plans ... they imagine they're doing something (!) – they just resist.

Later, a little later, I'll be able to give examples for very small things, showing how the Force acts, and what interferes and mixes in, or what is driven by that Force but distorts its movement, and the result, that is to say, the physical appearance as we see it. Even an example for a very small thing without any world importance gives a clear notion of the way in which everything occurs and is distorted here.

For everything, everything, all the time, all the time, that's how it is. And when you do the yoga of the cells, you realize it's the same thing: there is the action of the Force acting, and then ... *(Mother laughs)* what the body does with that Action!

*(silence)*

There immediately comes the why and the how. But that belongs to the realm of mental curiosity, because the important fact is to put a stop to the resistance. That's the important thing, putting a stop to the resistance so the universe may become what it must be: the expression of a harmonious, luminous, marvelous power, incomparably beautiful. Afterwards, once the resistance has ceased, if out of curiosity we want to know why it occurred ... it will no longer matter. But right now, it's not by looking for the why that we will be able to bring about the remedy: it's by taking the true position. That's the only thing that matters.

Putting a stop to the resistance through complete surrender, complete self-giving, in all the cells if one can do it.

They are beginning to have that intense joy of being only through the Lord, for the Lord, in the Lord....

When that is established everywhere, it will be fine.

Vol. 7, p. 152

## July 27, 1966

Yes, a few days ago the consciousness was under attack. All that is petty, sordid, ugly, oh ... poor, helpless, all that – it was such an avalanche! ... This poor body, it cried over its incapacity to express anything superior. And then, the answer was very simple – it was very clear, very strong – and the experience came: the only *solution* – *the only way out* of the difficulty is to BECOME divine Love. And the experience was there at the same time for a few moments (it lasted long enough, maybe more than half an hour). Then you understand that everything you have to go through, all these

342

ordeals, all this suffering, all these miseries, is nothing in comparison with the experience of what will be (and what is). But we are still incapable, meaning that the cells haven't the strength yet. They are beginning to have the capacity to be, but not the strength to keep That – "That" cannot stay yet.

And That has such an extraordinary power to transform what is! All our notions (and this had become visible), our notions of miracle, of marvelous change, all the stories of miracles that have been told, all of it becomes a child's prattle – it's nothing! Nothing. All that we try to have, all that we aspire to have, all that ... is childishness.

Only, it was clear that this isn't ready yet.

And it was so extraordinary that the cells felt they couldn't live on without ... without That. That was the impression: That, or else dissolution. And when That had gone away ... It didn't go by accident but deliberately, and with the clear notion: "Now no fuss, you must prepare yourself for That to stay." And it was so categorical *(gesture like a Command from above),* that there was no arguing. When That had left, there was a sort of suffocation. Then the Command came, with the rigidity of a wall: "No fuss, you must prepare yourself."

Then you return to your senses, and it all seems so ... oh!

There is the certitude – the certitude based on experience – that when That is here, it will be ... Or rather, while That is here (since It was here for a while), all the splendors you experience by rising, going out, leaving the body, are nothing. It's nothing, it doesn't have that concrete reality. When you have the experiences up above, you live up above and everything appears lackluster and useless in comparison, but even that appears vague in comparison with HERE. This is truly why the world was created: it's to add to that essential Consciousness something so concrete and so solid, so real, and with such tremendous power!

Only, to the body consciousness it seems long. Up above, of course, there is a smile, but for the body ... And strangely enough, there isn't in the body that joy of the memory of the experience. You have the joy of the memory of the experiences up above, but here, it's not like that! It's not that. The body might say, "It's no use for me to remember: I want to have the thing." Because wherever the mind comes in, the memory is charming, but here, it's not like that. It's not like that: on the contrary, it intensifies the need to be, the aspiration, the need. And life looks like something so stupid, false, artificial, meaningless, without ... "What's all this nonsense we constantly live in!" And yet, when That was there, nothing was destroyed, everything remained, but it was something else altogether.

Later ... *(Mother seems about to say something, then stops herself)* ... later.

No, it has made me understand something, but it's something very (how can I put it?), very intimate.... When Sri Aurobindo left, I knew I had to cut the link with the psychic being, otherwise I would have gone with him; and as I had promised him I would stay on and do the work, I had to do that: I literally closed the door on the psychic and said, "For the moment this doesn't exist anymore." It remained like that for ten years. After ten years, it slowly, slowly began to open again – it was frightening. But I was ready. It began to open again. But then, that experience surprised me when I had it; I wondered why it had been like that, why I had received that command and had to do it. And when there was in the body that identification with divine Love [a few days ago], after that had left, the cells were ordered to undergo a similar phenomenon [to what happened after Sri Aurobindo's departure]. And I understood why the whole material world is closed: it's to allow it to exist WITHOUT the experience [of divine Love]. Naturally, I had understood why I was made to close off my psychic, because ... because it was truly impossible, I couldn't go on existing outwardly without Sri Aurobindo's presence. Well then, the cells have understood that they must go on existing and living their life without the presence of divine Love. And that's how it took place in the world: it was a necessary phenomenon for the formation and development of the material world.

But we're perhaps nearing ... We are nearing the time when it will be allowed to open again.

*(silence)*

You remember, I don't know if it was in a letter or an article, Sri Aurobindo spoke of the manifestation of divine Love; he said, "Truth will have to be established first, otherwise there will be catastrophes...." I understand that very well.

But it's a long time in coming! *(Mother laughs)*

Up above, nothing is long. But anyway, it's here that we are ordered to exist and to achieve.

It's on this occasion, too, that I had an answer regarding death. I was told, "But they all want to die! Because they don't have the courage to be before That is manifested." And I saw – I clearly saw it was like that.

The power of Death is that they all want to die! Not like that in their active thought, but in the body's deep feeling, because it doesn't have the courage to be without That – it takes great courage.

So they began with a complete ignorance and general stupidity, participating in all that this life is outwardly (as if it were something wonderful!). But as soon as they begin to grow a little wiser, it stops being wonderful. It's like what I said about this flower [the lotus]: when you know how to look at a flower, at the so spontaneous and, oh, uncomplicated expression of this marvelous Love, then you understand how long the way is – all these attachments, all this importance we give to useless things, whereas there should be a spontaneous and natural beauty.

*If the world understood too soon, nobody would want to stay on, basically! That's the point.*

Yes, exactly! That's the point.

If they knew too soon, if they were able to see the opposition between what is and what must be, they wouldn't have the courage. One must ... one must truly be heroic – heroic. I assure you, I see these cells, they are heroic – heroic. As for them, they don't "know" in that mental way: it's only their adoration that saves them. That is, "What You will, Lord, what You will, what You will ... ," with the simplicity of a child's ingenuous heart: "What You will, what You will, what You will ... only what You will and nothing but what You will exists." Then it's all right. But without that, it's not possible. It's not possible to know what they know and to continue to be if That isn't there. You know, the feeling is, "At Your service, what You will, what You will ... whatever You will ... ," without discussion, without anything, without even a sensation, nothing: "What You will, what You will...."

This is the only strength, there is no other.

Well, some have to do it, don't they! Otherwise it would never get done.

And at that moment (it was a rather difficult moment), there was even in the consciousness ... it was like a sword of white light that nothing can shake and which gave the cells the sensation, "What! But you should be in an ecstasy of joy, now that you know what will be" – what there IS, in principle.

But it has caused a sort of detachment from the gestures, the outside, as if life weren't quite real – yet real at the same time, but the Reality isn't there.... There is the sense of the Presence; that's constant. And that's a good thing to begin with, it strongly counterbalances the sense and perception of all the Distortion. There is even an insistence from this Presence for That alone to exist and to increasingly reduce the reality of the perception of what must not be. There will be a great strength in the being when the perception of what must not be is dimmed, erased as something far away and nonexistent.

That's what is being prepared.

What makes the work a little more complicated is that it isn't limited to this *(Mother's body)*, it's everything, everything around ... and to a rather considerable distance. Because the contact in thought is almost perfectly established: it's impossible for someone to think [of Mother] without there being a response in the consciousness – a response, a perception. So, imagine what it is ... It's rather vast and rather complicated.

And there are kinds of rungs or stages – stages in the response of the consciousness; rungs and stages according to the degree of development and consciousness. It makes for, oh, not an immensity, but still a rather extensive world. In this perception, the earth isn't very large.

And there is a precision in details for tiny things, like what goes on in an individual's consciousness, for instance, or the response to certain events. It's very, very precise. But there is always a ban on saying things so as not to give them a power of concretization. But the work is being done like that, on all the planes; on all the planes (there are even planes beneath the feet), constantly, constantly, without stop, night and day.

Vol. 7, p. 156


## August 3, 1966

When the mind is active, or rather, as long as the mind is active, when you have dedicated your life and are fully convinced that it's your only raison d'être, you tend to imagine that if you work for the Divine, the whole being participates, and if you aspire to progress, the whole being participates. You are satisfied once all contradiction has disappeared either in the vital or in the mind, and once everything is in agreement and harmonious. You think you have won a victory. But then, now ... now that it's the cells of the body that want and aspire, they have been forced to note that suffering, difficulty, opposition, complication, all that is only to make them be wholly, completely, totally and CONSTANTLY in their aspiration.

It's extremely interesting, really very interesting.

I told you last time about those moments I had, which really were moments of realization [of divine Love]; then I clearly saw that it went away because "it" couldn't stay, and I immediately wanted to know why it couldn't stay. To just say, "Things aren't ready ... things aren't ready," is quite meaningless. Then the cells themselves observed a sort of ... it's something between torpor, drowsiness, numbness and indifference; and that state is mistaken for peace, quietude and acceptance, but it really is ... it really is a form of *tamas*. And that's the reason why it may last for what, to our consciousness, is almost an eternity. And there was, as I told you, an experience [a painful attack]; it recurred in another form (it never recurs in the same form), in another form, and then the cells noticed that that sort of intensity, of ardor of will taking hold of them, that something concrete in the self-giving, in the *surrender,* does not exist when everything is fine (what people are in the habit of calling "everything is fine," which means that you don't feel your body, there is no difficulty and things are just getting along).

It was almost a disappointment for these cells, which thought they were very ardent (!) and have had to realize that that semi-drowsiness was entirely responsible for all that's habitually called "illnesses" – but I don't believe in "illnesses" anymore. I believe in them less and less. Everything that comes is a particular form of disorder, resistance, incomprehension or incapacity – it all belongs to the domain of resistance. And there isn't really a deliberate resistance [in Mother's cells], I mean, what's conventionally called bad will (I hope this is true! If there is any, they haven't become aware of it yet), but those things come as keen indications of the different points [of work or resistance in Mother's body], so it results in what's called pains, or a sense of disorder, or a discomfort. (A discomfort, that is to say, a sense of disorder or disharmony,

348

is much harder to bear than a sharp pain, much harder; it's like something that starts grating and gets stuck and can't get back into place.) All that, in the ordinary consciousness or the ordinary human view, is what people call "illnesses."

There only remains the phenomenon of contagion (contagion of viruses or germs), but there, experience shows that phenomena of psychological disorder – all psychological disorders – appear to be, according to experience, of the same nature as the contagion of a contagious disease and of all viruses and germs (such as the plague, cholera and so on). There are psychological contagions of psychological states: states of revolt or violence, of anger AND DEPRESSION, are contagious in the same manner, it's a similar phenomenon. Therefore, since it's a similar phenomenon, it can be mastered. It's simply a question of words: we call them "illnesses" (but these [psychological contagions] can also be called illnesses) or we can call them any name we like, it's a question of words, that's all. But it's similar, it's the same thing: it's an opening to disorder or an opening to revolt. We can call it what we like. Only, it's in a different field of vibrations. But the character is identical.

And then, what discoveries I make! Extraordinary discoveries: how every experience always has an obverse and a reverse. For instance, the calm of a vision that's vast enough not to be disturbed by tiny infinitesimal points and is (I was about to say "seems to be," but it doesn't seem to be: it IS) the result of a growth of consciousness and of an identification with the higher regions, and at the same time that apparent insensitiveness that looks like the negation of divine compassion; there comes a point when you see both as having become true and being able to exist not simultaneously but as ONE thing. As recently as the day before yesterday, I had the perfectly concrete experience of an extremely intense wave of divine Compassion [in the face of one of those "psychological contagions"], and I had the opportunity to observe how, if this Compassion is allowed to manifest on a certain plane,

349

it becomes an emotion that may disturb or trouble the imperturbable calm; but if it manifests (they aren't the same "planes": there are imperceptible nuances), if it manifests in its essential truth, it retains all its power of action, of effective help, and it in no way changes the imperturbable calm of the eternal vision.

All those are experiences of nuances (or nuances of experiences, I don't know how to put it) that become necessary and concrete only in the physical consciousness. And then, it results in a perfection of realization – a perfection in the minutest detail – which none of those realizations have in the higher realms. I am learning what the physical realization contributes in terms of concreteness, accuracy and perfection in the Realization; and how all those experiences interpenetrate, combine with each other, complement each other – it's wonderful.

At the same time, I am little by little learning from demonstration the true use that must be made of mental activity. Its purpose is easy to understand: it has been used to educate, awaken and so on; but it's not something that after having done its duty and fulfilled its purpose will disappear. It will be used in its own manner, but in its true manner and true place. And it becomes wonderfully interesting.... For instance, the idea that you are what you think, that your knowledge is your power, well, it seems to be a necessity of the transition, of the passage from one state of consciousness to another, but it's not, as I said, something that will disappear when something else is reached: it will be used, but in its own place. Because when you experience union, the mind appears unnecessary: the direct contact, the direct action, do without it. But in its true place, acting in the true way, sticking to its place (a place not of necessity or even usefulness, but of refinement in action), it becomes quite interesting. When you see the Whole as a growing self-awareness, the mind enriches – it enriches the Whole. And when each thing is in its own place, it all becomes so harmonious and simple, but with such full and complete and perfect simplicity that everything is used.

And with all this, there is (it almost seems to be the key to the problem, to the understanding), there is a special concentration on the why, the how of death…. Years and years ago, when Sri Aurobindo was still here, there came one day a sort of dazzling, imperious revelation: "One dies only when one chooses to die." I told Sri Aurobindo, "This is what I saw and KNEW." He said to me, "It is true." Then I asked him, "Always, in every case?" He said, "Always." Only, one isn't conscious, human beings aren't conscious, but that's how it is. But now I am beginning to understand! Some experiences, some examples are given in the details of the body's inner vibrations, and I see that there is a choice, a choice generally unconscious, but which, in some individuals, can be conscious. I am not talking about sentimental cases, I am talking about the body, the cells accepting disintegration. There is a will like this *(Mother raises a finger upward)* or a will like that *(Mother lowers her finger)*. The origin of that will lies in the truth of the being, but it seems (and that is something marvelous), it seems that the final decision is left to the choice of the cells themselves.

I am not at all referring to the physical, vital, psychic consciousnesses, not to any of that: I am referring to the consciousness of the cells.

That's how the present moment is: the will may be like this *(Mother raises a finger upward),* or it may be like that *(finger downward).* Like that, it means dissolution; like this, it means continuation and progress – continuation with the necessity of progress. There is something which is the consciousness of the cells (a consciousness that observes, and which, when it is awakened, is a wonderful witness), and that consciousness is the one which goes like this *(same gesture)* or like that. This is expressed by a will to endure or to last, or by a need for the annihilation of rest. And then, when these cells are full of that light – that golden light, that splendor of divine Love – there is

351

a sort of thirst, a need to participate in That, which takes away all that is or can be difficult in the endurance: that disappears, it becomes a glory. Then ...

That's what is being learned.

*(silence)*

But to be able to observe (this is something being worked out on a parallel line), to observe exactly what goes on in this cellular realm, one must be perfectly free from and independent of other human beings' influence. And this is extremely difficult because of that habit of mixture.... It's the sensitiveness of the cells which has difficulty. So constant care must be taken to fasten all that sensitiveness on to the aspiration for the Supreme alone; that's the only way, the solution. You have to do that constantly, every time you feel the influence of others' contact. In ordinary life, of course, to get rid of influences you cut off the contact; well, that movement of withdrawal, recoil, isolation, all those psychological movements (through material isolation in the physical; in the vital, in the psychic, in the mind, everywhere, it always consists in cutting oneself off, in separating oneself), all that is false; it's contrary to the truth. The truth is to ... *(outspread gesture)* to feel the union. And yet, for the cellular work of cellular transformation, an isolation must be reached that isn't a contradiction of the essential unity. And that's a little difficult; it makes for a very delicate, very painstaking, very microscopic work which somewhat complicates matters. But it's possible, for instance, to touch someone, to take someone's hand, and for union to be achieved only in the deeper truth, while outwardly there is just a bringing together of cells.

The work is very intensive, very intensive indeed.

Vol. 7, p. 165

## August 31, 1966

*I've often had the experience (on another plane, I suppose) that the current inexplicably seemed to be reversed: things stop being harmonious, and there's no knowing why.*

The why is very simple: it's always separation – the individual separating himself, always. So, according to everyone's nature, there is more or less egoism, but there is separation. Now I see the false movement: it's when the consciousness falls back into an old habit. And as it's an old habit – very old habit – you don't feel it as a fall: it's a tiny little movement like this *(Mother twists something between her thumb and index finger).*

I know – this morning, it was very clear.

You see, everything is the Supreme's action to hasten the return of the individual consciousness to the Consciousness – the supreme Consciousness; so then, through the individual (I don't know if you'll be able to follow), the pressure of the Force to be accepted is turned into a will to make itself understood. That's the distortion. And you see, it's extremely subtle. But by "will," I mean a will in the human way, you understand. The pressure of the Force *(Mother lays her right hand flat on top of her left hand)* to make itself understood by the consciousness *(the left hand below),* the pressure of the Force on the consciousness to transform it is turned in the intermediary individual into a will to make itself understood.

Another thing. There is instinctively, that is to say, almost subconsciously, almost involuntarily, not a will or an anxiety, or even a curiosity, but a sort of habit of observation: the habit of observing the effect produced on others (it's not bluntly what they think or feel, their opinion; it's not as blunt as that because as soon as it assumes that proportion it makes one smile). It's a sort of habit, a habit of looking at every circumstance not only as you see it, but, at the same time, as, let's say, others see it. It's not an "anxiety" but you take it into account; you take it into account not for its result, but you automatically take it into account in the reaction of the consciousness: what others feel, think, their reactions; not exactly their opinion, but the feeling of their reaction. It's a sort of habit. And that is the fallacious distortion of the sense of Oneness. Of course, we are all ONE, and in the distorted consciousness this oneness is translated as a noticing, an observation (I am not referring to those who are concerned with themselves and for whom it's important, that's not what I mean: it's in the functioning of the consciousness). And that movement of observation has a place, but in this form, it's not a true place. So then, it's so subtle.... There is the sense of Oneness, that every movement of the consciousness has repercussions everywhere, in all consciousnesses because there is only one consciousness, and the distortions are different; it's the distortions that make for diversity.

*(silence)*

Yet another thing. There is an intense and constant aspiration for Union. It always begins with self-giving – the spontaneous self-giving to the Supreme. But then, there is, mixed into it ... (how can I express it?) the expectation (is it an expectation? It's almost just a noticing) ... it's not an anxiety for, but rather an *expectation,* yes, of the result. In other words, in that great will and aspiration for the manifestation of Harmony, of Love in the Truth, in that thirst of the whole, entire being for That which is the source of that Harmony, to the movement of aspiration is added the perception (it's more than the perception: it's the expectation), the expectation of the result, and then, it gets warped *(same twisting gesture).*

And what I am saying now isn't at all something I see, it's something I lived during my morning walk at 4:30. There were different successive experiences [which Mother has just described], and then, a very clear, very keen perception of the point at which the true experience *(same twisting gesture)* gets falsified. And it's not something violent, there's nothing dramatic to it, nothing at all, but ... it's clearly the difference between the Infinite and Eternal, the All-Powerful [being turned] into the individuality – the individual limitation. And for the ordinary consciousness, the usual consciousness – that is to say, the limited, individual consciousness – that experience itself is marvelous, but you are the "recipient," you are "the one who experiences." That's the point, it's the difference between the [pure] experience and, all of a sudden, "the one who experiences." And then, with that "the one who experiences," it's over, everything is distorted. Everything is distorted, but not dramatically, you understand, not like that, no. It's the difference between Truth and falsehood. It's a falsehood (how can I explain?) ... it's the difference between life and death; it's the difference between Reality and illusion. And the one IS, while the other ... remembers having been, or is a witness.

It's very subtle, really very subtle. But it's immense – immense and total.

This body lived the Truth this morning several times for a few seconds (which might have been eternities). But it's obvious that if everything were ready for "that" to be established, it would mean omnipotence.

There was so clear an explanation – obvious, tangible – showing how it happens all the time – all the time, all the time, everywhere. And unless one experiences it, there's no way one can even understand the difference; all words are approximations. But just when it is true ... (Mother smiles blissfully) ... And then, one doesn't know if it lasted or if it doesn't last: all that has disappeared. And it doesn't abolish anything, that's the most wonderful part! Everything is there, nothing is abolished. It's only a phenomenon of consciousness. Because at such a time, everything that is becomes true, so ... I mean it abolishes nothing of the Manifestation; you don't even feel that Falsehood is abolished: it doesn't exist, it isn't. Everything can remain exactly as it is; it becomes only a question of choice. Everything becomes a question of choice: you choose this way, choose that way.... And in a splendor of joy, of beauty, of harmony, a plenitude of luminous consciousness in which there is no darkness anymore: it no longer exists. And it truly is, so to say, the choice between life and death, consciousness and unconsciousness ("unconsciousness" isn't what we call unconsciousness, the unconsciousness of the stone, it's not that). One doesn't know what consciousness is until one has experienced "that."

If it could be translated into words, it would be so pretty (that's when I understand poets!). That ineffable Presence seems to be saying, "You see, I was always there, and you didn't know it." And it's lived at the very heart of the cells: "You see, you know that I was always there, but you didn't know it." And then ... *(Mother smiles on in a contemplation)* ... It's a tiny nothing – which changes everything.

That's how a dead man can come back to life. That's how: through that change.

The mind dramatizes, and that's why it cannot understand. Of course, it has been useful to refine Matter, to make it more supple, to prepare things – to make Life more supple and refine Matter. But it has a taste for drama, and that's why it doesn't understand. Violent emotions, complications are its game, its amusement. Probably because it needed them. But one must really leave that aside when the time comes, when one is ready for the experience.

*(silence)*

And immediately after that, the certitude – so peaceful – that everything was necessary – everything, but everything: from the most marvelous for the human consciousness to the most horrible, the most repulsive – everything was necessary. But strangely, all those things, all those experiences, all that life is what becomes unreal – unreal, worse than an act you put on for yourself: unreal. And it is in its unreality that it was necessary for the consciousness. All appreciations are purely human – purely human because they alter the measure, the proportion. Even physical suffering, material suffering, which is one of the things most difficult to feel as illusory: a lamentable act you put on for yourself, for the cells. And I am speaking from experience, with convincing examples. It's very interesting.

**September 3, 1966**

*(...[A]bout an old Playground Talk of April 28, 1951, in which Mother speaks of awakening the body not through coercion by the vital, but through collaboration from the body itself, and of the need for physical plasticity so as to be able to undergo all kinds of change.)*

I've had several hours of this very experience: how the body is automatically attached to its precise way of doing things, and how it must receive the light in order to be ready for anything. It must be able to say spontaneously and sincerely, "Your Will, Lord, nothing but Your Will...." But it accepts this from no one else or nowhere else than the Lord. Otherwise, nothing doing.

To me it's very interesting. Once again I note that I always experience what I am going to hear or to be read.

It's curious. Like an inner preparation.

\* \* \*

*A little later*

There was, yesterday afternoon and this morning, a long demonstration of how the Mind brought about and permitted a certain change in the evolution of Matter for the Divine's play, how rejection of the Mind is useful ONLY as a means of progress and evolution, and how it will be fully used when the new being – the complete, divine being – manifests. It was very interesting. A demonstration.

It's the continuation of the demonstration [of August 31] which showed that ALL that has happened is necessary.

But this can be really understood only when you have got rid of the Mind. As long as you are bound to it, you don't understand anything.

It takes place little by little....

What takes time is to prepare Matter, this cellular matter as it is now organized [since the awakening of the mind of the cells in Mother], to make it supple enough and strong enough to be able to bear and manifest the divine Force. That takes a lot of time.... It explains everything, everything – everything is explained. The day we can describe that in detail, it will be really interesting.

And there is a small beginning of how that being which Sri Aurobindo calls "supramental" will be – the next creation. A small beginning. And it is, as Sri Aurobindo said, an explanation from within outward – the "outward," the surface, has only a quite secondary importance and it will come at the very end, when it's ready. But it begins from within outward, and it begins in a rather precise and interesting way.

A great deal of time ...

Vol. 7, p. 191

## September 28, 1966

For a long time lately, that is, for days and days, there has been a very sharp perception, very intense and clear, that the action of the Force outwardly results in what we call "suffering" because it's the only kind of vibration capable of pulling Matter out of inertia.

Supreme Peace and Calm were distorted and disfigured into inertia and *tamas,* and precisely because it was the distortion of true Peace and Calm, there was no reason for it to change! A certain vibration of awakening – of reawakening – was necessary to emerge from that tamas, which was incapable of directly changing from tamas into Peace; something was needed to shake the tamas, and outwardly it resulted in suffering.

I am referring here to physical suffering, because all the other kinds of suffering – vital, mental, emotive suffering – arise from a wrong functioning of the mind, and those ... we can easily rank them in the Falsehood, that's all. But physical suffering is to me like a child being beaten, because here in Matter, Falsehood turned into ignorance, which means there is no bad will – there is no bad will in Matter, everything is inertia and ignorance: total ignorance of the Truth, ignorance of the Origin, ignorance of the Possibility, even ignorance of what needs to be done so as not to suffer materially. This ignorance is everywhere in the cells, and only the experience – and the experience of what, in this rudimentary consciousness, is translated as suffering – can awaken, arouse the need to know and be cured, and the aspiration to be transformed.

This has become a certitude because the aspiration has been born in all these cells, and it's growing more and more intense and is surprised at the resistance. But they have observed that when something is upset in the functioning (which means that instead of being supple, spontaneous, natural, the functioning becomes a painful effort, a struggle with something that takes on the appearance of a bad will but is only a reluctance devoid of understanding), at such times the intensity of the aspiration, of the call, grows tenfold: it becomes constant. The difficulty is to keep up this state of intensity; generally it all falls back into, I can't say "drowsiness," but it's a sort of slackening: you take things easy. And it's only when the inner disorder becomes hard to bear that the intensity grows and becomes permanent. For hours – hours – without flagging, the call, the aspiration, the will to unite with the Divine, to become the Divine, is kept up at its peak – why? Because there was what's outwardly called a physical disorder, a suffering.

Otherwise, when there isn't any suffering, there is now and then an upsurge, then it flags and falls back; then at some other time, another upsurge ... It never ends! It lasts for eternities. If we want things to go fast (fast relatively to the rhythm of our lives), the whiplash is necessary. I am convinced of this, because as soon as you are in your inner being, you treat this with contempt (for yourself).

But then, when that true Compassion of divine Love comes and you see all those things that look so horrible, so abnormal, so absurd, that great pain over all beings and even over things ... Then there was born in this physical being the aspiration to relieve, to cure, to make all that disappear. There is something in Love in its Origin that is constantly expressed by the intervention of the Grace; a force, a sweetness, something like a vibration of solace, spread everywhere, but which an enlightened consciousness can direct, concentrate on certain points. And that's just where I saw the true use one could make of thought: thought is used as a channel to carry the vibration from place to place, wherever it's necessary. This force, this vibration of sweetness is there over the world in a static way, pressing to be received, but it's an impersonal action, and thought − enlightened thought, surrendered thought, the thought that is nothing more than an instrument, that no longer tries to set things in motion, that is satisfied with being moved by the higher Consciousness − thought is used as an intermediary to make contact, to build a connection and allow this impersonal Force to act wherever it's necessary, on precise points.

*(silence)*

We may say in an absolute way that the remedy always goes together with the trouble. We could say that the cure for every suffering coexists with the suffering. Then, instead of seeing an "unnecessary" and "stupid" trouble, as people generally think, you see that the progress, the evolution which made the suffering necessary − which is the cause and the goal of the suffering − achieves the desired result, and at the same time the suffering is cured, for those who can open up and receive. The three things − the suffering as a means of progress, the progress, and the cure of the suffering − are coexistent, simultaneous, meaning that they don't follow one another, they take place at the same time.

If, when the transformative action creates a suffering, there is in what suffers the necessary aspiration and opening, the remedy is absorbed at the same time, and the effect is total, complete: the transformation, along with the action necessary to obtain it, and at the same time the cure of the false sensation caused by the resistance. And the suffering is replaced by ... something unknown on this earth, but which has to do with joy, ease, trust, and security. It's a supersensation, in perfect peace, and clearly the only thing that can be eternal.

This analysis expresses very imperfectly what we could call the "content" of the Ananda.

I think it's something that has been felt, experienced (partially and very fleetingly) through all ages, but which is beginning to be concentrated and almost concretized on earth. But physical Matter in its cellular form has, we can't say a fear or an anxiety, but a sort of apprehension of new vibrations, and that apprehension naturally takes away from the cells their receptivity and takes on the appearance of a discomfort (it's not a suffering but a discomfort). But when that apprehension is counterbalanced and cured by aspiration and the will for total surrender and the act of total surrender, then that sort of apprehension having disappeared, there comes supreme ease.

All this is like microscopic studies of the phenomena of consciousness independent of mental intervention. The need to use words to express ourselves brings in that mental intervention, but in the experience it doesn't exist. And it's very interesting because the pure experience holds a content of truth, of reality, which disappears as soon as the mind intervenes. There is a flavor of true reality which totally eludes expression for that reason. It's the same difference as between an individual and his portrait, between a fact and the story told about it. That's how it is. But it's far more subtle.

So then, to return to the letter, when you are conscious of this Force – this Force, this Compassion in its essential reality – and see how it can be exerted through a conscious individual, you have the key to the problem.

I've had experiences ...

## October 26, 1966

Sri Aurobindo wrote somewhere, I don't remember in what connection, that in a certain state of consciousness one had the power to CHANGE THE PAST. I found that very striking.

Because it's an experience I've had several times, and with all this work I am doing now, I understand better. You see, what seems to be perpetuated or preserved isn't individuals: it's states of consciousness – states of consciousness. Those states of consciousness manifest through many individuals and many different lives, and those states of consciousness are what progress towards a more and more luminous perfection. There are now, at present, all kinds of "categories" of states of consciousness that come one upon another in order to be put in contact with the Truth, the Light, the perfect Consciousness, and at the same time they have retained a sort of imprint (like a memory) of the moments when they manifested.

There is a big work of transformation of the material states of consciousness going on: the states of consciousness nearest to the Inconscient, the most material states of consciousness. They come like that [to present themselves to Mother], with one or two examples of their previous manifestation (perhaps even their first emergence from the Inconscient), and then I see the transition (along with what has transformed them, changed them or even simply altered them through successive manifestations), the transition up to the point when they are now presented before the supreme Consciousness for the final transformation. This is a perpetual work, so to speak, because, interestingly, it's a work I can go on doing while seeing people. Generally my work was interrupted when I saw people, because I was busy with them and that diminished and limited the work: they represented a small aggregate of difficulties that enormously shrank the Action [of Mother]. But now it's no longer like that. And the interesting point is that it places people in this or that "curve of transformation" of the consciousness. For some time I have been seeing a considerable number of people I had never seen before (with all the old or familiar people there was no difficulty, but with the new ones it generally caused a shrinking of the work), and now with this "study" of states of consciousness, people are placed: here, there, here *(Mother draws different levels in space)*. And if they are receptive, they must go away [after seeing Mother] with a new impulse to transform themselves. Those who aren't receptive just miss it; but they are no longer a disturbance: they come in and go out. And from that I know what state they are in – I can even do it with photos, but when I see people it's much more complete. Photos are no more than one moment of their being, while here, even what isn't being manifested is there, hidden behind, and can be seen, so I see the person more completely. It's very interesting. It transforms this whole burden of visitors into something interesting.

Vol. 7, p. 243


## November 30, 1966

... In my case, strangely, I seem to see through a thick veil, that is to say, everything is blurred. Then suddenly, for no apparent reason, I see an object, some thing or other, clearly, so clearly, precisely, with a detailed accuracy, as if it were shown to me. Or else when reading a letter, for instance, if I read it without paying attention to anything else, I see perfectly well, but if I start thinking of an answer or concentrate, if the consciousness starts working, everything disappears and I can't see anything anymore – the next minute, the words become clear again. Which means it doesn't depend on a defect of the sight or the material organ: it's something else – something else that one wants me to learn. Because it constantly comes back as if to show me something. But there's so much work and so many people that I don't always have the time to stop and concentrate to see what it is. I would have to catch the exact point when the sight comes and when it goes, and follow the conditions of the consciousness at that moment. I don't have the time.

It's really like an attempt to demonstrate to me that sight doesn't depend on the eyes.

The organ is in good condition, it doesn't have any lesion. But the sight isn't the same with this eye as with that one. With this one *(the right)*, it's only an overall, slightly blurred vision. With that one *(the left)*, it's a precise, clear vision, but there's a tiny spot in the corner, like a black spot, because of which I see everything clearly but with a patch in the corner. Then if I concentrate, I see that patch grow bright and luminous, like a dark blue star, and that star moves in front of me (it doesn't depend on the eye), it moves about, and if I fix my eyes on someone, for instance, I see that dark blue star go and rest here or there *(gesture at different levels of the person)*, at the exact spot where some work has to be done. So it means it doesn't depend on the eye, it's independent of the eye. And also if I look at a photo, with a certain position between the right eye and the left, I suddenly see the photo come alive, in three dimensions, with the person's head sticking out. That's how I can see the character. It's really strange, like an attempt to teach me to see in a different way.

We are learning our lesson.

Vol. 7, p. 283

## January 21, 1967

Something rather indefinable as yet is happening.

The body was in the habit of fulfilling its functions automatically, as something natural, which means that for it, the question of their importance or usefulness did not arise: it didn't have that mental, for instance, or vital vision of things, of what's "important" or "interesting" and what isn't. That didn't exist. But now that the cells are growing conscious, they seem to stand back *(gesture):* they look at themselves, they begin to watch themselves act, and they very much wonder, "What's the use of all this?" And then, an aspiration: "How, how should things truly be? What's our purpose, our usefulness, our basis? Yes, what should our basis and our 'standard' of life be?" To put it mentally again, we might say, "How will we be when we are divine? What will be the difference? What's the divine way of being?" And what speaks there is that whole kind of physical base entirely made up of thousands of small things absolutely indifferent in themselves, whose raison d'être lies only in their totality, like a support to another action, but which in themselves seem devoid of any meaning. And then, it's again the same thing: a sort of receptivity, of silent opening to let oneself be permeated, and a very subtle perception of a way of being that might be luminous, harmonious.

That way of being is still quite indefinable; but in this seeking there is a constant perception (which translates as a vision) of a multicolored light, with all the colors – all the colors not in layers but as though *(stippling gesture)* combined in dots, a combination of all the colors. Two years ago (a little more than two years, I forget), when I met the Tantrics, when I came into contact with them, I started seeing that light, and I thought it was the "Tantric light," the Tantric way of seeing the material world. But now I see it constantly, associated with everything, and it seems to be what we might call a "perception of true Matter." All possible colors are combined without being mixed together *(same stippling gesture)*, and combined in luminous dots. Everything is as though made up of this. And it seems to be the true mode of being – I am not yet sure, but at any rate it's a far more conscious mode of being.

I see it all the time: with eyes open, eyes closed, all the time. It gives a strange perception (with regard to the body), a strange perception at the same time of subtlety, permeability (if I may call it that), of suppleness of form, and not exactly a removal but a considerable lessening of the rigidity of forms (the rigidity is removed, not the forms: a suppleness in the forms). As for the body, the first times it felt that in some part or the other, it felt ... when it happens it's a bit lost, with the sense of something eluding it. But if one remains very quiet and waits quietly, it's simply replaced by a sort of plasticity and fluidity that seems to be a new mode of the cells.

It might probably be what, on the material level, must take the place of the physical ego; that is to say, it seems the rigidity of the form must give place to this new way of being. Of course, the first contact is always very ... surprising. But the body is getting used to it little by little. What's a little difficult is the moment of transition from one way to the other. It's done very progressively, yet at the moment of transition there are a few seconds that are ... the least we can say is "unexpected."

In that way, all habits are undone. It's the same with all the functionings: blood circulation, digestion, breathing – all the functions. And at the moment of transition it's not that one abruptly takes the place of the other, but there is a state of fluidity between the two which is ... difficult. It's only because of that great Faith, a perfectly still, luminous, constant, immutable faith in the real existence of the supreme Lord – in the SOLE real existence of the Supreme – that everything goes on apparently as it is.

There are kinds of great waves of all ordinary movements, ordinary ways of being, ordinary habits: they are thrown back, come back again, try to engulf and are thrown back again. And I can see that for years the body and the whole body consciousness used to rush back into the old way to seek safety, it used to find its safety in flight; but now, the body has been persuaded not to do it any longer and on the contrary to accept: "Well, if it's dissolution, let it be dissolution." It accepts what will be.

Mentally, when that happens in the physical mind (it happened years ago, but I had observed that), it's what gives people the feeling that they're going insane, and they get frightened (and with fear things happen), so they rush back

366

into ordinary common sense to escape. It's the equivalent – not the same thing, but the equivalent of what happens in the material: you feel all the usual stability is vanishing. Well, for a long time – a long time – there was that retreat into habit, and then you are quite at peace and you start all over again. But now, the cells no longer want that: "Come what may, we'll see soon enough!" The great adventure.

How will we be? – How will we be? How ... You understand, it's the cells asking, "How should we be? How will we be?"

It's interesting.

Vol. 8, p. 30

### February 8, 1967

I have some interesting things to tell you. It's about that cold. An extraordinary healing power ... All the phases in their most acute form, with the study of the process, going through each phase in a few hours, or a few minutes (depending on what it was). When you have a cold, you usually go through one phase, then another (you know how it is), then it goes lower down, then there is a cough, then ... All of it was gone through quickly, and in two days it was over. And with the whole process, but not the mentalized process, not at all: the vibratory process, showing how the Force comes and acts, and at the same time ... Oh, it was very, very interesting, because there was the part played by the inconscient, the part played by conscious reactions, the part played by the will (that's tremendous, an enormous part), the part played by mental suggestion (tremendous, too), and ... the action of the supreme Vibration. The whole thing in detail, day and night, constantly; to such a point that at times I stood still, like that, to follow the course. And it went on (I saw you on Saturday) for ... Sunday, Monday, Tuesday: those three days.

It's my fault it started; as I told you I had complained about these sinuses which were a constant nuisance, and there was also that constant inflammation of the mouth and the throat. So it had its effect. I can't say it's fully over because there still remains a lot, quite a lot of the old habit, but it came with the intention of changing things.

And all this has been learned in detail from a vibratory point of view. It's very interesting, I haven't wasted my time!

*Because what applies to a cold obviously applies to any disorder, doesn't it?*

It's the detailed process in each case. That was one of the manifestations of a cold.

*I mean, it could act with other diseases, too, couldn't it?*

Every disease represents its own vibratory mode. Every disease has its own vibratory mode; it represents a whole field of vibrations to be corrected. It's the EXACT measure of what in Matter resists the divine Influence – the exact measure, to the atom.

Oh, how interesting it is, if you knew how interesting.... Take coughing, for instance (not in the chest, in the throat). So, the first vibration: an irritation that draws your attention in order to make you cough. It has a certain kind of vibration which we may call "pointed," but it's not violent: it's light, annoying. It's the first little vibration. So with that vibration, awakening of the attention in the surrounding consciousness [of the throat cells]; then refusal to accept the cough, a rejection here [in the throat], which at first almost causes nausea (all this is seen through a microscope, you understand, they are tiny things). The attention is focused. Then, at that point, there are several possible factors, sometimes simultaneous and sometimes one driving the other away; one is anxiety: something goes wrong and there is apprehension at what's going to happen; another is a will that nothing should be disturbed by the irritation; and all of a sudden, the faith that the Force is capable of restoring order everywhere instantly (none of this is intellectual: it's vibrations).

Then, sometime yesterday morning, something very interesting took place: a clear perception that the vast majority of the cells, (in THIS case: I'm not talking about the whole body, I am talking about this particular spot – throat, nose, etc.), that the vast majority of the cells still have a sort of feeling – which seems to be the result of innumerable experiences or of habits (it's both; not clearly one or the other, but both) – that Nature's force, that is to say, the nature governing the body, knows what needs to be done better than the divine Power: it's "used to it," it "knows better." That's how it is. So then, when this new consciousness [the mind of the cells] which is being worked out in the physical being caught hold of that, oh, it was as if it had caught hold of an extraordinary revelation; it said, "Ah, I've got you, you culprit! You are the one who is preventing the transformation."

It's tremendously interesting, tremendously interesting!

All this is magnified in order to be expressed, but it's on the scale of the body's cells. And there was something like a flash of luminous Power as soon as that was discovered: it came down like that, brrm! *(gesture of a sword of light plunging into Matter)*

And it hasn't gone away since then. To such a point that I tried to recall that state of consciousness in order to note it down in detail – it no longer exists.

Those actions are ... really miraculous, but in tiny details, of course, which is why they don't look miraculous: they are only actions in details.

The attitude taken by the cells, the action of the will, the habit of Nature, the Intervention – all that was seen minutely, phase after phase. Because these cells [in the throat] were complaining; they were the ones that said things weren't changing and remained as they were. They clearly saw that things were kept under control, but without any sign of

369

transformation. And that cold came as a magnifying glass, you understand. It came and magnified everything so it would become more visible and more easily observed. And the detail of all that's going on is, oh, really marvelous: it's a whole world, and it's tiny little things that generally go unobserved because we observe mentally. But seen like this ... For instance, at a certain point in those successive phases, all the signs are there that the body's will is going to flag and that you are going either to faint or to fall "sick" for a while. Then comes the choice made within by the cells, which weigh the possibilities against one another from the standpoint of the progress of transformation: "What can act? What can be the most useful and produce the greatest result? Is it to yield and have an apparent fall (it's only apparent), and in that fall, to allow the Force to do its work without interference? Or is it to follow the course of conscious transformation?" And that's where this marvelous discovery of the cells took place: they really felt Nature knew better *(laughing)* how to go about it, because it was used to it. That was exquisite! Wonderful.

All this must be going on in everyone, but people are unconscious. It's the consciousness of the cells which has awakened, you understand. It's so interesting! And how illnesses can be avoided, how things ... All of it based on the experience of the UNREALITY OF APPEARANCES: a play is going on behind, which is altogether different from what we see or know.

I am now perfectly aware of the causes of allergy (studied in detail), and why cases of allergy are multiplying here in the Ashram. Naturally, it's based on ... *(Mother starts coughing and concludes:)* Ah, forbidden topic.

*(After a moment of silence, Mother resumes:)* It's the nerves that become increasingly receptive to the Force (and consequently, increasingly sensitive), and they don't have the wisdom or equilibrium necessary to counterbalance the increased sensitiveness. But then, the doctors' treatment is stupid! What would be needed is just the opposite: what's

needed is (how can I put it?) to infuse wisdom and peace, not to deaden the body.

....

It's true that now, as soon as the nerves (but you know, it's an observation of every second), as soon as the nerves start protesting ... It happens very often when they are interested in a sensation: they become interested in a sensation, they concentrate and follow it, then suddenly, it exceeds ... (how should I put it?) the amount they are used to considering as pleasant (it can be put that way), so there's a slight tipping over and they start going wrong, they start protesting. But if there is observation, there is the action of the inner "mentor" that tells them, "Now, all sensations can be borne almost to their highest degree: it's quite simply a bad habit and a lack of plasticity. Calm down and see what happens." (Something of the sort.) Then they are docile, they calm down, and ... everything falls flat. Falls flat, and then ... the allergic reaction is over. So I think I've learned the knack! ....It's very amusing. That way you learn things.

Only, how to communicate this to people? I don't know.

It's a subtle, keen, minute observation.

At the same time, there is another factor (oh, there are several methods). You have a small material action to do (quite uninteresting in itself, but anyway, it has to be done) and there is that same inner disquiet which can cause things to tip over on the wrong side any moment; if the consciousness – the total consciousness of the body – is busy with something else, the difficulty dies down without your noticing it. So the possibility is there of keeping the consciousness interested in something else. But then the possibility of illness or disorder isn't cured. So it's a constant choice between the work of transformation and (or) an equilibrium sufficient to go on with the general work.

I could write volumes, it's very, very interesting. It's being organized.

371

*We don't really understand the value of the microscopic.*
Yes! Yes, exactly.

Vol. 8, p. 44

## March 4, 1967

Yes, this problem of the transformation, I see more and more clearly that there are three approaches, three ways to go about it, and that in order to be more complete one should combine the three.

One – the most important, naturally – is the way we could call "spiritual," the way of the contact with the Consciousness – Love-Consciousness-Power, that is. These three aspects: supreme Love-Consciousness-Power. And the contact, the identification: making all the material cells capable of receiving Him and expressing Him – of BEING That.

Of all the ways, that is the most powerful and most indispensable.

There is the occult way, which brings all the intermediary worlds into play. There is a very detailed knowledge of all the powers and personalities, all the intermediary regions, and it makes use of all that. That's where one makes use of the Overmind godheads: it's in this second way. Shiva, Krishna, all the aspects of the Mother are part of this second way.

Then there is the higher intellectual approach, which is the projection of a surpassing scientific mind and takes up the problem from below. It has its own importance too. From the standpoint of the detail of the procedure, it reduces approximation, it gives a more direct and precise action.

If one can combine all three, then obviously the thing will go faster.

Without the first, nothing is possible (and even, the other two are an illusion without the first: they lead nowhere, you go round in circles endlessly). But if you clothe the first in the other two, then I think the action is more precise, direct, rapid.

It's the result of these last few days' "study."

Vol. 8, p. 72

## March 11, 1967

*There is a question of terminology. I would like to put a note at the beginning of the third volume of "Questions and Answers," in which I say: "We found it fit to begin this new volume with the Talk of February 29, 1956, because on that day, during the meditation that followed the class, there took place ..." What? "The first descent of the supramental forces into the Inconscient"?*

(Mother shakes her head) It was: Light-Force and Power. And it wasn't into the Inconscient, it was into the earth atmosphere.

*Light-Consciousness-Power?*

"Consciousness" is part of the totality, it will come later.

*Supramental Light-Force-Power?*

Yes.

*And is the word "descent" right?*

It's "manifestation," rather. The image was ... (I can't say there was "above" and "below," that's not how it was), it was the barrier being broken and the flow rushing forth. It's better to put "manifestation."

Vol. 8, p. 76

## April 5, 1967

Mon petit, when the cells get into this state, it's wonderful, you can't imagine! It changes life com-plete-ly. They are like that: a sense of wonder at the first Contact. "Is it possible? Can it be that beautiful! Is it possible?" Like that. And constantly, all the time, every moment, on any occasion: "Can it be like that?" Such a sense of wonder! Then you see how much difference there is from the old habits and everything people have crammed their heads with [renunciation, the beyond] – it's marvelous! Unbelievable. This whole morning again it was like that.... There comes a sense of discomfort (it always comes from outside, from this and that, in relation to this and that; that's how it comes), and immediately, instantly, they remember. They remember, they say, "No! What You will, Lord." That's their attitude, an attitude of such complete self-giving! Much, much more complete, much more simple, much more charming than in any other part of the being. It's "What You will.... You, You, You, what You will. To be ... to be You not with an idea of aggrandizement, but to melt, flow, disappear in You like that." And also, "But You are reality!" And all these words are a diminution. Diminution not in the sensation, but in the consciousness – it's a marvel of consciousness, you know: "You, You ... But You alone exist, You alone are." Then all discomforts, all pains, it all vanishes without a trace. It's a marvel, one can't imagine!

Sri Aurobindo once wrote somewhere, after an experience like this of the Divine Presence in the being, he wrote, *"If men knew how marvelous is the way.... But they don't know." He* wrote it, I can't quote because I'll quote it wrong, but he had this experience: "If men knew how marvelous it is, they wouldn't hesitate for a minute."

Now they still make a distinction: the "spiritual life" and the "ordinary life."

Only, one should have what I had when I was very young: the sense of material realization in its utmost perfection, the will for perfection HERE. One should have this in order not to fling everything out of the window and just remain like that *(gesture: dumb with bliss),* like an idiot sitting there uselessly. It's thanks to that old discipline that everything I do is automatically done with a will for perfection. It's an old discipline. Otherwise one would be sitting there, laughing at

374

everyone and everything: "Have my experience, you'll see what it's worth!"

It's really interesting.

Vol. 8, p. 96

## April 15, 1967

There is something interesting in this cellular consciousness: they have a sense of sincerity which is much sharper, and what they call in English *exacting,* than in the vital and the mind (even the material vital and mind). There is a sort of absoluteness in the sincerity which is very remarkable, and they have a severity towards each other which is quite wonderful. It's extremely interesting. If anything, any part, any movement, tries to cheat, they catch it like this *(gesture of nipping it and wringing its neck),* and in such a sharp and precise way.... In all vital or mental movements, there is always a kind of *(sinuous gesture)* suppleness, something that tries to adapt itself – while here, oh ... it's like this *(inflexible gesture).* So when there is invocation, prayer, self-giving, surrender, trust, all those things become so pure – so pure, so crystalline, you know, that ... oh!

And there is a growing conviction that a perfection realized in this very Matter is a FAR MORE perfect perfection than anywhere else. That's what gives it a stability it has nowhere else.... When there is the great offering and also the joyous self-giving, joyous surrender, if something comes in with even a very slight self-interest – for instance, a suffering in some little corner (a pain or disorder), which hopes for or wishes or expects some improvement – then it gets caught like this *(same gesture of nipping and wringing its neck)* and it's told, "Oh, insincere one! Give yourself without condition." Then it's magnificent.

It's very interesting.

And this joy, this enthusiasm at the possibility: that being wholly sincere should be POSSIBLE; that it should be, I might

375

almost say, allowed (these are words): "Life is such a disorder and muddle of insincerity that THAT is really what is expected of us, THAT; THAT is what's permitted, THAT is what must be realized: to be absolute in the joy of self-giving." It's a marvel, a marvel!

Also, the contact with all those beings of the Overmind, all those gods, all those Entities, all those divinities.... There is here, in the cells, a sort of ... (what can I call it?) rectitude, and, yes, sincerity and honesty that says, "Oh, what fuss they make! How all this is *(Mother puffs up her cheeks)* puff! puff! swollen up." It's very interesting, really very interesting. The vision of the world is quite different. It's far more honest – far more honest, far more sincere, far more straightforward. It's strange.

The consciousness expressed in transformed cells is a marvel. It justifies all those ages of misery. Reaching that was really worth the trouble. Really worth the trouble.

Especially all pretense, all exaggeration, all vanity, oh, it's all gazed at as through the ingenuous eyes of a very pure child (it's much better than that! The comparison is invidious).

*(silence)*

There is also a sort of internal code of regulations. When there is a pain somewhere, something that goes awry, you should see the others' attitude! ... A sternness that first says (I have to translate, and it loses all its charm), but first it begins with, "Don't you make such a fuss and to-do" (or "don't you all," it depends). Then, a pressure to surrender. And that action to make the Light circulate everywhere.... I am translating; with the translation, the mind always mixes in, unfortunately. The thing in itself doesn't think itself – it doesn't think itself, doesn't watch itself be, it's very spontaneous. Very spontaneous and, therefore, very sincere. It's pretty.

It's like an immense society, you understand.

And during the work there are ... (what should I call them?) aggregates, or very small groups of cells that have retained imprints, imprints made on them. Or sometimes here *(gesture to the brain),* but here it's full of a great light like that, compact; still there are corners – many dark nooks and crannies – and the memory of the circumstances, events, sensations, perceptions that built the imprint unfolds all of a sudden: it's all seen in the new Light, to be done away with. And then ... yes, as they say, you "travel," you travel in an immense world, indeed; and it's not things from the past, it's ... an immense Present in which you travel.

Only, you travel consciously and at your own will, rather than through the effect of a drug. That's superior.

This morning again, the lesson was repeated with, for instance, bits of old things still clinging, reactions, small movements (inner movements): "Only one solution, one single solution: self-annulment, perfect self-giving, the *surrender* of everything."

Then there's the joy of Light – the beauty, the joy ... a splendor!

*(silence)*

It's the only remedy.

Vol. 8, p. 110

## April 22, 1967

That there is a very great Pressure, a sort of intensity of pressure, is indisputable – everywhere, just everywhere. And, naturally, the reaction of Ignorance.

...

Among those who aspire, a small number are sincere, serious, level-headed, ready for anything: ready to go slowly, to go fast, to do much, to do little – but they are regular and quiet. And finally, a band of people like imbalance and, for them, it's an opportunity for all kinds of crazy things. But the Pressure of the Force is clearly making itself felt everywhere.

Sri Aurobindo always said that the most important, but also the most difficult thing, is to learn to keep one's BALANCE IN INTENSITY. To have the intensity of aspiration, the intensity of effort, the intensity of the march forward, while at the same time keeping one's balance – the balance of perfect peace. That's the ideal condition. But it's difficult.

*(silence)*

And for the cells of the body, the transition from the tranquillity of "tamasic" origin (the calm that was, in the distant past, the outcome of Inertia, and what still remains of that tendency for inertia), for this calm to stop being inert and, on the contrary, to belong to the calm of All-Powerfulness, there is a difficult transition. For the cells it's difficult.

These last few days, oh ... It's this transition that's being worked out in the details, and it's not easy.

It's like that habit of the cells of drawing the force from below (through food and so on): when you try to transform that into a constant habit of drawing the force from above, every instant, in every small detail, there's a difficult moment.... ("From above" is a manner of speaking, because if you think about it, it may also be from the depths: there's no sense of direction, high or low or anything of the sort.) But it's no longer leaning on the surface for support – for standing, walking, sitting, moving about....

There is also the pressure of external agitation (the world lives in ceaseless agitation), the external agitation: everything and everyone is rushing towards ... one really doesn't know towards what. They want to squeeze in ten times more things in a space of time than can be normally done, so it goes like this *(gesture of tremor).* And to have the strength to remain calm and steady in the middle of it, in that whirl ...

It's very interesting, really.

What people generally call force (in the English sense of the word *strength)* is something very heavy and tamasic. The true force is a movement of fantastic speed but ... in perfect calm.

There is no agitation; the movement is fantastically faster, but without agitation, in such calm! ... They generally don't even feel that Force, yet it is the one that makes – that will make – the transformation possible.

The difficulty is always the transition. You see, the body acts (it is carried, so to speak: things are done without the sense of resistance or fatigue, nothing of the sort, that doesn't exist), and then, if for some reason or other (generally some influence or some thought coming from someone else), if the memory of the other method (the ordinary method, the universal method of all human beings) comes back, the body suddenly seems ... (it's very strange), it seems to become incapable of doing ANYTHING, absolutely as if it were about to faint. Then, there immediately comes the reaction, and the other movement gets the upper hand again. But that makes for a difficult time. When these relapses become impossible, there will be security. But as it is now, it's difficult.

Only, now (in the past there used to be a dangerous moment), now there is immediately in the cells that movement of adoration, which calls, "You, You, You ..." Then it's all right.

Vol. 8, p. 116

## April 27, 1967

I told you about that experience, which has been growing increasingly concrete and constant, of the Vibration of Harmony (a higher harmony expressing the essential Consciousness in its aspect of love and harmony and, as it draws nearer to the manifestation, of order and organization), and of the nearly constant and general vibration of disorder, disharmony, conflict – in reality, Matter's resistance to this Action. The two vibrations are like this *(Mother slips the fingers of her right hand between those of the left)*, as if they interpenetrated each other and a simple movement of consciousness sent you to one side or the other, or rather, as if the aspiration, the will for realization, put you into contact with the Vibration of Harmony, and the SLIGHTEST slackening made you lapse into the other. It has become constant. So then, on the 24th, right from morning there was a constant aspiration, a constant will for the triumph of the Vibration of Harmony. Then I sat down at my table as I always do, some five or ten minutes before it [the meditation] began. And instantly, with a power – a power capable of crushing an elephant – this Vibration of Harmony came down like that, in such a mass ... that the body lost the sense of its own existence altogether: it became That, it was conscious of nothing but That. And the first quarter of an hour literally flashed by in a second. Then, there were three people in the room; one of the three, or maybe all three, felt ill-at-ease (nothing to be surprised at!), and that woke me up: I saw the light (I burn a candle on my table) and I saw the time, but it wasn't me – something saw. Then there was a sort of pacifying action on the place, and then – gone again. And one second later, the call of the end! (The gong struck to end the meditation.)

It's the first time that has happened to my body. It always used to remain conscious. Sri Aurobindo, too, told me the same thing, that he never, ever had samadhi in his body. Neither did I: I always, always used to remain conscious. While that ... only Force remained, there was nothing left but Force at work: there was a concentration here, a concentration on the whole country, and a concentration on the whole earth. And it all was conscious, like that *(vast gesture above the head)*, at work. But something massive, as powerful as an elephant – enough to crush you.

I didn't say anything to anybody, I wanted to know (because when I speak, people try to find something, while I wanted to know the spontaneous reaction). The first thing I received was a letter from G. saying that he was at the Samadhi, and just before it started, a force came down on him so strongly that he fell (he was sitting, he fell forward). So he asked me what it was. I haven't replied yet. Then there have been other people, other things.

That was unique for me, because it's the first time it has happened to me. But it has had a result: all that still clings within to that old habit of disorder and disharmony – which is the cause of, oh, everything, all mischief, all illnesses, everything – that has been ... Yesterday afternoon, I saw there was something that needed to be done away with, and it changed into a head cold. It's nothing.

It's nothing, and it has given me an opportunity to see that all the cells everywhere, even those that according to the old habit should be in discomfort because of the cold, are all in a blissful aspiration of transformation. And they truly and spontaneously feel that what's happening to them is to make things move a little faster. So they are very happy.

But things should move still faster; that is, all these things such as colds and so on should pass very quickly – come in and go out.

There are still lots of bad habits – that will pass.

And there was the consciousness – the Total Consciousness, in a light ... a light without any equivalent here, yet it was quite material. If you like, it might be like molten gold – molten and luminous. It was very thick. And it had a power – a weight, you know, like that, it was astonishing. And then, no more body, nothing anymore – nothing anymore, nothing but That. And the vision of That, like this *(gesture widening out above the head)*, in its immediate action, its action on the country, and its action on the whole earth. An action that doesn't cause any movement, I don't know how to explain it. A sort of pressure – a pressure in which nothing is displaced.

The pressure went away after the meditation, but the effect has remained, and when, out of the old habit, I got up afterwards to take something on the table over there, I nearly fell! The body no longer knew how to walk! I had to concentrate, then it came back.

381

Something still remained (but not as strong as that), something remained when I went to the balcony [in the afternoon of the 24th]. At the balcony I was different from what I usually am. I don't exactly know what it was. But then, the photographs are very different; there is something in the photographs that wasn't there before. There was a special atmosphere.

*(silence)*

I remembered something Sri Aurobindo told me sometime during the last months; he told me, "When the supramental Force" (which he was constantly calling down, of course), "when the supramental Force is there and for as long as it is present, you get a sense of all-powerfulness – an unconditioned all-powerfulness: an ALL-powerfulness." But he said, *"It goes into the background"* when the pressure of the Force is removed.

Vol. 8, p. 119


## May 3, 1967

... "What does 4.5.67 mean? What's going to happen on 4.5.67? Why..." It comes from every side into the atmosphere. So yesterday I said to someone, someone with great faith and some authority over a large number of people (they ask him all these stupid questions; he didn't tell me but said it mentally, so that I received it mentally), when I saw him in the afternoon I said to him, "So, you have been asked all these questions; well, here is what you are going to answer them very gravely (!):

| | |
|---|---|
| 4 means | Manifestation |
| 5 means | Power |
| 6 means | New Creation |
| 7 means | Realization." |

Now, let them do whatever they like with that!

It's to keep them quiet.

And indeed, he told me this morning (I replied, "You need not tell me, I know! "), he said to me, "Oh, as for me, I'd rather wait and see." I answered, "That's the true attitude, it's better to wait and see."

In any case ... I don't know – I don't know anything and don't want to know anything, I don't know. I wouldn't be surprised if nothing happened, but ... Because, for me, it has ALREADY happened. It came on the 24th, I told you, I had had all kinds of experiences (you too told me!), but never this one: the material personality, the body – absolutely dissolved. There only existed ... the Supreme Consciousness. And that, I must say, has remained. It has remained in the sense that ... I can no longer eat, I can almost no longer rest, I see really hundreds of people and things and papers and ... This poor body might say, "Phew!" – but not at all. And if the tension in others happens to cause a slight loss of balance, the body spontaneously says like this: "Oh, but You are here" – and it's all over. It's all over right away. So this is something.

We will see.

Vol. 8, p. 129

## June 24, 1967

Much to say, but ... It's better to reach the end. It's a curve – it's better to reach the end. It's too early to talk.

*(After a silence)* The near totality of the body's movements are movements of habit. There is, behind, the consciousness of the physical mind (what I call the "cellular mind") which, for its part, is constantly conscious of the divine Presence and anxious not to let in anything except That. So a whole work is going on to change, to shift the origin of movements. I mean that instead of that origin automatically being habit, the work is for the divine Consciousness and Presence to automatically be the prime mover *(Mother makes the gesture of forcing the consciousness into the body)*.

But it's quite ... quite inexpressible, that is, as soon as you try to express it, it becomes mentalized, it's no longer the thing. That's why it's very difficult to express. I can't talk about it.

But I think I told you not long ago about that habit of and taste for drama in the most material consciousness. That was the starting point. As soon as that part grew conscious, that habit became foreign, so to say, foreign to the true consciousness, so the transfer is now taking place.

It's a very delicate and difficult work.

It means fighting against a millennial habit, you understand. It's the automatism of the material consciousness which is, yes, dramatic, almost catastrophic; sometimes dramatic while at the same time imagining a conclusion that undoes the drama. But as soon as you express it all, it becomes much too concrete. It's better not to talk about it.

As soon as it's said, it becomes artificial.

It's as if, in order to replace that habit, there were a kind of effort to create another one (!) which is only an approximation. Does that state of consciousness, that way of being, that way of existing, reacting, expressing, does it strive towards the divine Manifestation? Is it in conformity with the tendency towards the divine Manifestation?... The thought is silent, still, so the imagination isn't working (all that is deliberate), and the movement is trying to be as sincere and spontaneous as possible under the influence of the divine Presence.... Words distort too much.

From time to time, now and then, all at once – the concrete experience, as in a flash: the experience of the Presence, of identification. But it lasts for ... a few seconds, then things revert to their former state.

It can't be expressed.

\* \* \*

*(Then Mother turns to the translation of two texts by Sri Aurobindo which she wants to publish.)*

"That is a great secret of sadhana, to know how to get things done by the Power behind or above instead of doing all by the mind's effort."

That's exactly the point.

Then:

"The importance of the body is obvious; it is because he has developed or been given a body and brain capable of receiving and serving a progressive mental illumination that man has risen above the animal. Equally, it can only be by developing a body or at least a functioning of the physical instrument capable of receiving and serving a still higher illumination that he will rise above himself and realise, not merely in thought and in his internal being but in life, a perfectly divine manhood. Otherwise either the promise of Life is cancelled its meaning annulled and earthly being can only realise Sachchidananda by abolishing itself, by shedding from it mind, life and body and returning to the pure Infinite, or else man is not the divine instrument, there is a destined limit to the consciously progressive power which distinguishes him from all other terrestrial existences and as he has replaced them in the front of things, so another must eventually replace him and assume his heritage."

(*The Life Divine*, XVIII.231)

I understand! I have been preoccupied with this all the time.

*(silence)*

But Sri Aurobindo's conclusion is that it isn't this [the body] that can change: it will be a new being.

*No! He says "if" man cannot, it will be a new being.*

No, I don't mean here in this text, I mean in the things he wrote afterwards.

*?...*

Besides, it's the same problem, because ... Can a body change?... It does seem very difficult – though not impossible.

385

It's not impossible, but ... it's such a formidable labor that life is too short. So even there, something needs to be changed, that habit of wear and tear is indeed a terrible thing.

*Yes, but where would a "new being" come from? He won't drop from heaven, will he?!*

Of course not, that's just the problem! The more you look at it ... It won't come that way *(Mother laughs),* it will obviously come in a similar way that man came from the animal. But we lack the stages between the animal and man – we may think them up, imagine them, they have found some things, but to tell the truth we weren't there to see it all! We don't know how it happened. But that doesn't matter.... According to some, the transformation can be consciously begun inwardly by forming the child. It may be, I am not saying no. It may be. Then he will have to form another more transformed, and so on – several stages, which will disappear just as the stages between the ape and man disappeared?

*Well, yes, that is the whole story of human improvement.*

We can call it what we like, of course. But a NEW BEING ... We can imagine, as you say, a new being coming down ready-made from start to finish! ... But that's pulp fiction.

*That's what Sri Aurobindo also says. That being must be worked out.*

After two or three – or four or ten or twenty, I don't know – intermediary beings, there would come the new way, the supramental way of creating.... But will it be necessary to have children? Will it not do away with the need to have children in order to replace those who go, since they will now live on indefinitely? They will transform themselves sufficiently to adapt to the new needs.

*All that is quite conceivable in the long term.*

Yes, in the long term.

*But Sri Aurobindo and you are here so it's done in the short term!*

No, Sri Aurobindo didn't conceive of it in the short term.

*Anyway, so it's done by you. Whether in the long or the short term, so it's done by you in this life and this body.*

But what I see ...

I am trying to do it – not out of an arbitrary will, not at all: there is simply "something," or someone, or a consciousness or whatever (I don't want to talk about it) which uses this *(Mother's body)* to try and do something with it. Which means that I do the work and am a witness at the same time, and as for the "I," I don't know where it is: it's not down here, it's not up above, it's not ... I don't know where it is, it's for the requirements of language. There is "something" that works and is a witness of the work at the same time, and is at the same time the action being done: the three things.

Because now, the body itself really collaborates as much as it can – as much as it can – with ever-increasing goodwill and power of endurance, and the self-observation is truly reduced to the minimum (there is still some, like something touching lightly now and then, but it doesn't even stay for a few seconds). Self-observation, oh, that means a thoroughly disgusting, repugnant and catastrophic atmosphere. It's like that, FELT like that. And it's becoming increasingly impossible, I see that, it's visible.... But there is still the whole weight of millennia of bad habits, which we could call pessimistic, that is, expecting decay, expecting catastrophe, expecting ... well, all those things, and, ugh! that's the most difficult thing to purify, to clarify, to remove from the atmosphere. It's so INGRAINED that it's absolutely spontaneous. That is the great, great, great obstacle – that sort of sense of inevitable decay.

Naturally, from the mental standpoint, the entire earth atmosphere is like that, but in the mind it hardly matters at all: one ray of light and it's swept away. But it's HERE INSIDE *(pointing to her body)*, that habit – that catastrophic habit – is what is terrible, terrible to contradict. And it's INDISPENSABLE that it should disappear so the other can settle in.

So it's a struggle every minute, every minute, all the time, all the time.

And of course, the being isn't cut off, the body isn't cut off: the body is something of a multitude, with varying degrees of proximity; and very near, there are all those who are here, and it's the same problem – the same problem. Because all that has been gained in the consciousness of this being hasn't been gained at all in the consciousness of others. So that increases the work.

The problem of mental, even vital, contagion is solved, so to speak, but the problem of material contagion still remains.

And in this material consciousness, there is this material mind which has so marvelously responded here [in Mother], but it doesn't yet have the power to assert itself spontaneously against what comes from outside, that never-ending contagion, constant, constant, every minute.

*(long silence)*

When, all at once, the Contact is conscious and the sense of Identity comes (for a few seconds, as I said), when it comes ... it's like a hosanna in all, but all the cells, they say, "Oh, so it's true! It's true indeed! ..."

And that's all-powerful.

It comes perhaps a hundred times a day, but it doesn't stay.

Vol. 8, p. 193


## July 12, 1967

That's how it is. All of a sudden, for two or three seconds, you seem to be holding the key. And all that's conventionally called "miracle" looks like the simplest thing in the world: "But it's perfectly simple, all you have to do is this!" And then ... it goes away. And once it's gone, you try and try – absolutely useless.

But when it's there, it's so simple, so natural! And absolutely all-powerful.

*(silence)*

A world of things that one could say. But saying them spoils them.

One thing that seems to be trying to come is the power to heal. But not at all as it's described, it's not that at all – it doesn't give a sense of "healing," you understand. It's ... *(Mother searches for words)* putting things back in order. But that's not it either.... It's a little something that disappears, and that little something is ... essentially it's the Falsehood.

It's very strange.

Basically, it's what gives the ordinary human consciousness the sense of reality. That's what must disappear. What we call "concrete," a "concrete reality" ... yes, what truly gives you the sense of real existence – that's what must disappear and be replaced by ... It's inexpressible.

*(silence)*

Now I can follow.

I remember, when I came back after having BEEN those bursts – those pulsations, those bursts of creative Love, when I returned to the ordinary consciousness (while retaining the very real memory of That, of the state), well, that state, which I felt to be pulsations of creative Love, is what must, is That which must replace here this consciousness of concrete reality – which is, which becomes unreal: it's like something lifeless – hard, dry, inert, lifeless. And to our ordinary consciousness (I remember how it was in the past), that's what gives you the impression, "This is concrete, this is real." Well, "this," this sensation, is what must be replaced by the phenomenon of consciousness of that Pulsation. And That *(Mother makes an intense gesture enfolding her whole face)* is at the same time all-light, all-power, all-intensity of love, and such FULLNESS! It's so full that ... where That is, nothing else can exist. And when That is here, in the body, in the cells, then all you have to

389

do is focus It on someone or something, and order is instantly restored in the person or the thing.

So, translated into ordinary words, it "heals." It heals the disease. But it doesn't heal it: it annuls it.... Yes, it annuls it.

*It unrealizes it.*

Absolutely. I have concrete proof of it.

Any disease, any disease whatsoever.

*(silence)*

And the condition of all the cells (the vibrations that make up this body) is undeniably what makes the thing [healing] possible or not; that is, depending on the body's condition, it serves either as a transmitter, or on the contrary as an obstruction. Because it's not a "higher force" acting in others THROUGH Matter: it's a direct action *(horizontal gesture, on a level)* from matter to matter.

What people generally call "healing power" is a very great mental or vital power that imposes itself through the resistance of Matter – but this isn't at all the same thing! It's the contagion of a vibration. And then it's irrevocable.

But it's gone in a flash. It's only a promise or an example of what will be: it WILL be like that, obviously. Obviously. When? ... That's another question.

*(silence)*

Right here, this Vibration is felt as ... *(Mother gestures as if everything were swelling)*. You understand, it [the body's ordinary condition] is tied up, it's tied and bound, I might almost say hardened, I don't know; and at such times, it seems to swell, to expand.

Only, it's momentary.

Vol. 8, p. 212

**July 19, 1967**

What do you WANT?

*(silence)*

*I know very well what I want.*

*(Mother goes into a long concentration lasting about a half-hour)*

Nothing to say?

*One should remember always.*

Remember ... Did you feel anything special?

*Yes.*

What?

I did something – not something special because I usually do it – but more totally, I might say, than usual. I'd like to know if you felt anything?

*I don't know.... It seemed so much THAT.*

Yes.

I told you the other day about what I call the "transfer"; for two days (more than two: several days, but especially yesterday and today), a work has been going on to make it continual, that is, to allow nothing except That.

Then there begins to come a kind of material power of EXTENDING – extending the zone, you understand, extending it like that *(encompassing gesture)* to what's immediately near. So today, instead of applying the Force like this *(gesture from high to low),* as I always used to do, I ... it was as if encompassing your body in the same movement of the cells.

It was successful enough! And I'd like to know if you felt a difference.

*I've never had such a strong impression of That, and ... so strongly THERE.*

Ah! Then that's it.

391

I do it at night for you, only it's more subtle than with the physical presence.

(silence)

It's being done.

It's being done in the sense that it's becoming more and more constant.

It is the action of a perfectly conscious aspiration, increasingly constant, and the Response which brings the immediate result of that aspiration.... But it's still a completely new field – new from that total, integral point of view. Formerly, everything going on in the body (I don't mean this one, I mean it in a general way) was a reflection and an effect of the "Thing," while now, it is the Thing itself. But the millennial habit of being otherwise is so strong that the impression is ... It's like ... (the comparison is poor, but anyway), like stretching a rubber band; so, as long as you keep it stretched *(gesture of keeping Matter at full stretch),* the effect is there; but if the tension stops, even for a second *(gesture of abrupt flattening),* it falls back out of habit.... Which compels you to constant tension. But it won't always be like that. It is the transition from one habit to another; once the other movement is established, then it will be natural, this constant tension won't be necessary.

We'll see how much time it takes.

And for the first time with you, I (because the result, too, was rather concrete and constant this morning), I tried to encompass. It's far from being what it should be, but there has been a result. It's very far from being "that" which it should be, but ...

(silence)

This extraordinary impression of the unreality of suffering, unreality of diseases, unreality ... It's very strange. Then that whole millennial habit comes along and tries to deny and say ... and say that it is the state you are in which is unreal! So then, it's there. Because there is no mental action or thought or any

392

such thing: it's all in the vibrations ... There are moments, you know, of inexpressible glory, but it's fleeting. And the other thing is there – pressing all around....

When you succeed in keeping the [material] mind absolutely inactive, it's relatively easier, but when the mind comes and assails, then ... Then you almost have to use violence to repulse the onslaught, to establish silence.

That's why until you reach that state in which the mind can be like this *(vast, calm gesture),* absolutely still ... When there is nothing except the consciousness, then it's all right. Before that, it seems impossible, an impossible work. But when the mind is replaced by the consciousness, then ...

There's no time left for anything. We'll work some other day!

*(Mother laughs)*

Vol. 8, p. 225

## August 2, 1967

*(Mother reads Satprem a quotation from Sri Aurobindo:)*

"To be perpetually reborn is the condition of material immortality."

*Sri Aurobindo.*

That's excellent.

\* \* \*

*A little later, following a meditation:*

That's how it is. Day after day, almost hour after hour, with the Power coming back ... You remember, I once said it had completely gone, and that was true, it had completely gone in order to leave the body absolutely to itself, for its conversion, if I may say so; but once there had been in this body consciousness the same aspiration and the same ardor of consciousness (with a far greater steadiness than in any other part of the being; there are no fluctuations as there are in the vital and mind, it's very steady), once that was established (through kinds of

393

pulsations, not distant from one another, but first on one detail, then spreading out and becoming generalized), since then the Power has been ... I might say it has been coming back. But at every stage of that return, all the old difficulties appear to be waking up again, they seem to spring up again (they had quite fallen asleep, you understand), and every time that happens, this body consciousness feels a sort of astonishment mingled with distress that the presence of the divine Power, the divine Consciousness, the Truth-Consciousness, should give rise to all those difficulties, which are essentially difficulties of ignorance and inertia – the incapacity to receive. And it comes back as memories, like that *(gesture from below),* like a snake rearing its head. And every time, the entire physical consciousness has the same call, "Why? How can these things be when You are here!" That's what astonishes it: "Since You are here, how can these things be?"

Till now, in most cases, that has signaled a conversion, a transformation, an illumination (depending on the case), but this case we were just talking about [the Tantric apprentice] came precisely as a result of that return of the Power (I knew it; he told me yesterday, but I knew it when he had his revolt). And all that came was just all the old revolts, all the old movements, which were previously so strong, so widespread, so ESTABLISHED, and had been as though halted in their expression by the withdrawal of the Power. So everyone was slumbering in his condition. Then, as soon as the Force started coming back and working again, it all woke up again.

But it's not the full Presence yet, not the complete Presence of the being, which, through an incontrovertible omnipotence, changes things. So then, the body, with something so very moving in the simplicity of its prayer and its childlike astonishment, asks, "Since You are here, how can that be? ... " And all that is ready to be transformed is transformed. But it isn't yet ... (how can I explain?) the compelling thing *(gesture of irresistible descent),* the absolute authority nothing can resist – it's not that, not yet, far from it.

394

There's no knowing how much more time it will take.

All that is on the verge of changing changes.

Otherwise, it's the slow underground labor, invisible, almost imperceptible, continually.

*(silence)*

The interesting point is that this body spontaneously, instantly and effortlessly – spontaneously – tries to find in itself, in the body's cells (it's a whole WORLD! A whole world), the cells try to find in themselves, "Oh, where is my incapacity? Where is my helplessness? Where is ... even my bad will or my stupidity or incapacity to understand and adhere?" Like that. And always the same answer, "Give everything, give everything, give everything.... I don't understand, I can't understand, I don't know, I can't know – I can't do anything, I am incapable of doing anything by myself: everything is for You, do it."

They try and try, everything tries to give itself perfectly, perfectly, that is, without exception – everything, everything.

It's a sort of ... not anxiety, but above all a vigilance, as if they were on the alert: "May we do nothing but what You want, think nothing but what You want, feel nothing but what You want, say nothing but what You want...." Constantly, uninterruptedly, night and day. In the middle of activity or in the middle of rest, everything asks, "To be what You want, to feel what You want, to do what You want, to exist ... without difference."

The slightest pain, any discomfort, the slightest clumsy gesture, the slightest thing, and immediately, "Ah! *(with a start)* This isn't You."

*(Mother goes into a contemplation)*

The subtle physical seems to be more and more transformed. There is still a mystery between the two. A mystery. They are coexistent [the physical and the subtle physical bodies], and yet ... *(gesture of a lack of connection)*, the subtle physical doesn't appear to have an influence on this [the body].

Something ... Something to be found ... something.

Vol. 8, p. 253

### August 16, 1967

What did you feel at the darshan yesterday – not "darshan," at the meditation?... Nothing special?

*No, Mother. It was fine, but I don't know.*

Ah ... *(in a disappointed tone).* You were at home?

*No, in Sri Aurobindo's room.*

Oh....

Do you know, I sat down when it was nearly time [for the meditation], maybe half a minute before, and instantly, without warning, like a staggering blow: such a powerful descent (I was completely stilled) of something.... At the same time Sri Aurobindo seemed to tell me (because the definition came along with the "thing" – it was a vision which wasn't a vision, which was absolutely concrete), and the word was *golden peace.* But so strong! And it didn't budge anymore. For the entire half-hour it didn't budge. Never before ... It's something new, I had never felt that before. I can't say.... It was perceived, but not like an objective vision. And other people spontaneously told me that as soon as they sat down for the meditation *(gesture of a massive descent),* something came with a tremendous power, everything was stilled, and a sense of peace as they had never felt in their life.

*Golden peace ...*

And indeed it gave a sense of supramental golden light, but it was ... such peace! A concrete peace, you know, not the negation of disorder and activity, no: concrete, a concrete peace. I didn't want to stop: they sounded the gong, but I stayed on for two or three minutes. When I did stop, it went away. And it made such a difference for the body – the body itself – such a difference that when the experience went away I felt in great discomfort and it took me half a minute to find my balance again.

It came and went away. It came for the meditation, then went away. For more than a half-hour: thirty-five minutes.

*Golden peace.*

....

But the minute (really the minute – it wasn't even a state in time, it really was the minute), the minute I made contact with what I call the Supreme, that is, the part that looks after the earth, throughout the years it has always been i-den-ti-cal-ly the same thing.

All that has differences is below. That is the summit. And the summit ... that's why I use the word "Supreme," because there's nothing other than "That," which is supreme Peace, supreme Light, a sort of supreme tranquil Bliss, a sense of supreme Power and a Consciousness ... an all-containing Consciousness, like that *(immense gesture)* ... and then it's over. It's still. Still – not "motionless," but far above movement, far above. And identical, with the sense that "it's like that forever." And it contains everything, but ... *(immutable gesture, the palms of the hand drawn back).*

As soon as you make contact with that, everything is fine.

Change, movement, newness is when you are on the way – on the way you keep having experiences, one upon another upon another; or when you are on the road to transformation, there is one thing, then another, then yet another. But when you make contact THERE, it's over *(same immutable gesture).* Every time you make contact there, it's like that. And it contains everything, but ... you are not concerned with that.

And naturally, it's supreme rest, supreme power, supreme knowledge, supreme consciousness ... and something more.

Vol. 8, p. 262

## September 30, 1967

*(After a long meditation, Mother, still deep inside and half in trance, starts speaking:)*

Did you feel anything special? ... Because the last two or three days, but especially last night and this morning, it was the body learning, the cells learning ... I told you that the work till now has been the change – the transfer – from acting out of habit and reaction to letting the divine Consciousness act. And this morning, for a part of the night and the whole morning until people started coming, with every action, every movement, every gesture, all the tiny little things (when, for instance, a problem is put by someone or a decision has to be made, for years the answer has been coming from above), but now with all material movements, also the inner movements, with the attitude of the body, of the cells, the absolutely material consciousness, with everything, everything – the old method was gone.

It began with the perception of the remaining difference between how things were and how they should be, then that perception disappeared and there only remained "that".... Something (how can I explain?) ... The English word *smooth* is the most expressive; everything is done *smoothly*, everything without exception: getting washed, brushing one's teeth, washing one's face, everything (as regards eating, for a long time that has been worked on in order that it should be done in the true way). It always begins with *(Mother opens her hands)* this sort of *surrender* (I don't know the right word, it's neither abdication nor offering but between the two; I don't know, there is no French word for it), the surrender of the WAY in which we do things: not of the thing in itself, which is quite unimportant (in that state there is no "big" and "small," no "important" and "unimportant"). And it's something so ... *(vast, even gesture)* uniform in its simplicity, there is nothing that clashes or grates or causes difficulties anymore or ... (all those words express things so crudely): it's something that moves forward on and on so ... *(same vast, even gesture)* the nearest word is *smoothly,* that is, without resistance. I don't know. And it's not an intensity of delight, it's not that: that also is so even, so regular *(same vast gesture),* but not uniform: it's innumerable. And EVERYTHING is like that *(same gesture),* in a single ... rhythm (the word "rhythm" is violent). It's not a uniformity, but something so even, and which feels so sweet, you know, and with a TREMENDOUS power in the smallest things.

For several days there was ... the vision of cruelty in human beings, and a very active work to make it disappear from the manifestation. That's part of the general work, with such a concrete power *(Mother clenches her fist)* to make it disappear. It began with visions of horrors (almost memories), which were seen – more than seen, you understand: things that aroused that reprobation, that sense of horror.... Then it was organized in its totality and the whole thing was taken up like that *(Mother opens her arms),* all those movements in time (time and space merge into something ... an immensity – immensity, infinitude, and, I might say, "multiplicity," but words are poor), anyway it was a totality taken up in the consciousness – a totality of ways of being and vibrations – and as if presented to the Supreme Consciousness so it may be transformed, so it may cease to exist.

That's how it began.

Then, once that was done, it got as if concretized, concentrated on this little point of a body, so it may, there too, become impossible for certain things, certain vibrations of unconsciousness to continue to exist. And today the outcome was that transfer, which was constant – constant, unalloyed for about four hours. Afterwards ... It's mostly the invasion of outside things that cuts off the experience. Yet there is no reproval of that invasion; the transformation – the TRANSFER – must continue AMID the contact with all that comes. Then it will be fine.

There are two things. There is all this crowd I see constantly, and as soon as I am there, as soon as the body is there to see the people, it's a long time (a "long" time, that is, humanly speaking) since it stopped being anything but a channel, a kind of ... *(gesture showing the Force flowing down through Mother to the people),* so the Consciousness of the Lord may flow through it and go [and do its work]. There isn't even, or there is as little need to receive as possible: it's an action like this *(same gesture through Mother),* the Force passing through. And when it takes place in that room over there [the "music room"] which is exclusively reserved for seeing people, the room fills with the Presence, and it's as if that Presence opened its arms to receive people, took them, enveloped them, and then let them go.

But as regards the things personal to this body, like all that has to do with washing, food, now it no longer takes place in the same way. I don't know how to explain. Here, it's an activity; over there, it's simply a Presence. Here, it's an activity: you have to fill a glass with water, pour mouthwash, brush your teeth – it's all activities. And, well ... there are no memories left, no habits; things aren't done because you learned to do them that way: they are done spontaneously by the Consciousness. In the transition between the old and the new movements there is a difficult little moment when the old habit is no longer there, nor is the new consciousness there permanently, so ... It results, for instance, in apparently clumsy gestures, gestures that are not exactly what they should be. But it doesn't last, it happens once in a while for a particular thing, just for the lesson to be learned – there is always a lesson waiting to be learned.

To replace the memory, the remembrance, the action, with ... For instance, if you want to know where someone lives, his address or house (that was last night's activity), the old method, the mental method has to be replaced with the new method of consciousness that knows the thing just when it has to be done: "This needs to be done." It's not, "Ah, I have to go there," no: you are every minute where you should be, and when you come to the place you had to go to: "Ah, here it is."

It's really very interesting.

So, between the moment when you act like everyone and the moment when you act – when it's the Lord that acts, between the two, there's a little transition: you no longer quite know this, and don't yet quite know that, so at times this poor body feels somewhat uncertain, clumsy. But it's learning its lesson very fast.

Really interesting.

*(long silence)*

Then you clearly understand why saints and sages, those who wanted to feel themselves live constantly in this divine atmosphere, had got rid of all material things – because they weren't transformed, and so they fell back into the old way of being. And there comes a moment when it's ... unpleasant. But if you transform that ... it's in-com-par-ably, vastly superior, in the sense that it gives an extraordinary STABILITY and consciousness and REALITY. Things become the TRUE vision, the TRUE consciousness; it becomes so concrete, so real!

Nothing – nothing else, nothing else can give that fullness.

Escaping, fleeing, dreaming, meditating, going into ... all that is very nice, but how poor it looks in comparison, how poor! So poor.

*(silence)*

The most difficult thing left is talking. That's the most difficult, it takes a great effort. This morning, while I had that experience, there was almost a kind of entreaty from the body: "Oh, don't talk, don't tell him." I didn't intend to talk, but *(gesture from above)* I am compelled to. The body doesn't intend to talk, it doesn't like to, but something obliges it to.

That's the only difficult thing.

Words are so inadequate! I have been asked that, too: how will they communicate, the wholly supramental beings (I mean, without the mixture of this material origin), how will they communicate? Simply like this? *(gesture of inner exchange)*

401

Talking takes such effort.

And it's not a "thought communication" like what they call telepathy, it's not that: it's ... movements of consciousness. That too will take place without clashes or resistance: movements of consciousness [in Matter]. If, for instance, something needs to be done but not by this body, by another, we are still obliged to say, "This needs to be done in such and such a way," and that represents ... you feel as if you have to lift a mountain, whereas if the other person were in the same state, it would get done quite naturally and spontaneously. I've had examples: now and then I SEE (not "think," but see), I see: "This needs to be like that" (very small things) and I don't say anything – the other body does it. It happens now and then, rarely – but it ought to be the constant state.... Oh, what an admirable life!

Vol. 8, p. 308

### November 15, 1967

*What I don't see is the process to break out of this inertia or unconsciousness.*

Process, what process? The process of transformation?

*Yes, it is said that the consciousness must act to awaken all this ...*

But it's doing it!

*Yes, it's doing it, but...*

It never stops doing it!

I tell you, the response is like this: there is a sudden perception (oh, all these things are very subtle, very subtle – but as a matter of fact, to the consciousness they are very concrete), the perception of a sort of disorganization, like a current of disorganization; at first the substance making up the body feels it, then it sees the effect, and everything starts being disorganized: that disorganization is what prevents the cohesion necessary for the cells to constitute an individual body, so then you say, "Ah *(gesture of dissolution)*, it'll be the end." Then the cells aspire, there is a sort of central consciousness in the body which aspires intensely, with as complete a *surrender* as it can make: "Your Will, Lord, Your Will, Your Will...." Then there is a kind of ... not something thunderous, not a dazzling flash of light, but a sort of ... well, the impression is of a densification of that current of disorganization; and then something comes to a halt: first there is a peace, then a light, then Harmony – and the disorder has vanished. And when the disorder has vanished, there is instantly IN THE CELLS a sense of living eternity, of living for eternity.

Well, that experience, such as I've told you, with the whole intensity of concrete reality, occurs not only daily, but several times in a single day. At times it's very severe, that is, like a mass; at other times, it's only like something that touches; then, in the body consciousness, it's expressed like this, with a sort of thanksgiving: one more step in the progress over Unconsciousness. But those aren't thunderous events, the human neighbor isn't even aware of them; he may note a sort of cessation in the outward activity, a concentration, but that's all. So of course, you don't talk about it, you can't write books about it, you don't do propaganda.... That's how the work goes.

None of the mental aspirations are satisfied with that.

It's a very obscure work.

*(Mother goes into a long contemplation)*

Vol. 8, p. 372

**November 22, 1967**

*(Mother takes flowers)* I'll put them in water.... Flowers are the beauty of life.

And there is a progress.

*Oh?*

403

At the end of the physical demonstration [on December 2], all the children will pray in chorus, and the prayer has been written by me. I will read it to you.

But I hadn't thought about it: they asked me for it, and I wrote it.

They must have read the *Bulletin,* and then they asked me for a prayer – a prayer that would really be the body's. I answered:

*THE PRAYER OF THE CELLS IN THE BODY*

*Now that by the effect of the Grace we are slowly emerging out of inconscience and waking up to a conscious life, an ardent prayer rises in us for more light, more consciousness:*

*"O Supreme Lord of the Universe, we implore Thee, give us the strength and the beauty, the harmonious perfection needed to be Thy divine instruments upon earth."*

It's almost a proclamation.

There. So we'll put it into French.

They will say it after their demonstration; it seems they are going to show the whole evolution of physical culture, and then, at the end, they will say, "We have not reached the end, we are at the beginning of something, and here is our prayer."

I was very glad.

*You said there is a progress?*

A progress! It's a tremendous progress! The thought had never occurred to them, never; taken as a whole, they had never thought of the transformation: their thought was to become the best athletes in the world and all the usual nonsense.

The body, you see, they've asked for a prayer of the BODY. They have finally understood that the body must begin to transform itself into something else. Previously, they were all full of the whole history of physical culture in every country, in which country it's most developed, the use of the body as it is, and ... and so on. Anyway, it was the Olympic ideal. Now,

404

they have leaped beyond: that is the past, now they want the transformation.

You understand, people were asking to be divine in their mind and vital – that is, the whole ancient history of spirituality, the same old theme for centuries – but now, it's the BODY. It's the body that asks to participate. It's certainly a progress.

*Yes, but one can see how in the mind the aspiration sustains itself, how it lives by itself. In the heart too, one can see how the aspiration lives. But in the body? How can one awaken that aspiration in the body?*

But good God! it's fully awakened! It's been for months in me! So it means they've felt it, they are feeling it.

How it's done? – It's being done.

*But how can one in oneself...*

No, no, no. If it has been done in one body, it can be done in all bodies.

*Yes, but I ask how.... Yes, how?*

Well, that's what I have been trying to explain for months.

It's, first of all, awakening the consciousness in the cells....

*Well, yes!*

Yes, but once it's done it's done: the consciousness keeps awakening more and more, the cells live consciously, aspire consciously. I have been trying to explain it, good Lord, for months! For months I have been trying to explain it. And so, that's just what pleased me: it's that they have at least understood the possibility of it.

The same consciousness which was the vital's and the mind's monopoly has become corporeal: the consciousness acts in the body's cells.

The body's cells grow into something conscious, entirely conscious.

A consciousness which is independent, absolutely independent of the vital consciousness or the mental consciousness: it's a corporeal consciousness.

*(silence)*

And this physical mind, which Sri Aurobindo said was an impossibility and something going round in circles which would do so forever, without consciousness, precisely, like a sort of machine, this physical mind has been converted, it has fallen silent, and in silence it has received inspiration from the Consciousness. And it has started praying again: the same prayers that were earlier in the mind.

*I quite understand all that can take place in you, but...*

But since it's taking place in one body, it can take place in all bodies! I am not made of anything different from others. The difference is the consciousness, that's all. It's made of exactly the same thing, with the same elements, I eat the same things, and it was made in just the same way.

And it was as dull, as dark, as unconscious, as stubborn as all other bodies in the world.

It began when the doctors declared I was seriously ill, that was the beginning. Because the entire body was emptied of its habits and forces, and then, slowly, slowly, the cells woke up to a new receptivity and opened directly to the divine Influence.

Every cell is vibrating.

Otherwise, it would be hopeless! If this matter, which began as ... Even a stone is already an organization; it was certainly worse than a stone: the inert, absolute Inconscient. Then, little by little, little by little, it awakens. One can see it, you know, one sees it: one just has to open one's eyes to see it. Well, the same thing is now taking place: for the animal to become a man, it didn't take anything else than the infusion of a consciousness – a mental consciousness – and now, it's the awakening of that consciousness which was there, deep down, in the very depths. The mind has withdrawn, the vital has withdrawn, everything has withdrawn; when I was supposedly ill, the mind had gone away, the vital had gone away, and the body was left to itself – purposely. And that's why, it's precisely because the vital and mind had gone that it looked like a very serious illness. And then, in the body left to itself, the cells little by little started awakening to the consciousness *(gesture of a rising aspiration);* once those two had gone, the consciousness which had been infused into the body THROUGH the vital (from the mind to the vital and from the vital to the body) started slowly, slowly emerging. It began with that burst of Love from all the way up, from the extreme, supreme altitude; then, little by little, little by little, it came down to the body. Then that sort of physical mind, that is, something totally and completely idiotic going round and round in circles, forever repeating the same thing over and over again, cleared up little by little and grew conscious, organized, then fell silent. And then in that silence, the aspiration expressed itself in prayers.

*(silence)*

It's a denial of all the spiritual assertions of the past: "If you want to live fully conscious of the divine life, leave your body – the body cannot follow." Well, Sri Aurobindo came and said, "Not only can the body follow, but it can be the base that will manifest the Divine."

The work remains to be done.

But now there is a certitude. The result is still very far – very far ahead, there is much to do before the crust, the outermost surface experience as it is, can manifest what takes place within (not "within" in the spiritual depths: within in the body). For it to be able to manifest what is within ... That will come last, which is very good because if it came earlier, we would neglect the work; we would be so happy that we'd forget to complete the work. Everything must have been done within, everything must be fully and thoroughly changed, then the outside will express it.

But it's all ONE SINGLE substance, the very same everywhere, which was unconscious everywhere; and so, the remarkable thing is that things are taking place AUTOMATICALLY *(gesture of points scattered throughout the world)*, quite unexpected things here and there, even in people who don't know anything.

*(silence)*

These material cells had to gain the capacity to receive and manifest the consciousness; and what permits a radical transformation is that instead of an ascent which is so to speak eternal and indefinite, there is the appearance of a new type – a descent from above. The previous descent was a mental one, while this is what Sri Aurobindo calls a "supramental descent"; the impression is, a descent of the supreme Consciousness infusing itself into something capable of receiving and manifesting it. Then, out of that, once it has been thoroughly kneaded (there's no knowing how much time it will take), a new form will be born, which will be the form Sri Aurobindo called supramental – it will be ... anything, I don't know what those beings will be called.

What will be their mode of expression? How will they make themselves understood and so on? ... In man, it developed very slowly. Only, mind has done a lot of kneading and, after all, has made things move faster.

How will we get there? ... There will certainly be stages in the manifestation with, perhaps, a specimen that will come and say, "Here is how it is." *(Mother looks in front of her)* One can see that.

Only, when man emerged from the animal, there was no way to record – to note and record the process; now it's quite different, so it will be more interesting.

*(silence)*

But even at this moment in time, the vast majority – the vast majority – of human intellectuality is perfectly satisfied being busy with itself, satisfied with its little progress like this *(Mother draws a microscopic circle)*. It doesn't even, doesn't even have a desire for something else!

Which means the advent of the superhuman being may well ... it may very well go unnoticed, or not be understood. We can't say, because there is no analogy; it's obvious that if one of the apes, the large apes, had met the first man, he would just have felt there was a somewhat ... strange being, that's all. But now it's different because man thinks, reasons....

But anything higher than him man has been used to thinking of as ... divine beings; that is to say, bodiless beings, appearing in the light, anyway all the gods in human conception – but it's not that at all!

*(long silence)*

Shall we translate this?

*(Mother translates into French the
"prayer of the cells in the body")*

*(silence)*

So?

Aren't you convinced?

Why don't you try?

*But I do! That's why I asked you the question. I am not doubting anything. I asked you how it's done, that's what I don't see.... For instance, I shave every morning. Well, in the morning you are dazed, tired, the mind doesn't work, the vital doesn't work....*

Yes, it's an excellent opportunity.

*Well, yes, so that's what I do! But I tell you, I just don't see, I don't. I don't know how it can be stirred – it doesn't stir.... It doesn't stir unless I apply the mind or the vital or the heart.*

Bah!

*It's not that I doubt! I say that my body is a donkey, quite possibly, but I don't doubt.*

It's not a donkey, poor thing! *(Mother laughs)*

*Doubt there isn't. But there is a question on the "how," that's what I don't know.*

That problem never arose for me, because ... When you do music or when you do painting, you very clearly notice how the consciousness permeates the cells and those cells become conscious. This experience, for instance: there are objects in a box, and you say to your hand, "Take twelve of them." The hand goes like that, without your bothering about it, and it finds the twelve (without counting, just like that), it takes the twelve and gives them to you. That's an experience I had long ago; when I was twenty I began with experiences of that kind. So I know, I knew how the consciousness works. You understand, it's impossible to learn the piano or painting without the consciousness coming into the hands, and the hands become conscious INDEPENDENTLY of the brain – the brain may be busy elsewhere, it doesn't matter in the least. Besides, that's what happens in those people who are called "sleepwalkers": they have a consciousness belonging to their body, which makes them move about and do things quite independently of the mind and the vital.

*I mean that when I am shaving in front of the mirror, if within myself I don't apply the mantra or an aspiration from the heart, well, it's an inert chunk shaving, and in addition the physical mind keeps running. But if I apply a mantra or a mental will ...*

No! It's THE BODY that ends up saying the mantra spontaneously! So spontaneously that even if you happen to be thinking of something else, your body will be saying the mantra. Don't you have that experience?

*No.*

And it's the body that aspires, the body that says the mantra, the body that wants the light, the body that wants the consciousness – you yourself may be thinking of something else, Tom, Dick or Harry or a book or anything, it doesn't matter.

But now I understand, I understand very well! In the beginning I didn't, I thought I had been made supposedly

410

very ill in order to stop the life I led downstairs – the life I now lead is far more busy than the one I led downstairs, so ... I wondered why, whether it was a transitional phase. But now I understand: cut off – I would keep fainting. What made the doctor declare that I was ill is that I couldn't take a step without fainting: if I wanted to walk from here to there, poff! I would faint on the way; I had to be held up so my body wouldn't drop to the ground. So the doctor's decision: to bed and no moving. But as for me, not for one minute did I lose consciousness! I would faint but remain conscious, I would see my body and know I had fainted; I didn't lose consciousness, the body didn't lose consciousness. So now I understand! The body was cut off from the vital and the mind and left to its own means; and then little by little, little by little ...

I remember, for instance, all that the doctors do: they give you vitamins, this and that. All right. So as soon as I had taken those vitamins, I saw that sort of physical mind start stirring and stirring and stirring: "Vitamins," I said, "I don't want them, they cause excitement in the brain." Then they changed and gave me something some other time, and that was good. And all that, all of it was simply THE BODY: all that it knew, all the experiences it had had, all the mastery from all the parts of the being, from the vital to the mind and above, all of that was gone! And this poor body was left to itself. Then, naturally, little by little something was rebuilt. For a long time I remained unable ... unable to do hardly anything (a little something, but hardly anything), but little by little it all was rebuilt, increasingly rebuilt: a conscious, purely conscious being – which is now chattering away! (It was unable to express itself.)

Yes, I understand. I understand. Well, perhaps that is what Sri Aurobindo meant when he said, "Your body is at present the only one on earth that can do this work." I thought it was a kindness on his part.... But it's true that it was cut off, I knew it – I saw it – cut off, the states of being were sent away: "Go away, all of you are not wanted anymore." Then the body had to rebuild a life for itself. And instead of having to go through all those states of being as it did before, through successive awakenings *(gesture of ascent from degree to degree, in the way of the yogis of old)*, up to the highest height, the highest height beyond the form, now it's no longer that at all, the body no longer needs anything of all that, it simply has ... *(gesture of a rising aspiration opening out like a flower)*. Something within opened and developed, which caused that idiotic mind to become organized and capable of falling silent in an aspiration. And then ... then there was the direct Contact, without intermediaries – the direct contact. That it now has constantly. Constantly, every single moment, the direct contact. And it's THE BODY: it doesn't go through all kinds of things and states of being, not at all, it's direct.

But once that has been done (this is something Sri Aurobindo had said), once ONE body has done it, it has the capacity of passing it on to others; and I tell you, there is now (I am not saying in its totality and in detail, probably not), but here and there *(scattered gesture to show various points on earth)* people suddenly get one experience or another. Some of them (most) get frightened, so naturally it goes away – that is because they weren't prepared enough within (if it's not the little routine of every minute, ever the same, they get frightened), and once they get frightened it's over, it means they will need years of preparation for the experience to recur. But still, some don't; suddenly, an experience: "Ah!" something wholly new, wholly unexpected, which they had never thought of.

It's contagious. That I know. And it's the only hope, because if everyone had to go through the same experience again ... Well, I am ninety now – at the age of ninety people are tired, they've had enough of life. To do this work one must feel as young as a small child.

It takes a long time, I clearly see that it has taken a long time.

And it isn't done, of course, it's BEING done – it isn't done, far from it. Far from it ... What's the proportion of conscious cells? We don't know.

From time to time, some cells scold others, that's very funny! They scold them, they catch hold of them, say a thing or two (in their own way) to those which want ... *(Mother draws a tiny circle)* to go on with the old habits: digestion has to be done in a certain way, absorption has to be done in a certain way, circulation has to be done in a certain way, breathing has to ... all the functions have to be done according to Nature's method. And when it isn't like that, they are worried. Then those which know catch hold of them and give them a good bombardment of the Lord, it's very funny!

There is something that translates into words (it's wordless, but something in there translates into words), and so there are conversations between the cells *(Mother laughs):* "You fool, what are you afraid of? Don't you see it's the Lord doing this to transform you?" Then the other: "Ah! ..." And then it falls quiet, opens out, and waits. And ... the pain goes away, the disorder goes away, and then everything works out.

It's wonderful.

But if by some mischance the mind comes in, starts watching or judging, then everything stops and falls back into the old habit.

*(long silence)*

Basically, it's the vital, mental – and so on – ego, it's all of that which was – poff! – taken away.

It was a radical operation.

So now there is a sort of suppleness and plasticity. And all this is learning (it's very much in touch with everything *[horizontal gesture]),* it's learning to find its whole support, its whole strength, its whole knowledge, its whole light, its whole will, everything like that *(vertical gesture, turned to the Supreme),* exclusively like that, in an extraordinary plasticity.

And then – the splendor of the Presence.

*(silence)*

There.

### December 6, 1967

I have a whole correspondence in French with S., who is learning French and puts questions to me. ... [H]e wrote me this:

*"Does the transformation not demand a very high degree of aspiration, surrender and receptivity?"*

I replied:

"The transformation demands a total and integral consecration. But is that not the aspiration of every sincere sadhak?

"'Total' means ...

Yes, it was on the following page (because I thought, "This man will wonder why I put 'total and integral' when the two words seem to mean just the same thing"). So I gave him the explanation:

"'Total' means VERTICALLY in all the states of being from the most material to the most subtle. 'Integral' means HORIZONTALLY in all the various and often contradictory parts that make up the outer being (physical, vital and mental)."

* * *

*(Then Mother listens to new, unpublished letters of Sri Aurobindo's:)*

*"How can I receive Sri Aurobindo's light in the mind?"*

"It can always come if you aspire patiently. But the basic condition, if you want that light, is to get rid of all other mental influences."

*"What is the meaning of 'to get rid of all other mental influences'? Is it this that I had better not read any other books except Sri Aurobindo's or not try to learn anything by hearing or admiring others?"*

"It is not a question of books or learning facts. When a woman loves or admires, her mind is instinctively molded by the one she loves or admires, and this influence remains after the feeling itself has gone or appears to be gone. This does not refer to X's influence merely. It is the general rule given to keep yourself free from any other admiration or influence."

Sri Aurobindo,
May 30, 1932

This is something people generally don't know. It's very true, but they don't know it. When they start admiring all sorts of things, it becomes a hodgepodge.

*(silence)*

This is one of the things I've learned lately through experience – universalization, the contact with everything *(horizontal gesture)* – and it has been shown to the body in such a precise way, in the detail of the vibration.... In the state of receptivity *(vertical gesture to the Heights)*, of receptive passivity (the opposite of action, that is), the body must be turned exclusively to the Supreme *(same vertical gesture):* the body and the cells have been taught that, and they've understood – they've understood and are now used to it. In the state of action *(horizontal gesture)*, when you are one with (well, let's limit the problem to the earth), one with the whole earth, there must be an ACTIVE radiating vibration of the supreme Force. Receptivity like this *(vertical gesture to receive the Force)*, and activity like this *(horizontal gesture spreading the Force out)*. And the cells have felt, they've understood, they can do it. And the relationship with everything around you, down to the smallest detail, is something so wonderful, with an influence radiating farther and farther away.

415

When you realize those two attitudes simultaneously, the contagion is abolished: the mental contagion (the very one Sri Aurobindo refers to here, the one you get when you "admire" something), the mental contagion, the vital contagion, and EVEN THE PHYSICAL CONTAGION – when the cells realize that, you stop catching illnesses. Because formerly (for a long time), whenever something occurred in the sphere of influence of the action, there used to be a repercussion [in Mother]. For a very long time, it was dangerous. Then it became limited to a sense of unease which would grow conscious, and conscious of the why – the why and the how. It was limited to a state of unease, but it was still ... troublesome. And now it's a sort of ... I can't say "knowledge," because it's not mental, but an *awareness* (there's no word for it in French), a perception – and nothing more, it doesn't have any action [or any repercussion in Mother's body]. So then, the whole problem lies there.

There are those who found this, the vertical ascent to the heights, and who isolated themselves from the world (they weren't able to do that completely because they didn't have the knowledge, but they tried). That's not the solution. Then there are those who want to help, the generous ones who are like this *(gesture of horizontal expansion),* and who catch everything, even the mental diseases of all the people around them. So the truth is the two together: this, the passive, receptive state *(vertical gesture),* and this, the active state of action and radiating influence *(horizontal gesture).* And the body has become wholly conscious of the dual movement and is working to realize it in detail.

A great problem has been solved.

And it's interesting because those two attitudes can be almost simultaneous, but they are ... On the level of vibration, of vibratory sensation, they are two opposites combining with each other: receptivity like this *(gesture),* towards the Consciousness, the Force, Power, Light, all that comes from above, and naturally Love (but about Love I will speak

416

later). And it comes *(gesture of descent),* it comes down and everything, everything is ab-so-lute-ly passive and receptive *(gesture of vertical opening):* it absorbs and absorbs and absorbs, like that, totally given, in the state of a sponge that absorbs and absorbs and absorbs.... At the same time, there is the relationship with the world *(horizontal gesture)* and the Power coming through and working, with the sense of the Force, the Action, the Thing imposing itself. It's magnificent. And in the SAME vibratory radiance of ... of "That." Always the same all-powerful Perfection being absorbed and acting *(gesture of flowing through Mother over the world in a perpetual movement).*

That seems to be the secret of all-powerfulness. There is no need at all to go through mental knowledge – that diminishes, shrinks, hardens.

It's a keen state of consciousness, that is, wholly awakened. In the cells of the body, it drives away all darkness. Naturally, it's a long and slow work, but it drives away, it's a state that drives away all darkness everywhere. And darkness is always the sign (sign or cause) of a disorder. So there is still plenty of it, one knows that. It's a slow work, a whole world! When you ... (how should I put it?) when you descend into (or I may say, concentrate on) this cellular constitution of the body, on the body's scale, it's a myriad world! A myriad world. Everything is as though made up of myriad tiny points, and each point has to be awakened and flooded with consciousness and light – a long work.

*(silence)*

So it's the solution to these two errors that constantly contradict each other: the error of shrinking, of an exclusivism of influence (which, when practiced on the mental level, becomes a limitation, a smallness, like all exclusive faiths); or else eclecticism without effect or force, which makes a sort of muddle with everything, with all ideas (mentally it doesn't matter, but on the level of the transformation, it's serious). So for these two opposites the problem has been solved.

417

The state I've just described is possible in the body's cells and in the body consciousness, also in the psychic consciousness; but vitally and mentally, even if you understand, it seems like an almost impossible realization because of a fixity, a fixity in the form: the form of thoughts and the form of sensations. Mentally it could only be translated as an acceptance of all thoughts, all formulas, raising them up towards ... something that's no longer a thought, no longer a mentally formulated thing, but a light, a light, a conscious light organizing and unifying all those thoughts. But if you take them all on the same plane ... You can accept everything, but everything as one standpoint – one among innumerable standpoints on "something" that cannot be expressed in words, because as soon as you put words on it, it becomes a formula, and the formula takes the power away. But physically, in the body's cells, it's very, very clearly perceptible and is lived quite spontaneously: you receive only from on high, and you spread it.

Vol. 8, p. 406

## December 8, 1967

The only somewhat new thing is that the body is beginning to be a bit ... *restless* at its decay. Before, it didn't bother about it, it didn't give it any thought; it knew it was going on, but ... Now, it's beginning to be bothered. So perhaps it's a sign, I don't know? It's beginning to be bothered – not psychologically, but like this: when it receives a Command to do something and there is, not exactly an incapacity, but a limitation to the possibility, that starts its unhappiness. So I wondered ...

Then at night it's the same thing, it says, "Why such a whole long period of diminishing consciousness?"

*Diminishing?*

You understand, it's happy and in what it regards as its normal state only when it's fully conscious of and vibrating with the Presence. But in the night's activities ... (how can I explain?) it's becoming more ... more like something one is used to, you know, like a habit *(gesture of a wave flowing);* there's no longer the joy of a vibrating observation, but a normal state of things, and it's not happy with that: it wants the same intensity *(vibrating gesture)* to be there at night. For instance, it doesn't tolerate the idea of fatigue, of the necessity of rest (although that never arises from the inconscient any longer), but rest as a sort of turning in on oneself, like that, to repair wear and tear – it doesn't like that: there must be no wear and tear, there must be a constant adaptation to anything asked of it. Later, it will probably not even accept effort – there isn't much "effort" left, but instead of effort, there's a sort of conscious receptivity that enables it to do things; and there are constant examples to show that if this receptivity isn't there, well, there's an awkward movement, or an impossibility, things like that, but it ... in the past, it used to feel that was unavoidable, but now it no longer wants it. Now it no longer wants it: things must not be like that. For example, to put something away or find it or do something, it sometimes feels a sense of difficulty (it's never quite impossible because nothing is asked of it which is impossible), but at times it's difficult – and a sense of displeasure comes over it. It feels that as an infirmity, as a lack of receptivity, you understand. Also the fact that it has become stooped: in the past it would say, "It'll get corrected"; now it's beginning to lose patience. That's quite new. It began on November 24. Because it's not a selfish turning in on itself, it's not that, it's not for itself, it's ... the sense of a lack of receptivity to the Force, of limitation arising from incapacity – it doesn't like that anymore.

Vol. 8, p. 410

**December 30, 1967**

...[U]sually (always so far, and more and more so), men establish mental rules according to their conceptions and their ideal, then they apply them *(Mother lowers her fist, as if to show the world under the mental grip)*. And that's absolutely false, arbitrary, unreal, so the result is that things revolt, or else waste away and disappear.... It's the experience of LIFE ITSELF that must slowly work out rules AS SUPPLE AND VAST as possible, in order that they ever remain progressive. Nothing must be fixed. That's the immense error of governments: they build a framework and say, "Here is what we've established, now we must live under it." So naturally, Life is crushed and prevented from progressing. It is Life itself, developing more and more in a progression towards Light, Knowledge, Power, that must little by little establish rules as general as possible, so as to be extremely supple and capable of changing according to need – of changing AS RAPIDLY as habits and needs do.

*(silence)*

At bottom, the problem almost boils down to this: to replace the mental government of intelligence by the government of a spiritualized consciousness.

It's an extremely interesting experience: how the same actions, the same work, the same observations, the same relationship with the people around (near or far), how they take place in the mind, through intelligence, and how they take place in the consciousness, through experience. And that's what this body is now learning – to replace the mental government of intelligence by the spiritual government of the consciousness. And it makes (it looks like nothing, one may not notice it), it makes a tremendous difference, to the point of multiplying the body's possibilities a hundredfold.... When the body is subjected to rules, even if they are broad, even if they are comprehensive, it is a slave to those rules and its possibilities are limited by them. But when it's governed by the Spirit and the Consciousness, that gives it incomparable possibility and flexibility! And that's what will give it the capacity to prolong its life, to last longer: it's by replacing the mental, intellectual government by the government of the Spirit, the Consciousness – THE Consciousness. Outwardly, it doesn't seem to make much difference, but ... My experience is like this (because now my body no longer obeys the mind or the intelligence at all, no longer at all – it doesn't even understand how that can be done), and it more and more, better and better follows the direction and impulsion of the Consciousness. But then, it sees, almost every minute, the tremendous difference that makes.... For instance, time has lost its value (its rigid value): you can do the same thing in very little time or in much time. Necessities have lost their authority: you can adapt yourself this way, adapt yourself that way. All the laws – those laws that were laws of Nature – have lost all their despotism, if I may say so: it no longer works that way. All you have to do is constantly and always to be supple, attentive, and ... responsive to the influence of the Consciousness – the Consciousness in its all-powerfulness – so as to go through all this with extraordinary suppleness.

That is the discovery being made more and more.

And it's wonderful, you know! A wonderful discovery.

It's like a progressive victory over all constraints. So naturally, all the laws of Nature, all the human laws, all habits, all rules, all that grows increasingly supple and finally becomes nonexistent. Yet it is possible to keep a regular rhythm that makes action easier – it's not contrary to this suppleness. But it's a suppleness in the execution, in the adaptation, which comes and changes everything. From the point of view of hygiene, health, organization, from the point of view of the relationship with others, all that has not only lost its aggressiveness (because for it to lose its aggressiveness, all you have to do is to be wise – wise and level-headed and calm), but also its absolutism, its imperative rule: that's entirely gone – gone.

And then, you see: as the process grows more and more perfect – "perfect" means integral, total, leaving nothing

421

behind – it NECESSARILY, inevitably means victory over death. Not that this dissolution of the cells which death involves stops existing, but that it would exist only when necessary: not as an absolute law, but as ONE of the processes, when necessary.

It's mainly all that the Mind has brought in terms of rigidity and absoluteness and near invincibility – that's what ... is going to disappear. And simply by ... handing the supreme power over to the Supreme Consciousness.

That may be what the sages of old meant when they spoke of handing the power of Nature or the power of the *Prakriti* over to the Purusha – handing it from the Prakriti over to the Purusha. Perhaps it was their way of expressing the same thing.

Vol. 8, p. 430

# International Publications

**Auroville Architecture**
*by Franz Fassbender*

**Auroville Form Style and Design**
*by Franz Fassbender*

**Landscapes and Gardens of Auroville**
*by Franz Fassbender*

**Inauguration of Auroville**
*by Franz Fassbender*

**Auroville in a Nutshell**
*by Tim Wrey*

**Death doesn't exist**
The Mother on Death, Sri Aurobindo on Rebirth
*Compiled by Franz Fassbender*

**Divine Love**
*Compiled by Franz Fassbender*

**Five Dream**
*by Sri Aurobindo*

**Vision**
*Compiled by Franz Fassbender*

**Passage to More than India**
*by Dick Batstone*

**The Mother on Japan**
*Compiled by Franz Fassbender*

**Children of Change: A Spiritual Pilgrimage**
*by Amrit (Howard Shoji Iriyama)*

**Memories of Auroville - told by early Aurovilians**
*by Janet Feran*

The Journeying Years
*by Dianna Bowler*

Auroville Reflected
*by Bindu Mohanty*

Finding the Psychic Being
*by Loretta Shartsis*

The Teachings of Flowers
The Life and Work of the Mother of the Sri Aurobindo Ashram
*by Loretta Shartsis*

The Supramental Transformation
*by Loretta Shartsis*

The Mother's Yoga - 1956-1973 (English & Frech)
Vol. 1, 1956-1967 & Vol. 2, 1968-1973
*by Loretta Shartsis*

Antithesis of Yoga
*by Jocelyn Janaka*

Bougainvilleas PROTECTION
*by Narad (Richard Eggenberger), Nilisha Mehta*

Crossroad The New Humanity
*by Paulette Hadnagy*

Die Praxis Des Integralen Yoga
*By M. P. Pandit*

The Way of the Sunlit Path
*William Sullivan*

Wildlife great and small of India's Coromandel
*by Tim Wrey*

A New Education With A Soul
*Marguerite Smithwhite*

# Featured Titles

## Divine Love

The texts presented in this book are selected from the Mother and Sri Aurobindo.

*"Awakened to the meaning of my heart. That to feel love and oneness is to live. And this the magic of our golden change, is all the truth I know or seek, O sage."*

Sri Aurobindo, Savitri, Book XII, Epilog

## A Vision by the Mother

On 28th May 1958, the Mother recounted a vision she once had of a wonderful Being of Love and Consciousness, emanated from the Supreme Origin and projected directly into the Inconscient so that the creation would gradually awaken to the Supramental Consciousness. The Mother's account of this vision was brought out a first time in November 1906, in the Revue Cosmique, a monthly review published in Paris.

## A Dream – Aims and Ideals of Auroville
### the Mother on Auroville

50 years of Auroville from 28.02.1968 - 28.02.2018
Today, information about Auroville is abundant. Many people try to make meaning out of Auroville – about its conception, to what direction should we grow towards, and, what are we doing here?

But what was Mother's original Dream and what was her Vision for Auroville back then?

## Matrimandir Talks by the Mother

This book presents most of Mother's Matrimandir talks, including how she conceived the idea for this special concentration and meditation building in Auroville.

## Memories of Auroville - Told by early Aurovilians

Memories of Auroville is a book about the very early days of Auroville based on interviews made in 1997 with Aurovilians who lived here between 1968 and 1973. The interviews presented in this book are part of a history program for newcomers that I had created with my friend, Philip Melville in 1997. The plan was to divide Auroville's history into different eras and then interview Aurovilians according to their area of knowledge. Our first section would cover the years from 1968 till 1973 when the Mother was still in her physical body.

## The Way of the Sunlit Path

May The Way of the Sunlit Path be a convenient guide for activating this ancient truth as a support for a Conscious Evolution.
May it illumine the transformation offered to us in the Integral Yoga.

## A Dream Takes Shape (in English, French, Hindi)

A comprehensive brochure on the international township of Auroville in, ranging from its Charter and "Why Auroville?" to the plan of the township, the central Matrimandir, the national pavilions and residences, to working groups, the economy, making visits, how to join, its relationship to the Sri Aurobindo Ashram, and its key role in the future of the world. This brochure endeavours to highlight how The Mother envisioned Auroville from its inception, some of the major achievements realised over the years, and some of the difficulties currently faced in implementing the guidelines which she gave.

## Mother on Japan

I had everything to learn in Japan. For four years, from an artistic point of view, I lived from wonder to wonder. And everything in this city, in this country, from beginning to end, gives you the impression of impermanence, of the unexpected, the exceptional... ...everything in this city, in this country, from beginning to end, gives you the impression of impermanence, of the unexpected, the exceptional. You always come to things you did not expect; you want to find them again and they are lost – they have made something else which is equally charming.

## Auroville Reflected

On 28 February 1968, on an impoverished plateau on the Coromandel Coast of South India, about 4,000 people from around the world gathered for a most unusual inauguration. Handfuls of soil from the countries of the world were mixed together as a symbol of human unity. Why did Indira Gandhi, the erstwhile Prime Minister of India, support this development for "a city the earth needs?" Why did UNESCO endorse this project? Why does the Dalai Lama continue to be involved in the project? What led anthropologist Margaret Mead to insist that records must be kept of its progress? Why did both historian William Irwin Thompson and United Nations representative Robert Muller note that this social experiment may be a breakthrough for humanity even as critics commented, "it is an impossible dream"?

## A House For the Third Millennium
### Essays on Matrimandir

Nightwatch at the Matrimandir...
A cosmic spectacle; the black expanse above, the big black crater of Matrimandir's excavation carved deep into the soil. The four pillars - two of which are completed and the other two nearing completion - are four huge ships coming together from the four corners of the earth to meet at this pro propitious spot...

## Passage to More than India

This book is a voyage of discovery. In 1959 the author, Dick Batstone, a classically educated bookseller in England, with a Christian background, comes across a life of the great Indian polymath Sri Aurobindo, though a series of apparently fortuitous circumstances. A meeting in Durham, England, leads him to a determination to get to the Sri Aurobindo Ashram in Pondicherry, a former French territory south of Madras.